CRITICAL SECURITY IN THE ASIA-PACIFIC

MANCHESTER
1824
Manchester University Press

New Approaches to Conflict Analysis

Series editor: Peter Lawler,
Senior Lecturer in International Relations,
Department of Government, University of Manchester

Until recently, the study of conflict and conflict resolution remained comparatively immune to broad developments in social and political theory. When the changing nature and locus of large-scale conflict in the post-Cold War era is also taken into account, the case for a reconsideration of the fundamentals of conflict analysis and conflict resolution becomes all the more stark.

New Approaches to Conflict Analysis promotes the development of new theoretical insights and their application to concrete cases of large-scale conflict, broadly defined. The series intends not to ignore established approaches to conflict analysis and conflict resolution, but to contribute to the reconstruction of the field through a dialogue between orthodoxy and its contemporary critics. Equally, the series reflects the contemporary porosity of intellectual borderlines rather than simply perpetuating rigid boundaries around the study of conflict and peace. *New Approaches to Conflict Analysis* seeks to uphold the normative commitment of the field's founders yet also recognises that the moral impulse to research is properly part of its subject matter. To these ends, the series is comprised of the highest quality work of scholars drawn from throughout the international academic community, and from a wide range of disciplines within the social sciences.

PUBLISHED

Christine Agius
Neutrality, sovereignty and identity: the social construction of Swedish neutrality

Eşref Aksu
The United Nations, intra-state peacekeeping and normative change

M. Anne Brown
Human rights and the borders of suffering: the promotion of human rights in international politics

Lorraine Elliott and Graeme Cheeseman (eds)
Forces for good: cosmopolitan militaries in the twenty-first century

Richard Jackson
Writing the war on terrorism: language, politics and counter-terrorism

Tami Amanda Jacoby and Brent Sasley (eds)
Redefining security in the Middle East

Jan Koehler and Christoph Zürcher (eds)
Potentials of disorder

David Bruce MacDonald
Balkan holocausts? Serbian and Croatian victim-centred propaganda and the war in Yugoslavia

Adrian Millar
Socio-ideological fantasy and the Northern Ireland conflict: the other side

Jennifer Milliken
The social construction of the Korean War

Ami Pedahzur
The Israeli response to Jewish extremism and violence: defending democracy

Maria Stern
Naming insecurity – constructing identity: 'Mayan-women' in Guatemala on the eve of 'peace'

Virginia Tilley
The one state solution: a breakthrough for peace in the Israeli-Palestinian deadlock

Critical Security in the Asia-Pacific

Edited by Anthony Burke and
Matt McDonald

Manchester University Press
MANCHESTER AND NEW YORK

distributed exclusively in the USA by Palgrave

Published by Manchester University Press
Oxford Road, Manchester M13 9NR, UK
and Room 400, 175 Fifth Avenue, New York, NY 10010, USA
www.manchesteruniversitypress.co.uk

Distributed exclusively in the USA by
Palgrave, 175 Fifth Avenue, New York, NY 10010, USA

Distributed exclusively in Canada by
UBC Press, University of British Columbia, 2029 West Mall,
Vancouver, BC, Canada V6T 1Z2

British Library Cataloguing-in-Publication Data
A catalogue record for this book is available from the British Library

Library of Congress Cataloging-in-Publication Data applied for

ISBN 978 0 7190 7304 5 *hardback*
ISBN 978 0 7190 7305 2 *paperback*

First published 2007

16 15 14 13 12 11 10 09 08 07 10 9 8 7 6 5 4 3 2 1

Typeset in Photina
by Florence Production Ltd, Stoodleigh, Devon
Printed and bound in Great Britain
by Antony Rowe Ltd, Chippenham, Wiltshire

CONTENTS

CONTRIBUTORS

Edward Aspinall is a Fellow in Indonesian Politics in the Department of Political and Social Change, RSPAS, at the Australian National University. He is the author of *Opposing Suharto: Compromise, resistance and regime change in Indonesia* (Stanford University Press, 2005) and, with Harold Crouch, co-author of the East West Center Policy Paper, 'The Peace Process in Aceh: Why it failed'. He is currently working on a book manuscript on the history of the secessionist movement in Aceh.

Mark Beeson is Professor of International Relations at the University of Birmingham. His research interests centre on the political-economy and international relations of the broadly conceived Asia-Pacific region. His most recent publications are *Regionalism and Globalization in East Asia: Politics, Security and Economic Development* (Palgrave, 2007), and the edited volume, *Bush and Asia: America's Evolving Relations with East Asia* (Routledge, 2006).

Alex J. Bellamy is Professor of International Relations at the University of Queensland. He is the author of *Kosovo and International Society* (Palgrave, 2002), *Understanding Peacekeeping*, with Paul Williams and Stuart Griffin, (Polity, 2004), and *Security Communities and their Neighbours* (Palgrave, 2004). He is also editor of *International Society and its Critics* (Oxford, 2005). He is currently writing a book on *Just Wars* (Polity) and working on a project on the role of the military in Asia, sponsored by the Australian Research Council.

Roland Bleiker is Professor of International Relations at the University of Queensland. From 1986 to 1988 he was Chief of Office of the Swiss Delegation to the Neutral Nations Supervisory Commission in Panmunjom. He has been a visiting fellow at Yonsei University and a visiting professor at Pusan National University. His most recent book is *Divided Korea: Toward a Culture of Reconciliation* (University of Minnesota Press, 2005). He is currently conducting research that re-views and re-thinks the emotional dimensions of security threats, such as terrorism and epidemics, through a range of aesthetic sources.

Anthony Burke is Senior Lecturer in International Relations at the University of New South Wales, Sydney. He is the author of *Beyond*

Security, Ethics and Violence: War Against the Other (Routledge 2007) and *In Fear of Security: Australia's Invasion Anxiety* (Pluto Australia 2001), as well as numerous journal articles on war and peace, international security, Asian human security, asylum seekers and security theory. He is the publisher and former editor of the journal *Borderlands*, and is currently working on an Australian Research Council-funded project on the politics and ethics of the use of force.

Richard Chauvel is Associate Professor and Director of the Australia Asia Pacific Institute at Victoria University. He has teaching and research interests in Indonesian history and politics, Australia-Indonesia relations and Australian foreign policy. He is the author of *Nationalists, Soldiers and Separatists: The Ambonese Islands from Colonialism to Revolt* (KILTV Press, 1990), and *Indonesia: Ending Repression in Irian Jaya* (ICG Asia Report, 2001). He is currently writing a history of the West New Guinea Dispute under the Peter Hastings Memorial Fellowship.

Simon Dalby is Professor of Geography and Political Economy at Carleton University in Ottawa. He is author of *Creating the Second Cold War* (Pinter, 1990) and *Environmental Security* (University of Minnesota Press, 2002) and co-editor of *Rethinking Geopolitics* (Routledge, 1998) and *The Geopolitics Reader* (Routledge, 1998, second edition, 2006).

Sara E. Davies is a lecturer at the School of Justice Studies, Queensland University of Technology. Sara is author *of Legitimising Rejection: International Refugee Law in Southeast Asia* (Martinus Nijhoff, forthcoming) and has published a number of articles concerning international refugee law and refugee policy in Southeast Asia. She is currently working on a book project titled *Global Health Issues* with Polity Press, to be completed in 2008.

Lorraine Elliott is Senior Fellow in International Relations at the Australian National University. She has published widely on global environmental governance, regionalism and Southeast Asia, non-traditional security, and Australian foreign policy. Her books include *The Global Politics of the Environment* (Palgrave Macmillan, 1998; second edition 2004) and, as co-editor, *Forces for Good: Cosmopolitan Militaries in the 21st century* (Manchester University Press, 2004). Her current research includes a major project on the global governance of transnational environmental crime and illegal resource activity.

Julie Gilson is Senior Lecturer in the Department of Political Science and International Studies at the University of Birmingham. She is the author of *Asia Meets Europe* (Edward Elgar, 2002) and co-author of *Japan's*

International Relations (Routledge, 2005). Her current research analyses the role of civil society forces in the Asia-Pacific.

Marianne Hanson is Reader in International Relations in the School of Political Science and International Studies at the University of Queensland, Australia. Her research and publications examine the legal and ethical, as well as the strategic, components of international security. She is a member of Australia's National Consultative Committee on Security Issues and of AUS-CSCAP.

Bryn Hughes is currently completing his PhD on Democracy, Identity and Political Violence at the School of Political Science and International Studies, University of Queensland. His areas of interest and publications are in the area of critical security studies, identity, and the Democratic Peace Theory. He was also awarded the Australasian Political Science Association's Travelling Scholarship for the best postgraduate paper at its 2004 Annual Conference.

Hazel Lang is Senior Research Fellow at Griffith University and Honorary Associate at the Centre for Peace and Conflict Studies at Sydney University. Her research interests include Burma/Myanmar, human security, peacebuilding, and global refugee issues. She is the author of *Fear and Sanctuary: Burmese Refugees in Thailand* (Ithaca: SEAP, Cornell University, 2002) and has also been commissioned to publish public documents, including with the UNHCR and the International Crisis Group. Hazel wrote this chapter while she was Lecturer in Asian Studies at the Australian National University.

Katrina Lee-Koo is Lecturer in International Relations in the Faculty of Arts, Australian National University. Her research interests include critical security studies, feminist international relations and contemporary Australian foreign and security policy. Her recent publications include articles in journals such as *the Australian Journal of Political Science* and *Borderlands*, and she is the editor, with Bina D'Costa, of the forthcoming book *Gender and Global Politics in the Asia-Pacific.*

Matt McDonald is an Assistant Professor in International Security in the Department of Politics and International Studies at the University of Warwick. His research interests and publications are in the area of critical security studies broadly defined, including an interest in the 'war on terrorism', asylum/immigration and environmental change. He is currently completing a book exploring the relationship between security and environmental change.

See Seng Tan is an Assistant Professor and Deputy Head of Studies at the S. Rajaratnam School of International Studies (RSIS), Nanyang Technological University, Singapore. He also directs the research programme on multilateralism and regionalism at RSIS. His publications include *After Bali* (World Scientific, 2003), *Asia-Pacific Security Cooperation* (M. E. Sharpe, 2004), and *The Role of Knowledge Communities in Constructing Asia-Pacific Security* (Edwin Mellen, forthcoming 2007).

Yongjin Zhang is Associate Professor at the University of Auckland and the Director of New Zealand Asia Institute. His major research interests are in International Relations theory and Chinese international relations. He has published in *Review of International Studies, European Journal of International Relations, Pacifica Review* and *The China Journal*, among others.

ACKNOWLEDGEMENTS

As is the case with any book, but perhaps particularly with an edited book, this text would not have been possible in its current form without the assistance, encouragement and insight of a range of people to whom we are indebted. We are grateful to Alex Bellamy who was closely involved in the conception of, and initial planning for, the project. Ken Booth provided inspiration and moral support as we sought to place the book with publishers. At Manchester University Press, Peter Lawler and Tony Mason were enthusiastic supporters of the project and provided incisive editorial advice. Thanks also to Xiangning (Sunny) Wu for her excellent work on the index at short notice. Some of our thinking and conception of the book's arguments was developed while the editors were studying and teaching at politics and international relations departments at the University of Queensland; the University of Adelaide; the University of Wales, Aberystwyth; the University of New South Wales; and the University of Birmingham. We are grateful to those institutions and our colleagues there for their support and for being great sounding boards for our ideas. Anthony Burke thanks Professor To-Hai Liou, Dr Kwei-Bo Huang and the staff and students of the Department of Diplomacy, National Chengchi University, Taipei, who hosted him at the Conference on East Timor and Asian Security in 2002, where some of the thinking for the Introduction was developed and refined. Matt McDonald thanks the students of his Masters-level Asia-Pacific Security course at the University of Birmingham and the course co-convenor, Julie Gilson, for helping to shape the structure and aims of the book. He also wishes to thank the staff and students of the Institute of Asia-Pacific Studies at the University of Nottingham who gave valuable feedback on an earlier version of his chapter presented in the Institute's seminar series in December 2005. We are of course grateful to the contributors, who under the burden of other commitments agreed to contribute far-reaching and high-quality chapters that we hope will greatly advance the debate and take-up of critical security thinking in the Asia-Pacific region. Finally, to our ever-supportive partners Jen and Helen: thanks for everything.

Anthony Burke
Matt McDonald

ABBREVIATIONS

ABRI	Indonesian armed forces (to 1998)
ACT	Australian Capital Territory
AEPF	Asia-Europe People's Forum
ANZUS	Australia, New Zealand and United States (Security treaty)
APEC	Asia-Pacific Economic Cooperation
APT	ASEAN Plus Three
ARF	ASEAN Regional Forum
ASEAN	Association of Southeast Asian Nations
ASEAN-ISIS	ASEAN Institutes of Strategic and International Studies
ASEM	Asia-Europe Meeting
ASIO	Australian Security Intelligence Organisation
AUS-CSCAP	Australian Committee of CSCAP (the Council for Security Cooperation in the Asia-Pacific)
BAKIN	Badan koordinasi Intelijens keamanan (Indonesian National Intelligence Co-ordinating Agency)
BJP	Bharatiya Janata Party
CAEC	Council for Asia-Europe Cooperation
CAPWIP	Centre for Asia-Pacific Women In Politics
CATW-AP	Coalition Against Trafficking in Women – Asia-Pacific
CBM	confidence-building measure
CCP	Chinese Community Party
CentCom	Central Command
CPA	Communist Party of Australia
CSCAP	Council for Security Cooperation in the Asia-Pacific
CTBT	Comprehensive Test Ban Treaty
DAWN	Development Alternatives with Women for a New Era
DFID	Department for International Development
DIMIA	Department of Immigration, Multiculturalism and Indigenous Affairs
DIO	Defence Intelligence Organisation
DKBA	Democratic Karen Buddhist Army
DPRK	Democratic People's Republic of Korea
ETIM	East Turkestan Islamic Movement
FALINTIL	The Armed Forces for the National Liberation of Timorleste

GAM	*Gerakan Aceh Merdeka*
GDP	gross domestic product
GNP	gross national product
GPK	*gerakan pengacau keamanan*
IDP	internally displaced person
IDSS	Institute of Defence and Strategic Studies
IFI	international financial institution
ISEAS	Institute of Southeast Asian Studies
JI	*Jemaah Islamiyah*
KEDO	Korean Peninsula Energy Development Organization
KNU	Karen National Union
NATO	North Atlantic Treaty Organization
NGO	non-governmental organization
NKRI	*Negara Kesatuan Republik Indonesia*
NPT	Non-Proliferation Treaty
NWFZ	Nuclear Weapon Free Zones
ODA	Official Development Assistance
OECD	Organization for Economic Cooperation and Development
OIC	Organisation of Islamic Conference
ONA	Office of National Assessments
OPM	*Organisasi Papua Merdeka*
PDP	*Presidium Dewan Papua*
PERKIM	Malaysian Muslim Welfare Organisation
PKI	Indonesian Communist Party
PLA	People's Liberation Army
PMC	Post Ministerial Conference
PPP	Unity Development Party
SCO	Shanghai Cooperation Organization
SDF	Self Defence Forces (Japan)
SEATO	Southeast Asia Treaty Organization
SLORC	State Law and Order Council (Myanmar)
SPDC	State Peace and Development Council
SSR	Security Sector Reform
TAC	Treaty of Amity and Cooperation
3D	dangerous, dirty and demanding
TNI	Indonesian armed forces (from 1998)
UMNO	United Malays National Organisation
UNDP	United Nations Development Programme
UNHCR	United Nations High Commissioner for Refugees
UNRISD	United Nations Research Institute for Social Development

UPM	unregulated people movement
WHO	World Health Organization
WMD	weapons of mass destruction
WTO	World Trade Organization
ZOPFAN	Zone of Peace, Freedom and Neutrality

Introduction: Asia-Pacific security legacies and futures

Anthony Burke and Matt McDonald

ON 26 DECEMBER 2004, a vast earthquake in the Indian Ocean triggered a devastating wave that minutes and hours later struck the coasts of Sumatra, Thailand, India, Sri Lanka, Bangladesh and Somalia. The wave caused enormous physical and economic damage, taking the lives of 283,100 people, leaving more than 14,000 others missing and creating over a million refugees. A third of the dead were children. The death toll dwarfed anything short of a major war or a planetary catastrophe.

However this tragedy, the threat of it, and the enormous human and economic damage it could do, was invisible to the small army of regional experts and officials for whom security is a career, a vocation and a *raison d'être*. It did not appear in any defence white papers, on the agenda of the ASEAN Regional Forum (ARF) or in the bilateral discussions and planning of regional nations. This is especially ironic given that the ARF had committed itself to a 'comprehensive' understanding of security that 'also addressed non-military issues' – one of which included fostering cooperation in disaster relief (Chairman's statement, 1998: 102). Despite a February 1998 inter-sessional meeting of the ARF on disaster relief having 'emphasised the need for enhancement of early warning capabilities on emergencies such as earthquakes, floods and severe storms', in 2004 the Indian Ocean region did not have a working tsunami warning system – unlike the Pacific (Co-Chairman's report, 1998: 113). ARF activities may have helped with the response to the disaster, but it was too late to save those who had already perished. Few recent events have been more destructive to the lives of millions of people, yet it did not register as a *security* issue, at least not in regional states' policies, official statements, intelligence analysis or academic scholarship. Security, it seems, is about other things.

In one of the worst hit areas, the north Sumatran province of Aceh, Indonesia had in fact been preoccupied with defeating an insurgency by the Free Aceh Movement (*Gerakan Aceh Merdeka*, or GAM) – a conflict which saw terrible human rights abuses by both sides, a long-standing atmosphere of repression, and entrenched patterns of corruption and illegal business by the Indonesian armed forces (TNI). As Edward Aspinall and Richard Chauvel argue in their chapter, Indonesian anti-separatist operations were aimed at preserving the 'integrity' of the 'unitary state of Indonesia' (*Negara Kesatuan Republik Indonesia*, or NKRI), and its coercive policy was known in Indonesian vernacular as the 'security approach'. The tragedy of the tsunami appeared to shock and embarrass both sides enough to break through their long-standing political deadlock: GAM announced a unilateral ceasefire to allow humanitarian aid (a gesture not reciprocated by the TNI, who continued offensive operations) and new President Susilo Bambang Yudhoyono sent a team of negotiators to talks with the GAM. A peace agreement was signed on 17 July 2005 (ICG, 2005: 6).

It is not the first time that the Asia-Pacific region has been surprised, and its dominant security paradigms found wanting, by a major crisis. The East Asian political and economic crisis that broke with the run on the Thai baht in mid-1997 – causing widespread bankruptcies, protests, rioting, pogroms, mass unemployment and the fall of governments in South Korea, Thailand and Indonesia – was also not foreseen by the region's governments and security elites. Yet it is arguable that the region's dominant economic, political and security systems played a major hand in causing, and in turn worsening, the crisis (Daly and Logan, 1998). While the growth of international currency and capital markets, and the liberalization of Asian capital controls in the 1990s, was one element of the crisis, another was the 'Asian' model of state–market coordination, which while having a valuable post-war development role as Mark Beeson argues, also enabled corrupt relationships between businesses, government and banks. When to that we add the dangerous political crisis that developed in the final years of the Soeharto regime, and the subsequent violence in East Timor after his successor B.J. Habibie allowed a referendum on self-determination, the Asian financial crisis demonstrates how established frameworks of development, governance and security can be both politically destabilizing and cause terrible human insecurity. It highlights a need for a more holistic understanding of the complexity of insecurity processes and a more people-centred approach to creating security.

In the light of such events, *Critical Security in the Asia-Pacific* aims to address some of the neglected problems, people and vulnerabilities of the Asia-Pacific region. Doing so requires a new empirical and theoretical focus on what we understand security to be and how it is to be achieved. This is based upon, first, a *critical theoretical approach* that, drawing on a variety of sources, interrogates the deeper assumptions underpinning security discourses and policies; and, second, a *human-centred policy approach* that avoids the state and elite bias of traditional security analysis and instead focuses on the security, welfare and emancipation of human beings and communities. It does not deny the relevance or importance of existing concerns with national security or strategic stability, but does question their priorities, frameworks and effects, especially in cases where they may in fact *undermine* the security of individuals and states.

Readers of this book will thus find a very different set of analyses and priorities than is contained in a conventional collection on regional or national security affairs. Rather than theorizing about deterrence, alliance systems, strategy and counter-insurgency, you will read about emancipation, human security, 'security politics', language and threat-construction. And rather than the familiar analyses of interstate conflict, great powers, non-conventional threats and naval security, you will read writings more concerned with internal conflicts, self-determination, human rights, the fate of minorities and refugees, environmental insecurity, economic justice, and women and gender. Where the book does turn its attention to traditional conflicts and security concerns – such as regional security institutions, nuclear proliferation, economic development, the Korean conflict, and the role of great powers such as China or the United States – it does so with a critical eye and new insights and recommendations. In short, *Critical Security in the Asia-Pacific* seeks to highlight forms of insecurity and suffering that have been neglected by traditional security studies, or been understood in inappropriate, misguided and damaging ways. In turn, it seeks to address these forms of insecurity with normatively and practically better solutions.

What is a critical approach to security?

This book takes as its starting point a deep dissatisfaction with the 'traditional' or realist security studies that have dominated the study and practice of security in international relations, at least since the onset of the Cold War. This approach, predicated ultimately on the preservation of the nation-state's sovereignty and territorial integrity from violent threats, is defined here as that which precisely needs to be problematized and contested: as part of the problem of global suffering and vulnerability rather than as a basis for potential solutions. This approach to security defines the state as the referent object and agent of security, in a world in which immediate threats to state survival are ubiquitous given the interaction of self-regarding actors with no higher authority to prevent the threat and use of force.

To be sure, this focus on states and their security can potentially be defended as part of a 'social contract' in which states are the (best) means through which individual survival and wellbeing is assured. However the basis of this communitarian rationale is systematically ignored or unarticulated in traditional security approaches, which fail to reflect upon or interrogate the extent to which states are 'doing the job' of providing for individual wellbeing and survival. As Bill McSweeney (1999: 13–22) has argued, the focus on states as the security referent involves a fundamental slippage in the distinction between means and ends, furthered by conceptions and practices that see regime security and the territorial preservation of states as ends in themselves. Beyond these normative concerns, which constitute the most important rationale for the book, traditional approaches to security are also limited in terms of their capacity to develop our understanding of international relations, given their problematic assumptions of political agency, limited capacity to explain change, reductionist characterizations of power and capacity (as exclusively material in nature), and their simplistic conceptions of the origins of states' 'national interests'. It is in the context of these normative and analytical failings of traditional security studies that this book articulates and advances a *critical* security approach.

Critical security here is defined broadly enough to encompass two central traditions of critical security theorizing in academic literature. These traditions are broadly consistent with Chris Brown's distinction between (upper case) Critical Theory and (lower case) critical theory, and Steve Smith's distinction between emancipatory critical security studies (as articulated by Ken Booth and Richard Wyn Jones) and the broader definition of Keith Krause and Michael Williams in their edited 1997 collection, *Critical Security Studies: Concepts and Cases* (Brown, 1994; Smith, 1999). This latter approach is critical primarily in the sense of Robert Cox's important distinction between critical and problem-solving theory, itself based on Max Horkheimer's distinction between critical and traditional theory. Cox distinguishes between problem-solving theories – which take the world, its power structures, ideas and social relations, as givens – and critical theories which are more concerned with questioning the way problems are framed prior to their solution and for *whom* theory works (Cox, 1981; Horkheimer, 2002).

The first approach to critical security can be defined as a *reconstructive* project, aimed at advancing alternative claims of what security is or should mean. Most prominent in this analysis, as noted, is Ken Booth's conceptualization of Critical Security Studies as a concern with advancing individual emancipation (Booth, 1991). For Booth, security should be defined as emancipation: the removal of structural impediments that prevent individuals from carrying out what they would otherwise choose to do. Within this approach, emancipation is defined ultimately as a process of freeing up space for marginalized actors' voices to be heard in global politics, with the prime ethical consideration in security practice being towards the most vulnerable in global politics. This finds resonance in this volume in discussions of refugees and displaced persons in Sara Davies' contribution, and in Lorraine Elliott's discussion of environmental change, with her emphasis on the need to recognize the particular vulnerability of future generations and impoverished people most at risk from such change.

It is also possible to locate the human security discourse as articulated by the United Nations Development Programme (UNDP) within this reconstructive approach to critical security, given its focus on articulating a vision of security predicated upon rejecting the unacceptable normative implications of traditional security approaches and reorienting ethical consideration towards individuals (UNDP, 1995). Its dual articulation of human security as 'freedom from want' and 'freedom from fear' reorients our attention to the individual, and is invoked by some contributors to this book in pointing to the disjuncture between states/regimes and individuals in traditional security discourses and practices. In her chapter, for example, Marianne Hanson invokes human security as a discourse that forces us to recognize and confront the unacceptable fears, opportunity costs and violence that inherently confront individuals in the context of the development, possession, proliferation and threat of use of nuclear weapons by (their own) states.

The second definition of critical security within the scope of this book concerns what might be termed *deconstructive* approaches to security: approaches that do not primarily offer definitive alternative conceptualizations but rather seek to point to the silences, exclusions and blind-spots of traditional approaches to security – to expose both their analytical limitations and their normative implications. Anthony Burke's discussion here of the relationship between identity politics and security politics in the contemporary Australian context can be located in this approach – in particular his argument that the use of fear, threat and representations of otherness by the Australian government is broadly consistent with the exclusion and violence at the heart of traditional security conceptions and practices. His argument that Australia's threat or use of force (in Iraq, for example) has served paradoxically to *create* adversaries – the 'self-fulfilling prophesy' in Richard Ashley's (1984) terminology – is also a theme that runs throughout the book.

Clearly, these various 'critical' conceptualizations of security differ in not unimportant ways. There are tensions within the reconstructive approach (between the human security and emancipatory security discourses, for example) about what precisely alternative security futures should look like. This is applicable to the vexed question of agency and the particular possibility of human security being 'coopted' to serve elite purposes or 'tacked on' to traditional security practices, as Julie Gilson and Lorraine Elliott argue in their chapters (see Bellamy and McDonald, 2002; Thomas and Tow, 2002a, 2002b). It is also applicable to questions of political economy and the tension between approaches arising from liberal and Marxist traditions, as Simon Dalby notes in his conclusion. Perhaps an even more fundamental tension between the reconstructive and deconstructive approaches are their differing views as to whether setting out alternative security futures is actually desirable, or may constitute an imposition of Western, Enlightenment values (an issue addressed directly by Katrina Lee-Koo in her chapter). These concerns ebb and flow throughout the book, and inform the goal of some authors to restrict themselves to an articulation of the costs and assumptions of traditional approaches; others to point to the distinction between elite-based and bottom-up interpretations of 'progressive' security discourses; and still others emphasize sensitivity in suggesting what alternative practices and arrangements might be 'better' in different contexts.

While retaining this valuable breadth of critical security perspectives, however, we can nevertheless talk about *a* critical security approach. All of the contributions to this volume share a dissatisfaction with the analytical and normative implications of traditional security studies with its predominant focus on the territorial preservation of the nation-state from external military threat. Ken Booth captures these concerns in defining the academic project of critical security studies as 'rethinking the common sense of (the realist) orthodoxy from the bottom up while exposing the extent to which political realism is part of the problem in world politics rather than being the problem-solver' (Booth, 2005a: 2–3). Defined in such a way, critical security studies is indeed a broad church. And there is clearly a need for such a broad-based definition in order to open the door to the range of ways of conceptualizing, understanding and potentially redressing human suffering and insecurity, particularly in a region in which problem-solving approaches to security continue to dominate both in academic offices and the corridors of political power. The Asia-Pacific region is certainly, as Simon Dalby argues, a 'hard case' for critical security studies, with conditions most favourable to the realization of either reflective or normatively progressive security practices in the region (a vibrant civil society and open political systems) frequently absent.

The limits of innovation and the critical challenge

For some, the task of rethinking security in the Asia-Pacific is already well advanced. Academics and policy-makers alike might point to the modification of exclusively statist and military security paradigms by ideas such as 'comprehensive security' and (national and regional) 'resilience'; the imposition of nuclear-free zones (and norms) in Southeast Asia and the South Pacific; the formation of the Association of Southeast Asian Nations (ASEAN) with its norms opposing the solution of regional interstate conflicts by force and the intrusion of great powers; and the growth of constructivist scholarship and analysis. In contrast to realist assessments of power and military capability, this latter stream emphasizes the influence of ideas and norms that have created a regional 'security community' among ASEAN states – a grouping, some scholars argue, that has 'developed a habit of peaceful interaction and ruled out the use of force in settling disputes within the group' (Acharya, 2001: 1; Bellamy, 2004). They could also perhaps cite the partial incorporation of new ideas about 'co-operative' security[1] into regional security practices with the formation of the ARF, with its declared stages of 'confidence-building measures' (CBMs), 'preventive diplomacy' and 'conflict resolution' (ASEAN Secretariat, 2004: 14). Other mainstream innovations include arguments for 'broadening' security to take in new forms of threat (Collins, 2003: 1–5).

To be sure, there is much about these developments that could be (and is in a number of the chapters that follow) defined as progressive: in institutionalizing cooperation between states, for example, or breaking down conceptions of security associated exclusively with strategy and military threat. Nevertheless, some of these 'innovations' have also worked to reinforce elite assumptions and frameworks, and have sometimes served to obscure or legitimize terribly violent and unjust approaches to security, especially *within* regional states. To the extent that such thinking embodies critique, it has thus been a dangerously limited one. Indeed by limiting its questioning it may have thwarted critique as much as allowed it to flourish.

For example, while the 'broadening' of security analysis to take in 'transnational' threats such as unregulated people movements (UPMs), environmental degradation and scarcity, climate change, drug trafficking, or pandemics such as AIDS or influenza usefully highlights important issues and gestures towards a more holistic understanding of security, it incorporates assumptions that many critical scholars take issue with. One problem is that in this work the major focus for security (its 'referent object') remains the state (and, more accurately, governments and national elites within the state), sometimes reinforcing coercive policies that undermine the security of individuals. This is especially true for the analysis of people movements and refugees, which remains overly concerned with their potential to undermine national stability and integrity.

This concern with people movements as threats is visible in the work of the RAND Corporation's Peter Chalk and the Lowy Institute's Alan Dupont. Chalk argues that UPMs 'have the potential to challenge the integrity of both sending and receiving states', and Dupont, while acknowledging that accepting a link between UPMs and international security 'masks sharp differences of view over whose security is being threatened – that of the refugees . . . or that of the receiving countries who care and provide for them', still claims that 'these are not mutually incompatible positions. UPMs are a measure of both human and national insecurity' (Chalk, 2000: 155; Dupont, 2001: 136). In a more recent analysis Dupont states that the 'sudden large influxes of people who are ethnically and religiously different from the indigenous inhabitants, strikes at the whole notion of nationhood' (2006: 114).

While we would not deny that people movements have sometimes been sources of instability, especially when associated with regional and civil conflicts such as those in Palestine, Lebanon or Burma, a critical approach is suspicious of claims that people movements can be uncritically analysed and resolved as *both* a national and human security problem. In practice, sovereignty and national security have tended to trump the security of stateless people and reinforce coercive and exclusivist approaches not merely to refugees but national cultural diversity. Critical approaches instead highlight the *construction* of state and national identities, rather than assume them, and put their ethical and practical implications under scrutiny. In some cases this extends to a sustained critique of the concept and history of national/state *sovereignty* as such (see Burke, 2007). While critical scholars would acknowledge that large movements of people can be a serious administrative or political challenge for governments – who certainly possess a legitimate interest in ensuring that refugees do not constitute a threat to national security – they would insist that the human security of stateless people be paramount and bound with the obligations of states under international law, especially international human rights treaties and the 1951 Convention and 1967 Protocol on Refugees. This view guides the chapters by Sara Davies, Hazel Lang and Anthony Burke.

The normative problem with the 'broadening' approach can also be seen in the case of the Southeast Asian concept of 'comprehensive' security, which is based upon a 'multidimensional' understanding of security taking in military, political and economic dimensions. As we argue below, this is still a strongly statist and elitist approach that legitimates violent approaches to political challenges. The roots of comprehensive security lie in the concepts of national and regional 'resilience' developed in the intelligence agencies of the New Order regime of Soeharto. BAKIN (Badan Koordinasi Inteligens Keamanan (Indonesian National Intelligence Co-ordinating Agency)) chief Ali Moertopo (who was responsible for running subversion operations in advance of the 1969 'Act of Free Choice' in Papua and the 1975 invasion of East Timor) is famous for transforming former Defence Minister Nasution's notion of the 'middle way' for the Indonesian armed forces (ABRI) into the 'dual function'. Whereas the 'middle way' saw the army as an ambiguous social-political actor, neither a government nor a dead force subordinate to civilians, *Dwifungsi ABRI* gave the military a dual role both in the external defence of the nation and in its internal security (Schwarz, 1994: 30).

The dual function was merely one element of the 'total people's defence and security system' (*Sishankamrata*) which incorporated an interlocking national and regional 'resilience'. As Moertopo explained:

> The concept of national resilience is aimed at the creation of an all-embracing national order or system that would embody the capability of the nation to defend itself and at the same time to foil any threat from within as well as from without to its security and its continued existence . . . national resilience in [a] total integral and strategic way covers all the aspects of the life of the State and the Nation: ideological, social, political, economic, cultural, technological, defence and security (Moertopo, 1976: 21).

It is this doctrine that has provided intellectual coherence to Indonesian security policy, shaped the self-perception of the armed forces, and given a façade of legitimacy to its actions against perceived threats to national security and stability. During the life of the New Order, a vast panoply of threats were subsumed under this rubric – student activists, independent trade unions, the Left, street criminals, Muslims, protesting farmers, artists and writers, journalists, critical academics and more. However the most serious perceived threats, to which most violence has been applied, were the separatist movements in East Timor, West Papua and Aceh. This was made clear in 1999 in East Timor, as the TNI laid waste to the land in a final paroxysm of revenge and rage, and continues now through Indonesia's difficult and problematic transition to democracy (see McDonald *et al.*, 2002). In an important study of the Indonesian military Robert Lowry argued that national resilience was 'a mantra justifying continued authoritarian rule'; that it formed part of a holistic world-view in which 'individualism has no place and deviation of the most basic element can cause the whole system to malfunction' (Lowry, 1996: xxi).

In this light, a critical approach to security in the Asia-Pacific requires not merely a critique of a traditional security studies concerned with state-based military conflict but an engagement with an elite practice and discourse of security which is already broader in its focus but still analytically and normatively flawed. Below we go on to outline the combination of theoretical, policy and institutional frameworks in the region and the ways that they can be challenged by a critical security analysis.

Traditional security thinking in the Asia-Pacific

For the purposes of this book the Asia-Pacific region is somewhat arbitrarily defined as the Pacific Rim plus East Asia (north and south) and Australasia, thus excluding South American states and Russia (in contrast to the list of APEC (Asia-Pacific Economic Cooperation) members) and South Asian/ Indian Ocean states. The book tends to follow those lines of greatest interconnection and dependence in regional security dynamics, although this may also indicate flaws in regional diplomacy and institutions (the tsunami obviously demonstrated the need for greater cooperation amongst Indian Ocean countries, for example). As editors we are also conscious that there are glaring omissions in this book – due largely to the problem of space and the myriad sources (and viable topics for examination) of insecurity in the region. A study of critical security issues in this region also deserves dedicated chapters on the South Pacific, Antarctica, the Indochinese countries and indigenous struggles, and we hope this book stimulates further work in these areas.

Northeast Asia: alliances and deterrence

The Asia-Pacific region is arguably divided into distinct – but interconnected – security paradigms that are governed by differing normative and structural frameworks and differing levels of greater power influence and involvement. The first is the 'San Francisco' system – the 'hub and spokes' system of bilateral alliances between the United States and regional countries, which dates from the Cold War and which is focused upon realist frameworks of military deterrence and US strategic power projection. While this is most strongly based geographically on Northeast Asia, it incorporates Australia and the Pacific Islands, and is central to US military access to the Indian Ocean and Persian Gulf. During the Cold War it also incorporated Southeast Asia and Australasia (with Southeast Asia Treaty Organization (SEATO) membership of Thailand and the Philippines and its coverage of Cambodia, Laos and South Vietnam) but drew significant hostility from Sukarno's Indonesia, India, China and North Vietnam. Despite the membership of the ARF by the US and Northeast Asian countries, Northeast Asia is driven by interstate competition according to realist logics of deterrence and strategic advantage, and hosts a number of serious potential flashpoints for conflict. Bilateral rather than multilateral cooperation and diplomacy has more influence, although the region has not been untouched by normative change in international society and ad hoc multilateral initiatives are occasionally resorted to.

The North Korean regime's nuclear test in October 2006 served to underscore the sense of volatility associated with the Northeast Asian region, for some indicating the primacy of traditional modes of thinking about security and threat. And yet if the tragic inevitability of the North Korean response to threats emanating from the US administration illustrated anything about security processes and dynamics, it should precisely be that traditional frameworks of thinking about and enacting security are themselves part of the problem rather than a form of solution. Indeed it is worth noting that the critical analyses and predictions undertaken on North Korea – particularly in earlier drafts of the contributions of Roland Bleiker and Marianne Hanson – were ultimately (even if regrettably) borne out in the events of October. At a time when critical approaches to security remain marginalized on the basis of their lack of applicability to the 'real world', it is worth noting that such approaches appear more capable of appreciating the self-defeating logic of hard-line security rhetoric and policy in Northeast Asia than the architects of such policy in the American administration. This said, astute realists such as Lawrence Freedman (2004: 20) and Jeffrey Record treat North Korean behaviour as a rational response to US threats, with Record saying that 'rogue state regimes see in such weapons a means of deterring *American* military action against *themselves*' (Record, 2003: 17). Critical scholars share such insights, but also interrogate the deeper forces driving the conflicts and seek novel and more enduring forms of resolution.

Therefore even as it may appear that alternative approaches have little purchase and relevance in Northeast Asia, in this volume Roland Bleiker, Yongjin Zhang and Marianne Hanson offer critical perspectives on the identity-constructs driving the Korean conflict, the politics of counter-proliferation, and China's evolving security discourse. Even mainstream scholars – such as William Tow, who argues for a 'convergent security' approach combining 'prudent realism' and multilateral institution-building – emphasize that liberal approaches have an important positive role to play in moderating conflict in the area (Tow, 2001a). Critical scholars agree with liberals in emphasizing that deterrence and power balancing are dangerous stopgap measures and risk being inadequate to manage sudden, or even slowly escalating, crises – and as Marianne Hanson explores in her chapter, the emergence of preventive war doctrines in the United States adds a further destabilizing ingredient. However critical scholars also argue that there is a need to explore the deeper cultural forces, politics and forms of identity and otherness underlying regional conflicts if they are to be resolved, potentially involving a critical analysis of liberal policy initiatives.

Southeast Asia: a 'comprehensive' security community?

After 1967 Southeast Asia began to develop a slightly different paradigm to that governing relations in Northeast Asia (at least *between*, rather than within, its states). It was the removal of Sukarno by the Indonesian armed forces and the destruction of the Indonesian Communist Party (PKI, *Partai*

Komunis Indonesia) – which was accompanied by an archipelago-wide campaign of massacres and detentions that killed as many as 500,000 people – that enabled the formation of the ASEAN and the emergence of a nascent 'security community' that challenged some dominant strategic norms. Its first members – Indonesia, Singapore, Malaysia, Thailand and the Philippines – agreed to eschew the use of force to resolve disputes between them, to respect each other's internal sovereignty (the doctrine of 'non-interference'), and to minimize the intrusion of great power competition, with the objective of 'strengthening the economic and social stability of the region and promot[ing] regional co-operation in Southeast Asia' (ASEAN Bangkok Declaration, 1967). ASEAN declared its desire to establish a 'Zone of Peace, Freedom and Neutrality' (ZOPFAN) in November 1971 – which reflected ASEAN countries' early signatures on the Treaty on the Non-Proliferation of Nuclear Weapons (1968) but was never quite achieved – and in turn agreed a treaty creating a Southeast Asia Nuclear Weapons Free Zone in December 1995. From the outset, ASEAN constituted a combination of liberal norms in interstate strategic relations and statist norms pertaining to the maintenance of 'internal security', in which sovereignty defined as non-intervention is paramount, and regime security a dominant objective. This tension was in turn embodied in the development of Southeast Asian security concepts: 'comprehensive' security, and national and regional 'resilience'.

The 'development of comprehensive approaches to security' is a core principle of the ASEAN Secretariat, 2004, Annex A, Principle 2), and it is probably the closest thing to a common and overarching security concept in East Asia, including Australasia, one whose common biases and features are present across an otherwise natural diversity of concerns and frameworks at the national level. Comprehensive security is a doctrine in which, in Muthiah Alagappa's (1998: 624) words, 'security goes beyond (but does not exclude) the military to embrace the political, economic and socio-cultural dimensions'. Examples of comprehensive security in action include Indonesia's concept of national resilience, noted earlier, Chinese policy that sees economic development and political stability as significant, and Malaysia's view that 'national security is inseparable from political stability, economic success and social harmony'. Vietnamese and South Korean policy-makers have begun to articulate security in broader, 'comprehensive' terms as well. While Alagappa (1998: 625) plays down the importance of comprehensive security as an operational concept, he believes that 'it does affect policy and behaviour' and works as an 'intellectual foundation for thinking about security at the highest levels of government, with consequences for the determination of national priorities, including budgetary allocation, and strategies to be employed in the pursuit of security'.

On the surface, comprehensive security appears to capture the holistic and interdependent nature of insecurity processes and to incorporate the kind of liberal norms present in numerous ASEAN documents. However when we consider the recent history of Southeast Asia and ASEAN's handling of major crises, and interrogate its underlying concepts of 'resilience', it is revealed as normatively and practically flawed. As we argue above, comprehensive security as 'resilience' links internal security paradigms preoccupied with the (often violent and repressive) defence of regime security and territorial integrity with regional frameworks that, while often embodying very positive liberal norms of interstate cooperation, diplomacy and arms limitation, extend the internal structures into region-wide paradigms that place a primacy upon sovereign freedom, non-interference and 'political stability'. What kind of 'security community' is this?

While writers such as Acharya are right to emphasize the value and significance of ASEAN's norms of cooperation and multilateralism regarding interstate conflict – which are motivated by 'ASEAN's misgivings about the potential unreliability of major power security guarantees that are integral to a balance of power mechanism' (2001: 180) – constructivist scholarship tends to soft-soap the darker side of the ASEAN way and the essentially statist (and internally coercive) character of its 'norms'. Norms can be either good or bad, or many shades in-between, and it is hardly progressive to highlight their function as 'constitutive' of social realities (Acharya, 2001: 24) if their ethical and political implications are not simultaneously interrogated. Cooperation in the ASEAN case tends to *strengthen* statist norms and insulate regional governments from scrutiny over their approach to human rights and internal claims to justice, separatism and difference.[2]

This was made sadly clear by the silence of Indonesia's neighbours as its military initiated the appalling spree of killing, terror and destruction in East Timor following its people's vote for independence, by their diplomatic obstruction[3] during the crisis, and their patchy participation in an intervention driven by Australia, the United Nations, Portugal, New Zealand and the United States.[4] While Malaysia refused to join the intervention force, Thailand and the Philippines did play valuable roles, even if they did so at the request of Indonesia and avoided placing their troops in front-line combat roles. In fact, the only Asian faces in the force in the first few days were British Ghurkhas (Ryan, 2000: 73, 134). The Timor crisis came in the wake of the economic crisis and efforts by Thailand and the Philippines to modify the non-intervention norm with the notion of 'flexible engagement' that – in the words of the former Thai Foreign Minister Surin Pitsuwan – could allow ASEAN 'to play a constructive role in preventing or resolving domestic issues with regional implications' (Acharya, 2001: 154). These efforts were thwarted at the 1998 ASEAN meeting and will be even harder to revive with Cambodia, Vietnam and Myanmar as members.

If this is a security community, it is a community of economic, political and military elites, and the security it provides is morally (and conceptually) incoherent, being all too often premised upon the insecurity of others. In such systems of social and geopolitical power a universal claim (security) is mobilized to support a particularist politics (stability and privilege). In this way constructivist security analysis avoids the basic question motivating critical security studies: that of the meaning of security itself (Burke, 2002; Walker, 1997; Dalby, 1997). While Acharya does support the opening of debate about the relevance of the 'ASEAN way' in the face of complex region-wide crises,[5] he seems reluctant in his work on ASEAN as a security community to identify the truly profound transformation of ASEAN norms – and the pressure it places upon elite meanings of security – this implies.

The issue appears to be the (apparent) disjuncture between the liberal norms operative at the interstate level in ASEAN and the more Machiavellian norms shaping domestic governance and internal security. In this light, constructivist writers such as Alex Bellamy (2004: 90) make a revealing point when they remark upon 'the similarity of ASEAN norms and those of pluralist international society'. Critical theorists, however, have long pointed to the dangers inherent in the identity-construct implicit in the Westphalian idea of sovereignty – that is, the essentially paranoid and repressive relationship between self and other that shapes understandings of 'regime security', 'subversion' and 'national integrity'. In short, there seems to be little normative value in speaking of a Southeast Asian security community if it serves to perpetuate human insecurity.

There is also a danger that such theorizing could help to legitimize and perpetuate repressive ASEAN norms if the human rights critique is not given a more central emphasis and power. Critical security approaches offer a simple solution to this dilemma: define security in human-centred terms and challenge states and regional organizations to harmonize their own norms and practices with it. How this applies in practice is to a significant degree context-specific, necessitating engagement with both the range of contexts in which human security is at risk and the possibility of security practices implicated in this process to be reoriented.

Sites of insecurity, sources of security

This book is divided into three sections: agents; strategies and contexts; and futures. The first section outlines a range of possible agents or actors potentially capable of redressing individual suffering and vulnerability in the region. Julie Gilson's chapter examines East Asian regional institutions and dynamics of regionalism as potential sources of 'progressive' security discourses and practices. While Gilson notes some emancipatory potential in these processes and institutions (particularly if associated with an increase in non-state actor involvement), she uses the example of the 'comprehensive security' and 'human security' discourses elaborated by the Japanese government and ASEAN to point to the continued centrality of the state (rather than individuals) and the extent of limits in a regional context to fundamental change in security conceptions and practices.

While a focus on the progressive security potential of regional institutions and regionalism has become increasingly prominent in literature on security in the Asia-Pacific (Acharya, 2001; Lawson, 2005), less common is a focus on militaries as potential agents of individual security. In their contribution, Alex Bellamy and Bryn Hughes argue that while militaries in Southeast Asia have traditionally been more likely to threaten the citizens of their own states than provide for their security, processes of democratization, security sector reform and increased regional cooperation provide bases for hope that military roles are changing and will continue to change in a manner favourable to redressing individual insecurity. This conclusion is tempered with warnings about the implications of the 'war on terrorism' for these dynamics, and the perseverance of scepticism within the region given the historical role of the military itself.

The theme of more traditional sources or agents of security is also taken up by Mark Beeson in his discussion of the state's capacity to provide for individual security in the context of developmental and economic imperatives. Beeson argues, contra the hegemonic liberal economic orthodoxy, that the state has played a key role in ensuring economic development in East Asia, with associated benefits for individual wellbeing. Beeson ultimately suggests that human security requires that the provision of basic needs *precedes* the provision of political and social rights, even while suggesting that this argumentation has been used in the region as an excuse for maintaining the power of elites rather than pursuing democratization. While many would take issue with this generous interpretation of the benefits provided by 'strong states' in the context of human development, his chapter serves as an important counterpoint to those who would dismiss the state as a potential agent for individual security.

The final contribution to the discussion of agents of security is See Seng Tan's analysis of epistemic communities in Singapore. Tan contests two common interpretations of the role of epistemic communities in the construction of security: that they are either passive sources of governmental legitimacy, or autonomous agents with the capacity of constructing or creating state interests. Rather, he suggests that the relationship between agents and structures in this context is mutually constitutive. This analysis is important given the emphasis often placed on non-state actors and civil society generally as sources of progressive change, manifested regionally in attention to the role of the Council for Security Cooperation in the Asia-Pacific (CSCAP) in articulating alternative discourses of security in the region. It also addresses the often ignored question, one central to normative security theorists, of the relationship between academic theorizing and political practice (see Wyn Jones, 1995).

The second section of the book deals with strategies and contexts, outlining a range of different sites of insecurity in the region, the ways in which dominant security discourses and practices emerge, and the extent to which such discourses are contested in different contexts. The first chapter in this section, by Edward Aspinall and Richard Chauvel, addresses the Indonesian government's approach to minority groups and separatism in Aceh and Papua. Aspinall and Chauvel argue that Indonesian security discourses have consistently defined political community in narrow terms, in which groups within Indonesia are defined as either completely loyal to the state or a separatist threat. For Aspinall and Chauvel this dichotomy (echoed decades later in the language of the 'war on terrorism') has enabled and justified repressive policies that have contributed to a cycle of violence and significant human rights abuses on both sides.

Hazel Lang takes up the issue of civil unrest and human rights abuses in her analysis of conflict in Burma, in which she focuses on the plight of the up to 500,000 internally displaced persons (IDPs). In doing so she highlights one of the central themes of the book: that states are often a source of threat rather than an agent of security for individuals, a maxim nowhere more applicable than Burma. Lang concludes by suggesting that while the Burmese regime appears unlikely to reorient its security priorities and practices of its own volition, increasing pressure from ASEAN (already evident in its refusal to allow Burma to take on the Chairmanship of the organization in 2006) has the potential to alter the approach of the Burmese government. This example serves to indicate the possibility for a movement away from the norm of non-intervention for ASEAN members, identified in a number of contributions as an obstacle to the emergence of progressive security discourses.

Displaced persons also feature in Anthony Burke's analysis of Australian security discourses, in terms of the failure of the Australian government to recognize or act upon ethical and legal obligations to vulnerable outsiders in the form of refugees and asylum-seekers. For Burke, this example (along with representations of Muslims in general after 11 September 2001) is indicative of the increasingly narrow definition of boundaries of political community and identity under the conservative Howard Australian government, in which outsiders are conceptualized as threats to national security. Indeed,

Burke argues, articulations of threat and insecurity by the government should be viewed in this context as attempts to justify particular policies (anti-terror legislation, for example), to underpin government legitimacy, and to deny the validity of broader conceptions of Australian identity or obligation to vulnerable outsiders.

Lorraine Elliott's chapter deals with the complex problem of environmental change in the Asia-Pacific and its relationship to security. Elliott analyses the extent to which environmental issues are constructed as security issues (i.e. 'securitized'), and the capacity for environmental change to produce widespread harm for the most vulnerable in the region. In highlighting pressing regional environmental problems (including deforestation, resource depletion, pollution, and increasing and unsustainable energy consumption), Elliott draws attention to the weaknesses of traditional and even some alternative accounts of the environment–security relationships. She concludes by suggesting that the emphasis in responding to environmental change in the region should be on the needs and suffering of those most vulnerable to environmental change, and their empowerment to 'speak' security. For Elliott, emerging civil society voices in the region, including in comparatively closed political systems such as China, are already contesting processes of environmental change.

The question of the suffering of the most vulnerable is central to the subsequent chapter by Sara Davies, who focuses on the plight and treatment of asylum-seekers in southeast Asia. Davies focuses in particular on the example of Malaysia. She argues that while Malaysia has not acceded to key international legislation relating to the treatment of refugees, this is understandable given the Eurocentric nature and development of this law and has not precluded some positive practices on the part of the Malaysian government (in the 1970s and 1980s, for example) in dealing with refugees and asylum-seekers. Nevertheless, she argues that international law does provide an important source of pressure on signatory states that is not applicable to Malaysia, allowing the rejection of moral responsibility to refugees, asylum-seekers and illegal immigrants more likely. Davies' contribution raises a series of complex questions about security and ethical responsibility, pointing to tensions between an imperfect but nevertheless important set of international norms or rules, and to the (often significant) gap between practices that meet immediate material requirements and practices that are based on a politics of recognition of ethical obligations.

Yongjin Zhang's contribution to this volume outlines security perspectives and discourses within China. Specifically, Zhang argues that academic thinking on security in China reinforces traditional (realist) perspectives of security because it is bound-up with the preferences of the Chinese government and underpinned by mainstream (particularly US) academic thinking on security. Zhang argues that this orthodoxy reflects the Chinese government's strategic interests in responding to internal security threats, and the primacy of the 'rising China threat' literature within traditional security studies academically. Zhang concludes by suggesting that the failure of Chinese security analysts to explore truly critical notions of security constitutes an important impediment to the emergence of alternative security discourses or practices in China.

The final chapter in this section analyses the consequences of US strategic thinking for security interests and dynamics in the Asia-Pacific. Matt McDonald's chapter explores the implications of the US-led 'war on terrorism', arguing that this has undermined human rights and democratization processes in the region and encouraged militarism and militarization in state's security policies. In locating the 'war on terror' in broader foreign and security policies of the United States, McDonald questions the (often taken for granted) conception of the US as regional security guarantor, instead pointing to the ways in which the US-led 'war on terror' has undermined the security of the most vulnerable and been inimical to stated goals of redressing the terrorist threat. He concludes by suggesting that contestation of the 'war on terror' from within the US and the region constitutes immanent possibility for individual emancipation, defined in terms of the diffusion of power to exclusively 'speak' security away from governments and elites to sub-state groups and individuals.

The final section of the book deals, appropriately, with security futures. While the previous sections have outlined the agents capable of advancing individual security and the contexts in which suffering and vulnerability has arisen in the region, this section deals specifically with the question of what alternative security discourses and practices might look like. The first chapter in this section, by Roland Bleiker, deals with international engagement with North Korea. Bleiker compares the US hard-line approach to North Korea with the engagement strategy favoured by South Korea. In an argument that appears throughout the book in various forms and contexts, Bleiker argues that a hard-line approach is likely to produce and further (indeed has produced and furthered) the 'threat' posed, creating the very conditions supposedly being responded to. Bleiker calls for a more nuanced engagement approach to North Korea predicated upon an attempt to recognize what the world (and in particular US power) looks like from a North Korean viewpoint, an approach that would be based on an 'ethics of difference'. He suggests that such an approach is necessary (indeed realistic) in order to understand North Korea's reaction to future policy initiatives, its pursuit of a nuclear programme and in order to prevent future conflict on the peninsula.

The final substantive chapter, by Katrina Lee Koo, outlines a feminist critical security discourse and examines its applicability to the Asia-Pacific region. For Lee Koo, traditional and dominant conceptions of security ignore the range of ways in which women are particularly vulnerable in the Asia-Pacific, including through practices such as the trafficking of women and militarized prostitution. For Lee Koo, there is a clear need, in light of these limitations, for a feminist critical security discourse. This ought to be based upon revealing the gendered nature of universalized theories of security and pointing to the centrality of constructed identities to conceptions of security and threat. In articulating this security approach, Lee Koo confronts key dilemmas of the emancipatory security project in arguing for the need to define processes of emancipation as context-specific rather than universal, and in arguing that in instances of extreme marginalization, we can be justified in speaking and acting *on behalf of* the suffering.

Simon Dalby's conclusion engages with the not insignificant task of drawing together the range of conceptual and empirical insights of a deliberately broad ranging text. His focus in so doing is on identifying and drawing out underlying themes across contributions, and in articulating crucial questions for the development of critical security studies. Dalby identifies a range of relationships touched on but not fully articulated in preceding chapters, including the relationship between dominant modes of political economy and regional vulnerabilities; and the relationship between notions of empire and geographical space and the power to define security. Dalby's reflections in this context remind us of the benefits of inter-disciplinary research, particularly for building consciously holistic approaches to individual suffering and vulnerability. More fundamentally, Dalby's concluding chapter serves to raise a series of issues central to the development of a critical security studies approach, including the potential tensions between different normative imperatives within critical security studies as defined here (i.e. human security vs. emancipatory security), and the vexed question of the relationship between the universal and particular in articulating prescriptions for progressive change. He concludes by reiterating the importance of security theorists remaining normatively engaged, even in the context of uncertainty and disagreement over precisely where we might be going.

Visioning emancipatory security futures

The continued marginalization of critical thinking about security in the Asia-Pacific, both politically and academically, does not make the analysis undertaken in this book any less applicable or germane. For us, and for the contributors to this volume, it is precisely the marginalization of critical security perspectives in the region that provides the most powerful rationale for this book. These perspectives can offer new insights into traditional security dynamics and action, can shine a spotlight on security stories unheard or ignored in traditional accounts of state-based violence, and can articulate visions for resolutions to pressing regional problems involving human suffering.

This is tied, of course, to the broader argument that there is much at stake in debates about the meaning of security. This is not, as Ken Booth (1995: 272–6) has argued, a mere exercise in academic navel-gazing. Given the capacity, noted by so-called Copenhagen School theorists as well as postmodern theorists, for the promise of providing security to enable certain types of responses and underpin political legitimacy more generally, the prospect of accepting traditional security conceptions and practices as 'the way things are' should be avoided at all costs (Buzan *et al.*, 1998; Huysmans, 2004; Dillon, 1996). And while perhaps we may not agree over precisely where we should be going or how we should get there, we can nonetheless begin to ask those most fundamental of questions: 'whose security are we talking about?'; 'from what threats?'; 'and by what means can their security be achieved?' This book constitutes an attempt, first and foremost, to ask such questions in the contemporary Asia-Pacific context and to outline a range of responses that are informed by a desire to problematize and reconstruct prevailing political orders.

This book is also committed to pointing out possibilities for change, possibilities *immanent* within clearly problematic and at times repressive existing political orders and institutions (Wyn Jones, 1999; Booth, 2005b). While there has been debate among critical security thinkers about whether to plump for 'realizable utopias'[6] or more radical political transformations, surely a significant part of the critical project is a recognition of the role of political and ethical *choice* in the construction of security in any particular context. This necessarily opens up space for security to be constructed in different ways, with different (and hopefully progressive) implications for redressing individual suffering. Such possibilities are located in the chapters that follow in the waning or changing role of militaries in the region, in processes of democratization, in burgeoning civil society forces and in increasing patterns of regionalism and regional integration. While none of these processes should be unambiguously embraced, all are identified in different contexts as crucial sites of possibility, consistently related to the diffusion of power in speaking security: that is, away from the exclusive preserve of state leaders to refugees, minority groups, trafficked women or the impoverished. Their plight demands new ways of thinking about what security means, for whom, from what threats and in what political, social, environmental and economic contexts. It is to this task that this book now turns.

Notes

1 This is a term championed by former Australian foreign minister Gareth Evans as encompassing 'collective', 'common' and 'comprehensive' security. See Evans and Grant (1995: 101–3).

2 As Alan Collins notes: 'ASEAN was designed to be first and foremost an association of states engaged in nation-building . . . it was not intended to be a supranational institution that would provide a legal framework for enhancing cooperation amongst all its members' (Collins, 2003: 128).

3 When the APEC meeting in Auckland proposed to discuss the post-referendum violence in the days it was reaching its height, ASEAN members protested at the presence of British Foreign Minister Robin Cook (a non-APEC leader) and shunned the special meeting on Timor. The Thai foreign ministry spokesman, Kobsak Chutikul, said: 'No ASEAN country is going [to the meeting] because this is a non-APEC issue' (AFP, 1999; Barker, 1999; *ABC News Online*, 1999).

4 This came on top of 25 years of support for Indonesia's claim to East Timor at the United Nations.

5 Acharya comments that the environmental and economic crises of the 1990s 'showed that the key goals of ASEAN regionalism . . . may no longer be guided by a consensus on a strict adherence to sovereignty and its corollary, the doctrine of non-interference'. He also argues that 'pressures to revise ASEAN norms such as non-interference . . . could help in revitalising ASEAN and further its development as a security-community building institution. Flexible engagement could facilitate the engagement of civil society elements within a broader framework of ASEAN regionalism' (Acharya, 2001: 156).

6 This term is Richard Wyn Jones' (1995: 230). For some critical comments see Burke (2007: 'Introduction').

Part I

Agents

1

Regionalism and security in East Asia

Julie Gilson

THE SHORT TITLE to this chapter conceals the host of complex geographical, historical, definitional and ideational factors inherent in any attempt to understand what is meant either by 'security' in a given region, or the very definition of 'East Asia' itself in this particular case. East Asia is not a legally definable entity; it is not bound by a common cultural heritage, religion or history; nor is it determined by commonly recognizable geographical boundaries. What is largely shared within the region, however, is a normative commitment to the protection of sovereign integrity, in particular through adherence to the principle of non-interference, one of the foundations of the so-called 'ASEAN way'. The full range of these principles comprises: sovereign equality; the non-recourse to the use of force; the peaceful settlement of conflict; non-interference and non-intervention; the non-involvement of ASEAN to address unresolved bilateral conflicts between member states; quiet diplomacy; and mutual respect and tolerance (Malik, 1993: 51).

These principles complicate any apparent attempts to shift the security referent from state to individual, and hence it is difficult to discern within East Asia any fundamental rethinking about the nature of security itself. Nevertheless, concerns over forest fires and their resulting haze; consternation over the likely environmental damage to be expected from rapidly industrializing states including China; the steep increase in mass migration; and the illegal trafficking of drugs and people represent some of the many challenges to the principle of non-interference, and as such to the very bases upon which East Asia has built its networks of relations since 1945. This chapter proposes that the potential for a shift in the regional approach to security lies precisely in these areas of interest, and it examines the extent to which such potential is being realized. The chapter does not focus centrally on the historical origins of the concept of 'security' within East Asia, which has been associated in particular with the concept of a 'security community'

(Acharya, 2000). Rather, it examines the contemporary application of the term 'complex security' in a region which encompasses a particular, historically determined and normatively held concept of security, and which emphasizes the importance of sovereign independence.[1] For the states in the region, the range of complex security problems today is underpinned by military and nuclear fears: from China's nuclear arms, Japan's potential for nuclear weapons, North Korea's nuclear threat, to tensions between China and Taiwan. Following the first testing of North Korea's nuclear weapons in October 2006, for example, China's concerns over the potential for military action enshrined in the United Nations' Chapter Seven led to the submission of a revised resolution against Pyongyang. And while the US refused to rule out the use of force against North Korea, it was careful to engage in a diplomacy-first strategy of trying to address the problem in conjunction with its Asian allies. Meanwhile, concerns continue to be raised over the future of the US–Japan Security Treaty and its relevance for regional security. Simultaneously, economic integration continues alongside rapid growth in military expenditure, and the complex interplay of trade and military affairs renders intra-regional diplomacy problematic.

For the most part the concept of 'civil society' and the very definition of 'non-governmental organization' (NGO) remain fuzzy, in a region where such groups are often funded by their own governments and lack coherence and international credibility. Without their greater inclusion in the regional security institutions, and without a reshaping of long-held understandings of what security means, it is difficult to see how security in East Asia can move away from its current emphasis on the preservation of the state. What is more, if the issues themselves are not commonly agreed upon in terms of priority areas, the collective mechanisms for addressing them also remain incomplete. The only arrangement for dealing with regional security matters collectively is the loosely constituted ASEAN Regional Forum (ARF) and its track-two discussion forum, the Council for Security Cooperation in the Asia Pacific (CSCAP). However, the composition of the ARF (including the US, the European Union and Australia, amongst others) makes it hard to detect its regional credentials, while the more recent development of the ASEAN Plus Three (APT) process (incorporating the states of ASEAN alongside China, Japan and South Korea) has yet to clarify its own *modus operandi* or to demonstrate any novel approach to security issues (Camilleri, 2005: 254). This chapter examines the extent to which a reordering of security boundaries is either desirable or possible in East Asia. Drawing broadly on a constructivist approach to identity and region-building around norms of behaviour and the role of ideas in supporting state security agendas, it takes Booth's concept of emancipation as a process of the diffusion and decentralization of the power to define 'security'.

Thinking security

Discussions about comprehensive security tend to focus on two parallel trends. On the one hand, comprehensive security is regarded as embracing a plurality of 'new' or 'soft' subjects within the security debate. On the other, it is consistent with an emancipatory approach to understanding security as a 'freeing' mechanism, which fundamentally shifts the referent away from the state and towards the individual and moves away from understanding regional security approaches as responses to hegemonic incentives, towards the interweaving of history, culture and norms alongside systemic pressures pertaining to regional security cooperation (Press-Barnathan, 2005: 281). This chapter illustrates how this immanent possibility resides within the concept of comprehensive security, and particularly within key institutions. It is no coincidence that the very concept of 'emancipation' in East Asia still carries a postcolonial idea of liberation; the imperative to protect still-young sovereign rights; to prevent a recurrence of intra-mural conflict within Asia itself; and to create a regional identity in order to achieve all of the above. Nevertheless, changes to the prevalent conceptualization of security may occur as nascent debates over human security begin to take root.

A constructivist view of how the regional security discourse is sustained and embodied in regional institutions illustrates how the very process of security interaction may embed ideas about security within particular communities. Indeed, it may alter the very identity of the community in question.[2] By addressing the dual nature of comprehensive security within East Asia, this chapter examines some of the tensions inherent within East Asian concepts of security. By considering the concept of human security, the chapter examines the possibilities and constraints for the emergence of more normatively progressive sets of security discourses and practices, and of space for a range of critical actors. In so doing, it underlines the obstacles to the realization of critical security in the region.

The chapter begins with an examination of how the concept of comprehensive security is misleading in East Asia, where the traditional notion of Westphalian sovereignty is 'alive and well, shaping and reshaping the terrain of regional peace and security' (Moon and Chun, 2003: 106). It presents an overview of security structures within East Asia, with a particular focus on their institutional and normative underpinnings and the impact of regional identification underlying them. The second part examines the significance of comprehensive security in the region and the potential for the full development of human security. In this context, it analyses the so-called 'track-two' approach and the role of other, non-state actors. The final section examines how these various debates unfold in Japan, which has an important role in the development of regional approaches to comprehensive security. The conclusion assesses the potential for the debate to move towards an emancipatory comprehensive security agenda in the region.

'East Asia' as a region

For the purpose of this chapter, the definition of East Asia comprises the member states of the newest regional project, the APT process; namely, the states of the Association of Southeast Asian Nations (ASEAN), alongside China, Japan and South Korea. The label 'East Asia' is itself contested and the whole issue of security is closely linked with the question of identity formation, but this chapter accepts that ASEAN has set the framework for the discourse of security within the region more generally. ASEAN was established in 1967, predominantly to address conflict among participating member states, and issues of identity were, from the beginning, entwined with the protection of newly obtained independence and national resilience. From the origins of the ASEAN Post Ministerial Conference (PMC) during the late 1970s regional leaders made a concerted effort to establish formalized meetings and to create a broader regional framework within which to discuss key issues and address disputes without recourse to violence. The ending of the Cold War combined with a changing regional role for the US and a gradual rise of China, to elicit at the 1992 ASEAN summit in Singapore the expression of a common interest in a developing a 'broader dialogue for extended security' (Palmujoki, 2001: 68).

Scholarship on regionalism in East Asia has begun to engage with the changing profile of security agenda, and Hettne's and Palmer's work on 'new regionalism' in particular illustrates this movement (Hettne *et al.*, 1999; Palmer, 1990). However, there has been scant examination of immanent possibilities for change in the perception of the role of the state itself in regional security. So far, then, possibilities for change in East Asia have been expressed in terms of simply broadening the scope of issues to be placed on the security agenda of states, and the ARF itself has been instrumental in that process. In practice, the security institutions of East Asia are underpinned by an accepted set of norms, which come to be cited and applied as the basis for the development and maintenance of regional security institutions and for the *de facto* approach to the concept of security itself.[3] Although there is a tendency among a number of East Asian states to place a greater emphasis on the localized norms of engagement (such as non-interference), universal norms (such as human rights) come to be linked as part of institutional participation and in this way may provide pressure points for change.[4] Over the longer term, such practices may lead to the creation of 'identifiable social conventions', or even to the development of shared expectations, which can then become infused with normative meaning (Young, 1989: 82; Krasner, 1993: 18). The ARF and other institutional arrangements have reinforced and challenged this framework, leading both to norm diffusion and dilution, as will be demonstrated below. The arrangement embodied in the APT process also represents a close association of an institution with the issue of regional identity, as it is *de facto* a contemporary realization of the controversial East Asian Economic Caucus (EAEC) of the 1990s. This example of the EAEC attests to the fact that debates over norms and institutions are closely associated with the whole concept of regionalism itself. In these terms, security, as Alagappa notes, relates to political survival and the survival of the state from its neighbours, with the effect that institutions become a mechanism for surveillance, a kind of 'neighbourhood watch' (2003: 24). The case of the ARF raises a number of additional questions, as its membership extends beyond that 'neighbourhood' context.

The ARF and the APT process

Despite (or perhaps because of) the fact that the original idea emanated from Japan and Australia, ASEAN quickly took the lead in developing plans for the ARF, which was, notably, an 'ASEAN' and not 'Asian' forum. The objectives of the Forum were set out in the first Chair's statement in 1994 and centred upon the need for a dialogue on 'political and security issues of common interest and concern'; to contribute to 'confidence-building and preventive diplomacy in the Asia-Pacific region'; and to 'create a more predictable and stable pattern of relationships between major powers and Southeast Asia' (Chanto, 2005). The ARF was designed as, and remains, a loose forum for dialogue, based around annual ministerial and senior officials meetings. Its founders also emphasized the promotion of dialogue among disparate regime and state types and regarded the Forum as a vehicle for incorporating ASEAN principles into the fabric of a wider geographical framework. The types of issues discussed by the ARF have included territorial and jurisdictional disputes in the South China Sea, self-determination for East Timor, nuclear proliferation in Northeast Asia and South Asia, weapons of mass destruction (WMD) and the impact of globalization (DFAT, 2002). These were precisely the types of issues which were already being raised in other multilateral arena, such as the ASEAN PMC, in United Nations agencies, and in the Asia-Europe Meeting (ASEM). The ASEAN concept paper on which the foundations of the ARF were based outlined a three-stage evolution from: confidence-building; to preventive diplomacy; and to the development of mechanisms for conflict resolution, as a means of establishing a minimal set of expectations for the ARF (Palmujoki, 2001: 72; Haacke, 2003: 77).

The ARF also placed on the discussion table topics such as relations with Myanmar and the issue of Aceh, which raise potentially challenging issues with regard to ASEAN norms of behaviour. However, there was a sense that these issues were simply being placed on an increasingly lengthy list of agenda items, and were being raised in response to Western concerns. There was neither a sense of prioritizing specific agenda items, nor of creating the basis for new a normative framework. Nevertheless, their inclusion does mean that the states of ASEAN have had to confront – often in the face of very public international criticism – different approaches to security challenges such as human rights. Thus, the ARF not only provides the channel for disseminating ASEAN norms more broadly, but also for advancing a wider spectrum of debate among the states of ASEAN themselves and for raising the profile of those universal norms most actively championed by the non-ASEAN participants of the ARF and ASEM. Fundamentally, however, ASEAN states themselves retain defence policies which 'indicate that they charge to the organization no major security role', with the result that the ARF's role as a forum limited to discussion has been reinforced (Palmujoki, 2001: 64).

Notwithstanding this approach to the Forum, institutional momentum has engendered a number of changes, as exemplified at the ARF meeting in Hanoi in July 2001, when the group agreed on the adoption of papers on Concepts and Principles for Preventive Diplomacy, an Enhanced Role of the ARF Chair, and the Terms of Reference of the ARF Experts and Eminent Persons' Register. The 2001 process of clarification acknowledged the contested nature of the term 'preventive diplomacy', but agreement was reached around the idea of 'consensual diplomatic and political action taken by sovereign states with the consent of all directly involved parties'. These developments should be considered alongside the introduction of the concept of comprehensive security in 1995, which represented an important recognition of the changing regional and global security environments, the need for a multi-level dialogue on diverse issues and the desire on the part of member states to develop the ARF as a de facto confidence-building measure (CBM). Nevertheless, even within this agenda-setting approach to comprehensive security, Amnesty International (1998) has criticized the ARF's unwillingness to date to 'address the *full* regional security agenda'. Ironically, then, the very concept of national comprehensive security – which might more usefully read 'inclusive' – renders a 'full' agenda impossible, while the delineation of comprehensive security at the heart of the ARF has tended to reinforce existing approaches to security in the region. As such, 'comprehensive security' fails to address the nature of security actors themselves or to create space for the articulation of an alternative interpretation of security. Despite this strong commitment to represent sovereignty and status quo as the keys to security among the states of the region, there have been several attempts in East Asia to erode or at least refine these norms. Proposed in the mid-1990s, the Thai concept of 'constructive intervention' was later revised to a form of 'flexible engagement' and designed as an intermediate position between interference and non-interference (Anwar, 2003: 558; Acharya, 2003a: 236). The proposal was supported by Malaysia and the Philippines but opposed by Indonesia, Singapore and Vietnam, where the long-held commitment to non-interference was strongest. For this reason, during the crisis in East Timor, ASEAN states were careful not to interfere in Indonesia's domestic politics and therefore, unlike Australia, no ASEAN member state offered its services to the United Nations until requested to do so by the Indonesian government.

The issue of human security illustrates not only how this state-centric security focus constrains security thinking in the region, but also highlights possible contradictions among the views of Western and Asian participants in the ARF, especially over human rights and democracy. While it is discussed in the context of the ARF, the United Nations Development Programme's (UNDP) focus on the individual is not shared by all East Asian participants. Nevertheless, the ARF has 'engendered an increasing awareness of regional norms among the major powers and has alerted the regional states to the changing values and perspectives arising from today's globalized environment' (Desker, 2001). In striking this rather optimistic note, Desker inadvertently summarizes the dichotomy of its existence: while the modalities of the ARF may draw heavily on ASEAN practices, the reality of the Forum is that it has forced difficult issues onto the table, but with no effective mechanisms or even a mutually comprehensible framework within which to deal with them.

In summary, then, on regional issues the ARF has enjoyed a modicum of success, such as over the discussions regarding the South China Sea, and it may have facilitated a certain level of interaction, mutual awareness and socialization among states. However, although regional institutions such as the ARF are important for attenuating some of these tensions, Ball is correct to assert that informal dialogue alone will be insufficient to establish the basis for talks on substantive issues (Ball, 1998: 107). More significantly, it does little to alter the basic parameters of the state-centric security debate and notably continues to neglect the potential for NGOs and other non-state actors to play a role in regional security.

The ARF tends to be cited as the only security arrangement in the Asia-Pacific. However, APT cooperation began in December 1997 when leaders of ASEAN joined an informal summit with their counterparts from Japan, China and the Republic of Korea. The process was institutionalized as a regular meeting two years later and now includes 48 mechanisms for coordinating 16 areas of cooperation, ranging from agriculture to information technology. Originated as a forum for economic cooperation in particular, the APT bears upon security issues in two ways: by addressing directly the security implications of economic transactions (such as the funding of international terrorism and the security implications of financial crises); and by raising economic security as the key to development issues, thereby engaging with core concerns of a human security approach. Positive assessments of the APT suggest that it has 'already begun to change the political and economic landscape of East Asia', creating in particular a gelling effect on the wider concept of region itself (Stubbs, 2002; Glosserman, 2004).

Such assessments may be rather premature. Nevertheless, the APT does address two potentially problematic facets of the ARF; namely, its wide membership and broad issue scope. First, the APT narrows membership to the immediate region. As such, the principal actors themselves regard the APT as part of a comprehensive security network in the region. Second, its activities to date regarding territorial disputes suggest that the APT could become the 'dominant regional institution' in East Asia for dealing with difficult local issues (Stubbs, 2002: 441). On a different note, however, the APT does not resolve the issue of state-centrism. Indeed, by being presented as a reincarnation of former Malaysian Prime Minister Mahathir's EAEC, it reifies the 'ideal of an "East Asian Community"' founded on the ASEAN way. In addition, the APT, like the ARF, continues to depend on the active participation of the ASEAN states: for while the 'plus three' states agreed to participate, the focus of their security agendas has remained fixed on narrower bilateral and wider global targets. Like the ARF, moreover, it illustrates how regional norms in Asia 'remain strongly wedded to the protection of Westphalian sovereignty' and in this way renders unlikely a novel approach to the whole issue of comprehensive security (Acharya, 2003a: 225).

Comprehensive security, human security and non-state actors

The idea of comprehensive security has particular roots in the East Asian region, as illustrated through the ARF process and within Japan (see below). It has been defined in the region as the 'pursuit of sustainable security in all fields (personal, political, economic, social, cultural, military, environmental) in both the domestic and external spheres, essentially through cooperative means' (Tan and Cossa, 2001: 32; Job, 2003: 245). The notion of comprehensive security, then, allows a broadening from traditional definitions of security, to incorporate issues as diverse as economic and environmental security (such as global warming, pollution, rising sea levels and deforestation), alongside other non-military concerns such as refugee issues and population movements. Economic security plays a central role in this approach to security issues, as it is frequently regarded as a means of stabilizing tensions in other areas of activity. As such, economic development – which has been an important pillar in managing East Asian relations – may be seen to lie at the heart of this definition of comprehensive security. This concept of comprehensive security also includes those threats that have a direct impact upon state security – such as secessionist movements and ethnic violence – and which lead to the 'general threat of the state's incapacity to govern effectively because of under-development' (Anwar, 2003: 563). Essentially, then, this is a form of comprehensive *national* security, comprising development for the good of the state and the protection of sovereignty and non-interference, and it thereby implies a central emphasis on the so-called ASEAN way. This assessment is not to deny that there is an alternative agenda under development. For, through the emancipation of the discourse of security within institutional and normative frameworks outlined above, the prospects for a critical engagement with the security agenda begin to rise. This may be seen in the emergent discussions over the concept of human security in East Asia.

Where comprehensive (national) security ensures a continued focus on the state, order and stability, the UNDP definition of human security offers the possibility of taking the individual as the referent, particularly through its attention to justice and emancipation. The UNDP Human Development Reports of 1994 and 1995 listed seven dimensions to a broader concept of security; namely, economic, food, health, environmental, personal, community and political (Snitwongse and Bunbongkarn, 2001: 149; UNDP, 1995). This represented a move away from accepted explanations of security towards a closer scrutiny of the roles of the individual and the community. Thomas provides a definition that encapsulates these changing circumstances, noting that human security 'describes a condition of existence in which basic material needs are met, and in which human dignity, including meaningful participation in the life of the community can be realised' (2000: 6). The thrust of the reports and the subsequent Commission on Human Security (co-chaired notably by Japanese representative Sadako Ogata, former United Nations High Commissioner for Refugees, and Amartya Sen of Cambridge University) are summarized by Alagappa:

> To focus only on the security of the state, particularly on the military threat to state security, is to miss the whole range of threats that make human existence unbearable. (2003: 564)

That there are significant impediments to such a redefinition in the Asian context is not disputed. One problem is that the very concept of human security is not novel: it has frequently been utilized as a means of expressing the interconnected nature of military, political, economic and social aspects of security, incorporating concepts which overlap with the definition of comprehensive security. The general use of the term has been grounded in the protection of state security, and therefore the view that the 'person' at the centre distinguishes human security from traditional security continues to be difficult to discern in this region. There is much discussion about this form of security within the ARF, ASEM and other forums that include East Asian member states. However, as the case study of Japan illustrates below, the concept of human security is, like comprehensive security more generally, open to diverse interpretations and in East Asia to date has not been fully exploited, in large part because of a lack of debate about the role of civil society or non-state actors.

Paralleling discussions of human security in East Asia is the debate over the role and relevance of non-state actors in the security arena. It would be incorrect to suggest that such groups do not exist or play any role in the security debates and agenda-setting in East Asia. At the same time, however, it should be realized that the terms 'civil society' and NGO in particular do not hold the same resonances in East Asia as in Europe. Typically, non-state actors are seen as part of an informal and gradual approach to discussing security in East Asia, within the track-two processes, or they may be seen as the largely marginalized groups of the NGO world (Terada, 2003: 261). The so-called track-two (or 'one and a half') approach brings together a range of state and non-state representatives, most visibly in forums such as the CSCAP, which parallels the ARF, or the Council for Asia-Europe Cooperation (CAEC), which shadows the summitry of the ASEM process. Although state representatives are supposedly present in a private capacity, the reality is often that these track-two processes form an extension of government activities. Thus, there is a 'complex and symbiotic relationship between the national and transnational, the unofficial and official, and Track 1 and Track 2 processes' (Job, 2003: 247). Track two not only refers to informal networking and unofficial communication, but also to the promotion of cooperative security and multilateral security regionalism. The agenda, then, remains focused on the state as referent for security interests, and no civil society groups are represented in track-two frameworks. What is more, the state organization fails to confer upon them a significant degree of legitimacy.

This is not to suggest that track-two processes are without any value: they provide a forum for socialization and have been credited with developing a regional understanding of 'preventive diplomacy', and contributing actively towards negotiations regarding territorial disputes and North Korea, particularly through the Korean Peninsula Energy Development Organization (KEDO). However, while there is a sense that track-two activities create opportunities for shifting attitudes, track-two activities can serve to further marginalize the role of NGOs, by coopting named representatives from non-state spheres. Moreover, the nature of the debates held within track-two forums remains 'largely irrelevant to the concerns of Asian societies', and ensures that the 'state remains the modern subject *par excellence* in Asian security discourse' (Job, 2003: 275: Tan and Cossa, 2001: 23).

If NGOs are viewed as autonomous entities, separate from the state and even committed to common sets of causes, East Asia appears at first sight to be mostly devoid of non-governmental activity. Certainly, NGOs in East Asia are under-developed and are not always recognized either by the state or by other non-state groups, receive relatively little media attention and do not tend to enjoy active participation within society. Well-known NGOs in the region include Indonesian environmentalists opposing deforestation in Irian Jaya and human rights groups in Thailand, while internationally active groups include the ASEAN People's Assembly set up in 2000, and the Asia-Europe People's Forum (AEPF), which was established on the margins of the ASEM in 1996. Even the AEPF, though, tends to be dominated by the better structured, financed and organized European NGOs within it. At the same time, there has been a growth in localized NGOs, but these are issue-specific and do not generally represent a challenge to government interests, as the local–national distinction is often unclear. One key problem in East Asia, then, is in defining what an NGO is: such groups not only vary according to the types of organization, membership, duration, budgets, staff, geographical locus, ideology and political conditions, but they also lack 'legitimacy, transparency, and transnationalism' (Princen, 1994: 33). It is clear in East Asia that there does not exist a Coxian notion of 'global civil society' as a 'basis for an alternative world order' among non-state actors (Cox, 1999: 10). Moreover, the traditionally close proximity of NGOs and state agencies in East Asia means that NGOs may obtain controlled inclusion into official dialogue, and thereby come to be coopted by the very states they have yet to criticize. While alternative security discourses such as human and comprehensive security are articulated, then, the complex relations between state and society and continued emphasis on state security make it hard to see what is really happening. The case of Japan exemplifies some of these tensions.

Japan

Japanese approaches to comprehensive security and human security illustrate how they originated and how even normative approaches to security in the region are limited. For various reasons, the Japanese have faced similar issues to ASEAN in their security policies, and the Japanese conception of comprehensive security adopted the same ASEAN-style principles in developing the ARF. Japan's approaches towards the regional security agenda have since 1945 been tempered by a need to alleviate neighbourhood concerns of a return to Japanese militarism or, more recently, to reassure other East Asian states that Japan is not about to penetrate them economically to the detriment of the host state's interests. The difficult legacy of history and the political posturing of leaders and their use of symbols (from the Yasukuni Shrine of the war dead to school textbooks denying Japanese war atrocities throughout the region) have perpetuated the sense of regional suspicion over the possibility of a remilitarized, and indeed nuclear, Japan. Increasingly, Japanese business involvement, tourism and cultural exports have reinforced Japan's presence across the continent. At the same time, Japan is keen to ensure that China becomes involved in multilateral relations: China's nuclear tests in 1995, military exercises against Taiwan in 1996, its inclusion of the Senkaku Islands in its 1992 Territorial Waters Law and its crossing of the meridian line in the South China Sea all added to growing Japanese concerns over the potential security implications of China's rapid economic growth. In part to assuage some of these concerns, and in part to be seen to be playing a burden-sharing role, the Japanese government since the 1990s has been actively seeking new ways of cooperating to promote regional security (Hook *et al.*, 2005). The most visible evidence of this posture is Japan's proposal for, and involvement in, the ARF. Indeed, the Japanese government removed itself from the forefront of this initiative as a means of playing down any suggestion that Japan was seeking any greater regional role, while at the same time underlined Japan's reported commitment to comprehensive national security.

Japan's initiative for 'comprehensive national security' arose from Prime Minister Ôhira Masayoshi's Comprehensive Security Study Group in 1980 (Chapman *et al.*, 1983). Although the recommendations were not adopted formally as government policy, they were important in helping Ôhira to resist US pressure to shoulder more of the defence burden than was deemed to be politically tenable, and to broaden the concept of security beyond military security. Representing a similar dynamic to ASEAN's later embrace of (a limited) human security discussion after the Asian financial crisis, the 1973 oil crisis encouraged Japanese government to consider broader issues as part of security debate, principally economic security. The six specific policies drawn up by the group included: an increase in military cooperation with the US; the strengthening of Japan's defence capability; the need to persuade the Soviet Union that Japan was neither weak nor a threat; a recognized need for greater energy security; the imperative for greater food security; and the improvement of the crisis management of large-scale national disasters such as earthquakes (Sudo, 2001: 289). The principal reasons stated by the government for this policy were to obtain a wider international role and to promote Japan's own defence goals. This state-centred approach was perfectly summarized by Prime Minister Nakasone Yasuhiro's 1984 report, entitled a 'Comprehensive Security Policy for the International State of Japan'. This report emphasized the state security aspects of the 1980 report and gave particular attention to increased defence spending and multilateralism. Although it, too, sought to strengthen the emphasis on economic security, this was presented as a means of protecting the state, not vulnerable individuals. Thus, Official Development Assistance (ODA) and other aspects of economic cooperation were proffered ostensibly as a means to address the root economic causes of social and political instability, but were explained as a way of preventing the generation of military conflict in the first place. As such, aid was regarded principally as an instrument of state control. In reality, then, the term comprehensive security was designed to create a space for economic security and Japan's own attempt to redefine its security parameters echoes the general, 'largely abstract' debate over contemporary security (Alagappa, 1998: 11). This parallels ASEAN's approach to comprehensive security. Interestingly one of the unintended consequences of Japan's comprehensive security approach, emphasizing non-military means for inducing interdependent socio-economic stability, has been the development of diverse networks of economic, political, cultural and diplomatic ties with a range of countries and interest groups.

The Japanese government has also been central to the development of a debate over 'human security', promoted as it was by the high-profile presence of Ogata in the United Nations system. Interestingly, the Japanese government has adopted an increasingly active rhetoric of human security as a means of claiming to offer a more significant contribution to international security and to escape the criticism that it engages only in 'chequebook diplomacy'. It has also been adopted by the state to convince the Japanese electorate of the need to introduce an anti-terrorism bill after 2001, as well as to push for major changes to the role of the Self Defence Forces (SDF), particularly with regard to their international peacekeeping activities. There is, then, an ongoing debate within Japan about the nature of national and regional security and how to achieve it, given changing international conditions. Non-state groups are quietly requesting inclusion in some of these discussions, and it remains to be seen how far the Japanese government is willing to make the human dimension a central plank of its security policies.

Conclusion

This chapter has attempted to illustrate how and why studies related to security in East Asia face two difficult and overlapping problems. First, the concept of 'comprehensive security' has a particular meaning in East Asia, with its own indigenous origins, which prioritizes the notion of comprehensive *national* security. Second, the membership of security-related forums in East Asia remains strongly centred around states. This is reinforced in the institutional frameworks in which security is increasingly debated, and which socialize member states to accept only adjustments to the profile of their security agenda, while retaining an emphasis on what is perceived to be a sovereign right of non-interference. At the same time, however, that very mechanism for socialization offers the best opportunity to influence the ideational significance and increasingly the practical realities of how to define and respond to a range of threats and challenges, and to rethink the tenets embodied in the ASEAN way. The boundaries of the human security discourse within East Asia provide space for the inclusion of non-state actors and for a serious attempt at placing a real emphasis on the role and needs of the individual. A number of factors will affect the likelihood of such a development.

First, regional institutions play an important part in providing a locale for socialization, particularly given their emphasis on dialogue and mutual understanding. Moreover, institutions such as the ARF and ASEM seek to accommodate tensions among the demands and normative prerequisites of both western and Asian member states. Components of the multifaceted civil society of East Asia may find their voices in direct response to such opportunities, as localized East Asian groups work with and parallel their European counterparts. To date, even where common ground exists on the need to address particular issues, notably by the Western participants bringing in issues such as human rights, the means to achieve those goals may often be expressed quite differently. For its part, the APT's narrower membership and clearer central focus on economic issues responds to some of the failings of the ARF, but it rests more strongly on the pillars of the ASEAN way and is even less likely to admit the full participation of non-state actors.

Second, ongoing debates about the possible nature of an 'East Asian Community' will continue to examine the security implications of economic and political cooperation. This may be limited to the development of a set of interstate agreements or may, if the political will is present and civil society claims coherent and acknowledged, interrogate the very nature of the region in question. To date, competing mechanisms and interests reflected in the structures of ASEAN, the ARF and the APT illustrate the different regional potential to be developed.

Third, the role of non-state actors has to date contributed little to the security debate in East Asia. Even in those areas where non-state actors are present, they are usually weak, narrowly focused or effectively coopted into state activities through the commonly adopted track-two formula. NGOs and other non-state groups themselves remain very localized or disparate and there is as yet no substantial regional NGO forum to lobby for access. A reluctance on the part of many East Asian states to grant full access to NGOs not only prevents the full development of institutional forums for addressing common dilemmas, but also challenges the very meaning of what the 'common' might represent. And yet, as the example of ASEM demonstrates, regional groups can lobby governments and mobilize interests where structures exist for them to either join or shadow state activities (Gilson, 2002: 141–72). Groups engaged in lobbying for the recognition of human rights, the protection of the environment and other causes are starting to recognize a value in working with European counterparts and in presenting common cause. The changing shape of East Asian institutions and debates over the very meaning of the region provide ample space for their legitimate inclusion.

Finally, does the putative pursuit of human security within East Asia provide a real opportunity to relocate the plight of the individual in society and become a key dimension of security? It may indeed be 'time for regional and international organizations to put human security at the top of their agenda', but the nature of the participants and significance of security itself must also be brought into question if East Asia is to move collectively into a new stage of security debate. The human security agenda may offer an important opportunity; for even if the concept of human security had no analytic utility at all, it would be worth employing as an 'advocacy tool', as a 'comfortable shelter' to engage with the critical security debate for both state and non-state actors (Anwar, 2003: 565–6). To work towards this new stage, advocates of human security must do what those pursuing comprehensive security have not done: create the promised space for non-state participants; remove the contingencies attached to aid debates; acknowledge the human aspects of economic development; and examine how the individual might become the primary referent of security in East Asia. Thus far, there is very little that is genuinely comprehensive about 'comprehensive security' in East Asia, where the focus on the need to preserve state primacy remains central. And while the opportunity for change exists through institutional learning and the pursuit of human security, it remains to be seen whether current discussions will be used as an additional tool for ensuring national comprehensive security, or whether East Asians can forge a path towards a truly comprehensive security.

Notes

1 As a result, it does not imply what Booth regards as the integration of theories of the 'good life' and survival (Booth, 1991: 322).

2 This chapter does not focus on the norm-creating and maintaining effects of 'security communities', but scholarship relating to them also illustrates how they may constitute a collective identity in the pursuit of fostering peace (Adler and Barnett, 1998).
3 Norms here are defined as 'shared (thus social) understandings of standards for behavior' (Klotz, 1995: 14; Jepperson *et al.*, 1996: 54).
4 The term 'institution' is understood here to signify not only channels for the reduction of bargaining costs, but also to represent the potential for increased mutual awareness among participants about their involvement in a common enterprise (Keohane *et al.*, 1993: 175; Jepperson, 1991: 145).

2

Emancipation and force: the role(s) of the military in Southeast Asia

Alex J. Bellamy and Bryn Hughes

THE STUDY OF THE role of the military in Southeast Asian security has, by and large, remained immune to intellectual developments in the wider field of security studies. This has created important blind-spots in our understanding of the military's relationship with human security in the region. Where it has imported new ideas, traditional approaches to Southeast Asian security have tended to interpret them in such a way as to leave dominant realist perspectives intact. Although there have been attempts to 'broaden' the scope of security beyond the military defence of the state, approaches to human security in Southeast Asia have insisted that if the term is to have any meaning at all it must be interpreted in ways that make sense to foreign policy elites (Kerr *et al.*, 2003; Thomas and Tow, 2002a; Tow *et al.*, 2000). The importation of human security concerns to Southeast Asia has thus been conducted in such a way as to reduce its impact on security politics by replacing its primary concern with individual insecurity[1] with the concerns and interests of elites. Similarly, the importation of 'constructivism' into Southeast Asian security studies to date has sidestepped confrontation with the realist dominated sub-discipline by ignoring many of its key facets. With some notable exceptions (Acharya, 1997, 2003/4; Haacke, 2003), the few writers that have employed constructivist or 'alternative' theoretical security approaches to Southeast Asia have suggested that states will learn to cooperate through the sharing of norms, identities and interests (Busse, 1999; Peou, 2002; Tow 2001a, 2001b). This makes it relatively easy to dismiss 'constructivism' because, as Tow points out, 'ASEAN was hardly the unified actor that constructivists would like to portray' (Tow, 2001a: 262). Leaving aside the fact that Tow conflates constructivism with neo-liberal institutionalism, the importation of constructivist approaches to security in this way does great disservice to both 'non-traditional' theories and our understanding of security practices in Southeast Asia by closing off any prospect of broadening or deepening the study of security in the region. It forecloses insights on the power of ideas, the role of social learning and non-state perspectives on insecurity. The ideational structure formed from traditional conceptions of security, in other words, constrains the agency of those who strive to point out alternate ways of conceiving security, and in doing so, security theory affects security praxis.[2]

Traditional East Asian security studies has therefore helped to conceal two critical issues in relation to armed forces in the region. First, its obsession with great powers, balances of power, and future wars in Taiwan and elsewhere not only contributed to its slow response to the emergence of terrorist and other forms of non-state violence in the region, but it also masked the fact that more of the region's citizens are threatened by their own militaries than by those of other states or – for that matter – by terrorists. Second, the realist presumption that militaries protect states, and hence citizens, overlooks the role that militaries play in protecting particular *regimes* against internal opposition movements. Until very recently, Southeast Asian militaries were primarily concerned with either the protection of particular civilian regimes or with the maintenance of a particular conception of state/national identity through direct rule. The military plays these types of role in Burma, Thailand, Vietnam and Indonesia. In short, rather than protecting their citizens, in practice the region's militaries have expended more effort controlling, killing, torturing and arbitrarily imprisoning them in order to maintain a particular order or regime. The primary purpose of armed force in the region has been to protect states and regimes from internal opponents rather than external aggressors.

Focusing on the military's role in projecting force externally also obscures some of the political and socio-economic functions that they perform which may contain within them immanent possibilities for reform and emancipation. These immanent possibilities are embedded in the practices and justifications of the region's security sector. Taking as its cue the Hegelian idea that critical security studies should acknowledge that the resources for criticism and reform 'can be found only "immanently", that is, in the already existing political societies from where the critique is launched' (Devetak, 2005: 144), we base our critique and search for reform on the security sector's own claim to be protecting citizens and the community's common values. We ask, in short, whether the practice matches the theory. Where there are discrepancies, for instance where a military claims to be protecting civilians when it is fact endangering them or where the security sector claims to uphold the law or 'democratic values' but in practice operates 'above' the law or beyond democratic scrutiny, then there are immanent possibilities for emancipatory reform. Four potential areas stand out in this regard: first, the idea of military professionalism can contribute to wider processes of democratic reform; second, in many parts of the region, the military sector provides much needed economic life through positive business activities such as building vital infrastructure; third, in some parts of the region force is necessary to maintain the rule of law and there is no reason not to think that, with appropriate military reform, force could be used lawfully, legitimately and prudently to protect the common good; and finally, the development of military professionalism and especially the idea of defence diplomacy opens up significant avenues for regional cooperation on a wide range of issues.

This chapter develops in three steps. First, we outline how mainstream Southeast Asian security studies conceptualizes the role of military power, showing that it helps to legitimize military force by reference to hypothetical threats and obscures the very real violence that the region's militaries sometimes unleash on their own citizens. The second part concentrates on the role of the military in Southeast Asia as a regime protector and highlights some of the more recent episodes of militaries using unlawful force against their own citizens. The third part explores the four areas of immanent possibility identified above, calling our attention to the need to think more carefully about what the region's militaries actually do, and what role they can play in the realization of alternative security futures.

Securing Southeast Asia

Southeast Asia is often taken to be a realist region par excellence because actors remain preoccupied with the preservation of the state. According to Mohammed Ayoob (1995: 14), security can only be 'broadened' (but crucially not 'deepened') to include the security of individuals once the state is secured and legitimized (as in Western Europe). In many parts of the 'Third World' where sovereign statehood has only arrived in the past 40 years, the protection of the state from external threat remains the principal concern. Southeast Asian security studies has certainly tended to identify threats to the territorial integrity of the state as constituting the paramount 'security issues', masking the way that security praxis has a more internal than external focus and legitimating the perpetuation of human insecurity by the region's militaries.

The question of what counts as security threats and legitimate means to deal with them are therefore pivotal not only in order to identify the ways in which traditional understandings of security help to render people insecure but also as a necessary prerequisite for identifying immanent possibilities. Typically, Southeast Asian security studies has tended to focus on three sets of threats: threats emanating from China and the necessity of 'balancing' Chinese hegemony; threats relating to territorial disputes produced by decolonization; and secessionist and Islamist threats. Between them these portrayals of threat constitute a powerful case for insisting on the centrality of military force to the provision of security from threats emanating from others.

Despite a number of mitigating developments since the end of the Cold War, the 'China threat' continues to loom large in regional strategic thinking. One contributing factor is the territorial disputes that persist between China and several Association of Southeast Asian Nations (ASEAN) members over the ownership of the Spratly Islands in the South China Sea. The underlying factor, of course, relates to the fact that China is a major military power with an armed capability much greater than that of all the Southeast Asian states put together. Thus, despite the general avoidance of violent confrontations between China and Southeast Asian states, the cornerstone of security thinking nevertheless remains the deployment of military capabilities and alliance formation intended to balance against a potential Chinese hegemon.

The second key cause of concern for Southeast Asian security studies is the myriad territorial disputes that arose in the region during decolonization. Experiences of decolonization in Southeast Asia helped to reinforce realist ideas within the region. During this period, there were a variety of challenges to the sovereignty and territorial integrity of several of the region's states, most of which emanated from within the region itself. These included the Indonesian policy of challenging the legitimacy of the new Malaysian federation (the so-called *konfrontasi* policy), and Malaysia's fractious relationship with Singapore and the Philippines. The 'Corregidor affair' serves as one illustration. Relations between the Philippines and Malaysia worsened in 1968–9 when the media in Manila reported that a secret army was being trained to attack Sabah by Filipino armed forces on the island of Corregidor. This affair threatened the very existence of ASEAN barely six months into its existence (Acharya, 2001: 49). An important point of these tensions is that, throughout the Cold War, the focus of security in the region was drawn to state sovereignty and territory rather than human security concerns.

The third principal threat that concerns the region's security analysts comes from terrorism, radical Islam and secessionist movements. Virtually every state in the region, with the possible exception of Singapore, has confronted a significant internal threat from ethnic secessionists, religious radicals or communists. Like the communist threat before it, the emergent radical Islam combines a physical threat to the regime and the state's citizens with an ideological threat. The first type of threat is obviously manifested through acts of terrorism such as the 2002 Bali bombing. Thailand and the Philippines have experienced significant acts of physical threat from radical Islamists as well.[3] Insurgency groups such as the Moro Islamic Liberation

Front in the Philippines, and *Jemaah Islamiyah* (JI) across the region, moreover pose an important challenge to the legitimacy of the state itself. These radical Islamic groups, which have proven particularly divisive in secular-based states such as Indonesia, Thailand and the Philippines, insist that the religious leadership should replace traditional political elites at the head of the state and that states should not foster relationships with the US and its allies. These types of threats have inspired an outpouring of scholarly literature, which serves in turn to validate their importance (Crispin, 2004; Martin Jones, 2004; Pearson, 2002).

Whilst each of these types of threats has some substance to it (some more than others), our concern here is not with the validity of the threats but with the *effects* of this discourse on human security: the security issues it omits and the concerns and practices it legitimizes. The region's governments are unified in their feeling of being threatened by both insiders and outsiders. To manage their insecurity they developed a regional society, revolving around ASEAN, predicated on norms and institutions designed to manage relations between them, provide a bulwark to potential Chinese expansionism and give them a free hand to deal with internal opponents however they see fit. There are three clusters of norms embedded within a narrowly constituted epistemic community of political leaders: non-interference in the domestic affairs of other states; a consensus based style of decision-making; and the non-use of force to settle international disputes (Acharya, 2001: 58; Ramcharan, 2000: 65). The centrality of non-interference and non-use of force is unsurprising and fulfils two important functions. First, they not only provide the region's states with a free hand to deal with internal opponents violently, they actually enable such strategies since neighbouring states can neither criticize domestic activities nor allow insurgents to use their territory. Second, it is a manifestation of the region's attempt to balance Chinese hegemony (Acharya, 2001: 51–65).

In short, traditional approaches to Southeast Asian security insist that security is predicated on defending the region's states from a number of mainly external but also internal threats. This discourse legitimizes the acquisition and deployment of military force but not its use against external threats. Thus, whilst masking the principal role of the region's militaries this discourse tacitly enables and legitimizes it.

Regime protection

The principal role of most of Southeast Asia's militaries is the protection not of the state, nor of its citizens, but of a particular regime and the interests of the military itself. The common glue that brought the state leaders together in 1967 to form ASEAN lay not in shared history or culture but in their shared experiences of trying to govern fragile states. Although ASEAN's goals were primarily the promotion of economic, social and cultural cooperation, the prime preoccupation was regional peace and security, which necessitated stability *within* states. The closing declaration at the first ASEAN summit (in Bali, 1976) illustrated this: 'the stability of each member state and of the ASEAN region is an essential contribution to international peace and security. Each member state resolves to eliminate threats posed by subversion to its stability, thus strengthening national and ASEAN resilience' (Leifer, 1986: 66).

Throughout much of the Cold War and even now for many of the region's states (particularly Indonesia, the Philippines, Malaysia, Cambodia and Burma), the paramount concern has been with the consolidation, legitimization and security of particular regimes and ruling elites, rather than the protection of the impersonal state. Seen this way, the common perception of threat that brought the leaders together to form ASEAN in 1967, and that continues to shape regional cooperation, was not fear of an expansionist China or Vietnam but the presence of opposition movements that threatened regimes from within (Ganesan, 2000: 260). ASEAN's primary goal was therefore the promotion of regional peace and security through the collective legitimization of states and limited cooperation to protect the security of the region's regimes from *internal* challenges. Quite often, Southeast Asian militaries abuse the citizens under their ostensible care for the purpose of regime protection.

This idea is clearly demonstrated by briefly considering three recent or ongoing cases. A 2004 incident in southern Thailand illustrates how the Thai government has used the need for national cohesion and internal order to justify human rights abuses committed by the military. In this particular instance of a decades' old conflict between the mainly Buddhist government and the mainly Muslim southern provinces, a crackdown by government security forces on protests by Muslim youths led to the shooting deaths of 6 and the death by suffocation (during transport) of around 80 others. After the event, Thai Prime Minister Thaksin Shinawatra praised the efforts of the government's security forces and claimed the actions were justified (Voice of America, 2004). Despite general condemnation from many voices in international and world society, including governments and Muslim leaders – both within and outside of Thailand – these egregious human rights abuses have been allowed to go unchallenged.

Similar occurrences have marred Indonesia's recent past. Most remarkable perhaps was the 1999 violence (both sanctioned and committed by the Indonesian military) unleashed upon East Timorese civilians prior to and especially following their vote for independence. East Timor, however, is only one of several regions where the Indonesian armed forces have used violence against civilians as part of its campaign against a regional insurgency. The province of Aceh is an area in which Indonesian government security forces have been accused continually of committing countless atrocities on the Acehnese population.[4] In West Papua, moreover, reports about the murder of pro-independence supporters by government security forces are not uncommon and the violence has even increased in recent years (Human Rights Watch 2003).

Although typically less visible internationally due to the general shroud of secrecy obscuring the state's internal activities, human rights abuses at the hands of the military have also been rife in Burma for many decades. The Burmese military regime has persistently used violence and forced relocation to fracture and repress the Karen community, which has claimed independence (Lanjouw *et al.*, 2000: 231–3). At war since 1949 with successive military governments, members of the Karen ethnic minority have endured significant suffering due to the generalized, state-led violence (Lanjouw *et al.*, 2000: 231–3). And the abuses have not abated.[5]

To recap: discourses of Southeast Asian security are predicated on the idea of external threats and territorially discrete states. This discourse serves to legitimize the development and deployment of military forces. In relation to Southeast Asia, traditional security studies provides an instrumental rationale for force with one hand, whilst on the other hand it paints an image of the region that ignores the myriad ways that military force is actually used to suppress opposition. Whereas traditional security studies assumes that force is used to protect the state against external enemies, militaries in Southeast Asian have seldom fulfilled this role. More often they employ force to protect either the *regime* or itself against internal opponents. To put it bluntly, we think many more Southeast Asians are threatened by their own militaries than by external opponents or, for that matter, terrorists. That this simple observation is not widely acknowledged by the traditional Southeast Asian security literature is a product of its overly simplified view of the regime/state/society nexus whereby the first two are understood as necessarily 'protecting' the third from external harms, its obsession with balancing China and more recent obsession with Islamic terrorism. We are not saying that Islamic terrorism or Chinese hegemony are not security issues but that from the perspective of most real people in Southeast Asia, they are much less of an immediate threat than their own militaries.

Given the centrality of a narrowly focused realism on security praxis in Southeast Asia, our claim that the military sector fosters insecurity among those it is meant to secure might be an apposite ending. However, this project, like the critical security studies project in general, is also concerned with identifying possibilities for positive reform. Evidently, neither the military sector nor their political partners are likely to retreat in the short or medium term. However, there are potentialities not only for improving the military sector's record vis-à-vis human rights but also for the military sector to make a positive contribution to other sectors. These potentialities are located within the rubric of the 'security sector reform' policy agenda pioneered by the UK and US especially from the 1990s onwards.

Reform potentials

The theory and practice of Security Sector Reform (SSR) is relatively new. Its origins lay in the growing recognition within the 'development' or 'aid' community in the West that development and security are interdependent but it speaks directly to the way that the security sector is legitimized in Southeast Asia. Indeed, although 'new', SSR is predicated on the actualization of the traditional security rhetoric outlined in the previous section. That is, it asks how the security sector might better secure citizens under its care or strengthen the rule of law. Both of these claims are central to the legitimation of the security sector, yet as the previous section demonstrated, there is a sharp contrast between theory and practice. Thus, although 'external' in origin, SSR is predicated on the immanent possibilities already present in Southeast Asia's security sector.

Long-term development or democratization programmes cannot succeed, Western advocates of SSR argue, without the provision of stable security by legitimate and democratically accountable security forces. Aid donors therefore have a responsibility to promote good governance in the security sector in order to assist broader development programmes sponsored by a range of non-governmental organizations (NGOs), individual states and international institutions such as the World Bank.[6] There has been a growing awareness in the development and aid communities that not only do 'repressive or corrupt security structures . . . undermine the stability crucial to maximising the benefits of aid programmes' (Cooper and Pugh, 2002: 5) but also that positive reform of the security sector can provide a catalyst for wider good governance and democratization programmes. A 'new aid paradigm' (Duffield, 1999) has developed which recognizes that self-sustaining security depends upon the creation of a legitimate, democratically accountable and effective indigenous security sector. Whereas during the Cold War the security sector was shunned by the development and aid communities as the source of the under-development problem, there is an increasing awareness that development and security are interdependent and that armed forces and police forces can make a positive contribution to wider processes of democratization and development (Duffield, 2001).

The upshot of this convergence between security and development was the so-called defence reform agenda vigorously pursued around the world by the UK and US. This focus emerged from the recognition that 'unprofessional or poorly regulated security forces often compound rather than mitigate security problems' (Hendrickson, 1999: 9). The UK's development minister, Clare Short, identified five key areas of defence reform that DFID (Department for International Development) intended to promote. They were:

- Supporting the establishment of structures of proper civilian control over the military;
- Training members of the military in international humanitarian law and human rights;
- Strengthening national parliamentary oversight of the security apparatus;
- Supporting civilian organisations that might act as watchdogs over the security sector;
- Supporting the demobilisation and reintegration of ex-combatants. (Cooper and Pugh, 2002: 16)

Within post-conflict programmes such as that in East Timor and Cambodia, defence reform may also include building local capacity for reconstructive activities such as de-mining, and encouraging armed forces to play a role in promoting regional stability through defence diplomacy and building peacekeeping capabilities. The key normative objective underpinning these policies is two-pronged: on one hand to improve the efficacy of the armed forces in the pursuit of their legitimately and democratically decided goals and, in doing so, to minimize the potential threat to human security that they pose (Cottey *et al.*, 2002). As Malcolm Chalmers (2000) and others have explained, the defence reform agenda is concerned with moving a state's armed forces – its practices, doctrines and management structures – towards Western norms of behaviour.

While the East Timor case stands out as the lone case of explicit externally driven SSR in the region, it is certainly not alone if one thinks about the whole panoply of the reform agenda. In the Philippines, Thailand and Indonesia there have been moves since the 1990s to develop at least civilian (though not democratic) control of the military. In Thailand, for example, Prime Minister Chavalit (1996–7) intervened in military decision-making to assert civilian primacy and promote his own supporters. Such moves have effectively entrenched greater civilian control over the military, despite failing to uphold the ideal of 'depoliticising' the military (Huxley, 2001: 9–12). Since then, the military has been brought firmly under civilian control and given a much smaller role in internal policing.[7] The fall of Marcos (Philippines, 1986) and Suharto (Indonesia, 1998), moreover, opened up the possibility for military reform in their countries, even though this possibility failed to materialize at the time largely because the military remained an independent political, economic and social actor and because there was little incentive to reform. In Malaysia, Singapore and Brunei, where civilian control of the military is entrenched there have been positive steps towards greater transparency and accountability, but in Burma, Cambodia (to a lesser extent Vietnam), Papua New Guinea and the Solomon Islands the security sector continues to act as a powerful barrier to development and democratization through their endemic corruption, human rights abuse, inefficiency, lack of professionalism, and the absence of transparency or accountability.

There are at least two reasons why the region's states would want to engage with the SSR agenda. First, American and European military assistance is to some degree tied to fulfilment of SSR-related goals. While it should be noted, as Matt McDonald's chapter argues, that some significant setbacks in SSR have occurred since 11 September 2001, efforts related to the 'war on terror' have nevertheless presented important opportunities to advance SSR. In the Philippines, for instance, reform of the military has been externally driven by the US' interest in curtailing 'internal security threats' (i.e. Islamic terrorism) there.[8] The 2003 Joint Defence Agreement between the US and Filipino governments tied military assistance aimed at enabling the Filipino military to better respond to Islamic and separatist terrorism to progress in wider reforms in the military sector. Furthermore, the US has made the delivery of aid to Indonesia conditional on measures to improve the transparency of Indonesia's military budget as well as progress on human rights (Antara News, 2004). Second, as well as improving the military sector's transparency, SSR is also interested in improving its effectiveness. Political leaders therefore have a vested interest in pursuing SSR even though this might also constitute an important limit on its emancipatory potential.

Before we continue, it is important to add two important caveats. First, it is important not to overstate the case for SSR. Critics argue, not implausibly, that SSR might foster instability by challenging key vested interests, that it runs the risk of further legitimizing the military sector, and that it privileges the military at the expense of other relevant social sectors and could draw resources away from health and education (Cooper and Pugh, 2002: 19–24). Second, it is important not to overstate the extent to which the immanent possibilities for emancipatory reform presented by SSR have been taken up in Southeast Asia. Although several of the region's states are talking the language of SSR, substantive reform has been limited. There is evidence in Thailand, for instance, that whilst the military may have been withdrawn from internal oppression campaigns in the south, its place has been filled by new police organizations.[9] Moreover, in Burma, Vietnam, Laos and Cambodia especially, the SSR agenda has had virtually no impact. What follows therefore are four areas of emerging reform in Southeast Asia that have the potential to alleviate the role that the region's militaries play in causing human insecurity.

1 *Military professionalism*. Indonesian moves towards a professional army were driven primarily by a significant increase in the proportion of officers given professional military education at Indonesian and foreign military academies in the 1960s and 1970s, new practices of promotion by merit and the depoliticization of the officer corps (Kammen and Chandra, 1999: 81–2; Honna, 1999: 254). This new, though still relatively small, group of military professionals has fostered a strategy of '*regenerasi*' (regeneration) aimed at professionalizing the Indonesian military. According to observers, this has had several direct and indirect positive effects. First, it has reduced the ability of senior officers to use military power to run corrupt regional fiefdoms, lessening the military's role in regional politics, its direct implication in human rights abuse and its exploitation of resources and personnel for the private benefit of military officers. Second, the creation of a professional ethos within the officer cadres has made it easier for advocates of reform within the military to make their case both in public and within military and government circles. Finally, the formalization of a merit-based promotion system has created incentives for officers and members of lower ranks to follow orders and abide by the law (Kammen and Chandra, 1999: 83–4). Coupled with these shifts in behaviour is an equally crucial infusion of the 'discourse of professionalism' which is helping to legitimize and internalize these practices (Honna, 2003). Together these developments point toward the potential for an Indonesian military less antagonistic to the human security of Indonesian citizens.

Similar developments have been observed in Thailand, where professionalization has been linked to the withdrawal of the military from domestic politics after military coups in 1973, 1976 and 1991. During the 1991 coup, the military opened fire on civilian demonstrators, killing at least 50. Under both domestic and international pressure, the military handed over to an elected government in 1992 and has not since threatened to intervene in politics. Suchit Bunbongkarn (1999) argues that professionalization has made intervention almost unthinkable and that, recent events noted above notwithstanding, the military is playing less of a role in the maintenance of domestic order today than it has at any time since independence.

2 *Socio-economic role of the military*. Although traditional approaches to civil-military relations insist that the military sector ought to play no domestic role[10] – beyond emergency assistance to the civilian power – it is important to recognize that some of the wider roles and functions fulfilled by

militaries in Southeast Asia can help to improve socio-economic conditions in some areas. For instance, through the adoption of mandates with development, relief and economic foci, an increased willingness by the military to protect and rehabilitate affected populations can be fostered. Evidence indicates that this has already occurred, albeit sporadically, throughout Southeast Asia. The Philippine military, for example, has a long history of 'civic action' missions whereby the military has been employed for public works projects (Berry, 1986: 226–9). Armed forces have been used to provide the necessary manpower and expertise to build much-needed infrastructure and move other common public goods to the benefit of the broader population. In Thailand, the military has also been involved in the promotion of the people's welfare (Bunbongkarn, 1988: 134–7). In the late 1950s for instance, the military provided rural economic development assistance as part of its effort to win 'hearts and minds' during a counter-insurgency campaign (Bunbongkarn, 1988: 140–2). Again in the 1970s the military offered rural assistance as part of its fight against communist insurgency movements. Bunbongkarn (1988: 160) concludes that through programmes which tie the building of infrastructure and regional development assistance with the maintenance of order, the Thai military has acted as an important bridge between urban rich and rural poor populations, an outcome which is clearly consistent with emancipatory goals. Finally, the extensive involvement of militaries from across the ASEAN region in the provision of humanitarian assistance for the victims of the December 2004 tsunami illustrates well the fact that, appropriately engaged, the militaries of Southeast Asia can provide essential emergency assistance to the region's most needy. Armed forces from around the region were employed widely to alleviate the human suffering and insecurity caused by natural disaster (ASEAN Troops in Indonesia's Tsunami-hit Aceh to Remain, 2005).

3 *Democratization and transparency*. Thailand provides a useful case to highlight the immanent emancipatory possibilities for reform associated with the wider impact of SSR on public transparency and democratization. Military reforms in Thailand, and especially the professionalization of the military, have enabled emancipatory reform in a number of areas of public life, making a direct contribution to human security. Three areas in particular stand out. First, since 1992 many senior military officers have advocated reform to improve the transparency and accountability of government policy-making which mirror those associated with reforms in the military.[11] Second, the withdrawal of the military from politics has enabled civil society to play a much more important role in politics. On the one hand, the withdrawal of the military has itself opened avenues for civil society engagement. On the other, in some cases the military has actually

encouraged this engagement as a means of making the civilian political authorities accountable. Finally, a point that should not be undervalued, the depoliticization of the military has facilitated wider moves towards the establishment of an independent bureaucracy, helping to transfer power from the bureaucratic elite to the political elite (Ganesan, 2001: 3). Wider moves towards democracy have taken many forms. Not least, the military played a critical role in fostering multiparty politics by, among other things, encouraging and supporting coalition governments (Bowornwathana, 2001: 309–10; Ganesan, 2001: 9). Similarly, a shift in norms, towards a more modernizing and Westernizing outlook has made the army more accountable by strengthening the role of parliamentary oversight (Morell, 1986: 138–9, 150–1). Together, these developments indicate ways in which military reform itself can indirectly support broader patterns of democratization.

4 *International cooperation.* International cooperation provides avenues through which human security concerns can ultimately be advanced. On one hand, SSR benefits can come from 'carrot' style approaches designed to encourage state militaries to reform. The US Justice Department, for example, has committed $40 million for a project to bring Indonesia's police more into line with Western democratic norms (McBeth, 2003: 18). This type of cooperation can be seen in other examples such as recent joint war exercises between US and Filipino militaries (Manila Bulletin, 2004). While the purpose of these interactions is largely to combat terrorism in the region as part of the US' 'war on terror', a likely side effect is that an improvement of their sometimes strained relations can open up further possibilities for SSR, increasing the potential for the military to play a positive role vis-à-vis human security. Recently, for example, the US based its resumption of military ties with Indonesia upon progress on SSR, particularly budget transparency and issues pertaining to human rights, demonstrating that whilst strategic interests may be the main driver of foreign engagement in the region, such engagement may help to stimulate measures that may enhance human security, however marginally ('Jakarta Rejects US Demand for Military Suspensons', 2004).

Finally, military cooperation can be driven by assistance for humanitarian causes. The reaction and involvement by a number of state militaries to the tragic 2004 tsunami, as mentioned above, illustrate this. Cooperation came in the form of direct assistance to the victims and it not only brought together the Indonesian military with the militaries of established democracies such as Australia, Japan and the United States, but it also led to extended interaction between the militaries of Indonesia and its regional state partners comprising ASEAN (ASEAN Troops in Indonesia's Tsunami-hit Aceh to Remain, 2005).

Conclusion

The purpose of this chapter has been twofold. First, to demonstrate that traditional approaches to Southeast Asian security provide, at best, a partial reading of security in the region. By focusing on the 'big issues' of Chinese hegemony, cross border disputes and Islamic and secessionist terrorism, it legitimizes the expenditure of large proportions of the region's income on the acquisition of military force whilst simultaneously blinding us to the way that force is actually used. The sale of British Hawk jets to Indonesia provides a simple case in point. In the late 1990s, the Indonesians argued, and the British government accepted, that the Hawk jets would be used to train Indonesian pilots in order to enable the state to defend itself from potential attackers. In practice, the Hawk jets saw action in East Timor, where they were used to support the brutal suppression of FALINTIL (The Armed Forces for the National Liberation of Timor Leste) and East Timorese people as a whole. This simple case is reproduced throughout the region; militaries legitimized by the appeal to external threats and – post 9/11 – Islamic terrorism – are more often than not used to silence internal dissent.

Yet, while the misuse of armed forces remains pervasive today, we have drawn attention to areas in which the potential for empancipatory reform exists. We have identified and explored four areas through which drives towards SSR can be fostered. Increases in the professionalism of the military can spill into and support the overall advancement of democratic practices; the armed forces – when properly guided – are able to deliver much needed economic and infrastructure assistance, as well as provide legitimate protection to the general populace; and, improvements in regional cooperation can be realized by promoting the principles of defence diplomacy and military accountability.

These hopeful possibilities are predictably not without caveats. First, any developments for the armed forces must be careful not to pull away limited resources from vital areas such as health and education programmes; we must remain mindful of potential opportunity costs to the most direct forms of advancing a human security agenda. Second, it is important to avoid the re-legitimization of state militaries in ways that may empower them to backslide into formerly abusive roles and practices. Moreover, the sincerity of any reforms should be perceived in a hopeful yet vigilant manner. There is little doubt that the temptation to appease external and internal pressure groups in the shorter term with ostensible moves towards SSR – for a variety of reasons to include financial and military assistance as well as to win votes – will continue. Thinly veiled attempts at SSR must not be mistaken for deeply embedded shifts in patterns of behaviour.

Despite these caveats, immanent possibilities for reform and progressive change exist. The challenge in the first instance, as this chapter has endeavoured to point out, is to expose how traditional discourses of security have masked the practices of insecurity affecting the overwhelming proportion of Southeast Asian cities each day.

Notes

1 As the UNDP *Human Development Report 1994* put it, 'human security is not a concern with weapons – it is a concern with human life and dignity' (UNDP, 1995: 7). The Commission on Human Security chaired by Sadako Ogata and Amartya Sen reaffirmed this commitment by calling for a new 'security framework focused on people and aimed at ensuring their security' (cited by Steve Smith, 2005: 53). Our overall aim for this chapter is to demonstrate how a concern for weapons can be turned toward a concern for human life and dignity.

2 See Richard Wyn Jones (1995: 304–8), particularly where he discusses the role of 'traditional intellectuals' and offers the example of how the notion of 'common security' became insinuated into political practice.

3 In August 2004, three people were killed by Islamic separatist terrorists in Thailand's southern provinces (*The Bangkok Post*, 2004). And in February 2005, bombs were set off in two cities in the Philippines (*Manila Standard*, 2005).

4 The 1999 massacre of a Muslim teacher and 56 of his followers is one example. See Human Rights Watch (2001).

5 Excerpts from the Human Rights Watch *World Report 2003* indicated that in May the Burmese military was involved in attacks on Christian Karen villages, hospitals and schools. See the Human Rights Watch (2004).

6 This case was first presented by Nicole Ball (1998).

7 Perhaps the notable exception here is that the Thai military continues to conduct commercial activities unchecked by the government.

8 Rosemary Foot observes that the US has expediently turned a blind eye to human rights issues in Southeast Asian countries generally in order to advance its 'war on terror' agenda. See Rosemary Foot (2004).

9 This is one of the interim findings of a research project by Mark Beeson and Alex Bellamy on 'Impediments to Security Sector Reform in Southeast Asia', funded by the Australian Research Council.

10 Samuel P. Huntington's *The Soldier and the State: The Theory and Politics of Civil-Military Relations* (1957) is perhaps the seminal text.

11 The Thai ombudsman for accountability notes that whilst there remain significant areas for improvement, transparency and accountability in government between 1998 and 2004 has improved. See Soontornpipet (2002).

3

The political economy of security: geopolitics and capitalist development in the Asia-Pacific

Mark Beeson

EVEN FOR A VOLUME concerned with critical security, it might strike some readers as rather eccentric to have a discussion of economic issues, let alone the nature of capitalist development. Yet not only is it widely recognized that the nature and effectiveness of economic organization is an absolutely central determinant of the most basic forms of individual and collective security (Beitz, 1979), but also many of the nations on the eastern side of the Asia-Pacific have been famously preoccupied with a 'comprehensive' form of security that explicitly includes economic issues. Indeed, ideas about the way economic activity should be organized and the sort of role states should play as a consequence tend to be more encompassing and decidedly different from their counterparts in 'the West'.[1] At the very least, such structural and discursive variations serve as powerful reminders that, even in an age characterized by global processes and ever greater degrees of economic and political integration, significant differences remain – differences that often have an enduring regional dimension.

The historical experience of the East Asian region, particularly its unparalleled, rapid and largely unexpected economic development over the last 50 years or so, has a number of important implications. Indeed, if economic development is taken as one of the most fundamental preconditions for the accomplishment of more encompassing forms of security that promote human emancipation,[2] then the East Asian experience is especially significant. It is, however, a story that has contentious implications for both the current economic orthodoxy promoted by powerful international financial institutions (IFIs) such as the International Monetary Fund and the World Bank, *and* for critical security studies. On the one hand the state-led development model pioneered by Japan stands as a refutation of neo-liberal economic orthodoxy. On the other hand, though, 'statism' is generally reviled by critical security studies theorists on the grounds that it entrenches the position and power of – frequently authoritarian – extant political elites and blocks movement towards more progressive or cosmopolitan international orders (Wyn Jones, 1999; Linklater, 2005).

While there is much merit in the latter view, I shall argue that it overlooks critical problems of 'sequencing'. At one level this simply means that economic development is a basic right that takes precedence over other desirable goals which cannot be met without it (Shue, 1980). In other words, economic development must precede other 'higher order' objectives if the latter are to be realized. In this context the East Asian experience remains an important exemplar of how this might be achieved, despite some well-known, justifiable misgivings about the nature of political regimes across much of the region. At another level the qualified advocacy of a 'statist' approach to development is justified, I shall suggest, because the current world order is dominated by states and corporations from the 'developed' world, which make development elsewhere more difficult (see also Ayoob, 2002). The East Asian experience suggests that effective state capacity is one way of overcoming such structural obstacles to development. The absence of global mechanisms that might facilitate development and take the place of states with all their inherent limitations means that – at this historical juncture, at least – states remain a potentially central part of achieving the basic economic development upon which other forms of emancipation are predicated. Desirable as some form of authentic 'global governance' may be, the reality is that the IFIs that presently approximate it invariably reflect the ideas and interests of the developed world generally and the United States in particular (Halabi, 2004; Hurrell, 2001). Until that changes, it would be inequitable and naive to expect 'the South' to rely exclusively on the IFIs to underwrite their security and development.

In what follows I initially explain why an understanding of the political economy of security is important, especially in East Asia. Consequently, I detail the geopolitical conditions that have made politics and economics such inextricably intertwined, mutually constitutive forces across the region.[3] Following this, I briefly introduce some of the more important theoretical innovations that have made the political economy perspective such an important part of contemporary debates about security and international relations. The second section of the chapter gives more detailed consideration to the East Asian experience, explaining what is distinctive about it, as well as how and why East Asian political elites have been keen to promote and defend their approaches to development. Although such strategies have clearly been highly successful in promoting economic development – without which broader notions of human security are impossible – political emancipation and 'good governance' has not followed seamlessly in its wake. And yet if greater political liberalization and reform is to occur in East Asia, it needs to be accompanied by a simultaneous process of reform within the overarching structures of emergent global governance, that are currently dominated by 'the West'.

The political economy of security?

Before considering why the East Asian experience represents such an important practical and intellectual challenge to both orthodox and radical accounts of security and development, it is important to place it in its specific geopolitical context and explain why the actual course of, and ideas about, development have generally been so different from the Western orthodoxy, and why a political economy perspective is especially useful in explaining this.

Academic life is necessarily specialized, and often parochial and self-absorbed as a consequence. While there are undoubtedly benefits from theoretical parsimony and disciplinary demarcations, there are costs, too. The artificiality of such disciplinary borders not only often makes it difficult to make sense of complexity and long-run historical change (Tilly, 1984), but also it can fundamentally misrepresent the nature of 'reality'. This was notoriously the case in the artificial separation of politics and economics that emerged in the late nineteenth and early twentieth centuries – something that encouraged the growth of a highly technical, abstract, and formal economics profession, on the one hand, and a brand of political science that until very recently almost entirely ignored economic issues, on the other.[4] Of late, political economy has made an overdue and welcome come back, partly out of sheer necessity: it became increasingly obvious that it was simply not possible to account for the evermore interconnected and transnational nature of economic and political activities in the contemporary era without explicitly recognizing and theorizing the inescapable connections between them (Strange, 1994; Keohane and Nye, 1977; Philips, 2005).

Comparative political economy

When thinking about the political economy or – more accurately – political econom*ies* of the Asia-Pacific, and the specific ways in which capitalist modes of economic organization have been realized in that broadly conceived region, therefore, there are a number of inter-linked conceptual issues that need to be borne in mind, issues that are thrown into sharp relief through comparative political economy. First, the 'Asia-Pacific' is a somewhat misleading label for the purposes of the present discussion. Concealed beneath this rubric are very different ideas about the ways economic and political activity *ought* to be organized, and quite distinctive sub-regional variations in political practices and economic structures as a consequence (Beeson, 2006a). In North America and Australasia, there has been much greater enthusiasm about adopting the sort of neo-liberal economic agenda that is associated with the so-called 'Washington consensus' of deregulation, privatization and market-oriented reform.[5] In much of East Asia, by contrast, the state has played – and by comparison to the Anglo-American economies – continues to play, a much larger role in economic activity, and there is still much less enthusiasm about neo-liberal policies (Beeson and Islam, 2005). There are, of course, major differences in the level of economic development between say Japan and Indonesia, or in the precise historical role of the state in China or Singapore. Yet despite these significant differences, it is still useful to distinguish comparatively between broadly conceived East Asian orientations towards the state and economic development, and those found in the Anglo-American countries.

To understand why politics and economics can look so different in East Asia, why the link between them is so critical, and how this can ultimately impact on both traditional and critical notions of security, we need to place regional development in a global historical context. The critical long-term dynamic here has been the spread of capitalism via colonialism and imperial expansion from Europe into the rest of the world. More recently, the key factor shaping and constraining patterns of economic development and organization has been the emergence of American hegemony. It is not possible to do justice to either of these enormously complex, long-run developments in the context of this chapter,[6] but they are sufficiently important that a couple of points merit brief mention. First, capitalism is a particular, relatively new type of economic organization with distinctive features – especially market-oriented commodity production, the private ownership of the means of production, and the development of labour markets – which meant that its introduction necessarily had a revolutionary impact on 'traditional' societies in Asia and elsewhere.

Whatever we may think of the feudal practices that characterized countries such as China and Japan prior to European imperial expansion, the introduction of capitalist production structures and social relations into East Asia was a security threat of the first order, at least as far as the ruling elites of the time were concerned. From the perspective of the political economy of security, the point to emphasize is that while European intrusion into East Asia was underwritten by the sort of superior military technology that orthodox security studies tend to emphasize, the breakdown of older social orders and the downfall of the political elites that dominated them was ultimately a function of economic imperatives and the transformative impact of integration into an expanding global capitalist economy.[7]

It has been East Asia's response to this challenge that has been so noteworthy and led to such distinctive political and economic practices in the region. The 'developmental state' pioneered by Japan, in which close cooperation between state agencies and business elites planned the course of Japan's post-war reconstruction, has clearly been a highly successful model with which to underpin economic expansion, but it occurred within the context of a form of 'soft authoritarianism' (Johnson, 1987). In a pattern that has been repeated across the region, political liberties were invariably sacrificed in the cause of economic development. Clearly, from the perspective of a critical security studies, concerned as it is with emancipatory politics, this is a significant compromise. At this stage I shall simply note that Japan's economic development ultimately underpinned the emergence of an effective, albeit flawed democracy, and allowed the consolidation of a deep-seated antipathy toward militarism across much of the country (see Curtis, 1999; Katzenstein, 1996).

What is significant in the context of a discussion of the contemporary international order at this point is that, having been forcibly incorporated into an increasingly ubiquitous international capitalist system, the countries of East Asia found themselves on the front line of the Cold War. As other chapters in this volume deal with the consequences of this period in some detail, it is sufficient to note here that the global nature of the confrontation between the United States and the Soviet Union meant that East Asia was profoundly affected by the wider geopolitics of the period, and that the development of individual East Asian countries and the region as a whole reflected this. On the one hand, East Asia was internally divided along ideological lines, making the prospects for any overall regional identity and organization impossible (Cumings, 1997). On the other, the political and economic development of the countries of the region was decisively shaped by this wider geopolitical context, encouraging the sort of state-led development and authoritarian politics that is such a distinctive a feature of the region's post-war trajectory (Haggard, 1990).

Economic development was, understandably enough, a priority for the generation of political elites that either oversaw the establishment of newly independent nation-states, or who attempted to rekindle economic development from the ashes of the Second World War. Crucially, the United States' newly acquired status as the leader of the 'free world' meant that it played a uniquely influential role in shaping the overall political, economic and strategic architecture in which development would occur. At one level this meant that – for the victorious capitalist powers and their allies, at least – economic reconstruction and expansion would occur under the auspices of the Bretton Woods regime. And yet for all the rhetorical emphasis placed on economic openness and the promotion of economic and political liberalism, the overarching context of the Cold War meant that the US did not press reform upon its client states in East Asian too stringently. On the contrary, strategic imperatives meant that the US generally turned a blind eye to the mercantilist, authoritarian, anti-democratic practices that frequently characterized the developmental states of the region for the decades after the war (Beeson, 2004).

Consequently, capitalist development in East Asia was quite distinctive and sharply at odds with the sort of normatively inspired, prescriptive policy regimes championed by the US and the increasingly influential IFIs it helped establish in the post-war period. These institutions have generated much criticism as a consequence of their perceived closeness to the US and because of their promotion of policies that have been resisted and resented in much of the developing world (Woods, 2003). And yet, for much of the Cold War period, a number of countries in the region managed to take advantage of their position as pro-capitalist states without necessarily adopting many of the reforms that were being encouraged upon them by the US and its institutional allies (Beeson, 2006b). Given the importance that is rightly attached to the US' dominant role in the international system, and its capacity to establish the 'rules of the game' for participants in the global political economy (see Beeson and Bell, 2005a), how are we to explain this apparent anomaly?

Theoretical innovations in international political economy

A political economy perspective offers important insights into the way the contemporary international order works, the manner in which various parts of the world are integrated within it, the implications this may have for economic development, and by extension for broader notions of security. One of the key figures in developing new conceptual approaches in political economy has been Robert Cox, who drew extensively on the ideas of the Italian theorist Antonio Gramsci (see Germain and Kenny, 1998). Cox's ideas provide a useful starting point for thinking about the way both material and ideational processes have become increasingly transnational, and the constraining impact this might have for would-be developing countries that wish to emulate the East Asian experience. Because it can help us to understand the development of the political economy of security in East Asia, it is worth briefly spelling out some of its basic assumptions.

A central theoretical innovation developed by Cox via Gramsci was the linking of material reality in the form of an increasingly global production structure, with the institutions that effectively govern its operations. A further key insight was that the particular ideas and norms that informed the rules of the international political, economic and even security regimes –

which such institutions enforced or encouraged – were a product of specific historical circumstances, and actively championed by the dominant power of the era. Underpinning a particular 'historical bloc' or dominant class formation was a hegemonic power which used its pre-eminent position to consolidate a particular regulatory and ideational order. In this context IFIs such as the IMF and the World Bank were expressions of specific amalgams of ideas and material power, which provided the ideational and regulatory 'anchors' of an overall hegemonic strategy (Cox, 1981). Crucially, and unlike traditional realist readings of hegemonic power (such as Gilpin, 1987; Mearsheimer, 2001), hegemonic domination relied upon the willing consent of other powers in the international system – or more accurately, on the acquiescence and support of dominant elites in other nation-states (Cox, 1987: 7). In other words, hegemonic domination in this Gramscian-inspired interpretation worked because there appeared to be clear benefits for subordinate elites, not simply because the hegemonic power of the era was able to directly or indirectly coerce compliance through superior material resources.

The idea that certain political and economic processes can become the 'naturalised', seemingly unchallengeable 'common sense' of a particular historical moment is something that has been of particular concern to radical scholars (Block, 1990; but also see Bourdieu, 1991). This claim about the ideological nature of discourse and the possibility that some ideas and policy regimes work to further some interests and effectively obscure social reality has been central to the sort of 'critical' approaches developed by Cox (1981), and his celebrated claim that theory was never neutral, but always operated in interest of some group, institution or set of actors. This is a potentially crucial insight anywhere, but especially so in the Asia-Pacific region for two reasons: first, this recognition serves as an enduring reminder that we need to adopt a critical orientation to the production of dominant discourses that may be intended to further the interests of hegemonic powers and their allies. As we shall see in the second part of this chapter, there has been a sustained effort to produce such reformist discourses by the US and the IFIs in East Asia. Second, we also need to remember that within East Asian countries themselves, particular discourses, especially those that revolve around the security of the nation, have been used to legitimate and justify frequently authoritarian, anti-democratic practices. As Tony Burke (2001a: 218) perceptively points out, in much of Asia 'security has not merely been seen as one good among many but as the good that guarantees the others', allowing local elites to define the very nature of security in coercive and exclusionary terms, and downplay concerns about issues such as human rights as a consequence.

In short, the historical experience of the East Asian half of the Asia-Pacific serves as a powerful reminder that international orders are ultimately *social processes*, which are realized within specific geopolitical circumstances (Agnew and Corbridge, 1995). Even if conflict is latent rather than actual, the overall dominance of a hegemon will directly or indirectly delimit the range of options open to subordinate powers. A Gramscian-inspired interpretation of a particular international order has a number of major advantages that are especially relevant at present: first, the emphasis on transnational social processes helps to explain the relationship between national political and social forces, and the increasingly important regional and global processes that individual states must mediate. Second, it also provides a basis for developing a conceptual framework within which to consider the political economy of security. As we shall see, such an approach offers a way of accounting for both the trajectory of development in East Asia and the distinctive notions of security that have emerged within it.

Economic development and security in the Asia-Pacific

Despite the fact that capitalism has consolidated its position as the dominant, almost universal mode of economic organization, it is striking that it continues to display remarkably different characteristics across individual nations and even regions. It has been powerfully and persuasively argued that such differences are less important in the context of long-run historical change than is the fact that capitalist modes of social relationships predominate virtually everywhere (Strange, 1997). This important caveat notwithstanding, however, the increasingly sophisticated and extensive varieties of capitalism literature reminds us that not only is difference possible (see Coates, 2000; Hall and Soskice, 2001), but also that ideas about national development and – by extension – security, are likely to differ as a consequence.

The possibility that notions of security are not simply different in various parts of the world, but that they may actually be centrally bound up with what are often seen as distinct economic and political questions is especially evident in much of the developing world. Mohammed Ayoob (1995) has demonstrated how the historical developmental experience of much of the 'Third World' has generated particular forms of insecurity that are necessarily 'explicitly political', as much of the failure to develop economically can be attributed to concomitant inadequacies in state development. It is partly the recognition of the importance of the state in the remarkably successful development experience in much of East Asia that gives the interpretation of the East Asian experience such prescriptive potential and ultimately geopolitical importance: if the East Asian exemplar can be discredited, and other nations can be persuaded by ideological suasion and/or political pressure to subscribe to a particular regulatory order, then there are potentially significant pay-offs for the country (or countries) able to champion and benefit from specific regimes. For example, US-based financial institutions have directly benefited from the opening of the formerly tightly controlled economies of East Asia, despite the connection between financial sector liberalization and the financial crisis of 1997 (Wade, 2001): the East Asian crisis not only undermined the governments in Indonesia, Thailand and South Korea, but also dramatically impacted on general human security as unemployment and the cost of living rose in the affected countries.[8] Ironically, such outcomes were directly linked to the liberalization of hitherto highly regulated East Asian financial systems in line with IFI orthodoxy.

The crisis highlights both the paradoxical nature of the international economic system, and the fundamental asymmetries of power and influence that continue to characterize it. Despite the opprobrium the 'East Asian model' attracted in the aftermath of the crisis, it is striking that the American economy has increasingly come to rely on uninterrupted flows of capital from Japan and China to underpin its consumption patterns, budgetary position and increased defence expenditures (Ravenhill, 2006). If the US were a Southeast Asian country, it is safe to say that its debt levels would have triggered the attention of the International Monetary Fund and international currency speculators long ago. It is not simply the inequity of the system that is so glaring here, but that the US can use its dominant position to press for the sort of continuing international capital liberalization that is so vital to its overall strategic position and so lucrative for US-based financial interests, despite its clearly demonstrated dangers, and the fact that the US has had its own scandals associated with 'crony capitalism' over the last few years (Stiglitz, 2002).

East Asia's ideational importance

Although increased international interdependence may have become a fact of economic life, there is still a major debate about the sort of regulatory architecture that is appropriate to manage it (Armijo, 2002). These divisions can be broadly divided between those predominantly Anglo-American agents that prefer to give greater power to market forces and those East Asian and European actors that wish to see greater regulation or political 'intervention', even at the transnational level. It is significant that the existent transnational or inter-governmental agencies charged with debating such issues continue to be dominated by the US and reflect a degree of 'hegemonic business as usual', rather than an open-ended debate about a possibly optimal regulatory environment (Beeson and Bell, 2005b). Given the preference for a liberal international order evinced by political and economic interests in the US, such outcomes are unsurprising: particular interests directly benefit from specific regulatory orders. Recognizing this underlying reality helps to explain why the US and the IFIs have made such an effort to discredit East Asian models of development, despite powerful evidence about their continuing potential efficacy (Beeson, 2004; Chang, 2002).

In the context of the Asia-Pacific, it is important to remember that part of the great scholarly interest in the East Asian experience was not simply that it appeared to refute dependency theory and earlier explanations about the lack of 'peripheral' development,[9] but that the growing economic importance of the region presented a potential challenge to American hegemony and the dominance of neo-liberalism. It is also important to recognize how contested the interpretation of East Asian development has been as a result. The World Bank's seminal investigation of the 'East Asian miracle' was the subject of highly contentious, politicized debates about its content and production, in which an increasingly confident Japan played a prominent part (Wade, 1996). More recently, partly as a direct consequence of the economic crisis of the late 1990s, there has been a major re-evaluation of the entire East Asian experience and a systematic attempt by the IFIs to discredit it and the distinctive political and economic relationships that underpinned it (Hall, 2003).

These sorts of highly political contests over the interpretation of the East Asian experience assume added importance because of Japan's role as a former developmental role model, and as the principal architect of a distinctly East Asian orientation to security. Despite the fact that the performance of the Japanese economy has, of late, undermined its comparative standing, for many years the 'Japanese model' served as a regional alternative to the neo-liberal consensus. Not only was the state a central component of this alternative vision of successful development, but also the strong state model was a vital part of the notion of the 'comprehensive security' approach that Japan pioneered, too. The most noteworthy and distinctive feature of the sort of comprehensive security doctrine that Japan developed in the 1970s was the importance of non-conventional security issues, especially economics. The 'oil shocks' of the 1970s and 1980s were crucial in shaping ideas about comprehensive security, and reinforcing the perception that Japan's resource-dependency made it especially vulnerable to changes in the external international political economy over which it had little control. The solution to this dilemma was a mercantilist approach to economic policy-making that not only repudiated the sort of approach to economic development that would crystallize in the Washington consensus, but which underpinned a systematic, state-directed attempt to diversify resource supplies and guide the course of industrial development (Hegeinbotham and Samuels, 1998). While it is clear that Japan is not as influential an economic model as it once was, Japan's distinctive approach to security has had an impact on some of the most important countries of the region (Hu, 2001).

Elsewhere in East Asia, notions of comprehensive security have been redefined to give greater emphasis to the survival of the state as the core concern of security practice (Alagappa, 1998), an outcome that is understandable given the significantly lesser degree of state capacity that exists in Northeast as opposed to Southeast Asia. In Southeast Asia the challenges of nation-building in the aftermath of decolonization, the difficulties of encouraging 'late-late' economic development in a region affected by economic imperialism, to say nothing of coping with superpower contestation throughout Asia, meant that the countries of the region became concerned with threats to internal stability. Such factors had a predictable and distinctive influence on the way security was conceived in much of the region, especially the overwhelming identification of security with the survival and integrity of the state.

It is at this point that more conventional analyses of security can be most usefully reformulated through critical readings grounded in political economy, as the latter have the potential to highlight a number of issues and paradoxes usually neglected in conventional analyses. If we assume that economic development is a critical determinant of both traditional notions of security and of a more expansive notion of human security that recognizes the importance of individual economic welfare, then it is clear that the appropriate role of the state is a more complex affair than both traditional *and* some critical readings of security generally concede. If it is accepted that there is still an important economic developmental role for the state in regions such as Southeast Asia, then the debate about the role of the state that has figured so prominently in the discursive contest between 'East' and 'West' is still relevant, too. At one level, this is manifest in the continuing interstate debate about the nature of public policy in a global era, especially when promoted by powerful agencies such as the International Monetary Fund and the World Bank. At another level, however, concern about East Asia's authoritarian, sometimes anti-democratic states has also animated global civil society and those concerned with the promotion of human security.

The limits to the East Asian exemplar

When viewed from the perspective of East Asia's distinctive historical circumstances, in which the combined impact of the West's political, economic and strategic dominance have profoundly delimited the possible trajectories of development, it becomes easier to understand why the region's elites have been preoccupied with constructing powerful states with which to promote both indigenous economic activity and a relatively insulated political space within which this might occur. Indeed, the impulse for political insulation remains, albeit one with distinctly regional overtones these days: the increased interest in developing regionally-based institutions with which to enhance East Asian political, economic and even security cooperation is – to some extent, at least – an expression of the desire to overcome East Asia's perceived vulnerability to external influences.[10] As Helen Nesadurai (2005) points out, the financial crisis that engulfed much of the region in the late 1990s overturned the assumption that economic globalization and security were complimentary, and highlighted the potentially disruptive social and political impacts that integration into the global economy contained. The downfall of the Suharto regime – welcome as it may have been in many ways – illustrated just how susceptible individual regimes could be to economic forces and external actors (Beeson, 1998).

In such circumstances, the growing interest in developing regional mechanisms to underpin a more collective approach to enhancing economic security becomes understandable. As Julie Gilson argues in this volume, the historical experience of the region – in particular a general suspicion of powerful, supra-national organizations – suggests that constructing effective regional institutions will not be easy, nor will they necessarily be as democratic and responsive to non-elite interests as we might like. The challenge is to make East Asian states more accountable as well as more capable. In other words, in addition to developing the capacity to oversee or promote economic development, it is equally important that East Asian states become more democratic and responsive to wider range of interests. The problem in East Asia is that there are few precedents for such a transformation, partly as a consequence of the region's successful development history and the institutionalized relationships that underpinned it.

Cooperation between political and business elites has clearly not only been central to East Asia's economic success stories, but it has also been synonymous with self-serving 'cronyism', corruption and patronage politics (Gomez, 2002). The problem from a critical perspective is that the worst aspects of East Asian political and economic practices may be transposed to a regional level, providing a veneer of legitimacy and collective solidarity to undemocratic, elite-driven political practices, in much the same way that the Association of Southeast Asian nations (ASEAN) has done (Narine, 2002). Yet, long-term changes in the way the East Asia's economies are being integrated on a regional basis suggest some sort of cooperation is inescapable. It is not coincidental that the issue area that has attracted most attention in this context has been monetary cooperation – something that 'globalization' would seem to necessitate, but which perceptions of regional vulnerability generated by the economic crisis has given a distinctly East Asian rather than global character (Henning, 2002).

A critical reading of such developments that draws its inspiration from the political economy tradition can help explain the long-run material changes in the nature of economic activity and integration that have made regional cooperation such a prominent and paradoxical part of globalization everywhere (Hurrell, 1995). What a focus on the interaction between ideas, institutions, and political and economic interests reveals is the complexity of the dynamics of regional institutional development. Traditional analyses of intra- and inter-regional relations may be right to emphasize the continuing importance of material power and the apparent desire many East Asian elites have expressed about continuing American strategic engagement in the region. However, there are other short- and long-term processes that make an exclusive focus on traditional notions of security simplistic and misleading: the fusion of politics and economics that has been so characteristic of East Asia's developmental experience has generated both distinctive notions of security and styles of state activism that are both different from, and a potential source of conflict with the, Anglo-American parts of the Asia-Pacific.

Welcome as such an empirical and theoretical recognition of East Asian ideas about economics, politics and security might be, the historical shortcoming of such discourses from the perspective of critical scholarship is that they are frequently self-serving and reflective of elite interests. Whatever one may think of the technical efficacy, normative underpinnings or structural logic of the policies associated with American-sponsored neo-liberalism (Gills, 2000), it is important to recognize that it also represents a direct challenge to entrenched, interconnected patterns of political and economic power across much of East Asia. As far as such elites are concerned, therefore, this represents an immediate, albeit non-traditional security threat of the first order.

Concluding remarks

The remarkable economic development that occurred in East Asia in the post-war period represents an unparalleled improvement in individual human security for millions of people across the region. It is a transformation that owes much to a unique set of geopolitical conditions that allowed state-led economic development, but which also often encouraged the darker side of the developmental state: authoritarianism and illiberalism. A critical, Gramscian-inspired reading of these events may be able to highlight the national, regional and global political and economic forces that have generated East Asia's distinctive developmental regimes, and the notions of security that have been deployed to legitimate them, but they are less useful in evaluating the future role of state power across the region. The great paradox and policy challenge that the East Asian experience highlights is that the process of successful, rapid economic development – compared to which, it seems to me, most other notions of human security pale into insignificance – has historically depended on the actions and leadership of a capable state. For much of Southeast Asia, where the development process is still incomplete, basic human needs would still seem to depend on *more* effective state capacity, rather than less.[11]

Differing views about the appropriate role of the state are not just an important source of tension and discursive contestation between the Anglo-American and East Asian wings of the Asia-Pacific – although this is a crucial, under-recognized aspect of the way the preconditions of security are contested across the region. Rather, the great challenge for those concerned with continuing human emancipation is reconciling continuing state activism in the development sphere with progressive reforms in the political sphere. Even if it is accepted that states still have an important and potentially useful role to play in underpinning economic development *and* in protecting basic political freedoms, it is not obvious how states should be allowed to perform the former while being encouraged to observe the latter. The principal criticism of the US's hegemonic role has been that it showed inadequate concern with political rights during the Cold War, and an excessive concern with economic reform in its aftermath.

The interaction of the local and the transnational remains central to ideas about, and the practice of security in East Asia. The decline of 'traditional' security threats in the post-Cold War period means that not only are other political and economic issues now more prominent security concerns, but also their management involves a greater array of actors. In this context the involvement of the IFIs and their preoccupation with 'good governance' could be expected to provide precisely the sort of independent regulatory oversight and technocratic advice that ought to be central to the sort of economic development that is a prerequisite of more encompassing forms of human security.[12] And yet what Andrew Hurrell (2001) describes as the 'deformity' of existent international institutions ensures that they entrench the established hierarchy of power in the global system and are not capable of reflecting a wider variety of inter-*national* ideas, never mind the mass of the populations of the developing world. In such circumstances, it is predictable that East Asians remain preoccupied with national sovereignty and the possibility of developing regional mechanisms with which to preserve it. Unless simultaneous reform occurs at both the national, regional, *and* transnational level, then progressive reforms in East Asia will remain problematic. At the very least, this means that the key inter-governmental organizations and IFIs that approximate global governance must be made more representative and inclusive.[13]

That East Asians have developed notions of security that are distinctive and at odds with the prevailing wisdom, and which reflect historically specific political and economic realities is unsurprising. What is more surprising, perhaps, is that such differences and their implications are frequently glossed over in much of the Western-dominated theorizing that seeks to explain security in the Asia-Pacific. But while we need to recognize the differences that exist in East Asia, we also need to acknowledge that Asian ideas about the appropriate relationship between state power, economic development and the ultimate definition of security may be no more emancipatory in the longer term than those espoused in the Anglo-American countries. Indeed, there has generally been much less room for the expression of plural views in Asia than in the West. The challenge is to ensure that Asian definitions of security do not become excuses for the continuing suppression of internal dissent, but remain rightly concerned with underpinning economic security for as many as possible. Without basic economic development, however, political emancipation and more sophisticated forms of ontological security will remain largely academic issues.

Notes

1 'The West' is, of course, a very crude but serviceable shorthand for a range of social practices and ideas that are generally associated with Western Europe and more recently the United States. Because of its rather imprecise meaning I shall generally refer to the 'Anglo-American economies', and have in mind a mode of governance associated with neo-liberalism. The Anglo-American economies are the US, UK, Canada, Australia and New Zealand, countries which have displayed a greater enthusiasm for 'deregulation', liberalization and market-oriented reform than their East Asian counterparts. See Hall and Soskice (2001).

2 It has become the conventional wisdom in critical security studies that 'security' involves much more than military security, and that the capacity to promote human emancipation is a key measure of its efficacy. See Booth (1991).

3 There are two quite distinct ways in which 'geopolitics' is currently used. First, it is associated with a form of thinking about relations between states and empires that became influential at the beginning of the twentieth century. In this version, the primary concern was with relations between the 'great powers', their control of physical space, and the grand strategies they employed to do so. More recently, as a result of the work of political geographers in particular, an altogether more critical use of the term has come into prominence, which uses the term geopolitics to describe the social practices and discourses that effectively create particular understandings of space and spatial relations. It is this latter sense that is of particular importance here, as the active, social and political construction of regions is an issue of continuing importance. See Ó Tuathail (1996).

4 On the evolution of economic thought, see Deane (1978). On contemporary political economy, see Murphy and Nelson (2001).

5 The term 'Washington consensus' was coined by John Williamson, and his explanation of the dominant economic orthodoxy remains highly influential, despite some recent modifications in the 'post-Washington consensus'. See Williamson (1994) and Higgott (2000).

6 On European imperialism, see Abernathy (2000). On American hegemony and the construction of the post-war international order, see Latham (1997).

7 On the comparative responses of China and Japan to European and latterly American influence and expansion, see Moulder (1977).

8 In Indonesia, there was a dramatic increase in the price of basic staples such as rice and cooking oil, with predictable impact on nutrition. For an overview of the crisis and its impact, see Haggard (2000).

9 It is also worth emphasizing that much of the scholarship of this period was animated by an approach that was 'critical' in the sense of repudiating the inequalities of the capitalist system, rather than in the theoretical sense developed by Cox *et al.*, although the two are clearly not mutually exclusive.

10 Such concerns were, of course, central to the emergence of the original ASEAN organization and its preoccupation with security concerns. The development of ASEAN+3 is intended to extend both the geographical and extent policy ambit of regional institutionalization. See Acharya (2001).

11 On the continuing importance of the state in economic development, see Leftwich (2000).

12 On the difficulties of achieving 'good governance' in East Asia, see Beeson (2001).

13 Despite the importance of China and Japan, East Asia remains strikingly under-represented on key bodies such as the International Monetary Fund and the World Bank. See Rapkin and Strand (2003).

4

Deconstructing the discourse on epistemic agency: a Singaporean tale of two 'essentialisms'

See Seng Tan

THE ROLE OF EPISTEMIC communities as producers, processors and purveyors of knowledge on national and international security affairs is no longer questioned today, not least by conventional scholars of security (Adler, 2005; Haas, 1992). Likewise, the notion of security studies communities based in Singapore – comprising constituents of the state's national security establishment, including those from semi-official and non-official circles – as epistemic agents is increasingly acknowledged by analysts for their perceived contributions to knowledge constitution in ways positive and negative (Ball, 2000; Evans, 1994; Hernandez, 1994; Jayasuriya, 1994; Jones and Smith, 2001a, 2001b, 2002; Katsumata, 2003).

At risk of oversimplification, two broad conceptual understandings arguably define how Singapore's epistemic communities – comprising security scholars based at local research and policy institutes as well as universities – and their contributions to regional discourses have generally been viewed. The first understanding presumes an intentional subject, already given, who constructs security knowledge through an instrumental action. The second understanding presumes that construction operates in a deterministic fashion, thereby potentially making a mockery of human agency (Weber, 2001). Thus understood, Singaporean epistemic communities are either autonomous, voluntarist actors with settled identities who construct the identity of the nation and influence its behaviour, or passive recipients whose subjectivity is but a product of pre-existing social structures or some ontologically prior constructor/author, and who exist principally to promote the interests and preserve the wellbeing of the state and the regime which rules it.

In contrast to both these essentialist interpretations, this present undertaking seeks to read Singapore-based epistemic communities neither (in the first instance) as 'autonomous origins of meaning, registers of social value, and irreducible agents of history-making', nor (in the second instance) as passive, abject targets under the totalizing control of the state, and void of meaningful agency (Ashley, 1988: 245; Butler, 1993: 3). Rather, they are understood here as subjects whose practices, linked interchangeably with associated discourses, socially constitute not only the political world and the 'sovereign' statist identities – namely, 'Singapore' – which make up that world, but also the very subjectivity of those same epistemic communities as legitimate agents of security. As such, they are subjects that 'emerge in history', alternately constructing and marginalizing subjects while their own subjectivity is in process of being constructed and/or marginalized by others, including the state (Ashley, 1987).

What I hope to provide below, at least in a preliminary way, is an understanding of subjectivity or agency in the Singaporean context which will allow for an investigation into its construction. Without valuing 'linguistic' or 'ideational' reasons over 'material' ones, my contention is that the constitution and instantiation of agency are intimately linked to security discourses generated by epistemic communities and students of them. As such, the very identities of epistemic communities – as legitimate, productive agents of security – are indebted to those articulations. On the other hand, perspectives that refuse any enquiry into the construction of agency tend to foster ideological conclusions which severely constrain possibilities for progressive change in the security discourses and practices in Singapore. This principally occurs through a shared desire for a settled subjectivity that is bounded, grounded and, in a sense, sovereign, not least that of 'Singapore' and, where local epistemic communities are concerned, non-state actors.

Yet at the same time, it is just such an idealized desire which, more often than not, gets in the way of thinking outside of a state-centred security discourse and towards a more holistic human-centred one, for the simple reason that the extant debate on the agency of Singaporean security studies communities (as we shall see below) remains for the most part state-oriented. To be sure, the emphasis on epistemic communities allows for the possibility of multiple social actors in the collective imagining of community. That said, the tacit assumption of contending perspectives that such collective imaginations tend to coincide with the boundaries of the Singaporean nation[1] – or, for that matter, those of an Association of Southeast Asian Nations (ASEAN) region or community, but ultimately a state-based one – also means that the parameters of security discourse, even for intellectuals whose ostensible mandate is (in the case of a leading local think tank) to 'ponder the improbable', are significantly constrained.

These foregoing concerns are by no means a mere exercise in academic navel-gazing, especially in the light of ongoing institutional developments in Southeast Asian regionalism which hint at the anticipated formation of an

'ASEAN Community' in 2020 and of an ASEAN Charter – key institutional elements of regionalism that would presumably render ASEAN and its member states more 'people-centred'. Whether this declared objective is attainable may well have to do with a conscious decoupling in discourses on security: of subjectivity and agency from the illusions of autonomy and 'sovereignty' with which the former are invariably saddled.

Debating epistemic agency

> Agency belongs to a way of thinking about persons as instrumental actors who confront an external political world. But if we agree that politics and power exist already at the level at which the subject and its agency are articulated and made possible, then agency can be *presumed* only at the cost of refusing to inquire into its construction . . . In a sense, the epistemological model that offers us a pre-given subject or agent is one that refuses to acknowledge *that agency is always and only a political prerogative.* (Butler, cited in Campbell, 1998: 220)

The above reflection of Judith Butler's highlights an oft-cited tension within modern understandings concerning sovereignty and subjectivity, not least those which underwrite views on Singapore's epistemic communities. This should not surprise us given the commitment of most of these views to an empiricist epistemology and positivist methodology (Ashley, 1989; Persram, 1999; Smith, 2000). Both essentialisms identified at this chapter's outset are found in writings which deal with Singapore-based security studies communities. (For functional reasons, I shall refer to these two broad understandings below as Essentialism 1 and Essentialism 2, respectively.) Despite the apparent readiness of both interpretations to allow for an appreciation of agency as a 'political prerogative', a careful reading would suggest a shared tendency among them to insist otherwise, with dire consequences for their ability to loosen themselves from particular ideological conclusions.

Essentialism 1: epistemic communities as instrumental agents

Arguments that reflect the first essentialism presuppose epistemic communities as pre-existing instrumental agents of their own volition. By focusing on the ideational influence of epistemic agents on policy outcomes, this approach highlights the efforts of individuals or institutions in shaping political outcomes in security policy (Goldstein and Keohane, 1993: 3). This understanding is especially prominent in works on 'track-two' diplomacy, a 'non-official' process which brings scholars and statesmen together in institutionalized settings towards the common object of promoting regional cooperation in the Asia-Pacific region through policy dialogues (Ball, 2000; Evans, 1994; Simon, 1995; Woods, 1993, 1997). Carolina Hernandez

(1994: 6) encapsulates what has become the conventional wisdom on track-two processes:

> Track-two diplomacy refers to the generation and conduct of foreign policy by non-state actors, including government officials in their private capacity. It includes the participation of scholars, analysts, media, business, people's sector representatives, and other opinion makers who shape and influence foreign policy and/or actually facilitate the conduct of foreign policy by government officials through various consultations and cooperative activities, networking and policy advocacy.

Their efficacy is thereby measured in terms of whether their ideas and proposals make it into the policy process, as well as the availability of institutionalized means by which such ideational transference can occur (Hernandez, 1994: 6).

More recently, Hiro Katsumata (2003: 97–100) has contended that at least three 'notable' ideas promoted by regional epistemic communities during the 1990s have since become 'reality': the ideas of common and cooperative security, which presume that regional security is indivisible; the formation of an intergovernmental forum for multilateral security dialogue, as evidenced by the establishment of the ASEAN Regional Forum (ARF); and the extension of ASEAN's diplomatic style throughout the Asia-Pacific region so as to promote regional cooperation. For Katsumata, these can all be traced back to efforts of the ASEAN Institutes of Strategic and International Studies (ASEAN-ISIS), a region-wide epistemic community made up of security studies think tanks from the ASEAN nations – a conclusion held by a number of other analysts (Capie and Evans, 2002; Kraft, 2000; Simon, 2002).

Based on these foregoing points, Singapore-based epistemic communities such as the Singapore Institute of International Affairs (which is the 'licensed' representative for Singapore to the ASEAN-ISIS) and the Institute of Defence and Strategic Studies (IDSS) (which plays the same role vis-à-vis the Council for Security Cooperation in the Asia-Pacific or CSCAP), by extension, are thereby understood as given instrumental actors whose ideational efforts have occasionally proved efficacious in shaping official policy directions and substance in Singapore and the region. Regarding the Asia-Pacific region, members of Singapore's security studies communities (including several from the IDSS) were evidently instrumental in the formulation of the concepts and principles of preventive diplomacy, and also played a key role in the drafting of the 1995 concept paper on the issue (Tan *et al.*, 2002).

This is not to say that ideas by themselves – certainly not those purveyed by the local scholarly community – invariably exert a causal impact. Indeed, ideas are more likely to influence policy if they 'fit' well with existing ideas and ideologies in a particular historical setting (Sikkink, 1991: 26; Goldstein, 1988). As one scholar has allowed, 'persuasiveness is an inherently relational concept, determined as much by the shape of current economic and political circumstances as by the shape of the ideas themselves' (Hall, 1989: 370). Perhaps more appropriate than most, however, is the view that the interpretive influence of epistemic communities is best understood in terms of their production of 'semi-official narratives that authorize and provoke certain sequences of cause and effect, while at the same time preventing counter-narratives from emerging' (Said, 1993: 324).

All this appears to have been the case with efforts by the ASEAN-ISIS and the CSCAP at promoting comprehensive security – a 'new organizing concept for security' for the region (ASEAN-ISIS, 1992, 1993a, 1993b; CSCAP, 1995). As Julie Gilson notes in her chapter, comprehensive security found resonance with Asia-Pacific nations because the concept legitimizes rather than undermines established regional principles, not least state sovereignty and non-interference (Alagappa, 1988; Dupont, 1995; Wanandi, 1991). And although regional governments seem somewhat less enamoured with cooperative security than comprehensive security, the same argument more or less holds; as Rolfe (1995: vii) has intimated: 'Cooperative security approaches acknowledge the *centrality of the state* in security processes and the *primacy of state interests* in the achievement of security.' Hence, in sponsoring and sanctioning the state as much as being state-sponsored and sanctioned, narratives that compliment the region's security studies communities can partly be considered as a form of *statecraft* that works to authorize the state and inscribe its agential powers, while at the same time excluding narratives that promote alternate subjectivities particularly at the expense of states.

In all this, the debate over just how efficacious epistemic communities in Singapore and the region have been in advancing their preferred security ideas and norms is nevertheless joined by the shared supposition regarding the instrumentality of epistemic agents. This much is clear in works that adopt a considerably less charitable view of local security studies communities. For instance, David Martin Jones and Michael Smith (2001a, 2001b, 2002) take umbrage to what they perceive as the willingness of those communities to forfeit their privilege of critique and role as the nation's intellectual conscience. Regarding Southeast Asian security discourse as a seriously flawed enterprise, they identify (by name no less) and summarily dismiss various security intellectuals from Singapore as 'scholar-bureaucrats' who flatteringly but fallaciously portray ASEAN as 'the basis of a new regional identity and dispensation' (Jones and Smith, 2001a: 844). Elsewhere, they fault the collusion between scholars and statesmen wherein the former provide the requisite ideological ballast to a dubious brand of regional institutionalism which the latter have erected, one full of talk but empty of substance:

> Such insecurity translated to a regional level produces a rhetorical and institutional shell. The shell delivers declarations, holds ministerial meetings, and even supports a secretariat, but beyond the flatulent musings of aging autocrats or post-modern constructivists pontificating in Track Two fora nothing of substance eventuates. However, because Southeast Asia's political elites along with their academic travellers have invested so heavily in ASEAN's 'alternative security' discourse, it is regarded as impolite to point out [ASEAN's] essentially ersatz quality. (Jones and Smith, 2001b: 58)

Hence, far from a 'new organizing concept', comprehensive security – or, perhaps more conspicuously, notions such as the 'ASEAN way' – serves as a discursive tool which practitioners and intellectuals of statecraft employ, knowingly or otherwise, to rationalize and legitimize political authoritarianism, not least in the Singaporean context. And if not as scaffolding for authoritarianism then certainly as a convenient excuse to eschew taking the tough but necessary steps towards economic and social reform – change which, in retrospect, could conceivably have mitigated the more debilitative effects of the Asian financial crisis (if not avoided it altogether) for countries such as Indonesia and Thailand. In the late Gerald Segal's inimitable words:

> You know the argument: 'sorry, we cannot possibly agree to such confidence building measures, it is not the way Asians handle security.' Such ethnic-chic is often used to explain why Asians do not always open their markets or why their economies are so successful. But as with many trendy explanations, this one has only the smallest grain of truth. In practice, there is little that is 'Asian' about Asian security, and Asians and others need to stop believing that such thinking is either politically or even scientifically correct. History does not become blood and the fate of Asian security is in Asian hands, not their genes. (Segal, 1995: 107)

In this sense, it may be said that the very ideas and norms advanced by local security studies communities 'have been used to codify existing practices rather than to initiate new forms of order. Ideas have not made possible alternatives that did not previously exist; they legitimated political practices' – reprehensible ones, Jones and Smith want to highlight – 'that were already facts on the ground' (Krasner, 1993: 238).

Such conclusions inadvertently foster the impression of Singaporean epistemic actors as without agency or instrumentality, or very little of which to speak. But this clearly is not what Jones and Smith seem to want to convey. After all, their criticism appears to be premised on the supposition that Singaporean 'scholar-bureaucrats' have essentially (and, presumably, shamelessly) ceded their moral-cum-political authority to speak truth to power – or at least truth that is un-beholden to and emancipated from the repressive power of an autocratic Singaporean state. Do Singapore's think tanks and licensed intellectuals, to borrow from William Wallace (1998: 229), 'maintain the delicate balance between intellectual political orthodoxy and openness to expert criticism and new ideas which they have so far successfully managed'? Do they skilfully speak truth to power without bitterly offending those in power? To these questions Jones and Smith's riposte is a resounding 'no' – not because those intellectuals cannot but that they *would not*.

The tacit liberal humanism in Jones and Smith's text is therefore unmistakable. More importantly, the form and extent of political subjectivity which these authors implicitly attribute to the community of 'scholar-bureaucrats' in effect involves a relatively high level of agency and instrumentality, without which the charges they level at the latter would be incomprehensible. In other words, the agency of these local security studies communities is better understood in terms of their decision to vigorously promote and protect the interests and agenda of their autocratic masters rather than dispute them; they instrumentally align their lot with the state.

Indeed, Jones and Smith's (2001b, 2002) dismissals of ASEAN as an 'imitation community' and a 'rhetorical and institutional shell' with an 'essentially ersatz quality' are possible only by refracting the Association's institutional practices and 'accomplishments' – and the scholarship of epistemic communities which celebrates and sanctions them – through the ideological prism which governs their text. Contrast their conclusion, however, with the following reflection by the late Michael Leifer, who was by no means an ASEAN apologist. Where Jones and Smith's scholars and statesmen pontificate futility and vainglory, Leifer's engage themselves vigorously (or are urged to do so) in 'conservation', namely, the incessant prosaic labours of constituting, buttressing and reinforcing the regional status quo:

> It is well understood that conservation cannot be achieved by standing still . . . Nonetheless, regional order in the practical sense for ASEAN will depend on adequate attention being paid to the commonplace, which requires special attention because it is commonplace and, therefore, in danger of being taken for granted. (Leifer, 1987: 21)

Regional order and institutionalism, Leifer seems to imply, is ultimately about instantiating and hence remaking boundaries and borders – the 'commonplace' elements which hold up the purported ontological integrity and primacy of states and, by extension, the state system. It is (as I have noted elsewhere) a delicate acknowledgement by this venerable contributor to regional security discourse that articulations of 'commonplace' anarchies, dangers and fears – spurring, in turn, appeals for collective vigilance – are at times necessary in order that the limits of state-centric discourse can be affirmed and sustained (Tan, 2005: 83). It is the fragile admission that 'sovereign states' and regional institutions such as 'ASEAN' are partly the effects of representational practices that can be made to work only so long as alternate or rival voices are excluded or silenced (Ashley, 1988: 252; Said, 1993: 324).

Essentialism 2: epistemic communities as abject subjects

Contrary to the way political agency and instrumentality are assigned in the first instance, a second essentialism involves the treatment, explicit or tacit, of Singapore's epistemic communities as abject and/or passive subjects, almost always at the mercy and service of a prior author or constructor. In this regard, an intriguing essay by Kanishka Jayasuriya (1994), which explores the efforts of Singapore-based epistemic agents in the post-Cold War construction of regional identity, is particularly illustrative of such reasoning and will be considered at length here.

Seeking to denaturalize the reification of 'region', Jayasuriya's text, following Neumann (1994), analyzes multiple regional identities as effects or products of state elite discourses, particularly in the case of Singapore. Noting the importance of understanding how regional definitions are produced as well as who produces them, the text concludes: 'In the Singapore case, we shall argue that while policy communities played some role in the management of various regional discourses, *the production of regional identities has been pre-eminently a state sponsored project*' (Jayasuriya, 1994: 412, emphasis added). Furthermore, he suggests that security studies communities in Singapore – the text fingers the Institute of Southeast Asian Studies (ISEAS) in particular – function primarily as 'cheer leaders' for Singapore's ruling elite by 'disseminating the language of regionalism'.

Most if not all Singapore-based research institutes claim, in their annual reports and brochures, that they are independent, private institutions or institutions semi-autonomous of the government (Noda, 1995: 431). But as alluded to in the preceding section, the agency of Singaporean epistemic communities is itself a difficult notion, not only for the reason that 'non-official' subjectivities are never quite autonomous actors whose actions are unmistakably independent of the state. Indeed, perhaps no other nation epitomizes the idea of the state as a dominating absolutist presence than Singapore, not least where reasoning about and policy-making in security are concerned. In short, the Singaporean state is often treated as the agent of security par excellence (Leifer, 2000; Worthington, 2003). In this respect, the notion of local 'non-state' agents of security working outside of the control and influence of the Singaporean state would seem inconceivable to not a few, as Jones and Smith's notion of 'scholar-bureaucrats', as we have earlier seen, readily attests.

Nevertheless, Jayasuriya's admirable analysis presents at least two conceptual conundrums. Here, I want to suggest, is where his text and those of Jones and Smith's part ways in their dissimilar ascriptions of epistemic agency. First, his implication that the discourse of regionalism is absolutized – totally captured and controlled – by state elites, such that local security studies communities end up as unofficial mouthpieces of the Singaporean government, is a tricky argument to sustain even if the impression is such. In response to the notion that 'the state spans the essential sector of disciplinary practices' – in short, state absolutism – Michel Foucault (1980: 72–3) answers:

> I do not mean in any way to minimize the importance and effectiveness of State power. I simply feel that excessive insistence on its playing an exclusive role leads to the risk of overlooking all the mechanisms and effects of power which don't pass directly via the State apparatus, yet often sustain the State more effectively than its own institutions, enlarging and maximizing its effectiveness.

Simply put, Singapore's intellectuals working to 'sustain the State', as Foucault has put it, may volitionally coopt with the state or be coerced into the task, but this does not mean that they are to be dismissed as mere stooges of their political masters, void of contestation – a contention even scholars of authoritarianism writing in the main, at least since James Scott's (1985) work on resistance, can make but only with great care.

Second, the contention that these intellectuals are merely 'disseminating the language of regionalism' for state elites suggests that regional security discourse is merely a collection of inert linguistic codes simply manipulated by knowing agents of and for the state who constitute meanings and then transcribe them into discourse. As such, purporting to conduct a 'genealogy of regionalism', Jayasuriya's explanation and attendant conclusion comprise a problematic totalization of the state's privileged role as sovereign actor in its will to power and truth via its regionalism discourse. Nevertheless, as with Foucault's unease over the notion of the absolutist state, so also should Jayasuriya's explanation be treated with caution. Witness, for instance, the following rejoinder by an ISEAS member to Jayasuriya:

> [A]ny intellectual discourse on the project of 'Asian' regionalism would have to take into account the existence of divergent and contesting 'projects' and 'practices.' As with every other conceptual entity, 'the region' is a historically contingent, social construction. State discourses very often possess a competitive edge in reality construction, but never a monopoly. A 'genealogy of regionalism' in which the construction of an imagined community beyond the nation-state

> is seen to have been the sole prerogative of state elites who enjoy a complete monopoly over the fabrication of ideas disavows the plurality inherent to society. Despite the 'hermeneutics of suspicion' it displays towards the state, Jayasuriya's account privileges – indeed, it absolutizes – the discourse of the state. (Wong, 1995: 688)

The notion that state discourses on regionalism do not monopolize but rather compete with discourses produced by epistemic communities and others implies a plurality to Singaporean society that liberal critics of authoritarianism may not find entirely persuasive, not least where Singapore is concerned. Be that as it may, it is precisely *because of* and not despite his 'hermeneutics of suspicion', I argue, that Jayasuriya's absolutist reading of state discourses is possible. The perceived deep, hidden meanings which purportedly underwrite the regionalism discourse, refracted through a Ricoeur-like hermeneutics of suspicion, understandably engender the conclusion that the Singaporean state is in fact in hegemonic control of discourses produced by various sectors of society, including epistemic communities (Dreyfus and Rabinow, 1983: xxii). In Jayasuriya's text, the People's Action Party government of Singapore has a firm hold on practically all walks of life in Singapore, so much so that all manners of representation, interpretation and signification of not only regionalism but also many if not most issues are, in the final analysis, 'state-sponsored'.

But it does not automatically imply that state elites therefore speak and act as pre-existing social subjects. Indeed, they are subjectivized themselves via the very discourse they aim to dominate. In contrast to the critical appreciation that all subjects without exception 'emerge in history', Jayasuriya's text tacitly presupposes that the Singaporean state subject remains very much outside of history and practice. Although it engages in the discursive construction of multiple regional identities, the state is, nevertheless, represented as a metaphysical given with no account of constitutive processes. Ironically, Jayasuriya's move to seek determinate causation through fixing the origins of the regionalism discourse in the state is rendered clearer when we compare his constructivist approach with so-called 'essential core' explanations which his study purports to eschew.

Whether his text avoids rendering an essential core explanation is highly debatable, and there are good reasons that imply his ultimate recourse to essentialism. Following Neumann (1994: 57) – on whose work Jayasuriya is reliant – essentialist views of regionalism are troubling precisely because they presuppose an objective entity independent of the social construction, say, of region by subjects. Essentialist positions assume that 'the construct [of region] does not assert its authority as an "imagined community," a cognitive construct shared by persons in the region themselves. Rather, it is the construct of one man – the allegedly sovereign actor.'

In fairness to Jayasuriya, the spirit of his analysis remains relatively faithful to Neumann's conceptual parameters. Yet in attributing regionalism discourse to the sole prerogative and purview of the Singaporean state, he paradoxically reifies the state – albeit as a sovereign collective, not individual, actor – thereby rendering it an ontologically prior given rather than social construction. Hence, despite the reference to the critical social strategy of 'genealogy' in his study, what Jayasuriya's text provides instead is a limited constructivist exercise that stops well short of pursuing fully the ramifications of constructivism. In this sense, it may be said of his analysis that it posits 'a limit to the limit-attitude' – a move that condemns it to replicating elements associated with the more conventional appropriations from which it wants to be distanced (Campbell, 1998: 224).

Towards a human-centred discourse

Both essentialisms critiqued above hold to certain assumptions about subjectivity that ultimately do not permit inquiry into its construction. Whether praised or pilloried as volitional instrumental agents (Essentialism 1), or reduced to abject subjects under a hegemonic state (Essentialism 2), such views of security studies communities are possible only due to prior acts of naturalization and reification. But if we accept the notion that practitioners and intellectuals of security function within a discursive space that imposes meanings and thereby create and maintain hyperrealist and state-centric world-views from which policy positions derive, then the notion of 'official policy community' need not be limited to important policy-makers as understood within conventional security studies (O'Tuathail and Agnew, 1992). It could also conceivably include nameless bureaucrats involved in the policy process, pundits who comment on security concerns, and academicians and analysts who supply the requisite intellectual ballast (Doty, 1993: 303).

As such, the conventional view that non-official or track-two diplomatic processes are 'endogenous to the Asia-Pacific, but exogenous to the individual state policy-making elites of the region' – at least from this critical standpoint – may be conceptually untenable (Higgott, 1994: 368). Rationalist-based efforts to glean an unadulterated causal linkage between a constructor and a constructed, which entail privileging either the Singaporean state or some 'non-official' epistemic agent as an originary presence, may simply be erroneous, since both state and non-state elements can equally comprise constituents of epistemic communities as well as the 'effects' of the latter's constitutive labours. But as we have seen, inscriptions of epistemic agency in principally instrumental and/or abject terms are largely insensitive to such alternative readings because of their ultimate recourse to settlements that privilege either intellectuals-as-actors or states without enquiring into their agency. Simply put, the idealization of a particular subject as an autonomous or sovereign actor arguably says more about our ideological preferences and collective constructions of political life than it does about the 'real world' we purportedly study (Doty, 2000: 139).

This said, the failure to take agency seriously as ultimately a political prerogative could prove detrimental to our efforts to grapple with contemporary regional developments, not least ASEAN's express aims to establish an ASEAN Community by 2020 and to institutionalize a charter (Roberts, 2005: 1; ASEAN, 2005). Equally interesting was the collective call by the region's legislators at an ASEAN Inter-Parliamentary Caucus gathering in September 2005 for the suspension of Myanmar from ASEAN, should its ruling junta fail to release Aung San Suu Kyi and other opposition members within a year – a move at odds with the policy of non-interference typically adhered to by ASEAN nations, including Singapore (Lawmakers Want ASEAN to Suspend Myanmar, 2005: 10). As of early 2007, Aung San Suu Kyi remains under house arrest, while Myanmar is still part of ASEAN. For some, these emerging region-wide patterns of liberalization and legalization are moulding an embryonic people-centred culture of 'participatory regionalism' – with regional epistemic communities at the forefront (Acharya, 2003b). As the current secretary-general of ASEAN has it, 'ASEAN's chosen approach in building social cohesion is people-centred and community-based. It has to be' (Ong, 2005). For others, such claims of progress are dubious: 'But what happened to the original vision of a united, cooperative and mutually supporting ASEAN for the people of ASEAN? Unlike the European Union, which has kept the interests of the nations and peoples of Europe firmly in the forefront, there has been precious little development towards a "people's ASEAN"' (Noor, 2005).

Against this backdrop, the perspective that epistemic agents are abject lackeys of a pre-given absolutist Singaporean state (Essentialism 2) may concede that the state is relaxing its hold on regionalism as its exclusive preserve, thereby permitting certain 'licensed' sectors of its population to participate in regional discourses. However, the highly limited agency which this state-centred argument affords Singapore's epistemic communities would likely give little credence to the aforementioned regional developments where promotion of a holistic, human-centred discourse in Singapore and the region is concerned. Much as the introduction of concepts such as comprehensive security and human security in Southeast Asia, in the view of some, have expanded rather than limited the purview of states, so too proposals for an ASEAN Charter and the like could paradoxically facilitate the consolidation and enlargement of extant powers enjoyed by regional governments (Suhrke, 1999; Tan, 2002; Acharya, 2005a).

The perspective that epistemic agents are instrumental agents in their own right (Essentialism 1), as we have seen, includes affirmative and negative views. On the one hand, the affirmative view (Katsumata) credits epistemic communities with a relatively high degree of agential freedom and sophistication. However, different though its assumptions are from Essentialism 2 assumptions, the outcome of its agency is more or less similar: the advancement of ideas and institutions that arguably enhance and entrench the dominance of the state. On the other hand, the negative view (Jones and Smith) castigates 'scholar-bureaucrats' for ceding their moral responsibility to speak truth to power in their volitional, instrumental embrace of authoritarianism. Of the three arguments examined here this likely constitutes the most plausible conceptual understanding of epistemic agency with the potential to transform the regional status quo. Yet its crass caricature of Singaporean security intellectuals as 'scholar-bureaucrats' who have sold out to an autocratic state ends up privileging the latter, if only inadvertently. Moreover, it is not immediately apparent whether its inherent liberal humanism can offer a sufficient basis for social change.[2]

The point here is not that these perspectives offer no useful insights; they clearly do. Nevertheless, their proclivity towards essentialism renders it difficult for alternative readings that could conceivably allow for the relaxation of the subjectivity–sovereignty nexus, which insists on a priori settlements about the ontological priority of states, on one hand, or of non-state epistemic communities on the other. If students of agency are serious about restoring a deeper appreciation for history and practice, then it must necessarily begin with the understanding that all subjects, including 'sovereign Singapore' or the 'ASEAN-ISIS' or even the 'ISEAS', are sites of ceaseless political contestation and whose identities – or, à la Butler (1993), 'materiality' – exist only via precarious balancing acts wherein diverse interpretive elements are variously included and, at times violently, excluded (Ashley, 1987: 410). By setting aside the incessant pitting of pre-given states against pre-given individuals, the path towards a non-essentialist notion of subjectivity that necessarily begins with an acknowledgement of its debt to its 'other' – without which agency would be unthinkable – becomes less implausible.

Conclusion

Numerous critical analyses emphasize the potential role of non-state actors generally, and epistemic communities specifically, as agents for reorienting security discourses in progressive ways. For such theorists, these agents are capable of articulating alternative security priorities and practices, most usually located in the language of 'comprehensive security' or 'human security'. Others are sceptical of such possibilities, pointing to the extent to which such discourses remain trapped (particularly in the Asia-Pacific) within dominant security paradigms, and these epistemic communities rely upon a level of engagement with orthodox thinking about security that ultimately precludes genuine innovation in security thinking. As I have argued above, this dichotomy is ultimately unhelpful in understanding the relationship between the role played by epistemic communities and the contexts in which they play them. Such a conclusion has important implications in this context for critical security studies, given the emphasis placed on locating possibilities for progressive change within prevailing orders. This emphasis requires a sophisticated understanding of the mutually constitutive relationship between security agents and structures.

Shortly after the Cold War ended, Ken Booth (1991: 313), in appealing for a new language of international relations that would better fit with new realities, gravely announced: 'Our work is our words, but our words do not work anymore.' For epistemic agents of security such as Singapore's epistemic communities and the intellectuals therein who contribute to national and regional discourses on security, their words do not only constitute their work. Indeed, it may be said that their words – and the words of scholars who study those communities – constitute and legitimize their existence, if ever and only tenuously so, as subjects blessed with agential privilege and power to produce security knowledge. In short, their life is their words.

Notes

1 This is reminiscent of Adler's (1997) logic that where imagined security communities are concerned, peoples' imaginations of their economic and security wellbeing converge more or less with the boundaries of states.

2 For example, no less an authority than Emmanuel Lévinas (1981: 127) has criticized liberal humanism as 'insufficiently human' owing to its inconsideration of alterity and otherness, which arises from its Enlightenment-inspired supposition of subjectivity and agency as ideally sovereign and essentialist.

Part II

Strategies and contexts

5

Constructing separatist threats: security and insecurity in Indonesian Aceh and Papua[1]

Edward Aspinall and Richard Chauvel

SINCE THE END OF the Suharto regime in 1998, the 'outlying' provinces of Aceh and Papua have caused great concern to Indonesia's national security planners. Both have been sites of substantial secessionist activity and considerable violence between Indonesian security forces and supporters of independence. Thousands of people have lost their lives; hundreds of thousands have been displaced or experienced other losses.

This chapter aims, first, to provide an assessment of the Indonesian state's approach to security in these territories. It argues that its security policy is not especially sophisticated, but is instead, as in so many other settings, based on simplistic but frequently unquestioned notions about political identity and loyalty. In particular, Indonesia's security planners interpret and construct a separatist threat through a prism that defines political actors as either loyal supporters of the unitary state or as their polar opposite – disobedient and disloyal separatists. Second, we show how this bifurcated schema is then used to justify the application of force and the stigmatization of dissent in the handling of complex political challenges in the state's periphery. The state's own security policies are in turn often interpreted as a source of insecurity and threat among the target populations and, far from achieving their stated aims, contribute to the alienation that feeds separatism. Finally, we ask whether, in the midst of the intensely conflict-ridden and securitized political climates found in these territories, there is space for the imagination of alternative conceptions of human security by local communities, as well as room for their application in practice.

Defining a security approach

In the late 1980s and early 1990s, when Indonesia's President Suharto allowed a limited liberalization of the country's then highly authoritarian political system, some senior government officials and military officers began to talk about the need to modify the country's 'security approach'. This term was not pejorative, but was routinely used by officials to justify the military's position at the centre of the political system and the use of repressive measures to control dissent. To justify the security approach, the army's leaders had long talked about 'latent' threats that endangered the nation. Such threats include, above all, communism or the 'extreme left', an 'extreme right' (which mostly referred to Muslims who, in the regime's eyes, wanted to establish an Islamic state) and various other maladies including liberalism, globalization, and 'national disintegration'. The authority of the regime, in other words, depended upon the cultivation of a constant state of anxiety and insecurity that 'penetrated profoundly into the everyday activities of ordinary Indonesians' (Heryanto, 1999: 156). The other side of this coin was that the regime also constructed an Indonesian 'national personality' that valued principles like consensus, decision-making through mutual deliberation, communitarianism and, in the most extreme 'organicist' version, effaced the very conceptual division between state and society (Bourchier, 1997). These notions were said to be embodied in the state ideology of 'Pancasila' (the five principles). The regime could thus depict its opponents and other miscreants not merely as threats to security and stability, but as opposed to the fundamental essence of Indonesia.

Indonesia, then, is a country where until recent times securitization occurred not merely with respect to a discrete issue (e.g. 'terrorism') or social group (e.g. 'asylum-seekers'). Instead, it infused the whole political and civil society. If security is understood as a 'move which takes politics beyond the normal rules of the game' (Buzan *et al.*, 1998: 23), little wonder that the reforming retired generals and politicians of the late 1980s and early 1990s talked not only about the need to end the 'security approach', but also about the need to 'normalize' politics and end the 'emergency conditions' that had characterized politics since the army's rise to power in 1965 (see for example Soemitro, 1992).

Indonesia has changed greatly since the downfall of President Suharto in 1998. Advocates of 'normalization' would be pleased with what they now see. Most formal restrictions on the media, labour unions, political parties and other associations have been lifted. Democratic elections have been held, including the first direct presidential election in 2004. The organicist ideology that sought to fuse state and society is, if not in tatters, at least severely weakened. Discussion of the old national security threats has not disappeared (for example, dissemination of Marxism-Leninism remains formally banned), but articulation of these threats no longer pervades Indonesian political and security discourse. Large parts of the political field have been effectively desecuritized.

There is, however, one exception to this overall pattern. In the place of Pancasila, which used to be mobilized to legitimate repression against potential opponents of the regime, the term 'NKRI' now punctuates the speeches and political language of politicians, state officials, military officers and other commentators. NKRI is an acronym standing for *Negara Kesatuan Republik Indonesia*, meaning 'Unitary State of the Republic of Indonesia'. NKRI has become a mantra that is reiterated obsessively and repetitively. Politicians, military officers and journalists warn of threats and dangers to the 'integrity' of the NKRI. They proclaim their loyalty to NKRI. They declare that maintaining the 'unity' of the NKRI must come before all other considerations.

While there are similarities between the two slogans, NKRI has more specific targets in the dissident provinces, whereas Pancasila was a much broader umbrella under which to impose ideological conformity. The shift in discourse away from 'defence of Pancasila' to 'defence of NKRI' does, therefore, partly reflect recent historical events, and responds to particular challenges to the state. After the downfall of the Suharto regime, which was not only authoritarian but also highly centralized, there was a wave of political mobilization and cultural reinvigoration in Indonesia's regions, leading Suharto's successor, B.J. Habibie, to launch a far-reaching decentralization policy (see Emmerson, 2000; Aspinall and Berger, 2001; Aspinall and Fealy, 2003). In some places, there was a revitalization of secessionist movements. The separation of East Timor, following an independence referendum and international intervention in 1999, encouraged reinvigorated secessionist movements at Indonesia's far eastern and western peripheries, Papua and Aceh. Conversely, the 'loss' of East Timor galvanized much of the national elite to defend what remained of NKRI. The new salience of NKRI in national political discourse is partly a response to these movements. It also points to the fact that in some parts of Indonesia, at least, the old securitization of the political and social field has not abated. Rather, it has merely taken different form.

Trajectories of conflict

Space prohibits a full treatment here of the history of Aceh and Papua's incorporation into Indonesia, the development of secessionist movements and violent conflicts in the two places, or even of how Indonesian nationalists have incorporated the two places into Indonesia's imagined community. Suffice it to say that their histories are very different. Papua was excluded from the transfer of sovereignty to Indonesia in 1949 and remained under Dutch administration until 1962. The 12-year-long conflict between Holland and Indonesia was resolved in the New York Agreement, under which administration of Papua was transferred to Indonesia. The Agreement provided for an 'Act of Free Choice' in 1969, when Papuans should have been given the opportunity to determine whether they wanted to remain in Indonesia or become independent. The Papuan belief that the result of the 'Act of Free Choice' in favour of Indonesia was manipulated by Indonesia is one of the core motivations driving their struggle for independence.

Aceh's union with Indonesia, by contrast, was relatively smooth. Aceh had been the site of a powerful independent sultanate that resisted the expansion of Dutch colonialism in the nineteenth century. Its leaders and population, though having few links to the pre-Second World War Indonesian nationalist movement, furnished enthusiastic and vital support to the Indonesian national revolution in the 1940s.

In both places, sporadic secessionist movements developed during Suharto's New Order regime. In different ways, these movements protested against the methods by which the territories had been incorporated into the Republic, as well as the ways by which they were being governed. In Papua, armed resistance to Indonesian rule commenced shortly after the transfer of administration to Indonesia. The *Organisasi Papua Merdeka* (OPM, Free Papua Organisation) was formed in 1964 and staged its first major revolt in 1965. The OPM proclaimed Papuan independence in 1971 in the hope that it would attract international recognition and to make clear that Papuans rejected the 'Act of Free Choice'. The OPM's resistance was local and ad hoc. Although it never threatened Indonesia control over Papua, Indonesia has never been able to eliminate it.

In Aceh, an early *Darul Islam* (Abode of Islam) revolt in the 1950s, which questioned the terms of Aceh's incorporation into Indonesia, rather than incorporation itself, gave rise to a compromise settlement promising 'Special Territory' status. When this status proved unable to withstand the centralizing and authoritarian tide under the New Order, a group of *Darul Islam* veterans and their children formed the Free Aceh Movement (GAM, *Gerakan Aceh Merdeka*) in 1976 and proclaimed Aceh's independence. The movement was initially weak as a military force, although it re-emerged with renewed strength in the late 1980s.

The New Order used military methods to suppress these movements. But suppression of separatism never had the centrality in regime discourse that the ubiquity of NKRI points to today. To be sure, the army reiterated that it was the only force that could keep Indonesia together. Security officials acknowledged a 'separatist threat', but they did so in ways that silenced or trivialized it. For instance, they disregarded the explicit grievances voiced by these groups and instead asserted they were motivated by the underdevelopment of their provinces, a problem that could only be addressed by the government itself (McRae, 2002). There was little open discussion of the extent or nature of these movements. For much of the final decade of Suharto's presidency, for instance, there was an intense military operation in Aceh that resulted in widespread abuses by security forces. But this was pursued without a formal declaration of martial law or even a frank acknowledgement of the nature of the security disturbance. Instead the authorities talked in terms of a law and order problem, depicting secessionists as being part of a 'marijuana mafia' or denigrating them as a mere 'security disturbers movement' (*gerakan pengacau keamanan* or GPK).

After the fall of Suharto, there was a brief 'spring' in relations between the centre and the regions in 1998–2000. Political liberalization allowed people in Aceh and Papua to express long-suppressed grievances and aspirations. In particular, there was sudden and dramatic public exposure of the abuses conducted by the security forces in previous anti-insurgency campaigns, as well as demands for more autonomy in politics, a greater share of resource revenues, and so on. Central government officials promised that the 'security approach' would be abandoned and replaced by a new policy of sensitivity towards local aspirations. For the first time for several decades (Aceh) or at all (Papua) critical voices from the regions themselves now figured in national political debate, for instance contributing to the creation of new 'Special Autonomy' laws for the two provinces (McGibbon, 2004).

The post-Suharto ferment, however, also gave rise to strengthened secessionist mobilization. In Papua educated urban activists, mostly people who had not been associated with the OPM – from the churches, non-governmental organizations (NGOs) and universities as well as from within the Indonesian bureaucracy and *adat* (customary, or tribal) leadership – rapidly mobilized support for independence. In February 1999 a group of 100 elite Papuans met with President Habibie and startled him when they demanded independence. In 2000, a new province-wide organization, the *Presidium Dewan Papua* (PDP, Papuan Presidium Council) with an independence agenda was formed, and a 'Papuan People's Congress' was held. Among the Congress' resolutions was the assertion that Papua was already independent, as of 1 December 1961, and that Papuans rejected both the New York Agreement and the 1969 'Act of Free Choice'. In Aceh, a large student-led movement organized huge demonstrations in 1999 calling for an independence referendum. At the same time, the GAM insurgency gained new strength, consolidating its control over much of Aceh's rural hinterland and launching attacks on government installations and troops.

In such circumstances, there was a rapid return to a 'security approach' in both provinces (although this label was now rarely used). In Aceh, this took the form above all of intensified military operations against GAM and, eventually, martial law. In the resulting climate of security panic, virtually any individual or group who questioned state policy could be deemed a security threat, enabling the authorities to act against civilian activists who used peaceful methods to agitate in favour of independence or a referendum. At first, it was primarily the Indonesian police forces (newly separated from the military as part of President Habibie's reformulation of security policy) that took the lead in these operations. Eventually, however, the military (TNI) (*Tentara Nasional Indonesia*, Indonesian National Military) reasserted itself. This reached a peak in May 2003 when, after the breakdown of an attempt to negotiate an end to the conflict with GAM, President Megawati Soekarnoputri declared a 'military emergency' in the province, leading to intensified counter-insurgency operations and a much expanded role for the military in local administration.

In Papua, President Habibie's successor, President Abdurrahman Wahid attempted a conciliatory approach. He made symbolic concessions to Papuan nationalist sentiments, permitting the name 'Papua' to be used for the province instead of the Indonesian preferred 'Irian Jaya', and allowing the nationalist Morning Star flag to be flown. He even provided funding for the Papuan People's Congress. The Congress, however, was the turning point in official policies. A series of leaked documents from security agencies from this point reveal a hardening of official attitudes. A confidential police strategy document from the end of 2000, for example, noted: 'The issues of democracy and human rights were used by the separatists to undermine the morale of government officials.' Such assessments of the threat by the rejuvenated nationalist movement prompted determination to close down the political space created in the 'spring' and return to policies more akin to Suharto's security approach. Authorities took a harder line against flag-raisings and other pro-independence activities. Political tensions escalated in November 2000 as the anniversary of Papuan 'independence' (1 December) neared. Two days before the anniversary the leader of the PDP, Theys Eluay and four of his colleagues were arrested and charged with treason. On 10 November 2001, before their trial had finished, Eluay was killed by Kopassus (Special Forces) soldiers, after having attended the Kopassus reception to mark Indonesia's National Heroes Day. In April 2003 a court martial sentenced Lt Colonel Hartomo, the most senior officer charged, to 3 years, while Pvt. Ahmad Zulfahmi, who confessed to strangling Eluay, and the other soldiers received 3 years (Laksamana, 2003). Perhaps more revealing of the authorities' values than the sentences was the comment of the Army's Chief of Staff, General Ryamizard Ryacudu, that he regarded the murderers as heroes performing duties for the nation (AAP, 2003).

Security discourse on Aceh and Papua

Much commentary on the return to repressive policies in Aceh and Papua emphasizes the political and material interests of the TNI. Clearly, the TNI has not merely been an instrument of the policy shift, but also an important initiator of it. In the immediate aftermath of the fall of the Suharto, the TNI was weakened politically. The 'dual function' policy by which it had been assigned a 'socio-political' as well as a defence and security role under the New Order was formally ended. There was press exposure and judicial investigations into past human rights abuses. By recasting itself as the defender of NKRI against separatist threats, the TNI has been able to deflect much of this criticism and to defend its basic institutional interests (although it has not been able to restore its former political pre-eminence). At the same time, the TNI's material interests have provided it with both a strong motive and a means to defend its prerogatives. In particular, it is widely argued that in circumstances when the military only covers a small proportion of its operating costs from the state budget, the opportunities afforded for extra-budgetary fund-raising in conflict zones (e.g. via the provision of 'protection' services for private firms) gave it a strong incentive to renew its presence and role in both regions.[2]

However, the ideological work involved in constructing a security threat has been equally important. The return to repressive policies in Aceh and Papua was widely supported by civilian politicians and large sections of the public. Various opinion polls, for instance, demonstrated strong support for the declaration of a 'military emergency' in Aceh. Nationalist out-bidding in the national parliament was intense, with civilian politicians sometimes appearing to compete with each other to appear tough on separatism.

In the ideological sphere, we may identify similarities with the methods that are used to construct security threats and responses elsewhere in the world.[3] Fundamentally, a two-part, yet simultaneous, process is involved. The first is the construction of an 'us', a community that is embodied in abstract (even fetishized) symbols and which is portrayed as fragile and beleaguered. The second is the construction of a dangerous 'other' that threatens that community and its symbols. In Indonesia, as in most places, the shared vocabulary of nationalism provides the tools for this endeavour.

Officials, intellectuals, journalists and other commentators routinely speak of national identity and national unity as being a precious and fragile inheritance of Indonesia's anti-colonial movement, rather than being an expression of a 'common project' (Anderson, 1999: 8). In part, this is a product of history. Indonesian national identity is a relatively recent concept and one that arose at least in part from purposeful efforts by early twentieth-century nationalists. These efforts have subsequently been mythologized by a nationalist historiography that stresses that forging 'national unity and oneness' (as one of the stock phrases goes) was an arduous task and that recurrent threats of 'national disintegration' have been overcome only with great difficulty. Megawati Sukarnoputri provided a good example of this sort of mythologizing in 1999 when she recalled a childhood conversation with her father, Indonesia's founding president, Sukarno. She had asked why he had visited Papua. It was so far away. To which he replied: 'Without Irian Jaya Indonesia is not complete to become the national territory of the Unitary Republic of Indonesia.' As vice president (later president), she wanted to maintain her father's vision. She appealed to the people of Papua that the territory had been entrusted to the nation through the sacrifice of heroes (in Tifa Irian, 1999: 8).

'Separatists' are depicted as threats to the precious inheritance of national unity by a series of techniques that dehumanize them and stress their deviance. For example, when security officials call on members of secessionist groups to surrender and 'return to the bosom of the motherland' they frequently describe them in language that is borrowed from religion, as people who are *sesat* (misguided or deviant) and who should *taubat* (repent). At other times they criminalize them, depicting them as delinquents motivated by desire for personal gain, or use metaphors of illness or other forms of bodily distress. In the words of one local official addressing a crowd in East Aceh in April 2004 separatism is like a 'boil' which would release pus if burst, but which must be dug out by the roots; if not 'it can become a cancer or could even more seriously destroy the life of the sufferer' (in Analisa, 2004). On other occasions, separatists are described as 'naughty children' who, having been reprimanded and still refusing to rejoin the 'big family' of the Indonesian nation, must be subject to stern action.[4]

Importantly, the internal separatist threat is invariably linked in the security discourse to external threats to Indonesia's sovereignty and territorial integrity. In the years since the East Timor referendum, senior military officers and national politicians have routinely made what to outsiders seem outlandish claims about (usually unnamed) foreign powers and the secret designs they harbour on Indonesian territory. Usually, the warnings are vague and imprecise, as when Army Chief of Staff Ryamizard Ryacudu warned: 'We must be vigilant, because they will mess with Papua and then separate it. After all, Papua has a lot of [valuable] stuff in it' (in Media Indonesia, 2003). Such warnings themselves draw upon Indonesia's nationalist history, beginning with the attempt by the Dutch to establish a federal government in the archipelago in the 1940s as a way of weakening the revolutionary republic, through to the foreign 'treachery' that allegedly explained the separation of East Timor in 1999. In this security discourse, criticisms from abroad about, for instance, human rights abuses in conflict areas can be dismissed readily as cover for strategic designs. Domestic critics of security policy can likewise be accused of being anti-nationalist tools of foreign interests. Overall, the discourse fuses the internal threat mounted by separatists with the external threat of international criticism, presenting separatism as a deep and existential threat to Indonesia.

In fact, in common with the language of security panic and threat construction in many countries, official Indonesian discourse on separatists is not usually sophisticated. It does not operate by careful argumentation and discussion of evidence, but rather by repetition of key themes, by simplification of complex political problems, and by the evocation of a mood of anxiety and danger. Security discourse thus becomes a framing mechanism that is diffuse yet effective, infusing daily political discourse almost imperceptibly and naturalizing military responses to 'separatist threats'. Indeed, the metaphor of defence of NKRI is so powerful that security officials often find it so self-evident that separatism is a base evil that they frequently state separatists should be 'destroyed' or 'exterminated' without feeling the need to further justify such an approach.

Outcomes

Security policies and approaches often, as critical security scholars have long argued, generate insecurity (see Booth, 2005e). Such has been the case in Aceh and Papua, where many local people and outsiders have observed that the state's policies have often had an effect opposite to that which was intended. In a dynamic mirroring the prosecution of the US-led 'war on terror' globally and within the region, the reliance on violence has *contributed* significantly to the popular alienation that underpins support for independence, and hence conflict.

Take for example, the army's policy in Aceh. In the late Suharto years, the military was responsible for many serious abuses against civilians in its campaign to eliminate GAM. When public unrest erupted in Aceh immediately after Suharto fell, state violence suddenly occupied a central place in the list of Acehnese grievances. Issues that had previously motivated Acehnese resentment, such as political centralization and exploitation of Aceh's natural resources, were relegated to second place. Human rights campaigners and independence supporters alike now depicted Aceh's incorporation into Indonesia as one that had generated great physical suffering for the Acehnese. Security officials themselves admitted that many of GAM's new recruits after 1999 were motivated by a desire to revenge the deaths or suffering of close family members.

Yet, after a period of experimenting with new approaches, and when the GAM insurgency revived, officials revived a security response based on old formulae. In May 2003, when the government declared a military emergency, it recycled techniques from the Suharto years. Troops were mobilized to kill or capture GAM insurgents, while the civilian population was closely monitored in order to cut the rebel supply chain. Military posts proliferated in villages, thousands of villagers were temporarily relocated to detention camps, and checkpoints, street-side inspections and searches of citizens' homes intensified. The population was mobilized in parades to demonstrate support for NKRI. The military also sponsored civilian militias whose task was to provide intelligence on GAM movements, guard villages at night and carry out other actions in support of the military's counterinsurgency operations. Each of these elements had been central to counterinsurgency operations in the past and suggested continued belief in the 'primacy of the military solution' (Sukma, 2004: 21).

This approach was packaged in a language that stressed that the army wished to 'win the hearts and minds' of the local population (only one of the more obvious borrowings from the contemporaneous US occupation of Iraq). Security officials stressed they intended to avoid repeating past mistakes and wanted to protect the population rather than oppress it. In fact, international human rights agencies (despite having limited access to the province) again reported that serious abuses were committed, including arbitrary arrests and killings, torture and looting (Human Rights Watch, 2003). Presumably, such acts only deepened the alienation of many civilians, including those who were obliged to attend the ceremonies where they declared their loyalty to NKRI.

What was most revealing about this security operation was the ideological climate which accompanied it. Local newspapers carried almost daily reports of speeches made by local army commanders at 'loyalty parades' and other events. Mostly these contained stock reiterations of the need to defend NKRI and oppose separatism.[5] The speakers frequently also implied, however, that they were unsure of the loyalties of those they were addressing. Instead, they cajoled or, more often, berated them. Take, for instance, comments by Major Yani, Chief of Staff of the local Military District in Tapaktuan, South Aceh: 'It is no longer permissible for people to act in a neutral manner when it comes to GAM, to say yes to GAM on one side and then yes to the Indonesian government on the other. Starting now it must be clear: if you are NKRI then you must always be NKRI' (in Serambi Indonesia, 2003). Other officers spoke at length about how public servants could no longer work for the Indonesian government but 'in their hearts' support separatism. Speeches like these provide some insight into how military officers viewed their task in Aceh, and the deep unease they had about the sympathies of the population. At the same time that security officials said their goal was to protect the local community, they also depicted it as the chief source of insecurity.

In Papua, security officials were anxious not only about the leaders of the independence movement, but also about the loyalties of the very group whom Jakarta has relied upon to integrate the province into national governing structures. This was because, in official eyes, the principal threat posed to Jakarta's authority came not from an armed insurgency, as in Aceh, but from the urban, Indonesian-educated elite. Thus, at the same time that officials took overt action against Theys Eluay and other leaders of the new independence movement, they also cast a suspicious eye at local establishment figures. A Department of Internal Affairs memorandum of June 2000 pictured the Papuan 'conspirators' as including not only the public leaders of the post-Suharto independence movement, but also some of the most senior Papuans in the Indonesian administration, including two former governors, the present governor, an Indonesian ambassador and senior officials of the provincial government, as well as senior church leaders and intellectuals. The memorandum argued that the provincial administration had been 'contaminated' by the issue of independence (Dinas, 2000). Later, the deputy speaker of the Indonesian parliament accused the governor of Papua, Solossa, of seeking support overseas for the independence movement. A police operation – *Operasi Adil Matoa* – launched in July 2002 cast a wide net not only to include 'individuals and social organisations whose vision and mission are to separate the Province of Papua from NKRI', but also 'individuals and social organisations who oppose the policy of the government by using violations of human rights as a cover and who engage in other activities that can undermine the authority of the government and the state' (Pastika, 2002).

Meanwhile, the authorities' response to sporadic violence from sections of Papuan society involved deployment of military forces and indiscriminate reprisals. On 7 December 2000, for example, some 300 people armed with traditional weapons attacked the police station near the Abepura market killing three members of the security forces. The police were unable to identify or capture the attackers, but on suspicion they were highlanders, they raided the student dormitories, attacked the sleeping students and detained 90 of them. In detention some of the students were tortured and three were killed. On 13 June 2001, an armed unknown group killed five police mobile brigade members. In response, the security forces conducted a 'Sweeping and Clampdown'. According to Elsham and Church sources, the operation resulted in detention, torture and houses being burnt. Elsham estimated that about 5,000 civilians fled their homes and stated that daily social and economic activities became completely paralysed, with everyone living in a state of fear (Chauvel, 2003). This pattern of indiscriminate reprisals by the security forces has continued since the election of President Susilo Bambang Yudhoyono (Amnesty International, 2005).

We do not seek to argue that the challenges facing Indonesian state officials in Aceh and Papua have been trivial or that they do not pose real dilemmas. Especially in Aceh, the state has faced a powerful armed insurgency that has itself sometimes used brutal methods against civilians. For a time the insurgency paralysed much of Aceh's state apparatus and the economy, exacerbating the suffering of the population through loss of basic services and undermining the government's ability to respond to local grievances. In Papua, too, as indicated above, there has been sporadic violence by non-state actors. Nor do we wish to suggest that the 'security approach' has been the *only* state response to secessionist sentiment in these two provinces. On the contrary, after the fall of Suharto, many senior officials believed conciliatory measures were necessary to undermine support for secession and generate confidence in Indonesia. Chief among these policies was the passage of new 'Special Autonomy' laws for both provinces in 2001. Even at the height of the military emergency in Aceh, TNI said they were running an 'integrated operation' that included alongside security operations elements like restoration of law and order and economic development. However, in practice it was always the emphasis on security (defined in statist and militaristic terms) that has dominated, frequently undermining other elements of the government's approach.

The more general point is that the government's security policies have been pursued in these provinces largely at the expense of the security of local communities, whose members often view the state and its agencies as *sources* of insecurity and threat. These policies have also probably been counterproductive on their own terms, because although aimed at the physical destruction of secessionist movements, by alienating local people they added strength to secessionist feelings. Sometimes this connection is very obvious: for example, Theys Eluay's assassination and his funeral procession were the occasion for the first mass display of Papuan nationalist feeling since the end of 2000. Whatever the motives of those responsible for his death, the effect was to reinvigorate Papuan national aspirations and to create another martyr to the cause of Papuan independence.

Alternatives

State perspectives on security in Indonesia's separatist provinces have not been uncontested. On the contrary, groups in these territories have tried to articulate alternative conceptions of security. In the brief 'spring' which followed the downfall of Suharto, a tremendous variety of civil society activity appeared in both Papua and Aceh. Among the new initiatives were many which promoted conflict resolution, human rights and popular control of local resources, often drawing upon both transnational civil society networks and indigenous cultural resources and frameworks.

The ideal of creating Papua as a 'Zone of Peace' emerged in the context of the transition of the Papuan struggle for independence from the armed struggle of the OPM to the non-violent struggle espoused in the immediate post-Suharto period. The concept was a Papuan response to Jakarta's resort to violence as the government attempted to bring an end to the Papuan 'spring' in the last months of 2000. A couple of days after violence in Wamena in October 2000, which involved highlander Papuan attacks on Indonesian immigrants and coastal Papuans, as well as security forces killing Papuans, the PDP proposed to the government that it proclaim Papua as a 'Zone of Peace', so that the government, the security forces and civil society refrain from using violence in the resolution of the Papuan problem.

The 'Zone of Peace' idea quickly gained currency among Papua's leading institutions and political activists. Papua's largest Protestant Church, the GKI (*Gereja Kristen Injili* (Evangelical Christian Church)), also greatly influenced by the violence at Wamena, 'appealed to the government and the people to proclaim Papua as a Zone of Peace, where problems were resolved through dialogue, where the State's weapons were not used to butcher (*membantai*) the people and Papuans did not did not fight and kill each other' (Kabar-Irian, 2000).

Initially, the 'Zone of Peace' ideal seemed to be used principally to appeal to the government to refrain from using violence to assert its authority in Papua. For example, after the killing of three teachers at the Freeport Mine in 2002, Papua's religious leaders wrote to Megawati to say that they had been propagating the ideal, but it appeared that there were 'certain groups' (*pihak tertentu*) who did not want peace in Papua. However, the violence in Wamena, especially that by Papuan civilians, shocked many within the Papuan elite who then used the 'Zone of Peace' idea as a means to persuade their own followers to desist from violence. The 'Zone of Peace' ideal was also evoked by the fear of ethnic and religious violence when *Laskar Jihad* (Jihad brigade) groups from Maluku (a site of severe communal conflict in 1999–2001) became active around Sorong, Fakfak and Merauke. Its advocates saw the 'Zone of Peace' as a means to establish the principle of religious freedom and encourage cooperation between religious leaders (Elsham News, 2002).

In Aceh, where both militarization and violent separatism have been much greater, there was initially less space for local communities and civil society groups to assert an agenda independent of the two warring sides. Indeed, military officers posted to the province have often reminded local people that they could not be neutral in the battle between NKRI and GAM. Activists from some civil society groups who had campaigned on human rights issues or supported an independence referendum were accused of being part of GAM's clandestine front and were arrested; a few were killed. Yet even in Aceh there were attempts to carve out a space of civil society activity independent of the warring parties and removed from the zero-sum conflict between NKRI and *merdeka* (independence or freedom).

Such efforts included a wide range of human rights, conflict resolution, and women's empowerment activities, too numerous to summarize here. Interestingly, some local NGOs and other political actors attempted to re-interpret the meaning of *merdeka,* saying that when they visited local communities, villagers often told them that they supported *merdeka,* but when given a chance to explain what they meant, say what they desire is *merdeka* (freedom) from fear, from abuse and from poverty.[6]

The ferocity of the armed conflict, however, meant that attempts to find agendas for peace ultimately mostly involved formal negotiations between the armed parties, the Indonesian state and GAM. Independent groups, let alone ordinary villagers, were excluded from this process. While the first attempt to negotiate a settlement failed when military officers and civilian politicians accused GAM of using the ceasefire to strengthen their campaign of separatism and threaten NKRI, a renewed effort to find a peaceful settlement eventually produced a more comprehensive agreement, signed in Helsinki in August 2005 (Aspinall, 2005). This process had produced dramatic de-escalation of the conflict and demilitarisation. The breakthrough was made possible when GAM leaders dropped their demand for independence and said they were prepared to settle for a solution that allowed Aceh to remain within the Indonesian state, though with expanded autonomy. As they saw it, and echoing the language sometimes used by villagers, they were trying to achieve goals while avoiding conflict over sovereignty. According to GAM leader Sofyan Dawood, for instance, GAM would not 'cease to struggle for justice, eliminate tyranny, wrongdoing, and all sorts of criminal acts that occur on the land of Aceh' (Serambi Indonesia, 2005). This was, in other words, an attempt to side-step the zero-sum language of contesting sovereignties, although it is an attempt that remains fragile.

Conclusion

The preceding analysis shows how security policies in Aceh and Papua have been founded upon a simplistic schema for understanding complex political and social phenomena in both territories. The binary opposite – 'loyalty to NKRI' versus 'separatism' – became a ubiquitous and powerful feature of Indonesian political discourse in the years after the collapse of the authoritarian Suharto regime. It also became an ideological template that naturalized, indeed mandated, repressive policies for dealing with political challenges in the dissident provinces. The major practical effect was the survival in these territories of a repressive security approach of a sort that had been at the heart of the previous authoritarian regime. This security approach, and the attendant violence, became a source of major insecurity and suffering for local people in both territories. It also arguably became the major contributor to the very problem that it was ostensibly designed to address (popular support for secession). State violence alienated local people and fuelled support for the secessionist cause. Ironically, therefore, the bifurcation in official discourse between 'NKRI' and 'separatism' reproduced itself in the politics of the dissident provinces themselves.

In the midst of highly militarized national security conflicts such as those in Aceh and Papua, it can be difficult for local people to articulate alternative conceptualizations of human security and emancipation. The zero-sum polarization of political identities generated by state security discourses is a deadening force, especially when criticism of or resistance to the state is liable to be depicted as sympathy for separatism and thus prompt repression. Independent groups in Aceh and Papua have advanced alternative ideas about how meaningful human security could be maintained in their territories, but their ideas remained halting and incomplete, mostly involving attempts to curb the most egregious of state excesses, while at the same time protecting their advocates from suspicion. Yet by highlighting the debilitating effects of state security policies on citizens in the conflict zones, and by pointing out that state action was often experienced as a major source of insecurity, they raised possibilities of transformation towards a more emancipatory approach to security.

Indonesia is still in the midst of a difficult transition away from a long period of authoritarian rule. Many forms of political action and discourse which were once viewed by officials through a traditional security lens and deemed threatening and un-Indonesian have become a normal part of everyday political life. Political pluralism, civil society activism, dissent and criticism of state policies have become well established. In places like Aceh and Papua there was a reversion to repressive policies, though as the recent peace process in Aceh shows, this was not necessarily permanent. However, the achievements of the broader process of democratization give hope that even in those places a move away from an exclusionary and violent conception and practice of security is a real possibility.

Notes

1 This chapter uses 'Papua' as the name for the Indonesian western half of the island of New Guinea. The name has been a matter of contention since the 1940s, reflecting the struggle between the Dutch and the Indonesians, then between the Papuans and the Indonesians. Papuans have generally preferred Papua or West Papua, while Indonesian governments favoured 'Irian', as in Irian Jaya or West Irian. In 2000 President Wahid permitted the use of Papua for the territory, while in 2003 President Megawati Sukarnoputri, in her instruction to divide the territory into three provinces, reverted to 'Irian'.

2 For one discussion of such issues see McCulloch (2003).

3 See for example the chapters by Matt McDonald and Anthony Burke in this volume.

4 This is a formulation once used by TNI commander General Endriartono Sutarto in *Kompas* (2003).

5 Sometimes this was very vivid, as when Lieutenant Colonel Jamhur Ismail told one crowd that the time had come to 'sharpen their machetes' and comb the hills to look for GAM members to destroy (*Serambi Indonesia*, 2003).

6 For example, one outspoken member of the Islamic-based Unity Development Party, PPP (*Partai Persatuan Pembangunan*), Ghazali Adnan Abbas, early on spoke of the Acehnese desiring 'six *merdeka*': freedom to implement Islamic law; freedom to enjoy the natural riches of Aceh; freedom from fear, violence and brutality; freedom to uphold the law; freedom to give succour to human rights abuse victims; and freedom for political prisoners (*Serambi Indonesia*, 1999).

6

'Freedom from fear': conflict, displacement and human security in Burma (Myanmar)

Hazel J. Lang

FOR MORE THAN four decades military solutions have been sought for Burma's internal crises and for this militarized polity its own citizens have become 'threats – and more characteristically – enemies' (Callahan, 2004: 5). For two generations, it has been the civilian populations living in the war-affected Burmese borderlands who have suffered the brunt of the conflict. Minority insurgency struggles and their suppression through counter-insurgency campaigns by military-dominated governments have been fought out over a battlefield of civilian populations (Lang, 2002: Chapter 3). Over the decades, the direct and indirect impacts of 'low intensity' conflict have been pervasive and destructive, resulting in extensive militarization and displacement. The first Thailand-based refugee camps were set up in 1984, and over two decades on there are some 165,000 people registered as living in the border camps (TBBC, 2006: 3), with a steady flow of new arrivals continuing each month. This makes Thailand host to the largest protracted (or 'warehoused') refugee situation in East Asia[1] – with prospects for a safe and sustainable repatriation unlikely in the present context of chronic human insecurity in their homelands. It is important to keep in mind that the scale of the Burmese refugee problem exceeds the registered numbers in camps. Thousands more displaced people survive outside the camp structure, including some 200,000 displaced Shans who have moved into Thailand's northern provinces since 1996, and over a further million Burmese nationals negotiate the migrant labour economy in Thailand. And within Burma, there are as many as 500,000 internally displaced persons (IDPs) within the eastern border region (TBBC, 2006: 22), many of whom have been chronically and repeatedly dislocated, living their whole lives on the run.

The prolonged and chronic security challenges in the Burmese borderlands resonate with key human security challenges in contemporary conflict in the wider Asia Pacific region and globally. As Andrew Mack (2004: 366) highlights, the realist focus on the state as the referent object of security is of little utility in explaining the civil wars that now constitute 95 per cent of all armed conflicts. Ramesh Thakur (2004: 229–30) similarly argues that 'traditional security threats proved quite unnecessary to destroy the lives and livelihoods of very large number of people', noting that 'in situations where citizens are killed by their own security and paramilitary forces, the concept of national security is immaterial, irrelevant and of zero utility' in dealing with phenomena causing the greatest insecurity. For Thakur and other advocates, human security brings practical meaning to the term 'security' in ways the traditional concept simply cannot. Thus, whilst acknowledging that problems of interstate rivalry and threats of interstate war have not vanished in the Asia-Pacific, in a region such as Southeast Asia, various forms of intrastate conflict – civil wars, secessionist movements and communal violence – persist as the main form of threat to the security of states and people.

Burma's protracted and seemingly intractable conflicts in its periphery qualify amongst the longest running in the world today (Human Security Centre, 2005: 27), with the scale and intensity of human displacement and suffering in this country long hidden from view in the international community. This chapter emphasizes the significance of a human security framework for examining the widespread and devastating implications of internal conflict for civilian populations living in the war-affected regions. The security consequences, of course, flow across state borders, as highlighted in the brief sketch of refugees and displaced persons in Thailand. National and human security in Thailand is inextricably entwined with the vicissitudes of Burma's long-term security troubles, demonstrating that putative 'internal' conflicts and chronic human insecurities spill across borders in multiple ways. Attention to the human security dimensions of internal conflict and displacement is vital for present and future efforts in resolving conflict, building durable peace and achieving a sustainable repatriation of refugees and IDPs. Security, stability and peace will elude this region unless the key dimensions of human insecurity, including the political underpinnings of the conflict, are meaningfully addressed in a holistic paradigm of security (Acharya, 2004: 355). Approaching human security in a holistic manner seeks not only to examine the symptoms or manifestations of human insecurity, but to understand and address root causes (Thakur and Newman, 2004: 3).

This chapter aims to examine and conceptualize Burma's internal conflict and displacement within the context of critical security studies, with particular reference to a human security approach. The chapter outlines the nature of conflict in Burma, provides an analysis of the key dimensions of the militarized entanglement of civilian populations in insurgency and counter-insurgency dynamics, and examines displacement and refuge in such a context. It is important to emphasize and elaborate on the ways in which the conflict is played out in the midst of people's everyday lives and to note that, without informed analysis of the human security dimensions of the conflict, policy responses will fail to deliver and sustain practical and meaningful security.

'Freedom from fear': a human security framework

> Within a system which denies the existence of basic human rights, fear tends to be the order of the day. Fear of imprisonment, fear of torture, fear of death, fear of losing friends, family, property or means of livelihood, fear of poverty, fear of isolation, fear of failure. A most insidious form of fear is that which masquerades as common sense or even wisdom, condemning as foolish, reckless, insignificant or futile the small, daily acts of courage which help to preserve man's self-respect and inherent human dignity. (Aung San Suu Kyi, 1991: 184)

The significant normative insights and practical applications of the human security concept underpin the analysis of conflict and displacement in this chapter. As noted above, narrower state-centric conceptions of security (premised on the military defence of territorial integrity) at the expense of human security (centred on the protection and empowerment of people) serve to deprive the concept of security of practical meaning in many circumstances (Commission on Human Security, 2003: 2, 11). As Thakur and Newman note, the empirical reality for a significant proportion of the people of Asia is that 'the greatest threats to security come from disease, hunger, environmental contamination, crime, and unorganized violence. For many indeed a still greater threat may come from their own state itself, rather than from an "external" adversary' (Thakur and Newman, 2004: 1–2). In fact, rethinking security in the sense of 'deepening' the concept to embrace a more extensive set of referents for security beyond the sovereign state (Booth, 2005a: 14) highlights the importance of re-evaluating key assumptions around sovereignty. As Newman (2004: 358) writes:

> Traditionally, state sovereignty and sovereign legitimacy rest upon a government's control of territory, state independence and recognition by other states. The role of citizens is to support this system. The human security approach reverses this equation: the state – and state sovereignty – must serve and support the people from which it draws its legitimacy.

In many practical circumstances, the state is more a security threat than a security guardian. So while in principle states are responsible for the protection of their own citizens – as implied in traditional state-centric conceptions of security – in reality, in various situations, the people may not be secure *from* the state. This may apply in circumstances in which states are governed by elites whose legitimacy is contested, and whose policies threaten their own polities or people(s) more than any other threat (Tow, 2000: 5). States – such as the larger states of the Association of Southeast Asian Nations (ASEAN) – may be obsessed with 'internal security' against challenges to the regime or national unity (Burke, 2001a: 218). And states may consolidate their power in the name of national security and law and order to suppress individual and group demands on the government, or to plunder the resources of a society (Thakur, 2000: 234).

Since its popularization in the 1995 United Nations Development Programme (UNDP) Human Development Report, the term human security has been controversial, but it has provoked important debates on security in normative, analytical and policy terms. The multidimensional, holistic approach promoted by human security 'sacrifices precision for inclusiveness' (Thakur, 2004: 347) which some argue is desirable while others – including those within human security camp – find the definitional expansiveness analytically troublesome. Roland Paris (2001: 96) concludes that the concept itself is too broad and vague as a framework for analysis. Others point out that the broad conceptualization of human security – embracing both the 'freedom from want' and 'freedom from fear' visions[2] – removes the analytical value of more precise definitional boundaries, becoming at a certain point a synonym for 'bad things that can happen' (Krause, 2004: 44). This chapter aims to move beyond the potential conceptual quagmire – avoiding the danger, identified by Tow and Trood (2000: 13–14), of intellectual chaos in an already crowded field – taking on the normative shift in focus from a state-centric to a human-centric referent, while for analytical purposes adopting a narrower conception of human security related to the protection and empowerment of people in the context of violent conflict (the 'freedom from fear' approach). In navigating this broad and expanding field of study, I draw on the United Nations University definition of human security which prioritizes human beings as the referent of security, whether as individuals or as social and political groups, and focuses on 'freedom from fear, danger and threat' (Thakur and Newman, 2004: 4).

This definition, and the approach framing this chapter, embraces a set of referents beyond the sovereign state ('deepening') and is centred foremost on the security of people. And since critical security approaches are concerned with 'politicizing security' (rather than 'securitizing politics') (Booth, 2005a: 14), uncomfortable tensions will arise as the state-centric and human-centric paradigms answer the question of 'security for whom?' in very different ways (Burke, 2001a: 226). However, recent discussions on reconciling traditional and human security have been important in advancing the possibilities for a transformation of security thinking and practices. It is necessary now to advance the application of human security approaches within specific contexts across the spectrum and to generate new thinking, research and policy-making informed by these insights.

Specifically, this chapter examines a context in which the citizens of the state are perilously insecure, in which the state's responsibility to protect the security and promote the welfare of its citizens has been grossly neglected over decades of military rule and protracted conflict in the minority-dominated border regions. Successive regimes have ruled through coercion in the name of 'national security', but at the expense of the (human) security of many of their citizens and ethnic minority groups. In addressing extreme human vulnerability neglected in the traditional security paradigm, this chapter prioritises an understanding of insecurity brought about by internal war and displacement – the underlying causes of displacement, external displacement as refugees and internal displacement. In doing so, it seeks to fulfil an important aim of critical approaches to security by thinking about security from the perspective of those people(s) without power and those traditionally silenced by prevailing structures (Booth, 2005a: 14). Indeed as Ken Booth (2005a: 16) writes, 'it is by the study of concrete examples that we can go beyond theoretical knowledge towards a more empathetic understanding of the many realities of insecurity in the world'. Future research and policy-making needs to move further in this direction. And while some would caution against the 'securitisation' of refugees and IDPs, for example, through the application of the language of security (Suhrke, 2003), I would argue that it is also possible to advance a progressive security discourse bringing refugees under the human security banner with an emphasis on protection from threats and extreme vulnerability and empowerment (or emancipation).

Burma: security of the state vs. the people

Burma, the largest country in mainland Southeast Asia, has a population of 53 million people and has since independence from the United Kingdom in 1948 remained one of the most strife-torn but little-researched countries in Asia. The modern polity has been dominated by the armed forces (the *tatmadaw* in Burmese), and this dominance has seen military officers as state-builders and the transformation of the military as an institution into the 'military-as-state' itself (Callahan, 2001: 429). Today Burma's military, with some 400,000 personnel, is the second largest in Southeast Asia (after Vietnam) (Selth, 2002: 253). It has more than doubled in size since the crackdown on the pro-democracy uprising and the restoration of direct military rule in the form of the State Law and Order Council (SLORC) in

September 1988, which in 1997 reincarnated itself into the State Peace and Development Council (SPDC). Indeed, over the past decade, Burma has been the only country in the entire Asia-Pacific in which the armed forces have steadily continued to expand (Selth, 2002: 253). As Burma scholar Mary Callahan (2004: 207) points out, in the four decades since the military took political power, 'the Burmese *tatmadaw* has created a choke hold on power unrivalled in the world'. In explaining how the military has managed to maintain a stranglehold on political power over the past four decades, Callahan examines the political history of military-led state-building and how the military solution to internal crises has transformed populations and citizens into potential enemies.

With the unitary Burmese state as the primary referent, the regime's 'national security' ideology conflates the state with the regime and the *tatmadaw*. The regime's security ideology is based on its so-called 'Three Main National Causes' – 'non-disintegration of the union', 'the non-disintegration of national solidarity', and 'the perpetuation of national sovereignty' – which are concerned with the promotion of 'national unity'. These slogans are not simply propaganda and rhetoric professed in state-run news media and signboards around the country (accompanied by omnipresent warnings to potential dissenters such as 'Crush all internal and external destructive elements as common enemy'); the *tatmadaw* is also thoroughly inculcated with this ideology. The *tatmadaw* claims a monopoly for itself as the only force capable of safeguarding national unity and state sovereignty. But as Curtis Lambrecht (2004: 155) laments, the Three Main National Causes are used to 'legitimize three implicit goals: dictatorship, militarization, and cultural assimilation'. These implicit goals may provide the military with its pathway to territorial integrity, political independence and sovereignty, but the coercion-based state-society relationship highlights a vital concern in human security studies, namely that 'secure states do not necessarily mean secure citizens' (Evans, 2004: 265). For the mosaic of minority peoples inhabiting the country's contested border regions, state-building through military means – underscored by perpetual conflict – has been aimed at assimilating ethnic identities at great cost to civilian populations and with little success.

Minority identities militarized

While historically the military has held a firm grip on power in the central heartland, in the border areas insurgencies have abounded with outlying areas operating large guerrilla zones or revolutionary base areas. The ethnic geography of modern Burma is generally described as having a Burman-dominated, central heartland surrounded by a horse-shoe shaped ring of mountain ranges peopled by over a hundred ethnic sub-groups from four main Tibeto-Burman, Karen, Mon-Khmer and Shan (Tai) linguistic groupings.[3] Non-Burman ethnic minorities constitute approximately 35 per cent, or 18 million, of Burma's ethnically diverse population. Burma's post-independence inheritance in which state–minority relationships remain unresolved persists as one of the most important and intractable challenges confronting the country today. The struggles between the centre and periphery for control over the modern territorialized state and its peoples have been fiercely contested and remarkably violent.

Burma's intractable minority issue is embedded in the domination of a centralized, ethnocratic ('Burmanized') and militarized state, which has failed to address the fundamental underlying root causes of the conflict. This enduring problem was further entrenched when Burma moved from a quasi-federal to a unitary state under military rule (see Silverstein, 1997). Under military rule since 1962, the nominal federalist structure of the civilian parliamentary period (1948–58; 1960–2) was dismantled and the trend to a more centralized state intensified. It has been Burmanized in the sense that attempts to unify the centre and periphery under a single territorial sovereignty have been overtly ethnocratic in character. State-building – the preserve of the military – has been aimed at assimilating (rebellious) minority identities, with attempts to homogenize an ethnically heterogeneous society underscored by an authoritarian and nationalistic reliance on repression to restrain minority nationalisms in the periphery. The issue has been militarized because minority problems have been addressed by military means rather than through political institutions and mechanisms. As noted above, the *tatmadaw* has ideologically invested itself with a monopoly of responsibility for the protection of national unity and state sovereignty at immense cost to the security of its citizens. And five decades of civil war have thoroughly entrenched the militarization of ethnic claims and their suppression.

Minority issues are thus embedded in a perpetual military struggle – fought out through insurgency and counter-insurgency – which has entrenched a militarized reality of minority–state relations in Burma. The militarization of ethnicity has been met with the militarized suppression of ethnic mobilization – a process reproduced throughout Burma's post-independence history. On the one hand, ethno-nationalist forces have portrayed Rangoon regimes as bent on their political and cultural destruction; on the other hand, the *tatmadaw* has emphasized the unrelenting threat of 'disintegration' posed by the rebellions. Civil wars, internationally, generate contending images of non-state and state parties, and each party, typically, feels itself to be justified in its actions and unfairly maligned by its critics. One the one hand, non-state/insurgent ethno-nationalist forces are represented in a state-centric bias as 'rebels', terrorists and so forth, as a means of legitimating the government's action to incorporate their lands and resources. On the other hand, state forces have consistently argued that allegations of human rights abuses are exploited and exaggerated for use as a political tool by opposition groups (Lang, 2002: 67). Coercion and military conflict have only further hardened the antagonism.

The *tatmadaw*'s counter-insurgency strategy, the *Pya Ley Pya* or 'Four Cuts' strategy (officially endorsed in 1968 and still in operation today) was designed to suppress internal insurgency by cutting the insurgents off from their support system, which is linked to the civilian population ('denying water to the fish'). Typically such civilian support systems help to provide food supplies, funding, intelligence and recruits to insurgents (Lang, 2002: 37–43). And so minority armed struggles and their suppression by the centre (i.e. through counter-insurgency campaigns) have not been restricted to the combatants. Rather, insurgency and counter-insurgency warfare has been fought on a battlefield of civilian populations.

Dynamics of conflict and displacement

The cycle of violence is embedded in the nature and consequences of low-intensity warfare. The problem with this kind of warfare, elaborated below, is that it effectively blurs the boundary between combatants and non-combatants.

Insurgency

In the context of insurgency, because civilians serve as the crucial support base for low-intensity guerrilla warfare, they become identified with the rebellions. Insurgency blurs the distinction between combatants and non-combatants because guerrillas derive support from their civilian base as a necessary part of their struggle. Guerrilla warfare tends to rely on small-scale, mobile, ambush and retreat tactics. There is usually no clear distinction between the frontline and rear areas. In this context, the support of the civilian base is crucial for providing information and other physical support. 'Low-intensity' warfare is characterized by the overlap of insurgent combatant, non-combatant and support system in a shared social and geographic space. This muddles any distinction between combatants and non-combatants and their respective properties, or territories, within this shared space. Civilians thus become identified with the rebellions. In short, insurgents militarize civilian communities and expose them to the risks of war (Lang, 2002: 60–75). The overlap of combatant, non-combatant and support system in a shared social and geographic space is fraught with danger for civilians.

Counter-insurgency

In counter-insurgency warfare, civilians become the targets in military campaigns of pacification and destruction precisely because the civilian base is so crucial for opposition soldiers. If guerrillas are eager to assert their alliance with the people, then counter-insurgents are eager to sever it. This is because the counter-insurgents recognize that the civilian base is so crucial for the opposition guerrillas. The counter-insurgents are inclined to assume that civilians in contested areas have allied themselves with the rebels. Typically, in this kind of warfare, the state forces deliberately target the civilian population because they define these civilians as potential collaborators or sympathizers. Counter-insurgency strategy, then, essentially seeks to break this link, to deprive the opposition of its support base, and undermine the will of the population.

So in the course of counter-insurgency, civilian non-combatants (as potential rebel collaborators), as well as combatants, become the general opponent and the deliberate targets for attack. In counter-insurgency operations, civilian communities are harassed and punished for their perceived sympathies and support for the ethnic opposition forces. Violence experienced by civilian populations, however, does not tend to achieve its aim to undermine the political will of the civilian populations inhabiting the contested areas, and indeed may constitute a self-fulfilling prophesy familiar to critical security scholars and analysts. In many cases, peoples' experiences of violence and suffering will reinforce – or force – an affiliation.

In sum, insurgency implicates entire populations, and counter-insurgency punishes entire populations. The boundary dividing the front-line (where combatants engage in battle) from the 'home front' (where combatants ideally pursue their daily lives) is fundamentally blurred (Lang, 2002: 182). The immediate precipitating causes of displacement arise out of these dynamics. Fear pervades everyday life and intensifies further the blurred boundary between civilians and rebels. Because people almost always run away when counter-insurgency/government troops arrive, the view that villagers are potential insurgents and sympathizers is reinforced because they flee (Lang, 2002: 65).

Displacement

In becoming the military target of counter-insurgency campaigns against its ethnic minority opponents, the civilian population has suffered the brunt of the conflict. Unfortunately, the dynamics of conflict and displacement in the eastern borderlands of Burma today resemble the same familiar cycles as when I first conducted my field research on the border ten years ago. In so-called 'low-intensity' conflict situations as this, the causes of displacement are multiple and people flee the direct and indirect impacts of armed conflict and militarization. Displacement is caused not only by direct armed hostilities and assaults on the civilian population (which may involve the raiding of villages and the seizure of food, livestock and other properties; interrogation, torture, rape and even killing of villagers), but also by the unrelenting requisition of civilian forced labour (to carry military ammunitions, or other forms of forced labour for use in military camps and projects), a steady stream of coercive financial demands (imposition of a variety of taxes and 'fees', extortion and ransom), confiscation of land, and forced relocation of villages. In areas directly affected by fighting, counter-insurgency forces will usually come to villages and accuse the people of supporting the insurgent forces and impose punishments on the villagers such as those noted above. But they will also target important sources of the villagers' livelihoods, including their livestock, rice stores and cooking pots. Indeed, as one report has noted, the theft of a cooking pot or a chicken by passing troops can be assigned greater significance than a beating, because of the importance of such items for survival (Heppner, 2005: 16). Civil war has meant that most villagers have come to experience a combination of these factors as part of their everyday lives. And protracted conflict in Burma has meant that, in many cases, this is the lived experience of people over two generations. Recent field research on the patterns of human rights abuses and displacement highlights the long-term, repeated character of displacement (Human Rights Watch, 2005), in which vulnerable people have suffered recurring, multiple and mutually reinforcing shocks to their lives and livelihoods (Heppner, 2005: 11).

Since 1995, forced relocation and depopulation have been carried out by the *tatmadaw* on a region-wide scale as a core military tactic, targeting entire regions of resistance, and getting every village not close to a road or (government) military base to move to relocation sites (Heppner, 2005: 19). For example, since 1996 some 300,000 people inhabiting the centre of the Shan State have been targeted for relocation and forcibly displaced in an attempt to cut the insurgent Shan State Army from its civilian base (Warr and Yin, 2002: 102). Typically, *tatmadaw* columns operating in an area will issue relocation orders, giving local villagers only short notice to leave their homes.[4] It is reported that *tatmadaw*-controlled relocation sites are now found across large areas of central and southern Shan State, in Karenni, Karen and Mon States and Tenasserim Division, as well as in parts of central Burma (Human Rights Watch, 2005: 47–51). While state-generated terror and counter-insurgency strategy has caused chronic insecurity, this does not claim innocence for the insurgency forces. People have had to deal with belligerents on both sides – one Karen villager described the situation as 'like standing in a leaky boat . . . being rocked from both sides' (Heppner, 2005: 16).

Refuge: between Burma and Thailand

Today, after more than 20 years, Thailand hosts Southeast Asia's largest protracted, or 'warehoused',[5] refugee situation. Thailand shares a porous 2,401 km-long border with its Burmese neighbour, and has hosted camps since they were first established in 1984. As I have documented elsewhere, the political geography of the borderlands has been constantly evolving according to shifting military developments within Burma and the cross border political relationships operating at various official and unofficial, or 'extra-state' (Nordstrom, 2000: 36), levels between Thailand and Burma. This complex series of vicissitudes and relationships has impacted the contingencies of sanctuary for the refugees (Lang, 2002: Chapter 6). The Royal Thai Government is not a signatory to the 1951 Convention on Refugees, or its companion 1967 Protocol, and under national law, asylum-seekers in Thailand are technically 'illegal immigrants'. In strictly formal terms, legal refugee protection, and even the terminology 'refugee', does not exist. However, in practice, the Burmese are recognized as de facto 'refugees' and as a group with genuine claims to asylum in the border camps. As Sara Davies argues in her contribution to this volume, this disjuncture between international conventions and contemporary practices does raise some important questions for the treatment of displaced persons and refugees in the region. With some exceptions, Thailand has generally adhered to the principles of refugee protection. In 1995, the relatively low-key existence of the camps in Thailand was dramatically destabilized when armed elements from a breakaway faction of the Karen National Union (KNU), the Democratic Karen Buddhist Army (DKBA, which mutinied in late 1994, with the support of *tatmadaw*), began crossing the border into Thailand and raiding and burning down the refugee camps. The DKBA (and its *tatmadaw* collaborators) regarded the camps as sanctuaries for the KNU and their families, highlighting the camps could not be viewed as neutral political spaces but rather as enemies to be attacked. This severely compromised sanctuary for the refugees and safety for the local Thai villages in these areas. The camps were consequently moved to a safer distance from the border, and eventually were consolidated into larger, more strictly guarded, and concomitantly more aid-dependent, entities. The largest Karen camp in mid-2004 contained some 48,000 residents, departing remarkably from the much smaller village-style character of the camps in the period before 1995.

With sources of human insecurity within Burma precipitating movement across its western border, Thailand's national security is crucially linked with its Burmese neighbour. These consequences include displaced persons seeking sanctuary in camps, hundreds of thousands of Burmese nationals (many undocumented) in search of work in Thailand, trafficked persons (especially, as Katrina Lee Koo's chapter highlights, women and girls recruited into the sex industry), massive flows of drugs (including heroin and methamphetamines) produced in the border regions (with the knowledge of the regime), and the crisis of HIV/AIDS which tends to also follow migration, trade and other informal and illicit trafficking routes into Thailand and the region.

The problem of IDPs has continued to grow in Burma's eastern border region, presenting possibly the most difficult, as well as invisible and inaccessible, challenge of human insecurity and protection. As noted earlier, in some borderland areas, the Burma Army is conducting its final stages of counter-insurgency, involving the relocation of hundreds of thousands of villagers into areas under its control. In late 2006, the scale of internal displacement in eastern Burma is estimated at a daunting 500,000 (TBBC, 2006: 22). From a human security perspective, a preoccupation with state sovereignty presents particular obstacles in protecting the internally displaced. As Francis Deng (1999), for many years the United Nations Representative on IDPs, has noted with respect to internal displacement:

> The primary responsibility to provide protection and assistance rests with the State. And yet, paradoxically, the State is often the principal source of their insecurity and deprivation, viewing the displaced not as persons to be protected, but as part of the enemy to be targeted, oppressed or eliminated, thereby creating a protection gap.

IDPs located outside the *tatmadaw*-controlled relocation sites are vulnerable to identification as 'rebel collaborators' because they generally hide (and move around in) opposition-held areas. Further, states are generally not inclined to admit the existence of IDPs and may want to conceal the extent to which their own policies or actions have contributed to displacement. At the same time, it is important to remember the ways in which, over the years, people have forged their survival through developing locally creative ways of resisting demands of counter-insurgency troops, such as hiding rice outside the village, keeping a tab on troop movements by obtaining information from opposition forces, periodically fleeing their homes to a temporary jungle location and, with extremely limited resources, continuing on with their lives as circumstances allow.

Ending violence and building peace

The preceding analysis has aimed to elaborate key dynamics of civil conflict and displacement in Burma's border regions. The situation remains precarious with conflict continuing in a number of areas, increasing militarization consolidated across vast areas along the border, chronic internal displacement and a steady stream of displaced persons seeking sanctuary in Thailand as their last resort. Thousands of families have lived their entire lives in flight as IDPs, and thousands more are encamped in military-run relocation sites with few resources. Even in locales where ceasefires are in place, such as in the Kachin and Mon States, people continue to live in heavily militarized environments with continuing threats to their livelihoods and little prospect of reconstruction and rehabilitation at present. Clearly extraordinary challenges remain for the people(s) of Burma as they look to emerging from conflict and build peace.

The imposition of a military solution on Burma's ethnic minority predicaments by the regime has clearly forestalled a lasting resolution to the substantive root causes and grievances underscoring the conflict, or indeed to the violence that has prevailed since independence. Until a constructive process can address the manifold dimensions of the problem politically and institutionally, with sustainable outcomes for all parties concerned, the state and its citizens will remain vulnerable to renewed conflict and insecurity. Clearly at present the state is more of a security threat than security guardian, but what are some of the possibilities for positive change? And what immediate practical challenges need to be addressed? This last section briefly outlines the nature of the ceasefires between the government and a range of Burma's insurgent forces as well as key conditions necessary for the future repatriation of refugees and IDPs.

The regime has since 1989 offered the former communist and ethnic forces its ceasefire policy, in which its former insurgent foes 'exchange arms for peace', 'return to the legal fold' and participate in the government's National Convention (intermittently stalled since its establishment in 1993 to draft a new constitution). The *tatmadaw*'s enhanced operational capabilities since 1988 have provided for unprecedented military successes in the field against the insurgencies, and today a majority of Burma's insurgent forces have entered into ceasefire arrangements with Rangoon.[6] The major non-ceasefire groups in late 2006 remain the KNU (the largest, and in the process of renewed talks since late 2003), the Karenni National Progressive Party, the Shan State Army/South, and several other smaller forces (which include various splinter factions from ceasefire groups). The *tatmadaw* continues to wage its counter-insurgency programme in the eastern border areas where these groups remain active.

So what does an end to armed hostilities mean for civilian displacement and insecurity? On the one hand ceasefires have brought respite from the more blatant fears and destabilization associated with direct hostilities – importantly the civilian population is no longer the 'battleground' of competing militaries – and have allowed space for the re-emergence of community-based organizations (South, 2004). Nevertheless civilians living in ceasefire areas experience continuing insecurity and displacement due to extensive militarization accompanying the Burma Army's expansion into previously contested areas. As military agreements between former belligerents, the benefits of the ceasefires are mostly limited to the vested interests of the ceasefire parties and have failed to deliver meaningful security to individuals and communities. Although direct conflict-induced displacement has ended in ceasefire areas, people continue to be displaced by militarization and the loss of their land as a result of natural resource extraction and infrastructure development (aimed at consolidating state control) (Lambrecht, 2004). At present these conditions are not propitious for long-term peace-building.

Since the late 1990s, repatriation has appeared as a regular item of discussion on the plight of Burmese refugees in Thailand. Thailand, of course, does not want to remain an indefinite host and refugees cannot live indeterminately as temporary guests in camps. The starting point to address the eventual repatriation of refugees from Thailand is ultimately located within Burma, and there are a number of key constituent elements essential for a safe and sustainable return. It is obvious to note that so long as fear and insecurity persist in the border regions, displacement will continue. However, in preparing for a positive change in the underlying causes of displacement, certain conditions prioritizing human security would need to be met for a future return (see Lang, 2001).

International standards require a 'voluntary repatriation in safety and dignity' to an environment in which 'the causes of flight have been definitively and permanently removed' (UNHCR, 1993: 104). Following a substantive change in their home regions, voluntary repatriations require elements of physical safety and material security, as well as legal safety (UNHCR, 1996). One immediate priority would involve addressing the pervasive problem of anti-personnel landmines. The number of casualties produced by these weapons – globally thought to be 80–90 per cent non-combatants – is considered to be among the highest in any country of the world. Not only are the injuries inflicted by landmines of an indiscriminate and horrific nature, landmines continue to kill and maim decades after being deployed. Also, landmines remaining in the ground long term render tracts of rural land unusable and potentially deadly. Nine out of 14 of Burma's states and divisions are mine-contaminated, with a heavy concentration in eastern Burma (ICBL, 2004).

Addressing material security involves rebuilding damaged infrastructures, community services, agriculture and economic development. Legal safety includes a formal agreement between the country of origin, country of asylum, the United Nations High Commissioner for Refugees (UNHCR) and relevant non-state actors concerned. A further crucial legal arrangement concerns the requisition of nationality (i.e. citizenship). The acceptance back of displaced persons is politically charged, and Rangoon's position has been that it will only take back those with Burmese identity cards – thus at present, for so many refugees without national identity cards for Burma, a change in status from 'refugee' to 'citizen' remains uncertain. Finally, a brief caution is necessary relating to the return of refugees and IDPs. While a future repatriation of refugees is desirable and inevitable, it is crucial to be sensitive to local contexts and dynamics so as to avoid converting refugees into IDPs when state authorities view their return as part of their aim to consolidate control. Also, eventual solutions for returning or resettling IDPs will require in-depth understandings of the long-term patterns of displacement in such a way that avoids strengthening a repressive state at the expense of empowering local people and achieving a holistic sense of security. People's security may be threatened once again if not carefully managed.

Securing people

As Ken Booth (2005: 22) proposes, '[t]he best starting point for conceptualising security lies in the real conditions of insecurity suffered by people and collectivities'; moreover, security is concerned with the possibility of fulfilling human potential and not simply survival. This chapter has sought to connect the normative innovations made possible within critical security studies, and the human security literature in particular, with some of the real conditions that feature in the substantive empirical case of Burma's civil conflict. The relentless imposition of the military solution on Burma's minority–state predicaments has not achieved true security for either the state or its citizens. Instead, the targeting of its citizens as threats and/or enemies has perpetuated severe insecurity, displacement and poverty. Internal crisis in Burma cannot be contained within that country; the consequences of insecurity and instability continue to extend beyond its borders within the region and internationally. Burma's neighbours such as Thailand may have established friendlier relationships at the official level, but Thailand's own security has long been troubled by instability and human insecurity in Burma. With flows of refugees, HIV/AIDS and other diseases, and illicit drugs across its borders, the mutually reinforcing relationship between human security and national security becomes apparent. Some members of ASEAN, notwithstanding the salience of the doctrine of non-interference, have viewed the lack of progress towards reform and human rights of concern for the region's political and economic future. A significant development occurred, for example, when Burma was pressured to forego the 2006 chairmanship of ASEAN following pressure from key members fearing that this could damage the body.

The focus of human security on the dignity and protection of individuals allows us to go to the heart of the underlying causes of forced displacement by understanding the key dynamics of conflict and how these impact on individuals and communities as the primary referents of security. Innovations within critical security studies and the human security literature are crucial for rethinking limited state-centric notions of security. The concept of human security will continue to be academically contentious and troublesome, but it is also possible to move beyond the larger intellectual controversies within the human security literature by specifying definitional boundaries and applying these within specific contexts, thereby advancing a critical understanding of the predicaments involved. In many circumstances, a human security framework is essential for resolving conflict and building peace. Attention to the concrete and practical realities of local dynamics helps to generate a process concerned with rebuilding societies and sustaining people from the individual and community level onwards, with benefits also for the security of the polity. States cannot and will not be secure unless people feel secure too.

Notes

1 USCR (2004: 38). About half the world's refugees today live in protracted situations. According to the UNHCR, a protracted refugee situation is one in which refugee and IDP populations of 25,000 or more are sequestered in refugee camps without right of mobility or employment for five years or more.

2 The 'freedom from want' vision, based on the UNDP definition, is about ensuring basic human needs in economic, food, social and environmental terms; the 'freedom from fear' vision is about removing the use of, or threat of, force and violence from people's everyday lives.

3 For an overview of Burma's ethnic mosaic, see Lintner (2003).

4 Recently, relocation orders are more likely to be issued verbally, usually at a meeting with the village leader (Human Rights Watch, 2005: 45).

5 For the USCR (2004: 13, 38), the term 'refugee warehousing' is defined not so much by the passage of time as the denial of rights.

6 For a listing of Burma's vast array of insurgent groups and splinter factions – in ceasefires and not in ceasefires – see Smith, Martin, T., (2005: 78–80).

7

Australia paranoid: security politics and identity policy

Anthony Burke

On 1 August 2005, less than a month after the 7 July bombings of the London underground, the Australian Attorney-General and former Immigration Minister Philip Ruddock held an interview outside the Hyatt Hotel in Adelaide, where he stated that 'a terrorist attack could occur in Australia at any time'. Having made such an alarming statement, he then offered governmental action as a panacea: 'I don't regard it as inevitable. Some people do. The reason I don't regard it as inevitable is I think we have to do everything that we can possibly do to secure Australia from such an attack . . . with good intelligence; with an appropriate framework of law; with strong border protection.' Reviving a particularly nasty tactic from 2001, he also linked terrorism with asylum-seekers, citing the fact that one suspect in the London bombings had been an asylum-seeker and that hence government policy was working to secure the country because 'Australia [has] a better handle on movements in and out, both lawfully and unlawfully, than Europe and North America have' (Ruddock, 2005).

Later that week Prime Minister John Howard called a press conference – timed perfectly for the Saturday papers – to announce that he was calling a special meeting of the Council of Australian Governments to address contingency plans. He warned that in the wake of the London attacks Australians needed to rethink their understanding of liberty in a democracy. 'The most important civil liberty I have, and you have', he said, 'is to stay alive and be free from violence and death'. At the same time he said that 'we need each other and we need to work with each other . . . to reassert the fundamental values of Australia' (Dodson and Kerr, 2005). The immediate politics at work included an attempt to rally support for new laws and policy approaches – 'harsher penalties for inciting terrorism and longer detention for terror suspects . . . including granting police wider powers to arrest and detain suspects' – and a deeper identity politics that was seeking to impose a particular vision of Australianness and reinterpret multiculturalism 'with an emphasis on shared values and secularism' (Colman, 2005; Kerin, 2005).

What this meant in practice became visible two weeks later, when a senior government minister and two Liberal parliamentarians made a series of inflammatory remarks about Muslim communities in Australia. First the minister for education, Dr Brendan Nelson, made a statement about the teaching of 'Australian values' in Muslim homes and schools. 'If you want to be an Australian', he said, and 'if you want to raise your children in Australia, we fully expect those children to be taught and to accept Australian values and beliefs. We want them to understand our history and our culture, the extent to which we believe in mateship and giving another person a fair go, and basically if people don't want to support and accept and adopt and teach Australian values then, they should clear off' (*ABC News Online*, 24 August 2004). Two days later the Liberal MP Bronwyn Bishop (following her colleague Sophie Panopoulos) stated that Muslim girls should be banned from wearing their *hijabs* (headscarves) to public schools. She argued that the *hijab* 'defied the equality between men and women that is basic to Australian values' and was being used as an 'iconic item of defiance. It is not just a headscarf, it is a challenge to our freedoms and way of life' (*Daily Telegraph*, 2005).

These comments were intended to be somehow helpful to Australia's national security, having been provoked by the revelation that the London bombers were 'homegrown' (even if their radicalism had mainly been sparked by visits to Pakistan). With this uncomfortable fact a crucial conceptual division in the 'war on terror', and security discourse in general, appeared to be breached: that which cordoned off the inside from the outside, the place of safety from the source of danger – a division most often marked by physical and ontological borders (Button, 2005; Chance, 2005; Schofield, 2005). A level-headed threat analysis might be interested solely in how the bombers' personal system of beliefs and convictions was built and channelled into appalling acts of violence, rather than insist upon reading their acts as symptoms of cultural pathology against a background discourse of societal identity and coherence. However Ruddock, Nelson, Panopoulos and Bishop betray a profound anxiety about the potential convergence between difference and terror and, with their remarks about border protection and exclusion, they seek obsessively to reconstitute the border between inside and outside. Yet we may also wonder if there is not more going on.

First, however apparently irrational such a reaction is, it is almost automatic because of the way in which security has historically been thought *in the very terms* of identity, especially nation-state identity – as productive of secure and bounded identities marked off and defended from the outside. This dates from the time Thomas Hobbes and John Locke conceived security as the basis for the social contract, in which men sacrifice a measure of freedom and autonomy for the promise of identity and security that the sovereign provides; a security that confines human existence within the dual containers of *citizenship* and the *body-politic*. Not only does such a mapping of security onto identity produce a strong (if dynamic and moveable) border between inside and outside, but it also reproduces it internally through its intolerance of difference and its perennial fear of secession and sedition.

Second, there is a dynamic 'security politics' at work, which uses images of otherness and threat to consolidate and manipulate *identity* either as a political tactic, or a political end, or both. With remarks that insinuated the potentially treasonous nature of Australian Muslims – *embodied in their religion and mores* – the Liberal Party ministers and MPs conjured a 'fifth column' scenario virtually out of thin air. (Even if this was of legitimate concern, it was limited to a very small minority at odds with the rest of the Islamic community.) Such tactics have precedents in Australian history: in the anxieties which motivated the white Australia policy in the 1890s and political and legislative attacks on trade unions, Left organizations and the Communist Party of Australia (CPA) between the 1920s and 1950s. And, with their artless invocations of Australian 'values' and 'way of life', they also link with broader security and foreign policy discourses that claim, as did the government's 2003 Foreign and Trade Policy White Paper, that in the 'new climate of international terrorism, Australians have become targets because of the values we represent' (DFAT, 2003: xi). Not only was this a stunning evasion of the role the 2003 invasion of Iraq (and Australia's involvement there) may have played in providing added motivation for terrorist violence, and thus undermined the security of those Australians and Indonesians most at risk, it raises important questions about how key tenets of Australia's defence and foreign policy such as the US alliance are motivated and justified.

Hence my subtitle to this chapter, which reverses the usual phraseology to suggest that identity, more than security, is the actual end of policy. Security is a means not an end of such a policy; nothing we can credibly describe *as* security will be its result. This ought to be of concern to the most pragmatic of policy professionals, let alone critical theorists of politics and society, if security (of individuals *or* the state) is to remain a significant objective of state policy and transnational cooperation.

Building upon the analysis in my book *In Fear of Security*, this chapter explores this paradox in two ways. First it advances an alternative conceptualization of security as a set of techniques rather than an achieved state, which can explain how and why such a politics operates, and help us to identify its strategies; and second, it traces this politics through the history of Australia's search for security and identity, relating past events to contemporary crises. The chapter shows how hegemonic attempts to define and solidify Australian national identity have always been contested and unstable, how they have been linked with tangible conflicts over land, injustice and power, and how they have been closely intertwined with anxieties about (and discourses of) insecurity. It then goes on to challenge these approaches on two levels: normatively, it argues that such a politics forestalls the achievement of a holistic and non-militarized security based upon the emancipation of human beings; and practically, it argues that the operation of security politics gravely distorts Australian defence and foreign policy and directly endangers both others and the state's own citizens. The chapter concludes by suggesting a range of ways in which the current practices and conceptualizations of security, identity and sovereignty in Australia need to be refigured if Australian defence and security policy is to be rebalanced and, most importantly, if the normative promise of critical security studies is to have any hope of being realized.

Security politics and representation

One of the most significant contributions of critical approaches to the study of world politics are their insights into the role of *representation* in the production and circulation of political and social power, especially those forms of power marked by the name and desire of security. I refer here not to political but *linguistic* representation – those metaphors, narratives, rhetorics, images and discourses (as present in media reports, political speeches and intelligence assessments) which purport to describe the real but are central to its creation in thought and fact. The problem here is a familiar one: to trace and critique the slippage between the real and the virtual, the inaccessible real and its all too vivid representation; to mark the vast distance, which is quite deliberately collapsed in political discourse, between things and their representation as cultural or political facts.

Representation is important to security analysis both in quite pragmatic terms – in the creation and circulation of threat assessments, and the consequent determination of policy priorities, for example – and more deeply, in the way the very limits and possibilities for modern politics and life have been determined under the overarching rubric of security. In this latter sense, security is seen less as a thing – a goal that politics understands and naturally seeks to achieve – than as a series of practices and strategies of power. While security may be a legitimate goal, it is better conceptualized as a *political technology* that operates through, between and across societies in an attempt to order bodies, minds, space and organizations in particular ways (Burke, 2001b: xxx–xxxv). It is thus important to place systems and processes of representation in security affairs, and politics more generally, under critical scrutiny.

There are two reasons for doing so. First, as any good intelligence analyst would know, the way in which threats to security are assessed and prioritized is absolutely crucial to successful policy-making – if they are overstated, underestimated, misidentified or wrongly understood, the result can be disaster. Threat analysis drives decision-making; and, when it is presented as systematic, unbiased and professional, it forms a bedrock of 'truth' upon which policy rests and to which it feels compelled to respond. Crucial to successful and appropriate threat analysis are not merely informational and organizational capabilities – systems of electronic surveillance, field agents, sources, teams of trained analysts, and cross-agency and transnational collaboration – but larger discursive (or paradigmatic) assumptions which shape and determine priorities. These can range from organizational cultures, political interference and ideological bias at the micro-political level, to sweeping macro-political formations of strategic doctrine, foreign policy philosophy and political ideology which are contained within totalizing paradigms of security and the state. Hence it is important to place both processes of threat assessment, and the overarching paradigms which shape and limit it, under close critical analysis.

Second, such processes of threat assessment and policy response intertwine with a deeper 'security politics' which seeks to use images of threat, identity and safety to shape individual subjectivities, exert social control, discredit political enemies and alternatives, and fortify particular institutions or organizations (McDonald, 2005a: 175). Such processes occur dynamically – according to daily cycles of news, political contest and media reporting – but can also manifest longer-run strategies aimed at reshaping societal and cultural values, drawing upon deeply rooted and often controversial images of the past. In the wake of 9/11 Graeme Cheeseman writes of how contemporary 'neoconservative political forces and actors [although the problem is both more widespread and of longer pedigree] are prepared, ruthlessly, to invoke national military myths, exploit popular fears and prejudices, and spend as much of their national treasures as is necessary to advance their own particular personal or party political interests' (Cheeseman, 2005: 81). When driven by such narrow and opportunistic political agendas, or by deeply suspect conceptual paradigms, we face the very real prospect that rhetorics and practices of security are aimed not at achieving something we can legitimately call security (in a holistic, emancipatory sense) but merely at the reproduction of particular actors, institutions and forms of political hegemony. As a result, they all too often produce and perpetuate insecurity. Such 'security' policies, I will argue, are dangerously dysfunctional and counterproductive, and ought to be of concern to the most pragmatic or conservative of readers. In such cases, the shape and consequences of such overarching *metadiscourses* of security and threat have a significance far beyond immediate policy challenges, which they certainly affect and distort. They are central to the future of entire societies.

Now and then: the politics of security and identity

Australia's approach to security rests upon an unresolved paradox: it has often been described as 'one of the most secure countries in the world' (Dibb, 1986: 1) because of its isolated strategic location, natural sea barrier and distance from major conflict, yet it has long harboured a deep sense of physical and existential insecurity. This has driven Australia's efforts to develop a substantial military capability in regional terms, to closely ally itself with the United States and join wars in Vietnam, Malaya, Afghanistan and the Persian Gulf, and to develop close security cooperation with Southeast Asian armed forces. Prior to 1942 Australia sought the protection of Great Britain and volunteered its citizens for services in wars in the Sudan, South Africa, and the Middle East and France during the Great War. It returned to the same regions again at the outset of the Second World War, and sent troops to the Pacific and Southeast Asia including Portuguese Timor. These deployments were accompanied by important events in the creation of a federated national polity (in 1901), the establishment of a 'white Australia' policy, the dispossession and attempted forced assimilation of the land's indigenous traditional owners, and efforts to imagine and consolidate a unified national identity that have always been tied to a powerful discourse of security.

However, it is important to understand that, just as hegemonic understandings of security have been challenged throughout its history, there has never been a single agreed image of Australian national identity; it has always been unstable and at times almost unviable. This was made clear by former Minister for External Affairs and historian Sir Paul Hasluck, who argued in his history of Australian society in the Second World War that the very tenability of the Australian idea was at stake in the conflict. The war, he wrote,

> made Australia face up to the double challenge of national survival . . . the two great practical tests of economic and social responsibility and of national security, and the far more searching test of the strength of those spiritual forces which hold a people together as a nation, giving the nation a reason for its being, an identity and purpose. (Hasluck, 1952: 1)

He argued that while nationalism had been 'fervent' when thousands volunteered for military service in 1914, 'nationhood was still the bold outline of an idea rather than a completed structure'. He was especially concerned about the impact of the Great Depression on Australia which had escalated class conflict to new heights. This, he lamented, 'tends to undermine mutual trust, to set the claims of class above the claims of all the people, and thus to weaken the identity of common interests and purposes on which national loyalties are nurtured'. In this text Hasluck reasserted the same generic signifiers of Australianness later revived by the Howard government: the 'spirit of Anzac' and the 'ideal of mateship' which had been weakened by talk of 'class struggle' (1952: 6–7).

Hasluck glossed over the terrible price paid – by Aborigines, unionists and the dead of the Great War – for Australia's earlier efforts to define identity in terms of the Anzac heroism and sacrifice, along with the very bitter political conflicts over conscription and workers rights in the 1920s, which had seen violent confrontations between strikers and police and the introduction of laws (through amendments to the immigration and crimes acts) to enable the deportation of seditious aliens. Another argument with startling contemporary resonances was that put by conservative Prime Minister S.M. Bruce in support of amendments to the Immigration Act (later disallowed by the High Court) that would enable the deportation of any immigrant convicted of 'an offence against the laws of the Commonwealth relating to trade and commerce or conciliation and arbitration':

> [A]mong those coming into Australia are a number of persons of alien race and blood who, although we offer to them the opportunity to enjoy our citizenship, refuse to become Australians, do not recognise our ideals, and are not absorbed into our national life . . . they voice here false doctrines and ideas and refer to social conditions in a language that is absolutely inapplicable to any that exist in Australia . . . it is absolutely dangerous to the national life of our country. (Hansard, 25 June 1925: 460)

When in 1950 the conservative Menzies government introduced a bill to outlaw the CPA, it claimed that it derived from the Constitution's *defence* powers: it 'is a law relating to the safety and defence of Australia. It is designed to . . . give the Government power to deal with the King's enemies in this country . . . a self-defending attack on treason and fifth-columnism wherever they can be found' (*Hansard*, 27 April 1950: 1995). Bruce and Menzies were concerned with communism and industrial militancy – however the similarity to Bishop's 2005 declaration that the *hijab* 'is a challenge to our freedoms and way of life' and Nelson's demand that those Muslims who refuse to teach Australian values should 'clear off', could not be more striking. What was being enacted in all these statements was a fundamentally insecure and exclusivist image of national identity in which physical exclusion from the *body-politic* remains the ultimate security tool.

Even if Hasluck worried that a secure national identity was fragile through the 1920s and 1930s, some consolidation was enabled by the experience of war against Japan. Via myth-making about the role of the US Navy at the Battle of the Coral Sea and post-war Labor's anxious efforts to interest the US in a 'Pacific Pact', this image of insecurity and otherness was channelled into a discourse that emphasized the inevitable dependence of Australia on US arms and friendship for its security. In an important 1951 speech Minister for External Affairs Sir Percy Spender emphasized the 'common tradition, heritage and way of life' shared with the United States which, by virtue of its status as 'the greatest Pacific power' required that Australia 'carry out [its] Pacific policies as far as possible in co-operation with [the US]' (Spender, 1969: 557–8). Such discourses of common identity (which were naturally assumed to lead to a commonality of interests and strategic judgements) underpinned the Menzies government's decisions to enter the ANZUS (Australia, New Zealand and United States) alliance and send troops to Vietnam. Australia's involvement in that conflict was not only based upon a powerful anticommunism and an acceptance of the 'domino theory', but also upon a profound existential anxiety vis-à-vis the future development of Asia: as Australian Ambassador to Washington Howard Beale explained in his 1977 memoir, 'we are a western outpost hard by Asia in revolution, and we need allies' (cited in Pemberton, 1987: 162). For conservatives, such anxieties were soothed by a commitment, however violent and dysfunctional, of US force to the region.

While such images were moderated in later years, they have been strongly revived by the Howard governments, who have used them in a new historical context to justify a zealous commitment to the Bush administration, the 'war on terror' and the invasion of Iraq. As Alexander Downer explained Australia's participation in the 2003 invasion of Iraq, striking a note very similar to Beale's: 'It wasn't a time in our history to have a great and historic breach with the United States. If we were to walk away from the American alliance it would leave us as a country very vulnerable and very open' (Allard, 2004). Such justifications – while often accompanied by transparently bad faith arguments and distorted intelligence assessments – also represent deeply held convictions that drive policy. Like the Menzies government, the Howard government has chosen to frame its key foreign and defence policy orientations in terms of identity. The 2003 White Paper states that 'Australia is a Western country located in the Asia-Pacific region with close ties and affinities with North America and Europe and a history of active engagement throughout Asia', subtly distinguishing with whom it is alike and those with whom it merely 'engages' (DFAT, 2003: xi).

I will address the very dangerous strategic implications of this world-view below, and critique its assumptions about insecurity processes, about security policy, and about the concept itself. However it must be said that the Howard government's attempts to harmonize identity and security, *to read each into the other*, are merely permutations of a general project that previous Labor governments have also sought to promote, albeit differently (see Burke, 2001b: Chapters 2 and 4).

Identity as security: a critique

In what remains of this chapter I will lay out and critique the deployment of a governmental 'security politics' in Australia over the past decade. This has seen a diabolical convergence of events and political forms: the excessive intrusion of ideology into policy-making and a determined effort to redefine the national identity coincided with the election of a radically neo-conservative administration in Washington, the 9/11 attacks and a 'fourth wave' of sea-borne asylum-seekers.

After its election in 1996, the Howard government came to power determined to implement a purist neo-liberal process of economic reform and assert ideological dominance over Australian society and culture. These two agendas were closely intertwined: attacks on aboriginal power and land rights cleaved with the interests of mining and pastoral corporations (which have been similarly opposed to action on climate change), while early in his first term Howard outlined a strategy with which he could promote the further globalization of the national economy and manage potential opposition. In a 1997 speech Howard outlined his concern that neo-liberal reform and Asian engagement could produce feelings of insecurity for many; but rather than modify his economic agenda, he sought instead to tame and challenge such anxieties by reviving Menzies' concept of 'home'. This he argued was a 'compelling notion in our psyche' which provides a 'sense of security': 'the loss of security challenges traditional notions of home and people feel the need to react to alienation . . . I want to provide Australians with this security as we embrace, as we must and will, a new and vastly different future' (Howard, 1997). Fiona Allon, however, points out that such 'debates over home and belonging' are signs of 'groups and governments negotiating the new types of citizenship and governmentality which the changes in the international economy and globalisation necessarily involve' (Allon, 1997: 1–25).

A range of writers – Allon (1997), Ghassan Hage (1998, 2003), Judith Brett (2003), Carol Johnson (1997), Joseph Camilleri (2004), Graeme Cheeseman (1996) and Robert Garran (2004) – have analysed this new politics of identity and 'home', and Garran, Cheeseman and Camilleri have related it directly to the government's international policy especially towards the United States. Cheeseman (1996: 258) argues that there is a 'white Australia[n] strategic culture' persisting into the present, and Garran, analysing Howard's 'new nationalism', argues that 'support for the US alliance became part of his definition of patriotism' (2004: 8). What is especially significant for my argument is that appeals to security have been absolutely central to this politics. Under the potent promise of security they mobilize a political technology that combines both state-directed 'totalizing' power, working at the level of economies and populations, and distributed 'individualizing' power, which works in detail on the bodies and minds of individuals. This 'security politics' has been remarkably successful for the Howard government, underpinning its electoral dominance for three terms of office and forcing remarkable transformations in social attitudes, but at the cost of undermining human rights and democracy within Australia and, in the view of this writer, grossly distorting its defence and foreign policy.

As flows of 'boat-people' to Australia through Indonesia grew after 1999, the government stepped up its policies of mandatory detention and began to undermine legal processes for the assessment of asylum applications. It deployed SAS commandoes to board the *MV Tampa*, then created a bizarre 'Pacific solution' wherein it deported the asylum-seekers to camps on Nauru and Manus Island (Papua New Guinea). It also began a major naval operation to intercept asylum-seeker boats and turn them back to Indonesia. This was accompanied by a skilful campaign of propaganda and lies which portrayed the refugees as threats to Australia's 'sovereignty' and 'territorial integrity', as 'queue jumpers' ignoring available legal avenues for seeking asylum (these in fact did not exist), and as desperates who would expose their children to the danger of drowning to 'intimidate' naval officers (see Gelber and McDonald, 2006). The *Tampa* crisis began just as the government was facing a scandal about tax fraud by the Liberal Party in Queensland, and it seized on the opportunity to create a diversion. Two weeks later New York and Washington were attacked by terrorists. The subsequent election campaign was dominated by government rhetoric about border protection and security and it won in a landslide. Polls at the time suggested that 70 per cent of Australians supported the government's approach to refugees. The policies of indefinite detention (including of children), offshore processing, and naval interception and deportation, involved clear violations of both the letter and the spirit of international human rights and refugee law. Detention centres saw increasing patterns of mental illness, self-harm, suicide and conflict; while accusations of guards bashing and mistreating detainees were commonplace but of little concern to the government (JSCDFAT, 2001; AAP, 2005a; Burke, 2001b: 322–331). Nor were Australian citizens safe from the prisons and extra-legal police powers granted to the Department of

Immigration, Multiculturalism and Indigenous Affairs (DIMIA), as the high-profile cases of Cornelia Rau (a mentally ill woman detained for two years) and Vivien Solon (wrongly deported to the Philippines) showed.

Closely linked to these policies was a new emphasis on counter-terrorism. The government introduced legislation granting increased power to Australian security agencies and gave wholehearted support for the Bush administration's 'war on terror' including plans to attack Iraq. John Howard, in Washington on the day of the 9/11 attacks, unilaterally invoked the security pact – the ANZUS treaty – between Australia, New Zealand and the United States, despite the fact that the attacks could in no way be interpreted as being in the 'Pacific area' as the treaty states. Australian forces were dispatched to Afghanistan in December 2001 and to Iraq in February 2003, and force contingents were returned to southern Iraq and Afghanistan in 2005. As if to underline the convergence of asylum-seeker policy and the US alliance, it was subsequently revealed that the same SAS regiment which stormed the *Tampa* off Christmas Island was dispatched to US Central Command (CentCom) in Florida prior to deployment to Afghanistan, and thence a joint-service liaison team led by Brigadier Ken Gillespie was placed in CentCom. The government's National Security Committee of Cabinet secretly decided to send Gillespie's team back to Florida in August 2002 to participate in the planning for war against Iraq (Wright, 2003: 29–37). Neither the broader Cabinet, Coalition party room nor the parliament were informed, and the prime minister publicly claimed that no decision to join the war was taken prior to March 2003 (Garran, 2004: 152–65).

Not only did the war grossly violate the lives and human security of Iraqis, given the very high civilian death toll and the chaos, human rights abuses and civil war which has followed; the Australian government's participation and diplomatic support for it have severely undermined Australia's intelligence machinery, its national security (particularly against terrorist threats), and the global security and non-proliferation regimes that are so essential to that security. Howard made patently false claims in parliament about Iraq's weapons of mass destruction (WMD) programmes and capabilities, even when advice from Australian intelligence agencies failed to support them (Garran, 2004: 170). The parliamentary inquiry into intelligence on Iraq found that, after September 2002, assessments from the Office of National Assessments (ONA) changed to reflect the hawkish US, UK and Australian government claims, when previously both ONA and Defence Intelligence Organisation (DIO) assessments had downplayed Iraqi capabilities (JCAAD, 2003: 31–5). This points to the overt politicization of the intelligence process, which follows similar allegations about ONA and DIO during the 1999 East Timor crisis and the use of the Defence Signals Directorate in 2001 to intercept phone calls with the *Tampa* (and thus spy, in violation of its charter, within Australia) (Burchill, 2002; Collins and Reed, 2005).

It is likely that Bush's 2002 State of the Union Address (which named Iraq, Iran and North Korea as part of an 'axis of evil') and the invasion of Iraq have helped to accelerate Iranian and North Korean efforts to develop nuclear weapons and placed the survival of the Treaty on the Non-Proliferation of Nuclear Weapons (1968) in jeopardy. Notwithstanding recent diplomatic progress, a failure to dissuade North Korea from developing nuclear weapons has the potential to stimulate a North Asian arms race with very dangerous implications for Australia and Southeast Asia. Yet the government strongly endorsed the radical new American doctrine and even incorporated it into its defence policy. The 2003 *Defence Update* (actually drafted as propaganda for war against Iraq) stated that Australia will 'consider requests to support coalition military operations to prevent the proliferation of WMD, including to rogue states or terrorists, where peaceful efforts have failed' (*Australia's National Security*, 2003: 16).

However the threats that Australian policy poses to its own (and regional) security are more immediate. During the 2004 election campaign *Jemaah Islamiyya* (JI) bombers struck the Australian Embassy in Jakarta, killing 12 Indonesians. When interviewed by police one of the bombers, Iwan Dharmawan (nicknamed 'Rois') stated that 'the intention to bomb the Australian embassy was because the Australian Government is the American lackey most active in supporting American policies to slaughter Muslims in Iraq. It had the aim of preventing Australia again leaning on Muslims, especially in Iraq' (Wroe, 2005: 1). The government has been constantly warned about the inflammatory potential of joining the war on Iraq, not least by Scott Burchill who asked after the Madrid bombings: 'Is it in our national interest to hitch our wagon so closely to the US if it means getting caught up in Washington's blowback?' (Burchill, 2004).

Howard has argued that 'the crucial long-term value of the United States alliance should always be a factor in major national security decisions taken by Australia'. That is true, but the government has been working with flawed assumptions about the security benefits of the alliance, the worth of the 'values' shared by the two states, and the nature and impact of US power. Christian Reus-Smit argues that the crudely instrumental image of power held by both the Bush and Howard governments is 'deeply dysfunctional' and fails to understand the centrality of international norms and the need for legitimacy. Hence the Howard government's 'bandwagoning with the US is blinkered to the point of being irresponsible' (2004). The US government's attitudes to international human rights law, the United Nations Charter and the Kyoto Protocol are deeply inimical to the long-term interests of both Australia and broader international society, yet they have been replicated by

Australia. The revelations of torture at the Abu Ghraib prison have deeply angered Muslims around the world, who cannot have failed to connect Australia to these crimes when it was revealed that the defence minister was told by Amnesty International of the abuses in mid-2003 and that an Australian army lawyer had been closely involved in drafting a US response to the Red Cross that came 'close to denying the inhumane treatment, humiliation and abuse' (McDonald, 2005b: 154–5).

The Howard government seems both unable to summon a basic human empathy for the victims of the war or to consider how their suffering might undermine Australia's own security. Instead, as Downer's remarks in 2004 show, the government clings to the view that to reject war on Iraq would provoke 'a great and historic breach with the United States' and 'leave us as a country very vulnerable' (Allard, 2004). As a model for public policy-making (even 'rational' cost-benefit strategic policy-making, which I see as lacking in important normative qualities) this is extraordinary and disturbing. Rather than consider the causal consequences of particular actions or consider them in relation to a holistic, dynamic and complex understanding of security, the government appears to believe that as long as its preferred identity-forms are preserved and strengthened, this will automatically generate security. As Joseph Camilleri argues, 'the United States assumes a pervasive presence in the Howard cosmology precisely because it finds in it much needed psychological comfort and sustenance' (Camilleri, 2004: part 7).

The government's suite of anti-terror laws similarly threatens to antagonize Islamic communities, undermine human intelligence gathering and the civil rights of Australians. The first series of laws was introduced in 2002, and sought extraordinary new powers for ministers and security agencies such as the ability to ban organizations that may have 'endangered, or [are] likely to endanger, the security or integrity of the Commonwealth or another country' and to detain anyone without charge or trial for an indefinite period, including children, who may have information about a terrorist event. Detainees were to be denied the right to silence and a failure to answer any question put by ASIO (Australian Security Intelligence Organisation) would have been punishable by five years in prison. After enormous public protest, a parliamentary inquiry and strong opposition in parliament, these powers were amended so that people over 16 could be questioned for 24 hours over a 7-day period and be represented by a lawyer (Williams, 2005: part 16; Hocking, 2003; Michaelson, 2005). However the law breached a significant legal principle by allowing the detention and questioning of persons *not* suspects in a crime. In the wake of the London bombings the government introduced a new bill that, among other features, introduces 'control orders' to monitor terrorist suspects, give police preventive detention and warrantless search and seizure powers, and sweeping sedition laws. This bill, allegedly based on an agreement reached with the state premiers at the meeting cited at the beginning of this chapter, drew objections from the ACT (Australian Capital Territory) and Queensland governments, and a senate inquiry recommended the scrapping the sedition clause and 52 other changes (Commonwealth of Australia, 2005; AAP, 2005b). These plans, accompanied by anti-Islamic remarks and the deportation of a US peace activist, have raised the spectre of accelerating state authoritarianism and a lethal backlash from potential terrorists. Australian Arabic Council founder Joseph Wakim (2005) has warned that the 'debate' will 'feed directly into the video speeches of Al-Qaeda's propagandists' and 'incite extremist Muslims', while in the course of a perceptive survey the Singapore-based scholar Suzaina Kadir (2004: 199) warns that 'an increasingly centralised and coercive approach to Muslim politics will, in fact, undermine the very objective of dampening international Islamic terrorism'. Yet these measures will no doubt be popular with a large number of Australians.

The simulation of security

Following his alarmist remarks after the London bombings Attorney-General Phillip Ruddock announced details of potential new anti-terrorism laws, including the use of tracking devices on suspect persons, on 8 September 2005. He was promptly accused by opposition foreign affairs spokesman Kevin Rudd of using the announcement to distract public and media attention from a series of damaging scandals about the communications company Telstra (*ABC Online*, 9 September 2005). If the last few years are any guide, Rudd's accusation is entirely plausible. The systematic resort to security politics has been tremendously successful for the Howard government, but it raises very serious issues that should be of concern not only to those who care about the vitality of Australian democracy and culture, but also about the integrity of national institutions and processes for security policy-making. As I have argued in this chapter, while this problem has long been a danger in Australian politics it has been especially virulent since 9/11. It seems that endless politicking, and the hegemonic control of national identity and individual subjectivities, has become the *raison d'etre* for Australian policy carried under the name and promise of security, while the outcome has been only greater suffering, danger and insecurity.

The problem then is not merely the inappropriate securitization of particular issues, as Wæver and others worried, but the securitization of the entire political field. It is as if the more powerful security becomes as a political technology the less meaning it has as a concept, becoming merely a byword for cruelty and the abuse of power. This is to introduce the worst kind of postmodernism into the heart of social life, enacting the dystopic vision of Jean Baudrillard who argued in 1981 that societies were becoming hostage to a process of 'substituting signs of the real for the real itself; that is, an operation to deter every real process by its operational double, a metastable, programmatic, perfect descriptive machine which provides all the signs of the real and short circuits all its vicissitudes' (1988: 167). While we can acknowledge that whatever 'real' security may be will always be contested, there is an important point to be made here. Security under Howard is a *simulacrum*: it has no meaning beyond the reproduction of political hegemony and particular security institutions; it has become a closed, self-referring system divorced from the (very real) consequences of its operations. This 'hyperreal' politics has an especially bitter flavour when we consider the constant repetition of mantras about 'values', 'freedom' and the 'way of life' in response to Islamist terrorism. Could it ever have occurred to those who so sanctimoniously mouth such phrases – or type them into foreign policy white papers – that the most visible signs of Australia's 'way of life' are not multiculturalism and the rule of law but racist taunts, imperialist wars, immigration prisons, the abuse of executive power, and countless civilians dead under cruise missiles and precision guided bombs?

It is clear that Australia is worlds away from being able to achieve a harmonization of national and human security, or security as emancipation. Even welcome past innovations in Australian policy, such as the disarmament, non-proliferation and 'cooperative security' initiatives of the Labor governments of the 1990s, were partial and problematic. Signs of genuine innovation in Labor thinking are few. External constraints – such as the Association of Southeast Asian Nations' (ASEAN's) dominance by statist paradigms like comprehensive security and national resilience, and the aggressive unilateralism of the United States – also limit Australia's potential room to move. However there has a been a widespread and robust debate within Australia in past years – on the treatment of asylum-seekers, Australia's obligations under international law, the US alliance, defence priorities, the war on Iraq, and human rights – which suggests that less coercive and more sustainable approaches can be easily found and implemented. Likewise in the region the sheer novelty of new security challenges (whether they be terrorism, economic instability or the vulnerability of regional states to environmental cataclysms such as the tsunami or climate change) and their resistance to conventional policy solutions, has opened up an important space for questioning and reform. 'Immanent possibilities' for change do exist, but this chapter has also highlighted some very serious obstacles to achieving such progressive visions of security; obstacles that are immanent in the very history of security as an idea and a politics. Change, if it is to be change at all, will need to be truly profound.

8

Harm and emancipation: making environmental security 'critical' in the Asia-Pacific

Lorraine Elliott

ENVIRONMENTAL DEGRADATION and resource decline, and the important matter of how to overcome them, have become crucial challenges for the Asia-Pacific. While the policy debate is usually driven by economic and social concerns, there is a growing acceptance that these challenges also figure in the regional security agenda and, indeed, that they complicate that agenda. There are few academic or policy commentaries on regional security that now do not make some reference to non-military or transnational security concerns, including environmental degradation. However, defining or identifying environmental degradation as a non-traditional or non-conventional threat reveals little about the nature of those threats, or who or what is made insecure by them. Nor does it provide much in the way of guidance on appropriate policy responses or ways of overcoming insecurities.

A central purpose of this chapter is to deploy a critical security studies approach to 'unpack' environmental security (and the relationship between environment and security) in the Asia-Pacific. I do so in the face of Shamsul Haque's pessimism about the immanent potential of a critical approach to environmental security in the East Asian context. He argues that

> the potential for deconstructing the prevailing concept of security does not really exist, especially since the region's realist security perception is hardly questioned or critically examined. (2001: 212)

In response, this is partly a story about how environmental issues are 'security' issues in the Asia-Pacific and it is also partly about how policy-makers and commentators have represented them as security issues. The two are not the same, but it is a critical security studies approach that enables us to investigate why. The 'securitization' of the environment in the Asia-Pacific – making the environment a security issue – rests not just on the material assessment of resource scarcity and environmental degradation but also on perceptions of and claims about the consequences of such scarcity. Those perceptions, in turn, depend on who is 'speaking' security and on the answers they give to the important questions: security for whom and from what?

The first section of the chapter elaborates on the approach to critical security that is deployed here. Three observations might be helpful by way of brief introduction. First, I take as a starting point the claim that 'emancipatory change constitutes the primary purpose' of critical security studies (Stamnes, 2004: 162). Second, security and insecurity are understood (and explained) in terms of harm and consent rather than threat. Third, critical security studies has a specific normative purpose that is reconstructive as well as analytical. In other words, exposing the dominant paradigm is only one component of a critical security studies approach.

Following a more detailed elaboration of these themes, the chapter examines the nature of environmental degradation in the Asia-Pacific. It explores the ways in which this is implicated in different versions of (in)security in the region and how this has been 'securitized' by those who are authorized to speak security in the region. The third section explores two versions of the non-traditional security discourse that links degradation to (in)security – taking first states and then peoples as the security referent but also questioning the 'taken for granted' assumptions and analyses in the policy community about environment and security. The final section turns to the reconstructive purpose of a critical approach, speculating on the contours of a non-statist and emancipatory version of regional environmental security.

Critical environmental security

The literature on environmental security, and the incorporation of environmental concerns into security policy, reflects a fundamental tension between two positions. The first is a modified realist approach which deploys the language of threat to anticipate a causal relationship between scarcity, violence and conflict. It takes as its particular concern the stability and security of states. Access to resources (scarce or otherwise) is 'taken for granted' as a fundamental right of states and therefore attempts to undermine such access, even in conditions of non-scarcity, are considered to be a threat to state security and sovereignty.

This adversarial model of security is flawed on a number of grounds. It runs the risk of militarizing environmental problems, drawing attention away from the underlying causes of environmental degradation. It overlooks the extent to which environmental scarcities might be amenable to cooperation rather than conflict. Investigations suggest that there are numerous examples in areas such as international water law to demonstrate that shared water resources can provide the basis for conflict resolution and the development of cooperative management schemes.[1] State-centric and national security interpretations of environmental security have also restricted who can contribute to the 'security' discourse. Defining and providing security is determined to be the responsibility of state actors, nationally and internationally. When this is joined with 'environmental' threats, it can preclude ideas and concepts that do not have states as the key structures or agents. Thus traditional security discourse is not only inappropriate as a basis for environmental security but it may also stand in the way of creative and successful solutions to environmental insecurity. As Bilgin puts it, the supposed 'commonsense' of statism 'forclos[es] alternative non-statist conceptions of security and the constitution of alternative futures' (2002: 100).

The second theme in the environmental security literature is inspired by a concern with human security, often seen as an antidote to more traditional security emphases and one that could support non-statist conceptions and alternative futures. The United Nations Development Programme (UNDP), whose 1995 *Human Development Report* impelled the term into the international lexicon, understood human security as 'a concern with human life and dignity' (1995: 22). It argued that 'for too long the concept of security has been shaped by the potential for conflict between states . . . equated with . . . threats to a country's borders' (UNDP, 1995: 3). Human security was thus expected to open space to identify and acknowledge threats not to states but to peoples and communities, and to reassess the probability of insecurities. The UNDP was clear that environmental issues such as clean air and water were central components of human security. In pursuing the 'antidote' line, the Commission on Global Governance observed that 'threats to the earth's life support systems, extreme economic deprivation, the proliferation of conventional small arms, the terrorising of civilian populations by domestic factions and gross violations of human rights . . . challenge the security of people far more than the threat of external aggression' (1995: 79). In his Millennium Report to the General Assembly, the United Nations Secretary-General (2000: 55–65) identified the degradation and in some cases destruction of the planet's ability to provide life-sustaining services as a fundamental global challenge to the security of current and future generations. These are, as Ken Booth suggests, 'problems of profound significance' and ones which place 'emancipation at the centre of new security thinking' (Booth, 1991: 318, 321).

The UNDP suggested that human security would both invoke and require a 'profound transition in thinking' (1994: 22). A human security approach provides a broader window on the relationship between environmental decline and insecurity. It accommodates situations, such as ecological disasters, where there is no violent conflict or social unrest but in which the lives of people and the stability of the ecosystem are clearly under threat. From a critical security vantage, however, this version of environmental security remains problematic. In part this is because, in the contemporary human security literature, states remain the 'social protection providers of the last resort' (Lawson, 2005: 109). While the 2003 report of the independent Commission on Human Security emphasized paradigm shifts, protection and empowerment, it nevertheless offered human security as a complement or adjunct to state security (Commission on Human Security, 2003). Identifying new referents and new threats has done little to unsettle the dominance of the statist commonsense of orthodox security noted above.

Cox's device of critical theorizing provides some purchase here, demanding that we not take 'institutions and social and power relations for granted but call them into question' by concerning ourselves with their origins and appraising their very framework for action (Cox, 1986: 208). For environmental (in)security, this functions at two levels. The first demands an interrogation of the structural causes of environmental degradation. It also resists the conclusion that environmental problems (in the Asia-Pacific as elsewhere) are the consequence solely or even predominantly of local causes such as population growth, subsistence lifestyles or lack of governance capacity. These factors may be relevant but they are insufficient as explanation without attention to the global structural context within which environmental degradation occurs.

The second aspect of an analysis driven by Coxian critical enquiry directs attention to the ideational aspects of environmental security and the importance of exposing the hegemonic practices associated with 'speaking' environmental security. The dominant paradigm for a human security response to environmental degradation is a neo-liberal one that defends privatization and commodification of common resources, the use of market-based strategies to 'price' environmental resources and the inviolability of liberalized trade as the best way to support and encourage sustainable development.[2] This neo-liberal discourse is a consistent theme in the normative claims and the policy demands of multilateral environmental instruments and declarations (such as the 1987 report of the World Commission on Environment and Development, the 1992 Rio Declaration, Agenda 21, and the 2002 Monterrey Consensus on Financing for Development). It instructs and confines the work of bodies such as the WTO (World Trade Organization) Committee on Trade and Environment and it informs the modalities adopted in legally binding agreements such as the emissions and credit trading schemes adopted under the Kyoto Protocol on climate change. What is revealed is not so much a tension between state and human security, but that even when human security provides the discursive context, it remains tied to a threat paradigm and to reliance on the state as the remedial agent.[3] From a critical security studies perspective, this remains a conventional approach to security and one that is seen to be 'practically dysfunctional as the discursive framework for any political arrangement' (Dalby, 1997: 21) that could respond either to environmental degradation or to the competition and tension which might arise as a result.

A critical approach to environmental security revisions security as emancipation, as 'freedom to' rather than 'freedom from'. Following Booth's critical approach to (human) security, emancipation is a process rather than an end-point and environmental insecurity a form of harm rather than threat. This emphasis on harm recognizes the ways in which the environmental consequences of economic activity are displaced spatially and temporally in such a way that the 'quality of the lives of others is shaped and determined in near or far-off lands without their participation, agreement or consent' (Held, 1997: 244). In other words, the liberal concern with individual autonomy is augmented with a sociological concern about the ways in which the individual or the atomistic expression of freedom (or choice) is bound up with possible harm and lack of autonomy for others. A critical approach also resists a disciplinary neo-liberalism as the paradigm for achieving 'freedom' or overcoming environmental harm. The specific content of and strategies for environmental emancipation are not pre-determined, and are ultimately context-specific. As Stamnes points out, this is about 'making things better without applying an external definition of what would be best' (2004: 163). The freedom embodied in this form of emancipation cannot be achieved at the expense of others. In contrast to the orthodox views of security, emancipation is not a zero-sum commodity or condition.

The environmental (in)security challenge

Environmental degradation and pressure on resources in the Asia-Pacific is a consequence of the region's changing political economy and modes of production, both of which are embedded in a globalized economy. Subsistence lifestyles that are heavily dependent on the direct exploitation of natural resources and environmental services constitute the basic means of survival for over half the region's population. However the major cause of environmental decline and resource scarcity in the region has been the 'industrialisation of Asia within the world economy' (Vervoorn, 1998: 157). The region's political economy is characterized by increasing rates of consumption, growing urban populations, rapid increases in energy demands and changing relations of production. By 2020, more than half of Asia's population is likely to live in urban areas, three times that of 1990. In Southeast Asia, primary energy demand averaged across all the Association of Southeast Asian Nations (ASEAN) member states is likely to increase by close to 60 per cent between 2000 and 2010 with the annual increase likely to be higher towards the end of the decade (ASEAN Secretariat, 2001: 36–7).

Industrial production and export-led development in the region have relied heavily on the extraction of natural resources, including non-renewable minerals and 'renewable' forest resources, to meet the demands of non-local consumers.[4] Resource extraction and primary production still contribute significantly to regional economies (ASEAN Secretariat, 2001: 28). Those countries in the region that have sought to reduce their reliance on primary production have expanded into manufacturing or value-adding (and often highly polluting industries) such as pulp and paper, chemical and textile production. The intensification of resource consumption associated with industrialization extends to rural modes of production. A bias against so-called 'primitive' but often more sustainable forms of agriculture means that shifting cultivation has been actively discouraged in favour of permanent, commercialized and more intensive agriculture.

The vesting of resource and access rights in private, corporate and state hands has been another major factor in large-scale exploitation and the unsustainable use of both renewable and non-renewable resources. 'Pre-existing forms of rights over forest, land and coastal resources' are being disregarded in favour of individual property rights (Pas-Ong and Lebel, 2000: 10). Customary rights to open-access resources, such as water and fuel-wood in rural areas, are poorly defined and poorly secured. In a number of Asia-Pacific countries, there is also fairly conclusive evidence of military collusion in environmentally destructive practices, including species smuggling, illegal logging and fishing, and the dumping of hazardous wastes.[5]

The environmental consequences of this economic activity are extensive. The region, according to the Asian Development Bank, has become 'dirtier, less ecologically diverse and more environmentally vulnerable' (1997: 199). Resources have been depleted and the environment polluted to the extent that so-called renewable resources and environmental services such as clean air and water are being exhausted in much the same way as non-renewable resources. Rates of resource depletion, the decline in environmental services and the production of waste and pollution are on the increase. Demands for energy and water – key environmental services – are growing faster than supply with standard estimates anticipating a threefold increase in regional energy consumption between 1990 and 2020.

A number of environmental problems stand out as particularly challenging. Commercial and illegal logging, together with land-clearance for plantation and industrial agriculture, have increased the rate of deforestation to an estimated 1.8 per cent per year, up from 1.4 per cent in the 1980s and almost twice the rate of other tropical zones (ASEAN Secretariat, 1997: 4–5). The average annual loss of forestlands increased by 48 per cent between 1990 and 2000 (ASEAN Secretariat, 2001: 83). Nearly one-third of the forest cover in Cambodia, Vietnam and Laos has disappeared in the last 20 years (Agence-France Press, 2000). Frontier forests remain particularly vulnerable and logging bans in one country (such as China or Thailand) simply displace the problem elsewhere, a form of what Contreras calls a 'predatory economy' (2002: 4). The depletion and degradation of forest lands is also severely implicated in the loss of biodiversity. Southeast Asia now contains over 200 of the world's threatened mammals, almost the same number of threatened bird species, close to 100 of the world's threatened fish species and almost 30 of the world's most threatened reptile and amphibian species (UNEP, 2000: 80, 82). Almost half the region's wetlands are subject to moderate or high levels of threat from logging, agricultural conversion, mining and oil exploration and pollution (ASEAN Secretariat, 2001: 63–5).

Changing land use patterns and land degradation further complicate the loss of other environmental services. Southeast Asia already has less land per capita (0.19 hectares on average) than the global average of 1.24 hectares. Land use patterns have changed more quickly in Asia than they have globally (UNEP, 2000: 76; ASEAN Secretariat, 2001: 20, 29).[6] Commercial or industrial agriculture has become increasingly unsustainable and environmentally destructive, drawing heavily on water resources through poor irrigation practices. Per capita water availability in the region is the lowest in the world (see Jha, 2005: 207). Soil and water pollution has been exacerbated by the increased use of fertilisers and pesticides in almost all countries in the region that have a substantial agricultural industry. The ecological consequences include soil loss, land degradation, silting of river systems and destabilization of water retention and run-off. As much as 14 per cent of the land area of the ASEAN countries is now affected by *severe* soil erosion (ASEAN Secretariat, 2001: 89). China loses almost 2,500 square kilometres to desertification every year and eastern China has suffered major decreases in cropland (Millennium Ecosystem Assessment, 2005: 30).

Terrestrial problems are mirrored in the pollution and depletion of atmospheric, water, coastal and marine resources and their related and dependent environmental services. The haze – particulate-laden smoke – which arose as a consequence of land-clearing fires in Indonesia has been the most publicly identifiable of the atmospheric pollution problems in the region. It is not, however, the only atmospheric problem facing the Asia-Pacific. Higher rates of fossil fuel combustion across a range of economic sectors, combined with inefficient energy use, have resulted in increases in sulphur dioxide and nitrogen oxide emissions.[7] The region faces increasing demands on water resources for domestic, agriculture and industrial use. Water quality is a serious problem. Chemical run-off from agriculture and industry, untreated wastewater and limited sewage systems ensure that water pollution is a major environmental and economic problem in Southeast Asia, especially (but not exclusively) in urban areas. Coastal and marine areas are also subject to pollution, with contaminant levels of heavy metals, bacteria, and faecal coliform, in some areas much higher than prescribed standards.

Coastal resources, including fish stocks and mangrove ecosystems, are also under threat as a result of uncontrolled waste discharge, oil spills and siltation caused by hinterland soil erosion (ASEAN Secretariat, 2001: 66). In a part of the world in which a very high percentage of people live within 100 kilometres of the coast and are therefore highly reliant on the integrity of coastal ecosystems, the social and economic costs are as high as the ecological ones. Marine resources such as fish stocks are under less pressure in the ASEAN region – the Western Central Pacific maritime zone – than in other parts of the world. Nevertheless, pressure on marine fishery resources has continued to increase, productivity in many species is declining and, according to the World Resources Institute, the region could well be close to fully fished (cited in ASEAN Secretariat, 2001: 78).

Environmental (in)security in the Asia-Pacific

As suggested above, thinking about environmental (in)security in the Asia-Pacific proceeds at two related levels. First, what are or might be the insecurity consequences of environmental degradation and resource decline (the questions of for whom and from what notwithstanding)? Second, what is the discursive context within which these insecurity consequences are identified and 'spoken'? The environmental security discourse in the Asia-Pacific has generally pursued an orthodox approach to non-traditional security, identifying new 'threats' and at times new referents but nevertheless remaining attached to a statist commonsense and an ideational and material concern with threat. In effect, we have two paradigms but one ontology, collapsed together in the Asia-Pacific version of comprehensive security.

Non-traditional security version 1: non-traditional threats

The regional consequences of environmental degradation and resource scarcity are widely although not necessarily deeply acknowledged but the 'securitizing' process is a selective one. In its 1994 review of functional cooperation, the ASEAN Secretariat was clear in its warning that 'any drastic and irreversible reduction in the region's resources will . . . have far-reaching implications for the region's ecosystem and quality of life' (ASEAN Secretariat, 1994: 33). At the same time, but for different reasons, strategic analysts inside and outside the region have come to rank the environment (or environmental scarcities) among the new security issues.[8] Almost all of the region's environment and resource problems have been identified as a possible source of insecurity but the nature of the causal relationship is rarely explained.

The most orthodox version of the environmental security agenda retains a discursive emphasis on the possibility for environmental degradation and resource scarcity to generate conflict, cross border confrontation or the corrosion of political relationships. Some commentators, inspired by this approach, have counselled on 'troubling prospects' (Winnefeld and Morris, 1994: 65) and offered a 'pessimistic account of likely future conflict' (Lim and Valencia, 1990: 3) over resources and environmental decline in the Asia-Pacific. The agenda of environmental security concerns includes activities within one country that have a severe impact on environmental quality in other countries. It includes competition over scarce resources and environmental services, including living resources (fish and forests, for example), non-renewable resources, particularly energy resources and supposedly replenishable resources such as water. Resource competition is assumed to be exacerbated in areas where environmental vulnerabilities coincide with political vulnerabilities associated with land and maritime border regions. For example, competition for energy resources in the South China Sea is assumed to be made more conflict-prone because of overlapping and competing sovereignty claims. Asymmetric geopolitical relationships in the Mekong basin are posited as a factor that could exacerbate conflict over the sovereign rights of riparian states to draw on the river's water resources.[9] The extent to which riparian states rely on the river is a factor in possible upstream/downstream interstate allocation conflicts. As Goh (2001) points out, riverine allocation is not simply a matter of access to water resources. It also involves ecological feedbacks and the consequences of land or water use in one part of the Mekong basin for fish stocks or important siltation and stream flows elsewhere.

The usefulness and accuracy of the conflict model is of course disputed. Alan Dupont argues that 'there is no compelling evidence that environmental problems have been the primary cause of any major sub-national or inter-state conflict' in the region (1998: 75). Stuart Harris, taking a slightly different line on the same theme, has argued that the 'historically common approach to accessing resources' (through contest and conquest) 'has become largely obsolete' in the region (1995: 44). Yet the deployment of military capability or the threat of such deployment in the face of competition for resources is another matter. Troops are deployed to protect borders regions against illegal logging on mainland Southeast Asia (although this is complicated by various forms of military complicity in illegal logging as well). The case of illegal fishing is perhaps the exemplar case in which disputes over access to and authority over resources is 'interactive with . . . threat perceptions' (Ganesan, 2001: 520). The Indonesian government has cited illegal fishing (and the economic losses associated with this) as a major reason for seeking to strengthen its naval capabilities. Illegal fishing is a continuing source of tension between Thailand and its neighbours, particularly Malaysia, involving naval and border patrol activity on both sides. Shots have, on occasion, been fired.

While actual violent conflict between states in the region might be unlikely, political tension is not. And the region's history means that governments and elites are fearful of the consequences of political disagreements. Thus transboundary tension and disputes over the use of resources, such as water or energy, or the border-crossing environmental impact of economic activity, such as the haze, is thought to be a worrying factor in unsettling political relationships in the region. In Southeast Asia, the haze provides an example of real and at times publicly expressed tension between Indonesia (the source) and neighbouring countries which are affected physically and financially by the consequences. In Northeast Asia, China's growing demand for energy and exploitation of offshore energy resources in the South China Sea may well lead to 'festering relations' with other Asia-Pacific countries (see, for example, Lee, 2005). Regional commentators have also been persuaded by arguments that environmental degradation can contribute to instability through the 'disruption of legitimised and authoritative social relations' (Homer-Dixon, 1991: 9) or that 'civil turmoil and outright violence' are likely consequences of environmental scarcity (Myers, 1989: 24). Certainly economic activity in the region is frequently characterized by 'competing groups of users includ[ing] tribal communities, peasants, fisher[people], miners, loggers and corporations' (Lim and Valencia, 1990: 3). While social tension can be a feature of such competition, what prove to be sometimes incommensurable interests are also a factor in the burgeoning of local resistance to the environmental consequences of government and corporate projects, a trend explored further below.

Governments and regional security institutions have offered a contained and selective response to the non-traditional security literature. At the same time, the ways in which such institutions have come to own and 'speak' non-traditional security informs much of that literature. Both the ASEAN Regional Forum (ARF) and the informal, track-two process under the auspices of the Council for Security Cooperation Asia-Pacific (CSCAP) have adopted the language of comprehensive and cooperative security. The ARF members inscribed the 'comprehensive concept of security, including its economic and social aspects, as it pertains to the Asia Pacific region' on the agenda of their very first meeting in 1994 (see ARF, 1994). Non-military issues 'which would have a significant impact on regional security' remain a regular feature on ARF agenda (ARF, 1998: 2). It is notable, though, that comprehensive security remains firmly directed towards issues such as drug trafficking, people smuggling, transnational organized crime and, more recently, terrorism rather than the environment. The track-two CSCAP process has also adopted the non-traditional security agenda, establishing working groups on comprehensive and cooperative security, on transnational crime and on maritime cooperation. The annual track-two Asia-Pacific Roundtable has featured plenary sessions on environmental security as well as on other themes in the non-traditional security lexicon.

At the same time, fears have been expressed that a focus on transnational issues could come at the expense of more traditional security concerns. The primary security problematic remains one that focuses on the maintenance of regional order and stability and the protection (or securing) of those values that are associated with statehood. The core values to be protected – made secure – are those associated with the region's stateness: political independence, territorial integrity, internal order. As Anwar observes, 'the nation-state [is] perceived as the ultimate good' even in the context of comprehensive security (2003: 536).

Non-traditional security version 2: human security

As suggested earlier, a necessary component of a critical security studies-inspired interrogation of environmental security involves a reassessment of the referents – the 'who' of security. Within the non-traditional security literature, this usually takes the form of asking questions about the security of people and their communities. Thus security becomes embedded in and defined by the condition of human life, human dignity and human welfare. Environmental degradation in the region compromises this condition directly and indirectly.

A neo-liberal approach to human security has generated a concern with the indirect (in)security consequences of externalities and the ways in which environmental degradation is bound up in a regional economic security dilemma. The pursuit of economic growth (economic security) in the Asia-Pacific is a central cause of resource depletion, pollution and habitat destruction which, in turn, is a key determinant of economic insecurity. The industrialization of most economic sectors generates levels of pollution which are socially, ecologically and economically costly. Every $US 1 billion increase in Asian gross national product (GNP) generates about 100 tonnes of hazardous and toxic waste and pollutants (cited in Arif, 1995: 124). These externalities rarely figure prominently in the region's economic security calculations, despite a commitment to the ethic of sustainable development found in regional submissions and reports for global events such as the 2002 World Summit on Sustainable Development. The costs are not insubstantial. According to Andre Dua and Daniel Esty at the Institute for International Economics, environmental decline costs countries in the region an average of 3 to 8 per cent of their gross domestic product (GDP) per year (cited in Barkenbus, 2001: 2). The annual cost to the city of Jakarta to make polluted water potable, for example, is estimated at $US 20 million to $US 30 million (Shin, 1997: IV-59). A World Bank survey estimates that air and water pollution cost the Chinese economy approximately $US 54 billion in damage to human health and lost agricultural productivity, about 8 per cent of Chinese GDP (Edwards, 1997). The Indonesian government has estimated the annual cost of illegal fishing in Indonesian waters at $US 4 billion (the legal fishing industry was worth only about half that, $US 2.2 billion) (Anon., 1999). The costs of the haze pollution cause by land-clearing fires in Indonesia, in the major event of 1997–8, were conservatively estimated at $US 1.4 billion in health costs and lost tourism revenue, and $US 3 billion though losses in 'agriculture, non-timber forest products, hydrological and soils conservation and . . . biodiversity benefits' (Schweithelm, 1998).[10] The World Bank estimates that in countries such as the Philippines pollution-related health costs could be as high as 15 to 18 per cent of urban income and up to 7 per cent of GDP (cited in Bengwayan, 2000).

However, the human (in)security costs are not simply to be measured in GDP lost. Environmental scarcity and degradation is not simply a matter of market failure, externalities or zero-sum calculations about resource allocation. These externalities have direct consequences for the people of the region. It is they who ultimately bear the cost of environmental harm through increased vulnerability, poverty and ill health. Environmental degradation results in shortfalls in food production, food insecurity, poverty and conflict over land tenure. Mortality rates from air pollution, along with the incidence of chronic respiratory illness are also increasing, according to studies by the World Bank and the Stockholm Development Institute.[11] Solid waste and effluent pollution of water are implicated in health problems ranging from diarrhoea and dysentery to cholera and typhoid. Food insecurity is a real-life consequence of over-fishing and intensification of agriculture. Communities are dislocated by the environmental consequences of development projects. Indigenous peoples are displaced culturally and physically from forest lands.

The human security dimension of environmental degradation *is* acknowledged in the Asia-Pacific, in official policy discourse and in what might be called the 'commentary' and research community. One of the most notable, of course, is the Trust Fund for Human Security established in the United Nations Secretariat but arising from an initiative of the government of Japan. Human security concerns feature in track-two dialogues and colloquia, in the various non-official annual regional security overviews, in regional development reports and in regional submissions to events such as the World Summit on Sustainable Development. But the regional caution about permitting 'human security' to make too many inroads into the *formal* security apparatus or dialogue extends to this non-traditional version of environmental security. The resistance to 'human security' arises because of concerns that it will open a Pandora's box of human rights issues, or authorize commentary on the internal affairs of countries in the region. As Tan argues, the region's human security discourse is state-centric 'precisely . . . [because] it is deployed for the ongoing inscription or production of the state as an ontological entity' (2001: 2).[12]

Critical (environmental) security: emancipation and recognition

Environmental insecurity is not just about 'threat' and environmental harm is not just about physical danger and damage. As Linklater suggests, harm also involves 'distress, suffering, apprehension, anxiety or fear' (2002: 327). Or, as Axel Honneth suggests, harm is implicated in the problems of recognition: a lack of solidarity (or 'depreciation of the social value of forms of self-realization'), in physical maltreatment or humiliations, and in social exclusion and the denial of rights where 'human beings suffer in their dignity through not being granted the moral rights and responsibilities of a full legal person within their own community' (Honneth, 2001: 49).

Environmental harm arises in part through the costs to life and health associated with environmental degradation and unsustainable development. But it is exacerbated by differences in environmental endowment. This includes access to resources and environmental services, disproportionate vulnerabilities to environmental degradation (often out of proportion to contributions to pollution and waste) and unequal and inequitable authority and control over resource use. Environmental harms of the kind explored above can therefore be argued to do more than compromise the ability of people to carry out what they would freely choose to do (a version of autonomy). They illuminate Honneth's ethics of 'recognition': lack of solidarity in the disproportionate use of resources by the rich; physical maltreatment in the disproportionate impact of environmental degradation on the poor; and social exclusion in the politics of marginalization from decision-making and consent. Those who are already the most vulnerable and marginalized in the region – the poor in both urban and rural communities, indigenous peoples, women and children – often suffer disproportionately from the impact of unsustainable development and environmental degradation. The poor are the most disadvantaged and impoverished by environmental degradation, pollution and resource depletion and they are the least able to buy their way out of its consequences. This animates the importance of consent which has two related components. First, as Henry Shue argues, people 'are entitled to decide for themselves whether they wish to accept additional risks' (1981: 593), and this includes the risks that characterize environmental harms. Second, consent is also a process by which those who are most vulnerable, powerless and marginalized are *empowered* to refuse, negotiate and contest (see Linklater, 1998).

The dominance of a statist approach to security – even non-traditional, non-military comprehensive security – limits the responses available for dealing with or preventing the problems of harm. Confidence-building measures (CBMs), preventive diplomacy and early warning mechanisms – the comprehensive security mechanisms that characterize the debate within the ARF for example – are intended to manage tensions and increase cooperation among states. States may not be the most appropriate providers of environmental security and, indeed, the pursuit of states' interests (through economic and military security for example) is a likely cause of environmental harm of various kinds. In the Asia-Pacific, particularly for those countries that fall into the category of 'developing' states, strategies for overcoming environmental degradation and resource decline are often constrained by an uneven capacity for environmental policy-making and for implementation of those policies that are adopted. Indeed, policies inspired by the dominant neo-liberal orthodoxies which influence developmental paths in the region can contribute further to harm and complicate the potential for achieving environmental security. Market pricing of resources such as water, corporate or government control of access to forest land and resources, or the construction of dams to address water issues can exacerbate rather than overcome inequities. As so much of the critical literature on globalization points out, people are being made less environmentally secure by the practices of a global political economy.

If security is defined as freedom from harm and as emancipation then, as David Capie (1995) argues, 'more radical, alternative mechanisms need to be considered if genuine regional security is to be attained'. As well as rethinking policy and practice, those who are most affected must be able to contest and 'speak' the conditions of their own (in)security. This is about making their claims to security count. Tan argues that the possibilities for emancipation lie 'in the aspirations and attempts of critical social movements to open . . . political spaces for new modes of political thinking' (2001: 3). The development of civil society and a public space in the Asia Pacific is often made difficult by the non-pluralist nature of many of the region's political regimes (or what Contreras (2002) refers to as an elitist-statist mode of governance) and also by the orthodoxies of the region's security discourse in which local resistance is seen as a measure of state and regional instability. On the other hand, there has been a burgeoning of civil society and non-governmental environmental politics at local, national and regional level although in many countries in the region civil society remains on the margins of policy-making. The 'public space' is reflected in an often spontaneous local politics of resistance. Thus, for example, one finds local communities organizing against the Pak Mun dam project on the Mekong. In China, non-governmental organizations (NGOs) have mobilized protests against the environmental consequences of dam construction. Local villagers have engaged in mass protests against the environmental threats posed by pharmaceutical factories. This is not just about oppositional politics. It is also a space for 'imagining [security] alternatives' (Contreras, 2002: 10). Demands for a more just version of security, in which environmental concerns and harm are embedded in social rights, have been articulated by civil society actors such as indigenous peoples organizations and women's organizations in the region. The theme in much of this environmental resistance is not simply demands for better environmental policy but for knowledge, access and consent – key components of an emancipatory version of security.

Notes

1 See, for example, Dimitrov (2002) and Sadoff and Grey (2002).

2 For more, see Elliott (2002).

3 For more on the idea of environmental harm as a global phenomenon, see Elliott (2006).

4 While living resources are, in theory, renewable in that they can be replaced and replenished, the extent of timber extraction in the region is such that forests are being seriously and potentially irreversibly depleted.

5 For examples see Shepherd (2002), Environmental Investigation Agency (2005), and NGO Forum on Cambodia (2005).

6 The figures on hectares per capita of arable land exclude Singapore and Brunei Darussalam. In Cambodia, arable land per capita has increased as the clearance of landmines enables previously unusable land to be brought back into agricultural production.

7 ASEAN's major urban areas are well over the World Health Organization (WHO) guidelines on total suspended particulates. They are below the guidelines for emissions of sulphur dioxide and nitrogen dioxide although both are increasing in volume (see ASEAN Secretariat, 2001: 100–10).

8 See, for example, Morrison (1998: 18).

9 See, for example, Goh (2001) and Emmers (2005).

10 Other estimates put the figure as high as US$ 9.3 billion, see Millennium Ecosystem Assessment (2005: 57).

11 See Bengwayan (2000) and Jha (2005: 216) for useful summaries of estimated environmental costs in selected countries in the region.

12 See also Anwar (2003).

9

Seeking security for refugees

Sara E. Davies

THIS VOLUME IS CONCERNED with identifying – and exploring possibilities for redressing – the suffering and vulnerability of people in the Asia-Pacific, particularly that arising from the primacy of traditional security thinking and practices. In particular, proponents of critical security studies seek to point to the normative limitations of traditional security approaches that position the state as the best means of realizing individual wellbeing in an anarchic international environment. Other chapters in this volume (rightly) contest such an assumption on the basis that the state frequently *threatens* rather than *protects* its own population. But nowhere are the normative and ethical limitations of traditional security frameworks – and the Hobbesian social contract underpinning them – more profoundly apparent than regarding the stateless: refugees and asylum-seekers in global politics. Refugees and asylum-seekers point both to the failure of some states to live up to their obligations of providing for the wellbeing of their populations, and to the ultimate inability for traditional security approaches to register suffering outsiders other than as a potential threat to social cohesion (or 'societal security') or sovereignty defined as non-intervention. This chapter explores these dilemmas in the context of asylum-seekers in Southeast Asia. In doing so, it points in particular to the role of international refugee law in mitigating against sovereignty as exclusion, but also explores how and why international refugee law falls short of redefining state obligation in the region in such a way as to effectively redress the suffering of asylum-seekers.

International refugee law exists mainly to identify those who can legitimately leave their state and enter another without permission from either state. From a traditional security perspective, however, the preservation of a Westphalian conception of sovereignty overrides legal allowances for movement of asylum-seekers. In this regard, some states invoke security concerns in arguing that refugees reveal the permeability of a state's borders and constitute a source of threat, in turn necessitating harsher responses to refugees and greater levels of militarized vigilance. Clearly, these securitized perceptions of refugees neglect the 'human security' needs of the individual refugee, even to the point of enabling states to take measures that exacerbate these individuals' insecurity. In this context, states may seek to provide a legal rationale for strategies of rejection, by labelling these individuals as 'illegal migrants' or 'non-genuine refugees'. Such characterizations can be effective in convincing domestic populations to reject responsibilities to asylum-seekers (Huysmans, 2006). Further, the rejection of these ethical responsibilities is also made possible through the selective application of legal responsibility in international law: it is ultimately still the state's prerogative to decide when international refugee law does or does not apply to people seeking entry into the state (Chalk, 1998; Dupont, 2002).

Within a traditional realist security framework, the most vulnerable – the refugee – therefore remains the most insecure. Although international refugee law is conventionally understood as constraining state power on behalf of vulnerable individuals, it is also important to note here that it is unevenly integrated into national legal frameworks and considerations, and can even exacerbate asylum-seekers' vulnerability. In this chapter I argue that there are two distinct consequences of Southeast Asian states' resistance to international refugee law. First, non-accession to the key international refugee law instruments, the 1951 Convention Relating to the Status of Refugees and the 1967 Protocol Relating to the Status of Refugees (hereafter referred to as the 1951 Convention and 1967 Protocol respectively), has enabled Southeast Asian states to argue that the instruments do not apply to their asylum-seeking populations, thus denying the legitimacy of a potential normative framework for the appropriate treatment of asylum-seekers. Because Southeast Asian states have not acceded to international refugee law or developed receptive policies towards refugees, these states are able to claim that asylum-seekers are 'illegal migrants', which is technically true. Second, the majority of Southeast Asian states have not been compelled to accede to the international refugee law instruments or take humanitarian responsibility for their asylum-seeking population. In this chapter, I argue that because refugee security is unable to be enforced through international law when it is not acceded to by states, there exists a disconnection between the law's potential and its applicability in Southeast Asia. Therefore, international refugee law is limited in being able to emancipate[1] asylum-seekers in Southeast Asia.

Emancipation in critical security studies is primarily about achieving a more equal distribution of power and influence, enabling those who cannot at present speak for themselves to represent their concerns and insecurities (Linklater, 2001: 30). In this chapter, I seek to ascertain what makes asylum-seekers insecure, through highlighting how the state and international refugee laws create and exacerbate the insecurity and suffering of these people. This chapter also attempts to identify alternative possibilities by which state responses to asylum-seekers might enhance human emancipation (Wyn Jones, 1999: 1–6). The chapter proceeds in three main parts. First, I demonstrate how Southeast Asian states have come to justify their rejection of international refugee law, and explore why these reasons have not been successfully challenged in international society. Second, I outline how the failure to ensure refugee security through the application of international refugee law has resulted in extreme insecurity of asylum-seekers in the region. Finally, I focus on the case of Malaysia, which despite its arguably more generous asylum reception policy than many of its neighbours, still remains outside the framework of international refugee law. This has been invoked to justify policies towards asylum-seekers that heighten their insecurity and demonstrate the inability of present international refugee law to compel states to protect asylum-seekers. However, the Malaysian case also sheds light on alternative, if somewhat problematic and unsatisfactory, possibilities for emancipating the vulnerable trapped within this framework of insecurity.

Southeast Asia and international refugee law

The importance of the issue of asylum in the Southeast Asian context cannot be overstated. Southeast Asia has the highest number of individuals seeking asylum from a single United Nations High Commission for Refugees (UNHCR) branch office (Malaysia) and the second highest number of asylum-seekers submitting claims for refugee status from any single country (Burma) (UNHCR, 2004a). Furthermore, Southeast Asia hosts a large number of potential asylum-seekers, who are forced to live as 'illegal migrants' because these states have no refugee recognition policy and many fear being refused refugee status by the UNHCR. Beyond the limited assistance provided by the UNHCR, there is a lack of agreed procedures and bureaucratic infrastructure in Southeast Asia for determining refugee status (Muntarbhorn, 1992). This means that most humanitarian relief is provided on an ad hoc basis. Of the 12 states in the Southeast Asian region, only 2 – Cambodia (1992) and the Philippines (1981) – have acceded to the 1951 Convention and 1967 Protocol, and neither has incorporated the international instruments into their domestic law. The Association of Southeast Asian Nations (ASEAN) has also failed to demonstrate a collective interest in creating a regional refugee instrument that would at least provide all members with a common legal or political framework for responding to refugees in the region. However, the need for either a collective ASEAN response to the region's refugee situation or a higher number of state accessions to international refugee law instruments has been recognized (see *inter alios*, Muntarbhorn, 1992; Hans and Suhrke, 1997: 99–101; Nadig, 2003: 364; UNHCR, 2003a).

The persistent rejection of international refugee law by the majority of Southeast Asian states has had a number of effects on the human security of millions of people. First, there are large populations of people in each Southeast Asian country without refugee status who are usually labelled 'illegal migrants'. These people live difficult lives, choosing not to seek refugee status from the UNHCR in case they are rejected and their presence made known to the host government (Alexander, 1999). Second, the absence of international refugee law places a large burden on the UNHCR to monitor and manage refugee flows, while conducting its own refugee status determinations whenever possible (Rosero, 2003). Third, it has created an impetus for the region's asylum-seekers to seek refuge outside the region, for instance in Europe, the US and Australia. The problem is that the UNHCR is not equipped to meet every individual asylum-seeker's claim in Southeast Asia, leaving these people vulnerable. This has resulted in people seeking asylum through the only means available, which are often 'illegal', such as utilizing people smugglers or arriving without visas. Either option in seeking entry by boat to Australia, for example, is expensive, dangerous and usually leads to long-term detention. Clearly, the question of why most Southeast Asian states have not acceded to international refugee law is an important political puzzle that has a direct impact on the human security of refugees and asylum-seekers.

The world's primary international refugee law instrument – the 1951 Convention – contains a *general* definition of the refugee. The 1951 Convention was designed to deal with *European refugees* after the end of the Second World War (Chimni, 1998). The legal instrument was a political product of Cold War concerns and its application was limited to persons who fled 'as a result of events occurring before 1 January 1951' and met other certain criteria.[2] Crucially, the 1951 Convention insisted that each refugee make an individual case for flight and that the receiving state evaluate each case on its merits. Further, each state party had the option of limiting the meaning of 'events occurring before 1 January 1951' to 'events occurring in Europe before 1 January 1951'. Evidently, the concerns addressed by the 1951 Convention were specific to European experiences and neglected African and Asian experiences and perceptions. This neglect was a product of two factors. First, because decolonization was still underway in 1951 there were very few Asian or African representatives in the preparatory discussions. As a result, a broad consensus based on European experiences was allowed to emerge. Second, even though Asian and African voices were not entirely silent, they were marginalized. This resulted, of course, in a

Eurocentric interpretation of the refugee experience which led to a very narrow, ethnocentric interpretation of the 'refugee' (Hathaway, 1992: 6).

The 1967 Protocol was in many ways a direct response to the 1951 Convention's Eurocentrism. It was created as a separate legal instrument in order to remove the temporal and geographic constraints on the 1951 Convention and to strengthen the UNHCR's presence outside of Europe. However, the Protocol retained the Convention's Eurocentric understanding of the refugee, and concerns continued to be expressed by several postcolonial states. The UNHCR itself pointed out that African and Asian experiences with refugees were quite different from the European experiences that shaped the 1951 Convention (UNHCR, 1965). One key difference was the tendency of refugee movements in Africa and Asia to involve mass influxes which was compounded by the fact that most receiving states lacked the bureaucratic infrastructure to deal with refugees in the manner prescribed by the Convention (Chatelard, 2002). Furthermore, by the time the 1967 Protocol was signed, a consensus was emerging amongst Asian states that international refugee law was flawed in at least two important respects. First, it was created in response to European problems and would not be able to address the very different refugee problems confronting the recently decolonized developing states. Second, international refugee law was widely viewed as imposing a heavy economic burden on developing states and relieving the world's wealthier states of their humanitarian responsibilities. The 1967 Protocol was a compromise between the short-term humanitarian needs of refugees and the interests of states in Europe, Africa and Asia, which effectively sidelined serious discussion about many of the key sources of tension.

In short, international refugee law developed in the 1950s and 1960s was rooted in Western values and interests. The result was that these instruments failed to reflect a genuinely inclusive global understanding of, and response to, refugees. It is hardly surprising in this context that Southeast Asian states had a limited sense of ownership of the law and felt no obligation to accede to the 1951 Convention and 1967 Protocol. Subsequently, people seeking refuge in Southeast Asia have no formal means of seeking such status and to the extent that these states have invoked international law at all, it has been in the form of selective interpretations to justify narrowly defined national interests (Davies, 2005: 29). In general, however, Southeast Asian states have challenged the legitimacy of this international law on the grounds of Eurocentrism, which has in turn weakened the law itself and reduced the costs associated with refusing to abide by it.

As noted, over time Southeast Asian states began to cite the law by using it to explain why, within the parameters of the legal framework, their irregular migrant populations were 'non-genuine' refugees. These states would legitimize their description of asylum-seekers as 'illegal migrants' or 'economic migrants' in contrast to the 'genuine' refugee as expressed in the 1951 Convention and 1967 Protocol. This has enabled a variety of practices inimical to the human security of refugees and as the next section demonstrates, has led to international refugee law being used as a justification for *not* providing a secure status to supposedly 'illegal' migrants and prevented some from seeking protection for fear of being labelled as 'illegal'.

Southeast Asia and refugee identification

The 'illegal' label has arisen because there are no refugee policies in the receiving countries. Piyasiri Wickramasekara argues that a great majority of migrants in Southeast Asia who do not meet the narrow definition of refugee are not necessarily economically motivated migrants or illegal immigrants (Wickramasekara, 2001: 37–8). The only time refugee status determination procedures are carried out in Southeast Asia is when an individual asylum-seeker approaches the UNHCR (Alexander, 1999: 251). Otherwise, the majority continue to live in uncertain situations, under 'illegal' status with the threat of deportation always hanging over their heads.

In many cases, the UNHCR's branch offices in the region have identified groups of 'illegal migrants' as being eligible for refugee status (Rosero, 2003). However, this does not resolve two important problems. First, even if a refugee is recognized by the UNHCR, it does not guarantee the refugee any rights in states that do not recognize that the status brings special rights and imposes special duties (Alexander, 1999). The most significant product of favourable refugee status determination by the UNHCR for the refugee is that they are eligible for resettlement in a third country that has acceded to the 1951 Convention – but this can take a long time (UNHCR, 2003a: 366–87). In addition, states that have acceded are *not obliged* to offer refuge to these refugees. Second, what becomes of 'illegal migrants' who are not accorded refugee status by the UNHCR? The system of refugee status determination is not foolproof, and there are many occasions where recognition has only been granted on appeal, and many more cases where it has not been granted at all. In Southeast Asia, an asylum-seeker's ability to resubmit an application dramatically decreases once their presence has been made known to the authorities (an inevitable occurrence upon seeking asylum in a UNHCR branch office). In addition, living conditions tend not to substantially improve even after being granted refugee status whilst living in Southeast Asia. The risks therefore of exposing one's presence by seeking recognition tend to outweigh the potential benefits of gaining refugee status and being resettled in a third country (Kibreab, 2003).

In Southeast Asia there are 'illegal migrant' populations in nearly every state. In recent years, the civil war in Afghanistan has contributed the highest number with Afghans believed to be located in Indonesia, Malaysia and the Philippines (UNHCR, 2000; USCR, 2002: 11). As Hazel Lang notes in her contribution to this volume, an estimated 300,000 Burmese currently reside in Thailand without refugee status, and unless in possession of one of the very few licenses to stay, are classified as illegal (USCR, 2002: 11). Many Vietnamese, Laotians and a small number of Cambodians are in a similar position in Thailand and Malaysia (USCR, 2002; UNHCR, 2004b). Malaysia and Bangladesh also receive populations from Burma. The lack of formal procedures for claiming asylum guarantees in these states also mean that the Burmese remain labelled as 'illegal migrants'.[3] The UNHCR in Malaysia receives populations seeking entry from Indonesia, Burma, Philippines and Vietnam, and it is believed that a number of people from these four countries live illegally in Malaysia (USCR, 2002; UNHCR, 2004b). Only a small number of these migrant populations seek (and therefore receive) asylum because of a widespread fear of forcible repatriation. Due to their illegal status these populations survive by working in dangerous, dirty and demanding (3D) jobs paying low wages in urban or rural areas (Wickramasekera, 2002). These dynamics are particularly evident in the case of Malaysia.

Malaysia

The Malaysian government's refusal to sign the 1951 Convention and 1967 Protocol is often explained as a manifestation of its racist attitudes (Wain, 1980; O'Connor Sutter, 1990; Suhrke, 1993; Robinson, 1998). However, careful scrutiny demonstrates that its reasons for not signing the instruments are, as with most Southeast Asian states, based on a more complicated set of concerns. With a minority Malay population since the independent state of Malaysia was created in 1963, the primary concern of the United Malays National Organisation (UMNO) which has held government since, has been to assert the 'special rights' of Malays (Berger, 2004: 35). The remaining ethnic Chinese and Indian populations, most of whom migrated to Malaysia during its period under British colonization to work the tin mines and tap the trees in rubber plantations, had citizenship rights. Post-independence, however, special privileges have been granted to the ethnic Malays (Allen, 1970: 158).

Therefore, there is some justification for the argument that Malaysia's response to refugees was reflective of a racist domestic structure. However, two points suggest otherwise. First, throughout the Indochinese refugee crisis (1975–95), Malaysia accepted high numbers of boat people and refugees, second only to Thailand (Robinson, 1998). Second, Malaysia has a strong Islamic tradition and a history of accepting refugees because of their Islamic faith (regardless of ethnicity). These actions do not reflect those of a 'racist state'. Indeed, in 1984 the UNHCR praised Malaysia for 'fully adhering to the letter and the spirit of that agreement [1979 Geneva Conference Agreement] [as] exemplary' (UNHCR, 1984a: 2). Likewise, Muntarbhorn's appraisal of Malaysia during the Indochinese refugee crisis was that generally, the 'principle of *non-refoulement* was respected'.[4] Robinson (1998: 190) agreed, suggesting that despite its policy of push-backs[5] (Malaysia was not alone in this policy, which was pursued also by all ASEAN states at the time), Malaysia 'maintained a creditable record of generosity, granting temporary asylum to more than 250,000 Vietnamese'. These responses are in marked contrast to the majority of other Southeast Asian states during the crisis. Moreover, the sheer volume of refugees who fled to and were accepted by Malaysia – the majority of whom were ethnic Chinese – questions the 'racist state' argument (Suhrke, 1993).

The primary reason why Malaysia chose not to sign the 1951 Convention or 1967 Protocol was that like its neighbours, it did not see any benefit in doing so. Malaysia formulated its own refugee response policy, which was based on religious preferences and recognition of its responsibility to provide minimal temporary asylum for all. Thus, it found more benefit in maintaining its own ad hoc practice than in signing the 1951 Convention and possibly losing control over such decisions. In 1959, the UNHCR requested that the then Federation of Malaya consider accession to the 1951 Convention. The communication noted that at the time, Malaysia's accession could provide a 'useful example' (UNHCR, 1959a) to other Asian states. It was reported though that the Federation of Malaya's response was unenthusiastic (UNHCR, 1959b). In 1969, the UNHCR's representative, William McCoy, reported on his discussion with the Malaysian government and their attitude towards the 1951 Convention and relatively new 1967 Protocol. The first point made by McCoy was that there had been a need to '*dispel some misconceptions and to clarify some misunderstandings* on the Convention and Protocol and also on the Mandate of the High Commissioner' (my emphasis) (UNHCR, 1959a: 1). McCoy reported that there was interest in the instruments, but accession 'in the near future is not probable' (UNHCR, 1959a: 1). Pressure on Malaysia by the UNHCR to sign on to the 1951 Convention and 1967 Protocol continued (unsuccessfully) throughout the 1970s, with the organization pointing in particular to benefits in relations between countries that had transparent refugee policies related to accession to international refugee law (UNHCR, 1977: 1).

Malaysia's continued reluctance to accede to the 1951 Convention and the 1967 Protocol was partly driven by the principle of non-interference in the domestic affairs of other ASEAN states, central to ASEAN's Treaty of Amity and Cooperation (TAC). Under TAC, the non-interference norm was widely considered tantamount to preventing criticism of a neighbouring state, or providing any form of support to any splinter group which may be destabilizing a member state (Acharya, 2001: 58). However, the 1951 Convention requires that a refugee be identified by a *legitimate* claim of persecution from their state of origin. Such recognition would be understood as interfering with the norms that TAC tried to institute in ASEAN in 1976. Thus, Malaysia's provision of asylum to its neighbouring countries' citizens is worth evaluating further in light of the TAC and their refusal to align their provision of refuge with the 1951 Convention and 1967 Protocol.

Since the early 1970s, Malaysia has had a history of allowing predominantly Muslim people to seek refuge. However, such populations were not provided with formal refugee status. The following three examples of Malaysia's response to asylum-seekers from the Philippines, Cambodia and Indochina, nonetheless suggest the possibility for emancipation. Emancipation 'involves the lifting of scope restrictions and greater sensitivity to radically different world views' (Linklater, 2001: 30), and in doing so to discover 'immanent, unrealised or unfulfilled possibilities within the reality of any given order' (Wyn Jones, 1999: 25). So while Malaysia's current relationship with asylum-seekers is understood as a strict 'rejection' relationship, as the following cases reveal, there is the possibility for alternative responses to asylum-seekers that do not involve immediate rejection.

Filipino asylum-seekers

Between 1972 and 1985 the Malaysian state of Sabah gave citizenship to between 40,000 to 90,000 Muslim Filipinos[6] who were fleeing an armed conflict between the predominantly Christian Philippine state and the Muslim separatist group, the Moro National Liberation Front, in the Mindanao Islands. Malaysia was in essence sheltering people that were either by religious or direct association part of a separatist group that had encouraged the Philippine government to declare martial law (McKenna, 1998). The fact that the West Malaysian state of Sabah accepted this group as refugees was therefore not well received by the Philippine government (Zolberg *et al.*, 1989: 175). However, these people were not given formal refugee status by the Malaysian government (although the UNHCR and Sabah local government did grant them refugee status) and a large proportion was portrayed as simply fulfilling a labour shortage that existed in the state at the time (Rachagan, 1987; UNGA, 1985). Malaysia has never had domestic legislation providing asylum-seeking or refugee status procedures (UNHCR, 2003b: 1). Therefore, a person arriving in Malaysia without a permit, pass or on 'special compassionate grounds' was still considered an illegal migrant (Rachagan, 1987: 253).

These laws eventually hindered the Filipinos in 1985, when the Sabah government changed hands from an Islamic majority to a Christian-based party. The Kadazan Party revoked the liberal residence permits. As a result, up to 58,000 Filipinos in Sabah remain without citizenship status, which would, if granted, provide them with more security of residence (UNHCR, 2003b: 2). What the Filipino Muslim case demonstrates is that although the Malaysian government allows refuge to be sought in its territory, it does not want to provide anything *more than* that to the population. Moreover, it simultaneously took measures to uphold the TAC in its relationship with the Philippines. This is evidenced by the fact that though Malaysia allowed Sabah to provide refuge to those seeking asylum from Mindanao, it also took steps to block Libyan attempts to place the discussion of the Muslim uprising in the Philippines on the agenda of the Organisation of Islamic Conference (OIC) during the 1970s.

What is important about the Filipino case is that it does not demonstrate a complete rejection of the refugee population per se, rather that Malaysia continually rejected the idea that these groups be defined as refugees according to international refugee law. As will be discussed further below, this suggests possibilities that exist in Malaysia, and Southeast Asian states in general, towards populations if emphasis is placed on the provision of non-persecutory asylum as opposed to a formal provision of refugee status. The possibilities that this could provide for asylum-seekers are further demonstrated in the Cambodian Muslim case below.

Cambodian Muslim asylum-seekers

In 1975 Malaysia accepted 1,275 Cambodian Muslims who had fled the Pol Pot regime, and during the Indochinese refugee crisis Malaysia continued to allow a select number of Cambodian Muslims to integrate locally. By 1992, it was estimated that 10,000 Cambodian Muslims had been allowed to settle in Malaysia, assisted by the Malaysian Muslim Welfare Organisation (PEKIM) which received funding from the UNHCR and the Malaysian government. In the early 1980s, Malaysia also permitted the local settlement of a small number of Rohinga Muslims fleeing Burma and Acehnese Muslims fleeing the violence from Indonesia (UNHCR, 2003b: 2).

In these contexts, the Malaysian government has allowed people to seek refuge at the risk of breaching the TAC. Malaysia has been able to strike a balance between solidarity with other Muslims and adherence to the TAC.

This balanced approach may not be in accordance with the 1951 Convention, but it suits Malaysia and has the potential to suit those wishing to seek asylum without fear of being labelled 'illegal'. Robinson (1998: 283) quotes the director of PERKIM:

> I don't think this country is interested in proclaiming itself as a haven for Muslims around the world . . . The government will not accede to the Refugee Convention but it needs to recognize that selected groups are in need of protection and assistance. Sri Lankans, Burmese Rohingyas, Bosnians have a case. There are also others who are not Muslims but who say their lives are in danger. Do we treat them simply as illegals and deport them? Generally, the government does not do this but they have not recognized them as refugees either.

The first thing to note here is that the Cambodian Muslims accepted in Malaysia during the same period were not Malay – they were Cambodian. This point is emphasized to cast further doubt on the idea that Malaysia's refugee policy was racist. Though racial issues certainly played a part, they were not Malaysia's primary concern and thus do not explain Malaysia's refusal to provide a secure refugee status to asylum-seekers. Rather, the emphasis on international refugee law reveals that it is unable to secure asylum-seekers emancipation in Malaysia.

Indochinese refugee crisis

During most of the Indochinese refugee crisis, Malaysia's level of cooperation was considered 'exemplary' by the Malaysia branch office of the UNHCR until at least 1987, when Indochinese refugee numbers rose again (UNHCR, 1984a: 2). Significantly, Malaysia provided cooperation only on the condition that all Vietnamese boat people were resettled in third countries. Overall the UNHCR considered Malaysia's upholding of the agreement to continue providing temporary asylum as an attitude that was 'all the more praiseworthy in the face of confirmed and persistent reports of pushbacks practiced elsewhere in the region by states which have assumed similar commitments as Malaysia to grant the boatpeople a temporary refuge' (UNHCR, 1984a: 2). For instance, when resettlement numbers declined during the 1980s, states such as Thailand and Indonesia refused to rescue boat people, or allow passing cargo ships that had rescued people often drowning in leaky boats, to dock on their ports. As a result, many asylum-seekers during this time died of drowning and at the hands of pirate attacks as ships would be told to refuse rescue to boat people (UNSEC, 1984: 11).

The main position taken by Malaysia was that they should not be expected to take all those who sought asylum for permanent refuge. Malaysia argued that the Indochinese refugee problem was not one that only

Southeast Asia should have to solve. Rather it was 'incumbent upon all countries . . . to work towards a solution of the problem, particularly through speedier resettlement and by attacking the problem at its roots' (UNGA, 1982: 7). Although Malaysia's Indochinese refugee population fluctuated, during the early 1980s the UNHCR rarely reported concern about whether Malaysian cooperation would continue (UNGA, 1985). In fact, Malaysia often took the boats that Thailand had pushed back from their shores (Muntabhorn, 1992: 114). As indicated, Malaysia had the highest number of Indochinese boat people throughout the crisis, second only to Thailand in terms of total refugee numbers, yet their provision of protection was one that the UNHCR derived most assurance from (UNHCR, 1984a). Malaysia's overriding concern in this context was that it not be expected to provide limitless asylum (UNGA, 1982).

Malaysia's refusal to sign the 1951 Convention was primarily instrumental. The Malaysian government continued to demonstrate a reluctance to sign the instruments for a number of reasons. First, the lack of accession allowed Malaysia to act more freely and in a way of its own choosing (UNHCR, 1984a). The Malaysian government believed that it had a sovereign right to decide how its state was run, who could enter and who could not. If the Malaysian government subscribed to the UNHCR's legal instruments, it believed that it would lose this independence. Second, the need to maintain sovereign independence in the treatment of asylum-seekers becomes all the more evident when observing to whom Malaysia was providing asylum – often citizens from neighbouring states (UNHCR, 1984b). The ad hoc provision of asylum was substantially different to the 1951 Convention, where granting refugee status would require Malaysia to essentially declare that its neighbours were mistreating their citizens and breach the conditions of TAC. The third reason for Malaysia's refusal to accede was that it did not wish to provide asylum to all who entered. Under this regime, not even Muslim asylum-seekers were guaranteed inalienable rights. The Malaysian government afforded itself considerable room for manoeuvre by not acceding to international refugee law. For instance, in the case of the Filipino Muslims, approximately 48,000 are yet to be granted citizenship (UNHCR, 2003b). The Filipinos, like the Acehnese and the Rohingya Muslims, were welcomed in the 1980s when the need for labour made their presence more welcome (UNHCR, 2003b). However, as labour patterns have shifted, these groups – in spite of their shared Muslim identity – are no longer any more secure than the Vietnamese refugees. They are also now subject to arrest, detention and forced deportation (UNHCR, 2003b: 1–2).

By refusing to accede to or even recognize international refugee law instruments, the Malaysian government freely positions and re-positions its migrant population. The Acehnese, Rohingya Muslims and Chins from Burma – welcome in the 1980s – had by the late 1990s had become categorized as 'illegal' migrants by the Malaysian authorities (Rachagan, 1987). The UNHCR has protested and made public announcements alerting the Malaysian authorities to the possibility that these people may be 'persons of concern', but has been unable to prevent a number of deportations since the late 1990s. The lack of state institutions 'responsible for protection, assistance or solutions for asylum seekers and refugees' leave most 'subject to arrest, detention and deportation' (UNHCR, 2003b: 1). For instance, in August and September 2003, hundreds of asylum-seekers waiting entry into the UNHCR Kuala Lumpur branch office were arrested as 'illegal' migrants. In March 2005, the UNHCR attempted to secure the release of over a dozen 'illegals' from Aceh and Burma before they were deported. The 400,000 'illegals' who had sought work in Malaysia experience a tumultuous time where they fulfil clear labour needs, but the failure to provide them with asylum means they are labelled as illegal and are constantly vulnerable to deportation (Kent, 2005). Without the ability to seek refugee status or even claim asylum, most are forced to live in these precarious circumstances.

Possibilities

The Malaysian case demonstrates that international refugee law is not currently being used as a resource (or normative-legal framework) for the protection of asylum-seekers in Southeast Asia. Rather, the language of 'illegal' migrants and 'non-genuine' refugees is used to *legitimize* the representation of these people as undesirable and outside the law, in contrast to what international society understands as a 'genuine' refugee. Therefore, international refugee law has not been able to present its purpose to Southeast Asian states and failed to be of protective use for asylum-seekers. The provision of social welfare and legal protection based on meeting a particular definition of 'refugee', as expected under the 1951 Convention, has been rejected by the majority of Southeast Asian states. However, what has not been completely rejected by these states is the provision of non-persecutory asylum, as demonstrated in the Malaysian case. At the moment, neither the 1951 Convention nor the 1967 Protocol has a specific provision for the right to asylum. But the Universal Declaration of Human Rights, which all states recognize in order to be members of the United Nations, does contain this right. A Declaration on Territorial Asylum was adopted by the United Nations General Assembly on 14 December 1967, however attempts in the 1970s to have this declaration developed into Convention status failed. Yet this failure does not mean that the adoption of regional provisions is impossible in Southeast Asia. An emphasis on non-persecutory asylum as opposed to refugee status opens up the potential for these states to continue to refuse refugee protection and avoid criticizing neighbouring states treatment of their citizens, while enabling the insecure to live in these states without the label of 'illegal' migrant. The core obligation sought in granting asylum at this stage would be to end forced refoulement, with the hope that provisions for social services, education and even citizenship might be granted at a later date. The emancipatory imperative at this stage is to end illegal migrants' perpetual insecurity in Southeast Asian states.

Conclusion

International refugee law currently provides the most commonly referred to, but certainly not unproblematic, framework of legitimization for an illegal migrant's entry into a host state, and the label that is afforded to an entrant is a central determinant of how they will be treated. Southeast Asian states' rejection of international refugee law instruments has resulted in people not being able to seek refuge in the region, and pointed to the failure of international legal instruments to ensure the protection of those the law was designed to protect (Soguk, 1999).

Of course, we may ask more fundamental questions of the process of identifying or recognizing asylum-seekers and refugees: whose identification of these groups as refugees do we rely on, and to whom does it matter? In practice, recognition is constitutive of refugee status, and recognition in general is, as Axel Honneth has argued, the foundation of emancipation and emancipatory potential (cited in Wyn Jones, 2005). Globally, the process of refugee recognition is both political and legal. This fact is given heightened importance in Southeast Asia because international refugee law has not been integrated domestically within states in the region, either through internal acceptance of the legitimacy of this law or external compulsion to adhere to it.

The protection of asylum-seekers is dependent upon political actors recognizing the sanctity of international refugee law, which calls upon asylum-seekers not to be immediately refouled until their refugee status is determined. As a result, if a state or collective number of states chooses not to recognize international refugee law, asylum-seekers can be labelled 'illegal migrants' or 'non-genuine' refugees and granted few, if any, human rights and privileges.[7] In Southeast Asia asylum-seekers are therefore not able to *seek asylum* and thus while there is security for states in this response, there is none for the asylum-seekers. This chapter has revealed that there is emancipatory potential for asylum-seekers, as the case of Malaysia shows, but this requires a radical reconceptualization of what we expect of international refugee law. Those seeking asylum need the provision of asylum without persecution and there is the potential for Southeast Asian states to grant this and the language of 'illegal' migrant to no longer have any meaning. Currently the politics of international refugee law renders the most vulnerable even more insecure in Southeast Asia. However, in seeing the concerns of Southeast Asian states in conjunction with asylum-seekers' needs in this region – we see the emancipatory possibility in non-persecutory asylum. Awareness of what international refugee law has failed to do for asylum-seekers in Southeast Asia allows us to see what states are willing to provide so that asylum-seekers can live in host states without fear. This recognition does not spell the end for international law or states, but the beginning for refugees' emancipation in Southeast Asia.

Notes

1 Here, I use Ken Booth's (1999: 41) definition of 'emancipation' not as a state of being, but as 'the condition of becoming'.

2 The 1951 Convention stated that the term refugee shall apply to any person who: 'As a result of events occurring before 1 January 1951 and owing to well-founded fear of persecution for reasons of race, religion, nationality, membership of a particular social group or political opinion, is outside the country of his nationality and is unable or, owing to such fear, is unwilling to avail himself of the protection of that country; or who, not having a nationality and being outside the country of his former habitual residence as a result of such events, is unable or, owing to such fear, is unwilling to return to it.'

3 Malaysia's asylum-seeking numbers, as with the majority of Southeast Asian countries, are not provided with a 'breakdown' of nationalities that comprise the total number. Nor is the total number of refugees/asylum-seekers completely indicative of the actual situation, for the numbers mentioned are only of those who sought asylum through UNHCR.

4 Muntarbhorn (1992: 119). *Non-refoulement* is a key principle of international law (see Article 33 of the 1951 Convention) and specifies that a person who seeks asylum and is then determined to be a refugee, cannot be returned or *refouled* to the country they originated from.

5 Push-backs involved the forced removal of boats carrying asylum-seekers from domestic water back into international water.

6 Muntarbhorn (1992: 115) says that there were between 60,000 and 80,000, while Robinson (1998: 283) says that there have been 50,000.

7 Law is conceived here as a 'powerful, rhetorical tool' that shapes political decisions. See Kratochwil (2000: 45).

10

Discourses of security in China: towards a critical turn?

Yongjin Zhang

CRITICAL SECURITY STUDIES', either as 'an issue area study' within the discipline of international relations (Booth, 2005a: 16) or as 'a call to develop self-consciously critical approaches to security' (Neufeld, 2004: 109), is said to have mounted a formidable challenge to the problematic of the prevailing orthodoxy in security studies in the last decade or so. It has generated a wide range of scholarship, so much so that Ken Booth claims recently that critical security studies 'has established an institutionalised life of its own, with courses and programs in a number of universities, as well as a steadily growing body of research'. He argues that it remains 'a subject without much explicit literature', having achieved 'an academic presence that exceeds what has been written in its name' (Booth, 2005b: vii–viii).

To what extent are such claims true of security studies as a field of enquiry *globally*? Can similar claims be made of critical intervention in security studies outside Europe? Has this alternative, and indeed antithetical, approach to the orthodoxy in security studies – either characterized as that of 'problem-solving' or that of 'political realism' – established its own institutional life in the Asia-Pacific?

In this chapter, I interrogate the above questions through an examination of recent security discourses in China, using 'critical' lenses provided by 'two main streams' of critical security studies identified by Steve Smith (2005). While identifying governmental discourses of security, the focus is particularly on discourses of security as elaborated by Chinese security analysts in the academic community. More specifically, I argue here that these 'academic' discourses are inexorably bound up with the preferences and interests of the Chinese government, and underpinned by mainstream academic thinking on security. As such, security discourses in Chinese academia reflect an absence of critical reflection on core questions of security (such as 'security for whom?') that can be understood within two particular contexts. One is the context of the hegemonic orthodoxy of traditional neo-realist approaches to security; and the other, the context in which governmental interests condition academic debate about Chinese security preferences. Even apparently 'alternative' readings of security, then, are ultimately discourses of, and for, the powerful.

An analysis of contemporary Chinese debates on security is important for a number of reasons. First, it is not just because China is a rising power, but also and more importantly because the Chinese state today has a profound sense of insecurity. A critical examination of security discourses of and for an insecure power goes a long way to address the question of what impedes the shift from a focus on militarism and statism embedded in traditional security studies to that on individuals, community and identity advocated by critical security studies.[1] Second, China has recently experienced a fundamental transformation from an isolated revolutionary power to an increasingly globalized state.[2] Yet it remains a non-democratic state. Such a transformation of the state imposes changing perceptions of threat and induces different practices of security. And third, China is still perceived as a major problematic for regional and global security. How such a perception influences the Chinese outlook on its security environment, and subsequently debates about security conceptions and practices, is a crucial question in understanding the potential for the arrival of critical scholarship in security studies in China.

Contextualizing security discourses in China

The political moment symbolized by the end of the Cold War and the subsequent systemic transformation of international relations have had a paradoxical impact on Chinese conceptions of security and the assessment of China's security environment. Such conceptions and assessments are further complicated by the unprecedented economic transformation of China, a revolutionary process that shapes and constitutes a new form of the Chinese state. If the production of discourse is a matter of political choice, with pre-existing understandings of history, culture and identity serving to constitute the realm of that choice, state transformation of China and identity politics in international relations after the end of the Cold War are two important contexts that condition security debates and discourse production in China.

State transformation

The transformation of China from a revolutionary power to a reformist state in the 1980s has long been noted (Zhang, 1998; Zheng 2004). The implications of such transformation of the Chinese state for national security have only recently been teased out more explicitly. During the Maoist period, when China was unequivocally a revolutionary power, Nan Li (2001: 18) argues, there had been a hegemonic class-based, transnational revolutionary discourse, which took socio-economic class, not the nation-state, as 'the central category defining internal identity, organization and security, and external insecurity, threat and struggle'. Li notes that the military's security discourse in the 1980s involved a particular attempt to construct or restore the nation-state as the 'central category'. Assuming the identity of a nation-state naturally dictates China to focus on the preservation of the nation-state (rather than individuals within it) and to formulate and implement its security policies with the considerations of an often narrowly defined set of 'national interests' at heart. Chinese security analysts claimed that such a shift is 'an inescapable choice for any country intending to join the ranks of great powers' and it was therefore necessary for China 'to strengthen research on national interests and clarify how such interests dictate the status, role and functions, and tasks of national defence' (Li, 2001: 18).

What Li fails to note is an unexpected implication of China's shift from revolutionary internationalism to conservative nationalism. China's enthusiastic embrace of the 'national interest' as central in governing its foreign and security policy-making was meant to signal the changing world-view of a revisionist power and the 'normalization' of a revolutionary state. Instead, it was soon to be seen as evidence of China's realpolitik view and reactionary outlook on world politics in the context of the post-Cold War transformation in international relations (Christensen, 1996; Deng, 1999). Debates within China in the mid-1990s on China's national interests, surrounding the publication of *An Analysis of China's National Interests* written by Yan Xuetong (1996), would further entrench such a perception.

The Chinese state is undergoing another profound transformation, linked to the government's desire to be embedded in the global market economy. In order to accommodate the exigencies of the global economy, the Chinese government has adopted commonly accepted norms, principles and standards in its domestic economic system. The 'forms' of Chinese state, in other words, have changed. This new form of the state has already informed the redefinition of security, interests and threat for the Chinese state and in the academic community. The prominence of economic security and energy security in the discourse of non-traditional security, as will be discussed later, must be understood in this context.

Insecurity and threat perceptions

Identity politics surrounding the end of the Cold War complicated the Chinese government's assessment of its international security environment.

Geopolitically, Chinese elites readily acknowledge that the end of the Cold War significantly reduced the likelihood of interstate violence in the international system. The disintegration of the Soviet Union and continued improvement of Sino-American relations have helped to remove immediate military threats along the Chinese borders. The People's Republic, many argue, has a largely benign military security environment for the first time since its establishment.[3] They are also keenly aware, however, that the non-democratic China, as the 'last bastion of communism' and the 'remaining Leninist state', has been increasingly cast as the 'other' in the construction of a collective identity of the West.[4] This conception underpins most claims of the inherent threat posed by a 'rising China' and the raging debates in the United States in the 1990s on alternative strategies to contain, to engage, or to constrain the rise of China (Shinn, 1996; Shambaugh, 1996; Segal, 1996; Goldstein, 1997). This debate, as will be noted, has played a significant role in conditioning academic debates *within* China as to its role and interests in global security politics.

For the leadership of the Chinese Community Party (CCP), the casting of China as a 'rising threat' constitutes an ultimate challenge to its rule and legitimacy. It follows that there is a deep sense of unease among the CCP leadership in particular about a strategy of 'peaceful evolution' allegedly orchestrated by the United States for democratic changes in China. A series of incidents in Sino-American relations in the late 1990s, particularly the bombing of the Chinese embassy in Belgrade and the successful military projection of American power in Kosovo, have reinforced an acute sense of insecurity and encouraged a popular sentiment about the meaning of American power: as a scheme to contain China globally (Sun and Cui, 1996; Yan, 2000).[5]

From both perspectives, what helps define debates about the 'China threat' is not so much China's rising power but the nature of the Chinese state. Even Michael Doyle could not resist the temptation of wading into the debate about China's possible threat to (liberal) peace. The prospect of China becoming the largest economy in the world under the conditions of globalization in 2020, in his words, 'should make everyone content' from an economic point of view. He continues:

> But from a geopolitical point of view, China's growth entails a massive shift of world political power eastward. That makes the statesmen of the US and Europe nervous, especially, if . . . China has not democratised [by then]. (Doyle, 2000: 90)

Many liberal analysts outside China would probably share Doyle's ambivalence about the implications of China's intensive engagement with economic globalization for global security, if the Chinese polity remains undemocratic.

Two security discourses in China: a critical anatomy

Given the profound state transformation that China has been going through and the acute sense of insecurity for the Chinese regime and the Chinese state, it is perhaps not surprising that over the last decade or so, there have been exciting and contentious debates within China on national security and on the emerging global order (Pillsbury, 2000; Garrett, 2001; Ye, 2004). Two security discourses, the discourse of multipolarity and the non-traditional security discourse, are particularly dominant. They stand out as reflective of mainstream academic thinking about the theory and practice of security in China, also reinforced significantly in governmental security discourses. A critical anatomy of these two discourses illustrates that discourses of security in China remain a fertile ground of dispute and confusion, and that there is a clear deficit of Chinese scholarly engagement with critical security studies.

The discourse of multipolarity: beyond new geopolitics

In search of an emerging global order after the end of the Cold War, Wyn Jones (1999: 93) once claimed, 'we are travelling without maps'. Indeed, for Simon Dalby, the intellectual disorientation in North America about the future order is compellingly illustrated in various striking claims from 'clash of civilizations' by Samuel Huntington to 'a new geopolitical game in the global chessboard' by Zbigniew Brzezinski, 'the coming anarchy' by Robert Kaplan and 'the domination by global corporation' by Richard Barnett and John Cavanagh, among others. In a more descriptive characterization of the period, Dalby commented ruefully that the period 'is still defined in terms of a pervious era', which suggests 'a period in which geopolitical identities are in flux and a period in which there is no hegemonic understanding of the world order and the roles that particular states play' (Dalby, 2000: 1).

Such geopolitical uncertainty about the future is as perplexing to Chinese analysts and the policy establishment as it is bewildering to their counterparts in North America. The acute sense of insecurity of the Chinese political establishment, however, has prompted an internal debate about the so-called 'new international security environment' for China. Central to this debate is a discourse concerning the emerging multipolarity through which Chinese analysts offer their own understanding of the coming world order (Pillsbury 2000; Johnston; 2003; Ye, 2004).

The 'multipolarity discourse' is a dynamic and ongoing discourse about the future configuration of power in the international system (*guoji geju*) with a diverse range of views and pluralistic perspectives.[6] At face value, the multipolarity discourse focuses on a debate on 'an objective trend' in global politics. More specifically, it is about what constitutes a pole; how many poles there are and might be; who they are; whether a decline of the American power is likely to lead to multipolarization; where China is situated in current or future multipolar orders; and whether a multipolar world represents a normative good. While a broad and delicate consensus is said to have been reached among Chinese scholars,[7] it is interesting to note that these ongoing debates increasingly challenge the officially sanctioned presumptions that multipolarization and multipolarity is not only desirable for China, but also constitutes a normative good for the new global geopolitics. It asks whether the wider international community accepts such presumptions. It questions the unqualified claim of the decline of American power. And it is unhappy with the characterization of a 'turbulent transition' from unipolarity to multipolarity as an open-ended process.[8]

At the heart of this discourse is a dynamic understanding of American power, and ever-changing interpretations of the meaning of American power. Chinese analysts seem to be more concerned with how American power confronts Chinese power than how it defines the systemic configuration of power in the future order. As Dalby (2000: 2) acutely observes, '[s]ecurity is usually a political *desideratum* well before it is an analytical category'.[9] For the Chinese government, the political desiderata of security are uncompromising and indisputable. The Cold War confrontations are unending from the Taiwan Straits to the Korean peninsula, and a hub-and-spoke formation of the American military alliances, especially between the United States and Japan, persists in the Asia-Pacific. The security dilemma for China is unrelenting also because of the 'Cold War mentality' manifested mostly clearly in the American policies towards China. These concerns are reflected in Beijing's policy agenda and ultimately underpin broader security discourses within China.

Any global projection of American power, successful or otherwise, therefore, constantly throws Chinese assessments of the multipolarization of the emerging order into flux. The NATO strikes on Yugoslavia and its intervention in Kosovo, for example, has led to a revisionist reading of American power and a more pessimistic view of multipolarization. Following the NATO (North Atlantic Treaty Organization) operation in Kosovo, Wang Zhuxun (1999) argues in *Liaowang* (Outlook Weekly), the most influential Chinese weekly on world affairs, that the United States as the sole superpower,

> occupies a relative prominent, single, superpower position of domination. . . . Right now multipolarization has lost its momentum for 'accelerated development'. Multipolarization in history may be more complicated and tortuous than once thought. . . . The early part of the 21st century may see a situation characterized by 'single power domination, and pluralistic disputes'.

The war against Saddam Hussein's Iraq, on the other hand, has inspired different assessments of the American power. It is true that the invasion demonstrated formidable hard (military) power of the United States and its determination to go it alone. Chinese analysts argue, however, that the failure of the United States to legitimate its actions through the United Nations Security Council, combined with its broader preference for unilateralism, has undermined its 'soft power': an indispensable component of American power in asserting the US hegemony. Its subsequent military occupation of Iraq further exposes serious limitations of hard power of the United States in solving the stubborn problems in the Middle East (Yuan, 2003).

One recent discussion of multipolarization is of special interest in our discussions here. Four popularist writers teamed together in late 2004 and published their conversations on the future multipolar world order entitled *The Coming of a New Warring States Era* (Wang *et al.*, 2004). The fact that the book is published by Xinhua Publishing House, a subsidiary of the official Xinhua News Agency, is a strong indication of the government sanction of the publication.[10]

The Coming of a New Warring States Era harks back to the image of the warring states periods in ancient China and projects the arrival of 'a new era of warring states' in future international relations. It claims that the war against Iraq is a prelude to 'a global transformation that would only take place in every one thousand years'. It argues that coming 'new warring states' are not defined principally by geopolitics, but by currency zones (*huobi quan*) and monetary and financial sphere of domination (*jinrong quan*). Great powers are vying for the so-called 'currency hegemony' (*huobi baquan*) because the 'American model of hegemony' is effectively economic hegemony supported by military hegemony. It speculates on equilibrium in a different global order in the future, the defining feature of which is not a balance of power among sovereign states, or among any political or financial alliances of nation-states, but a balance among non-governmental organizations (NGOs), global multinational corporations and sovereign states. It sees the world not evolving into unipolarity (as the United States can no longer effectively exert its hegemony), but into three spheres of influence defined by the possible shrinking dominance of the US dollar around the world, the maturity and expansion of the euro zone, and the forthcoming Asian economic zone led by monetary and financial integration of China, Japan and Korea.[11]

Such bold claims and speculations can be considered as either continued disorientation or an innovative reading by Chinese analysts about the future global order. This discussion, however, does take a tentative step to move the multipolarity discourse out of militarism and traditional geopolitics.

Though not perhaps self-conscious, the convergence of a discourse of globalization with that of multipolarity has produced a new security agenda for both academic enquiry and policy considerations.[12]

Of course, central to the multipolarity discourse are great-power relations, particularly between China and the United States (Shen, 2005). Chinese officials and analysts are, however, increasingly careful not to pitch multipolarity as a hostile challenge to the hegemony or primacy of the United States. They are keen to present multipolarization as 'antithetical to the self-help, unilateralist approach to security and development associated with traditional great-power game' (Deng and Moore, 2004: 123).

The discourse of non-traditional security: widening but not deepening

Until a few years ago, the discourse of non-traditional security remained largely marginalized in China, a state dominated by traditional security concerns from tensions across the Taiwan Straits to territorial disputes in the East and South China Seas. It has gained some prominence as a coherent and separate discourse only recently, as issues such as environmental degradation, drug trafficking, people smuggling, and transnational crime came to be considered as security issues in the minds of policy-makers and in academic discussions. In contrast to the multipolarity discourse, it is a less contentious discourse and promises unequivocally to expand the security agenda beyond the traditional fixation on military security and strategy of sovereign states. It is a discourse that both stimulates and is stimulated by an alternative understanding of the meaning of security and threat in the twenty-first century.

The Chinese government has long-standing concerns about 'transnational threats' such as environmental degradation and people smuggling as well as internal security problems caused by secessionism and social unrest. In the mid-1990s, these issues entered into the security discourse first within the framework of the Council for Security and Cooperation in the Asia-Pacific (CSCAP) as integral to a concept of comprehensive security.[13] The Asian financial crisis in the late 1990s highlighted China's economic and financial vulnerability to global capital and unregulated market. The new security concept pronounced by the Chinese leadership in the middle of the crisis incorporates firmly the idea of economic security, calling for regional and global efforts to jointly create a stable and secure external economic environment. This new thinking about security reflects the recognition that with its ongoing economic transformation and changing regional and global security context, China has diversified security interests, which are much broader than the single pursuit of militarized security that China used to pursue.

After the terrorist attacks of 11 September 2001 on the United States, terrorism and religious extremism were seen as the most challenging non-traditional security threat, even while (as Matt McDonald argues in his chapter in this volume) the government at times invoked these 'increased concerns' to justify taking a hard line against secessionist groups. In its evaluation of the international security situation, China's 2002 defence white paper warned that 'non-traditional security issues are looming large in some countries' and that threats to world security are 'diversifying and globalising' (Information Office of the State Council, 2002). In an official paper submitted to a US–China cooperation forum, it is further declared that

> [t]errorism, illicit drug(s), HIV/AIDS, piracy, illegal migration, environmental security, economic security, information security and other non-traditional security issues are more pronounced. The hallmark of these issues is that they are, in most cases, trans-national or trans-regional and are detrimental to the stability of all countries. (Garrett and Adams, 2004)

The Declaration on Cooperation on Non-traditional Security Issues jointly made by China and the Association of Southeast Asian Nations (ASEAN) in November 2002 promises close cooperation on a wide range of non-traditional security issues.[14] Well before that, and at a different regional security forum, the Shanghai Cooperation Organization (SCO), China persuaded its members, Russia and five central Asian republics, to pledge their cooperation in fighting three evil forces: terrorism, separatism and extremism.

It was perhaps the SARS epidemic that erupted in China in 2003 that helped to collapse the final political and intellectual resistance to including non-military threats on the security agenda. For most Chinese security analysts, two broad lessons have been learned from SARS. One is that the traditional approach to security, though still central in China's geopolitical concerns, is incapable of dealing with new sources of contemporary threats and insecurity. And the other is that 'non-traditional threats can imperil China's security environment and strike China's vital interests in social stability, national unity, and economic development' (Deng and Moore, 2004: 128). On the extensive security agenda, as it is generally agreed now, there are six principal categories of non-traditional security threats to China's security environment. These are related to financial security, environmental security, information security, epidemics, demographical changes, and secessionism (Su *et al.*, 2004).

Even the Chinese military has acknowledged and accepted that the considerations of national security should include non-traditional security issues. In a recent speech, for example, General Xiong Guangkai (2005) emphasized that non-traditional security threats are 'new challenges to the peace and stability of the world'. He highlighted also the intertwining nature of traditional and non-traditional threats.[15]

Why then has 'non-traditional security' as both a new generic concept and analytical term gained such an ascendance in Chinese academic and political security debates? Here, political interests and changing security conceptions are intimately related. First, the dichotomy pitching traditional against non-traditional security does not challenge the continued importance or more importantly the central assumptions of traditional security, i.e. the centrality of the security of the state in terms of military, sovereign and territorial threats. Second, defining a whole diverse range of sources of insecurity against traditional security does not only highlight their distinction, but also the intertwined nature of threats. As Julie Gilson argues in her contribution to this book, such a conception paradoxically can be viewed as reaffirming the state. Usually in the Chinese government's discourse, such concerns about insecurity continue to be discussed in terms of threats to 'national security' and the state continues to be perceived as central to the solution of all non-traditional security problems.

Third, it conveniently subsumes human security, and the potential challenges its discourse poses to the state as referent object of security, under the 'non-traditional' security framework. The Chinese discourse has consistently resisted the very foundational insight of human security, namely, that sometimes the state may constitute the very threat to its population (Yu, 2004; Geng, 2004). Despite China's professed interests in the nexus between development and non-traditional security, the 1995 United Nations Development Programme (UNDP) report on human security does not seem to have provided significant stimulus for China's discourse on non-traditional security. Subsuming human security under non-traditional security reduces the need to problematize the Chinese state.[16] Finally, such a generic term is useful to masquerade a political agenda. Internal secessionist demands and separatist movements can now be conveniently categorized as non-traditional security threats. The legitimation of national unity policies concerning Taiwan as a traditional security problem can now be applied to this non-traditional dimension as well.

The discourse of non-traditional security in China has been largely prompted by a series of crises, domestic and international. The broadening of the security studies agenda, if any, under the umbrella of non-traditional security has been dominated by considerations of policy concerns of the state (He, 2004). It has been very much a top-down process of rethinking security, even while reflected in academic debates. There has so far been little reflection on the politics behind it. Neither has there been any serious intellectual interrogation of the political role that security analysts play in such a discourse. It is a long march from here towards an understanding that 'attitudes and behaviour in relation to security are derivative of underlying and contested theories about the nature of world politics' (Booth, 2005a: 14). Certainly, the power dynamics and political interests inherent in these debates appear fundamentally inconsistent with a critical security studies project.

Power, scholarship and the deficit of critical engagement

If the foregoing anatomy of the two security discourses in China exposes a clear deficit of critical scholarly engagement with security studies in China, how to explain this deficit? Power matters, of course. But in what sense can such attitudes and behaviour in relation to security be regarded as derivative of power? In which way does power discipline the scholarship in this particular instance?

Power and the political project of legitimation

Security discourse is always a political project, either explicitly or implicitly (Eriksson, 1999a, 1999b). 'The distinction between scholarly analysis and legitimisation practice in discussions of security', in Dalby's words, is 'very blurred' (Dalby, 2000: 2). Different notions of security are imagined to serve different political projects. Security discourse, therefore, plays a distinctive role, enabling or constraining, in policy-making, implementation and legitimation. What are the political projects behind these two discourses? In what sense do they serve the interest of political power?

It is no coincidence that two dominant security discourses in China in the last decade have been the discourse of multipolarity and the non-traditional security discourse. The two discourses per se are not necessarily officially orchestrated. However, there is no doubt that they are officially directed. This does not mean naked interference by power. It does mean that these discourses are heavily dictated by the security policy agenda of the state, often predetermined, which sets the parameters of debates and determines central analytical questions for those discourses. It also means it is important to recognize that it is political choice that decides that multipolarity is a normative good, and that human security should be subsumed under the label of non-traditional security.

The official dictates from the Chinese government for the discourse of multipolarity are the changing power relationship between great powers, particularly between China and the United States. The underlying political project is to legitimize the strategic choices that Beijing has made in its approach to power politics in the new order to counter the hegemony of the United States. Not surprisingly, the discourse has been frequently used to justify and sustain China's much-touted diplomatic initiatives in developing strategic partnerships with various state actors, including Russia and the European Union, as its own distinctive approach to overcoming the security dilemma, simply because it fosters multipolarity. Iain Johnston has noted 'a strong post hoc, faddish flavour' of Chinese commentary on the question of multipolarity (Johnston, 2003: 30).

Equally, the non-traditional security discourse is deeply embedded within the context of domestic political and economic transformation and the changing identity of the Chinese state. It is first and foremost a political project that seeks to legitimate certain new state security practices such as China's security cooperation within the frameworks of both SCO and ASEAN and its relentless pursuit of energy security at all costs. The broadening of the security agenda in this sense is by no means 'critical' in any self-conscious sense. It continues to equate security with the state. The expanded notions of security in this instance serve only to help traditional security concerns to find a new home in non-traditional security discourse.

Both discourses are then political projects of and for the powerful. They provide *post hoc* justification and legitimation for, and also constitute the process of, the Chinese state's new security policy-making and implementation. For some this means exciting opportunities will have the ear of Chinese leadership, and therefore, power, which often brings professional as well as personal rewards.[17] For many others, the lack of critical distance between the scholarly community and power in China simply obscures their understanding that their discursive engagement constructs the meanings and practices of security and that power is deeply embedded in their production of security studies scholarship.

Disciplining power of the security discourse about China

Critical scholars have been frequently warned of 'considerable disciplining power' of political realism and neo-realist orthodox in security studies. Keith Krause (1998) in particular has given an elaborate discussion of disciplining practices of traditional security studies.[18] Such disciplinary power, however, has made more subtle exertion on security discourses within China. It is through a realist-dominated discourse about China as a major security problem in the emerging global order that an 'iron cage' has been produced, which has served, in combination with the strategic interests of the Chinese state itself, to discipline Chinese security discourses. This is an engaging discourse carefully constructed over a decade around debates about the China threat and Chinese realpolitik, largely dictated by American policy concerns about the rise of Chinese power.

The powerful problematics presented to the global international relations community by even the moderate voice of this engaging discourse are framed in terms of China's role in the security dilemma in East Asia; how China's new grand strategy signals a 'neo-Bismarkian Turn'; and whether China is a status quo power or a dissatisfied power (Christensen, 2003; Goldstein, 2003; Johnston, 2003, 2004). Discussions conducted in these terms by prominent China specialists in the United States tend to perpetuate the dominance of the neo-realist orthodoxy in Western academic representations of China as a regional and even global security problem. Looking more closely, the want of critical scholarship either in the Coxian sense or in the Frankfurt School tradition is glaring in what Pillsbury calls 'the analytical foundation laid by the pioneering scholarship' of American China specialists (Pillsbury, 2000: iii). China is simply looked upon as a problem to be understood, and to be resolved. These 'pioneers' have seldom if ever reflected upon how the(ir) perceptions of China as a security problem is derivative of particular prevailing power relationship, or how the China problematic has in fact been constructed by this particular discourse.

This neo-realist discourse is particularly powerful in disciplining Chinese security discourses in two ways. One is that it has produced a particular discourse within China refuting claims of the China threat. Ironically, the analytical concepts and theoretical assumptions of this counter-discourse are defined in the orthodox neo-realist terms characteristic of the China threat discourse.[19] Indeed, the constraining power of the China threat discourse is so considerable that any counter-discourse, including that of 'China's peaceful rise', has to be conducted in such a way 'without triggering fear that Beijing harbours revisionist intentions' (Deng and Moore, 2004: 123). The other is that the US-based scholarship produced for this discourse in the neo-realist model is often presented as normatively objective/neutral, methodologically sophisticated and epistemologically scientific. For a nascent international relations research community in China that has to import topics for its theoretical debates, such a positivist model of scholarship is seen as the one Chinese international relations scholars should aspire to follow.[20] In this regard, the lack of critical international relations scholarship in China is an accomplice.

Towards a critical turn?

The deficit of critical engagement in the two dominant discourses of security in China examined above is an indication that the prevailing orthodoxy in security studies has not been seriously challenged. Militarism is still dominant. Statism has found new expressions and sites in non-traditional security studies. Critical security studies has little institutionalized presence in China. In fact, 'critical security studies' as a specific term has yet to be translated into Chinese to enter into discourses of security in China's academic and policy communities.[21]

Arguably, necessary intellectual predispositions for meaningful and promising critical intervention in security studies are not present in China. For one thing, there has been no widely shared intellectual dissatisfaction, discontent and disillusionment about realism as the dominant paradigm in general and the orthodoxy in security studies in particular in Chinese academic community. The end of the Cold War and the opening of China's scholarly engagement with global international relations scholarship have ironically helped to entrench realism and its dominance in Chinese international relations scholarship. The fixation on statism, militarism and scientism characteristic of traditional security studies seems to have provided a comfortable focus for generating a meaningful research agenda of security for both the Chinese academic international relations community, as disoriented as their Western counterparts, and for the Chinese government, with its intense sense of insecurity.

Until very recently, critical international relations/IPE (international political ecconomy) scholarship was almost unknown to Chinese academics, apart from occasional mentioning of Robert Cox. One publication by Guo Shuyong (2005) in *World Economics and Politics* can be counted as pioneering in that it has systematically introduced critical theory in international relations to the Chinese audience, which organically links critical theory to Marxism, the Frankfurt School and constructivism.[22] Putting it bluntly, critical security studies has no intellectual roots in China.

Political difficulties in China apart, such lack of critical international relations scholarship poses the biggest intellectual impediment to any critical turn in security studies in China, which limits the possibilities for a move to critical practices of security. It hinders a critical understanding that 'security is essentially a derivative concept' and that central ideas that inform traditional studies of security derive from 'a combination of Anglo-American, statist, militarised, masculinized, top-down, methodologically positivist, and philosophically realist thinking' shaped by the Cold War (Booth, 2005a: 13). It means that Chinese security studies analysts are generally not critically reflective of their scholarly and political responsibility, which should not be exclusively for the state, but more importantly for the civil society, and ultimately for individuals. There is little awareness that the meanings and practices of security are constantly constructed by their discursive engagement and that the production of security studies scholarship in China so far has been largely dictated by power.

Consequently, there has been little self-conscious effort among Chinese security studies specialists to develop a critical perspective that 'seeks to stand outside prevailing structures, processes, ideologies, and orthodoxies while recognizing that all conceptualizations of security derive from particular political/theoretical positions' (Booth, 2005a: 15–16). From here, fulfilling the critical promise to 'develop an emancipation-oriented understanding of theory and practice of security' (Wyn Jones, 2005: 215) and to promote emancipatory politics in international relations has a long way to go in China.

Notes

1 Note here in particular Mohammed Ayoob's criticism of Booth. 'Booth's definition refuses to acknowledge that a society or group can be emancipated without being secure, or vice versa. . . . Such semantic acrobatics tend to impose a model of contemporary Western polities . . . that are far removed from Third World realities' (quoted in Steve Smith, 2005: 44).

2 On the concept of a globalized state, see Ian Clark (1999).

3 Such assessment, however, categorically makes the exception of the situation across the Taiwan Straits.

4 On security and the 'other', see Peter J. Kazenstein (1996: 18–23).

5 A popular assertion of China's identity vis-à-vis the United States can also be seen in a wave of publications between 1996 and 1998 on the general theme of 'A China that Can Say No'.

6 Michael Pillsbury (2000) has traced the origin of this discourse to 1986. For Johnston (2003), Mao's conception of three worlds provides the starting point to understand Chinese ideas about polarity in world politics. One prevailing myth in the Chinese foreign policy establishment is that the idea of the strategic triangle guided China's successful manoeuvre in the balance of power between the US, the former Soviet Union and China in the 1970s and the 1980s.

7 According to Ye (2004), such consensus concerns the following: (1) polarity refers to a particular configuration of power in the future international relations; (2) a 'pole' refers to a relatively independent power centre, or a group of states that asserts considerable influence on world affairs because it possesses comprehensive power attributes which encompasses political, economic military, cultural and scientific power; and (3) only the United States at the moment can claim to be a pole, though a few other states or group of states have the potential to develop into a pole. There is also uncritical acceptance among Chinese scholars of the official claim of the normative good of multipolarization for world stability and peace as well as to China's strategic and security interests. Ye calls in particular for transcending the strategic thinking of multipolarity.

8 In addition, there is also dissatisfaction about the ambiguous claim of 'one superpower and many great powers' (*yichao duoqiang*) as the current power configuration in the international system.

9 Italics in the original.

10 It is worth noting that this book is the product of teamwork. The team consists of two military writers, Qiao Liang and Wang Xianghui whose work *The Unlimited War* published in 1997 caused a sensation both within and outside China. The other two authors of the team are Wang Jian, an economist and deputy director of a think tank for the National Development and Reform Commission, and Li Xiaoning, a popularist speaker and commentator.

11 The ideas, arguments and claims presented in this volume are much richer and such a short paragraph can only provide a caricature that can hardly do any justice to them.

12 For a discussion of debates within China on globalization, see Garrett (2001).

13 For example, in September 1997, on the eve of the Asian financial crisis, environmental security, food security and energy security were the topics for CSCAP's Working Group on Comprehensive and Cooperative Security in Kuala Lumpur.

14 A more elaborate list of non-traditional security issues is found in the *Declaration*, which includes trafficking in illegal drugs, people smuggling including trafficking in women and children, sea piracy, terrorism, arms smuggling, money laundering, international economic crime and cyber crime.

15 Xiong was speaking in the capacity of the President of China International Strategic Studies Association. He was formerly the Chief of Staff of the People's Liberation Army (PLA).

16 Linguistics has also played a role here. The Chinese translation of 'human' does not easily take the discussion to the individual level of security in terms of freedom from fear and from want.

17 For a broad debate on the critical role of international relations scholarship in theory and practice, see Wallace (1996), Smith (1997) and Booth (1997).

18 Ken Booth issues similar but stronger warnings most recently. See Booth (2005a).

19 One good example is that China's 2000 defence white paper accepted unproblematically the concept of 'soft power' and uses the exact measurement of comprehensive national power (CNP) to describe its relative power vis-à-vis the US.

20 One Chinese researcher argues in particular that although the Chinese scholarly community participated in global debates on 'democratic peace' and the 'clash of civilizations', these topics are imported and the parameters of debates are set by the Anglo-American scholarship. See Ren Xiao (1999).

21 Interviews in Beijing, Hangzhou and Sydney, November and December 2005.

22 The same issue of *World Economics and Politics* carries six more introductory essays on 'non-mainstream' international relations theories, including 'The Critical Theory of Robert Cox: Origins and Special Features' by Li Bin, 'The English School of International Relations: Evolution, Contribution and Inspiration' by Tang Xiaosong, 'Postmodernism and Post-modern International Relations: Some Reflections' by Zhuang Liwei and 'Voices from the Margin: Feminism and Current Studies of International Relations and their Prospects' by Li Yingtao. All these essays had been earlier presented at a symposium on Non-mainstream International Relations Theories organized by the Institute of World Economics and Politics on 22–3 April 2005.

11

Nuclear weapons in the Asia-Pacific: a critical security appraisal

Marianne Hanson

THE ASIA-PACIFIC IS ONE of the most intensely nuclearized regions in the world. It is the only region where nuclear weapons have been used in attack, it has elicited grave international concern about nuclear proliferation – namely in India, Pakistan and North Korea – and it is home to three key recognized nuclear weapon states, China, Russia and the US, all of which possess sizable arsenals and which show every indication that they will retain these indefinitely. While this book's focus has been on a more limited designation of what constitutes the Asia-Pacific geographically, the current chapter broadens these geographic parameters to look also at US and Russian nuclear issues. This is done so in the belief that the nuclear policies of these two states are of paramount importance to issues of nuclear proliferation elsewhere, and certainly in the Asia-Pacific region. Additionally, the region has been the preferred centre for numerous tests of nuclear weapons between the 1950s and the 1990s. While an imminent threat of nuclear exchange might not be seen as an overwhelmingly strong feature of current security concerns in the region, this history and distribution point to a danger of eventual use, either deliberate or inadvertent. Such a prospect raises profound ethical, humanitarian, environmental and political questions, all of which are highly germane to a critical security analysis.

Nuclear weapons and the associated arms control regimes that accompany them have overwhelmingly been viewed as a traditional security issue, representing as they do a hallmark of Cold War activity and being associated firmly with realist reference points of the predominance of the state, preparation for military attack (in this case as part of nuclear deterrence strategies), and the pursuit of self-help in an anarchical international environment. And notwithstanding that the Cold War – the crucible which nurtured the development of nuclear strategy and especially policies of deterrence and mutually assured destruction – is long ended, nuclear weapons continue to remain central to the traditional security doctrines of nuclear weapon states. Yet although these weapons remain firmly linked to traditional security thinking in the minds of most security analysts, it is hard to find a case more pressingly in need of the kind of critique afforded by a critical security studies perspective.

This chapter aims to do the following: in line with the express intention of a critical security approach, it examines the issue of nuclear weapons with a view to understanding the origins and consequences of nuclear policies, as opposed to simply describing these or calculating their strategic effects. The argument presented here is that traditional security policies that have established nuclear weapons as a means of achieving security among states have led instead to what is termed here a fundamental nuclear *in*security, that is, the constant fear that such weapons might actually be used, exposing human populations to unprecedented destruction. By way of questioning the orthodoxies associated with nuclear weapons, the chapter explores briefly three key factors associated with their use: ethical and humanitarian concerns, the implications of nuclear deterrence and nuclear use on citizen–state relations, and the implications of nuclear war for environmental and development projects. The third section of this chapter will canvass the state of nuclear issues in the Asia-Pacific, focusing on the nuclear crisis in North Korea, proliferation in India and Pakistan, and the status of nuclear weapons in the US, China and Russia. It also provides a brief overview of some recent and non-traditional initiatives emanating from the region to foster nuclear arms control and disarmament.

Nuclear weapons, strategic studies and security: a critical appraisal

The possession of nuclear weapons and the threat of their use is an accepted and indeed doctrinally articulated policy in a number of key states in the world; these are the United States, United Kingdom, Russia, China and France. It is the very normality of nuclear weapons as a central part of national defence for these states that is remarkable. The possession, threat and use of nuclear weapons are not expressly forbidden, as are other activities claiming the attention of critical security studies, such as starvation, ethnic cleansing, genocide and other inflictions of harm on a widespread scale, deemed automatically and intuitively to be 'wrong'. To the contrary, even though there might be great unease about, and even a global norm against, weapons of mass destruction (WMD) – although even this is often abstractly put and selectively applied – we continue to see some states privileged with the apparent right to cause devastation and loss of human life on a massive scale using weapons of unprecedented power. For other states, denied this recognition conferred by the inequalities in the Treaty on the Non-Proliferation of Nuclear Weapons (1968), acquiring such weapons while outside the Treaty or even within it has become a clear goal. But does this relative acceptance of nuclear weapons as a fact of life – and for some a desirable and essential component of security policy – mean that the issue should still be seen through the lens of traditional security studies? I argue not, although it is revealing to trace the way in which it continues to be seen as such within the worlds of international security and defence analysts.

For decades, traditional security focused almost exclusively on strategic studies, and within this domain, nuclear issues were dominant. As with most 'explanations' of events associated with traditional security, not much was questioned, and the world of nuclear arms races and deterrence was taken as given. Smith (1999: 72) notes how 'naturalized' the world of strategic studies seemed, bringing with it a range of experts on nuclear weapons. These experts invariably accepted the mantra that the nuclear 'genie' was out of the bottle and all that could be done was to determine how to minimize the risks of a strike against one's own state while allowing for that same awful possibility against opponent states. It was a peculiarly technical environment that permeated strategic studies for many decades, and never more so than in nuclear policy debates. Booth notes the 'obsessive interest in the technological dynamics of security policy' whereby 'relations between states were often reduced to technology and technocracy', and where a 'security specialist' was all too often consonant with someone who possessed technical, rather than political skills (Booth, 2005a; see also Mutimer, 2000). There was no explicit place for emotion or for normative impulses. Questioning what security was, what it meant for whom, or whether specific policies were morally acceptable seemed hardly possible. Carol Cohn wrote compellingly of the separate world inhabited by the nuclear expert, where the language spoken was 'technostrategic', representing the 'intertwined, inextricable nature of technological and nuclear strategic thinking' and where 'human factors were irrelevant to the calculus of gain and loss' (Cohn, 1987: 4). It was at once a language that was incomprehensible to outsiders, but self-sustaining and feeding authorized government nuclear policies. Her examples were telling. Pointing to the ease with which nuclear 'experts' would label types of nuclear weapons – in this case fusion, rather than fission bombs – she noted that '[a]nyone who has seen pictures of Hiroshima burn victims or tried to imagine the pain of hundreds of glass shards blasted into flesh may find it perverse beyond imagination to hear a class of nuclear devices matter-of-factly referred to as "clean bombs"' (Cohn, 1987: 691).

It is with such direct attention to human costs that critical security approaches make their case. Following Robert Cox's distinction, critical theory differentiates itself from traditional approaches seen as unreflective and which have been categorized as 'problem solving theories' (Cox, 1981). The difficulty of course was that 'problem-solving theory', the positivist-inspired attempt to explain international relations was not problem-solving at all and rarely looked at the implications of international security policies on individuals. As Smith notes, traditional attempts at explaining international relations and achieving 'security' took existing political and strategic dynamics and practices as the given starting point for analysis; these 'certainties' were rarely deconstructed or challenged, and it was within such conviction and clearly defined parameters that attempts were made to see how problems arising from these could be solved or ameliorated (Smith, 1999: 89). Moreover, this was invariably within the context of lessening problems or risks for the *state* rather than for individuals. Equally, 'problem-solving' rarely brought with it any real commitment to changing fundamental structures and policies that were the very cause of such problems. The voices of victims of nuclear attack heard in Cohn's work were rarely articulated in traditional strategic studies' works on nuclear strategy.

There was, however, some challenge to this vast monopoly of traditional strategic thought. At a civil society level, there was never such an easy acceptance of nuclear policy as appeared at the government – or specifically, defence policy – level. Anti-nuclear groups remained active in many parts of the world for decades, evident most in the US and its allied European states, with a particularly poignant variant in Japan. At both an intellectual and practitioner level, it was the emergence of alternative defence and common security thinking in the early 1980s that most challenged prevailing state orthodoxy. The 1982 Palme report warned of the folly of aiming for a nuclear 'victory' and urged instead that in the light of potential nuclear destruction and the complexity of world politics, security could only be achieved *with* one's opponents, rather than *against* them (Independent Commission on Disarmament and Security Issues, 1982). These themes found resonance with Mikhail Gorbachev who incorporated them into his 'new thinking', itself instrumental in ending the Cold War, and even, for a tantalisingly brief moment at arms control negotiations with Ronald Reagan in Reykjavik in 1986, allowing for the possibility of a nuclear free world, although this aberration was soon dismissed.

The 1990s brought fresh impetus for rethinking the place of nuclear weapons in the world and a more intrusive questioning of nuclear orthodoxies than seen before, with the publication of a number of innovative reports urging the elimination of nuclear weapons, most notably the various Stimson Center reports and especially its final report (The Stimson Center, 1997), the Canberra Commission report (*Canberra Commission on the Elimination of Nuclear Weapons*, 1996), *The Tokyo Forum Report* (1999) and numerous other declarations by military and political leaders. These argued that nuclear weapons have no utility in either warfare or as a response to terrorism, biological or chemical weapon attacks and that retaining them only served to urge proliferation elsewhere and increase the likelihood of use (either deliberate or accidental). A phased and balanced move towards zero nuclear weapons was seen as the most rational course to pursue. Collectively, the findings of these various studies represent one of the most interesting and prominent challenges to the basic tenets of traditional security studies (albeit emanating from fairly mainstream sources) challenging as they did the central assumptions inherent in nuclear doctrines, doctrines firmly established as authorized state policy, but which nevertheless also promised catastrophe for the planet.

Despite this push, it would appear that things remain very much the same within the sphere of security doctrine in the nuclear weapons states as they did in earlier decades (Hanson, 2002). Cohn's observations were made almost 20 years ago, but little has changed in the strategic mindsets that continued well beyond the ending of the Cold War. Former US General Lee Butler, writing in 2000, warned of the dangers of old style thinking in a changed world, noting that 'this abiding faith in nuclear weapons was inspired and is sustained by a catechism instilled over many decades by a priesthood who speak with great assurance and authority' (Butler, 2000: 183). A decade ago, the Canberra Commission report warned that in a world beset with problems of ethnic cleansing, poverty, environmental degradation, poor governance, natural disasters and other new forms of threat, nuclear weapons had no useful role to play (*Canberra Commission on the Elimination of Nuclear Weapons*, 1996). Yet despite this lack of utility, they remain retained by all the original nuclear weapon states, have been acquired by non-NPT states (Israel, India, Pakistan and most recently North Korea) and are possibly sought by Iran, with current numbers of weapons standing at between 20,000 and 30,000 globally even after substantial reductions in arsenals made especially by the US and Russia in the past decade. Not even the terrorist attacks of September 2001 and the subsequent shift in focus for international security – with world politics heavily dominated now by the 'war on terrorism' – have done anything to lessen a reliance on nuclear weapons, even though such weapons are clearly ineffective against groups of terrorists whose whereabouts may be unknown. The effective conflation of non-proliferation of WMD and counter-terrorism, largely engineered by the US, has severely lessened the chances of the nuclear weapon states moving towards elimination of their nuclear arsenals.

Nuclear weapons, deterrence and the implications of use: a brief critical appraisal

Three major factors related to the possession, threat and use of nuclear weapons are examined here.[1] The first, and arguably most important, of these revolves around ethical and humanitarian concerns: nuclear weapons are targeted at civilian populations and, under typical strategic thinking, rely for their effectiveness on the threat of a massive loss of life – civilian life – in the state of a targeted adversary. Essentially, under the policy of nuclear deterrence, civilian populations are held hostage to a military system that uses weapons of a destructive nature vastly different to any previously devised. Notwithstanding attempts to move away from a counter-city targeting strategy and towards a counter-force strategy (focusing on military hardware and personnel) during the Cold War, nuclear deterrence remained tied to the threat of widespread destruction of civilian areas and massive loss of civilian life (even if this was not overtly stated to be the case).

At its heart, the use, and by implication the threat of use, of nuclear weapons violates fundamental principles of international human rights and humanitarian law governing the conduct of warfare. Principles requiring that parties to a conflict must distinguish between combatants and non-combatants and that prohibit superfluous injury or unnecessary suffering would be violated in the extreme by any use of nuclear weapons. Suffering and injuries would also continue in subsequent generations, as the deformities and illnesses of post-war Hiroshima and Nagasaki children have demonstrated, thereby raising additional legal and ethical questions of intergenerational justice.

It seems surprising therefore that nuclear doctrines, especially the policy of nuclear deterrence, were developed without an overt and publicly articulated assessment of their humanitarian consequences.[2] Nuclear weapons, used even in retaliation to a first strike, raise challenging questions about means, proportionality and effectiveness. That is to say, even in the event of a nuclear attack there are serious moral impediments to responding in kind by killing large numbers of civilians for the actions of their political leaders.

There had of course, developed a strong taboo against the use of nuclear weapons after 1945, and this taboo even appeared to underwrite the actual government practice of refraining from using nuclear weapons (Price and Tannenwald, 1996). But this only serves to reveal the huge disjuncture between official security policies that relied on nuclear deterrence and the widespread sentiment (even if not overtly acknowledged in policy-making circles) that the actual use of nuclear weapons would be too terrible to consider. Andrew Butfoy (1999: 166) in outlining the paradox of a security policy dominated by a concept of deterrence that involved the use of what are (because of moral restraints) essentially unusable weapons, referred to the boffins of nuclear strategy as living in a 'parallel, abstract world divorced from day to day diplomacy'. One might add that it was equally divorced from common humanity.

The second factor examined here is that of citizen–state relations and the risks and fears imposed on a population whose leadership possesses or seeks to acquire a nuclear weapons capability. At stake here are primarily questions of representation and consent in the relationship between the citizen and the state. Also at issue is the state's ability and responsibility to provide security and protection to its citizens.

Even in democratic states, where processes of government are transparent and accessible, individuals may have relatively little say in determining the security policies of their governments, and far less during security crises.[3] Stansfield Turner, former head of the CIA and a prominent military commander noted that during the Cold War that

> many civilian and military experts who shaped policy on nuclear weapons simply lost focus in concocting sophistic theories that never made sense . . . if ever scrutiny by the public was needed because scrutiny by the bureaucracy was so limited, this was it. Today, adequate citizen input to policies concerning weapons of mass destruction is still lacking. (Turner, 1999: 144)

Any decision to embark on a process of nuclearization, as happened for instance in India and Pakistan in 1998, and for that matter to all nuclear weapon states since 1945, brings with it nuclear risks to all citizens. This factor of responsiveness and responsibility to civilians becomes even more problematic in undemocratic societies where the processes of decision-making may be even more closed to citizen – or even non-military – input. In all cases, the burden of threat is not confined to military targets or even to political elites but rather casts a massive shadow over all citizens.

At a wider level, nuclear weapons raise key questions about the role of the state as security provider. Under nuclear deterrence, survival depends not on the actions of one's own state or on any set of defensive arrangements made by that state, but rather on the rational behaviour of one's opponents. John Herz, a realist thinker who nevertheless differed from his peers in his views on the fragility of the international order and the weakness of the state, was one of the first writers to point out that the advent of nuclear weapons called the territorial function of the state into question (Herz, 1959).[4] More fundamentally, the claim within critical security studies – that it is often the state that is the source of insecurity for its own citizens – finds some resonance here: in the case of nuclear weapons and the threat of waging nuclear war, we have a situation where it is the state that is the absolute locus of insecurity and fear. It is at once curious and alarming that a capability so vehemently denied to sub-state actors because of its horrifying implications (namely the justified fears of WMD falling into terrorist hands) should have so easily become accepted as a legitimate and almost revered capacity of *states*.

A third factor in any deconstruction of nuclear weapons policy concerns the enormous environmental implications attendant on their use, in warfare, but even in the less pressing instance of nuclear testing. Even this latter, relatively non-aggressive, practice has drawn widespread condemnation on environmental grounds, and raised important questions about neo-colonialism and the wanton disregard of local sensitivities, especially in the South Pacific. And although the present moratorium on nuclear testing is holding, the lack of entry into force of the Comprehensive Test Ban Treaty (CTBT) means that this tranquillity can be broken at any time. Among Asia-Pacific states, the US, China, India and Pakistan – each by refusing to sign and ratify the CTBT – are delaying any prospect of a legal ban on nuclear tests.

Clearly, a nuclear weapon strike would result not only in widespread casualties, but it would also render uninhabitable vast tracts of territory and increase levels of radiation over an even wider region. Uniquely among weapons devised by humans, nuclear weapons have the potential to destroy in an instant and possibly for decades – depending on the scale of the attack – areas previously host to a variety of animal and plant life forms. The capacity of societies to restore normal life in such an area would also be more pronounced in under-developed states, such as India and Pakistan. The use of nuclear weapons would have severe impacts on human environments, on prospects for reconstruction or development and subsequently on long-term economic wellbeing, all of which would collectively diminish the quality of life for those able to survive such an event.

The human rights and environmental concerns noted above are particularly applicable to the Asia-Pacific. Between them, the nuclear weapon states located in the region possess up to 30,000 nuclear warheads. Precise figures are difficult to calculate, and the total estimates include tactical nuclear warheads which are often inexactly counted even by their possessing government, as is the case especially in Russia. Including maximum numbers of tactical warheads then, the breakdown is as follows: the US possesses approximately 10,000 warheads, Russia up to 20,000, and China approximately 400 warheads (China does however own sufficient fissile material to produce a much larger arsenal if it wishes to do so). India and Pakistan currently have fissile material for between 40–90 and 30–50 warheads respectively, and North Korea is thought to have developed a 'handful' of nuclear weapons, although quite how many is difficult to confirm (The Nuclear Threat Initiative, 2006).

Nuclear weapons in the Asia-Pacific: an overview of crisis points

Within the general context of this level of nuclearization and the critical factors noted in the previous section, three areas of concern are broadly discussed here: the case of North Korea, the Indian and Pakistani acquisition of nuclear weapons capabilities, and the ongoing problem of nuclear arsenals possessed by great powers in the region, China, Russia and the United States.

The North Korean nuclear crisis

The demonstration in October 2006 that North Korea (the Democratic People's Republic of Korea – DPRK) had acquired nuclear weapons, together with an increasingly sophisticated ballistic missile system, represents one of the most serious challenges to peace and stability in Northeast Asia. The current crisis has been frequently framed as beginning in October 2002, when US observers announced that North Korea (in violation of the Agreed Framework negotiated to avoid a similar crisis in 1994) had apparently admitted to a clandestine uranium enrichment programme. The state subsequently dismissed weapons inspectors, announced its intention to withdraw from the nuclear NPT and restarted its Yongbyon reactor. Long branded by the US as a 'rogue state' and as a member of George W. Bush's famous 'axis of evil', the DPRK had subsequently openly talked of possessing nuclear weapons, and to the dismay of many in the international community, withdrew from the NPT in January 2003 and tested its first nuclear weapon in October 2006.[5]

It would be a mistake however, to see the crisis simply within the dates outlined above. October 2002 might have represented the actual rupture, but in reality the issue had been inflamed by a difficult relationship between North Korea and the US, and a contentious policy adopted by the Bush administration shortly after it came into office in 2001. As Roland Bleiker's chapter in this volume suggests, there is some reason to believe North Korea's leader is genuinely concerned about a possible US pre-emptive strike, especially in light of the build-up to the war in Iraq, where it appeared that the US was not to be deflected from its aim there of achieving regime change. Paradoxically then, the US's objective of preventing WMD proliferation in Iraq may have had the unintended consequence of speeding up nuclear proliferation in the DPRK. Nevertheless, the proliferation of nuclear weapons in North Korea cannot be seen as anything less than a major setback and a critical issue for the safety of millions of Koreans and others living in Northeast Asia. The DPRK's recent actions can have done little to build security and confidence in the region; apart from its 2006 weapons test, its testing of a long-range nuclear-capable ballistic missile in August 1998 represented one of the most overtly aggressive actions seen in the region in the past decade.

The series of six-party talks (involving North and South Korea, the United States, Russia, China and Japan), which has been in place since 2003, has been protracted and for the most part, unproductive. Not wishing to be seen to be rewarding North Korea for its violations of nuclear non-proliferation norms, the US was especially resistant to requests for bilateral negotiations. North Korea, for its part, often provided conflicting information and threatened to walk out of the talks. The fourth round of talks, held in September 2005, did seem to signal some improvement in relations and the possibility of a complete denuclearization of the Korean peninsula. These talks, in which China played an instrumental and constructive role, resulted in North Korea agreeing to abandon all civilian and military nuclear weapon programmes and return to the NPT. In return, other members of the six-party talks provided security assurances, and promised stronger economic relations and political normalization (Kerr, 2005). The agreement seemed to promise a significantly new phase in US–North Korean relations in particular, underscoring the importance placed by the DPRK on security guarantees – on simple statements of declaration that aggressive action will not be directed towards it.

Ultimately, however, the optimism surrounding the talks gave way as North Korea withdrew from the talks weeks after the September 2005 round of negotiations in protest over US financial sanctions, and tested its first nuclear device on October 9, 2006. Six-party talks resumed in late December 2006, but little progress was made, the DPRK still insisting that US financial sanctions imposed upon it were part of a 'hostile' US policy, and that negotiations on the nuclear issue could go no further until the sanctions issues were resolved (Kerr 2007). China had played an important role in reconvening these talks, but the progress and potential success of any future talks will almost certainly be complicated by the DPRK's blatant demonstration of its nuclear capability and its indication of intention to conduct further tests and US and Japanese continuing demands that North Korea unequivocally renounce its nuclear program (BBC 2006). Certainly, the prospect for a hard-line stance to yield real change in North Korea's nuclear policy and broader security outlook must appear questionable in light of the developments of October. Beyond the risk of nuclear conflict inherent in proliferation in and of itself, North Korea's announcement on the nuclear stage could place pressure on South Korea and Japan to consider their own nuclear options, a factor which would quickly have destabilising effects on the entire region.

Beyond the real and growing problems of interstate tension and regional instability, there is also the troubling issue of opportunity costs associated with North Korea's decision to develop a nuclear arsenal and the effects this has had on an already poor economy. It is possible – within a broad human security or critical security context – to argue that the acquisition of a nuclear capability by the DPRK is made all the more objectionable when considering the poor standard of security and safety afforded to North Korea's own people by the ruling regime. That it remains one of the poorest nations on earth is not contested, yet its military posture is hugely out of proportion to this status. Serious under-development and continuing poor governance cannot also but severely restrict any informed public input into the security policy of that state.

India–Pakistan nuclear proliferation

The history of nuclearization in South Asia, while it might be seen as less pressing an issue eight years after the fact of proliferation in 1998, is nevertheless of very real concern in the region, occurring as it is between two states with profound security disagreements and who are engaged in a long-running border war.

Neither India nor Pakistan had ever joined the NPT, believing that the discriminatory nature of that treaty violated the principle of equality of nations; indeed India had long been active in the United Nations in calling on the nuclear weapon states to move to the disarmament of their nuclear arsenals. The peculiar security dynamics between India and China, as well as between India and Pakistan, coupled with a particularly strong blend of nationalist fervour in the ruling BJP (Bharatiya Janata Party) in Delhi resulted in India blasting its way forcefully into the nuclear club in May 1998; Pakistan followed suit a few days later.[6]

The testing of their nuclear devices provoked widespread condemnation, economic sanctions and the disruption of political ties, as well as disapprobation from a wide range of civil society forums (as had the nuclear tests conducted by France in the South Pacific in 1995–6). Both states were criticized for acquiring weapons seen as outdated, immoral and irrelevant to modern life. And while tensions have been reduced on some issues (for example both states have recently concluded a ballistic missile notification pact – see Creegan, 2005: 9), the likelihood of a nuclear strike remains unacceptably high. Indeed both nations came 'very close' to a nuclear exchange in 1999 over their dispute in Kashmir (Hain, cited in Rogers, 2000: 55).

Clearly, the alleged benefit of nuclear deterrence has not prevented the continuation of conventional warfare between the two nations along their disputed border. It is also claimed that both states are in greater danger of sliding into a nuclear war than their Cold War counterparts might have been, as they have not developed the wide range of control and communication mechanisms deemed essential to minimizing the risks of accidental or inadvertent nuclear attack (Bowen and Wolven, 1999). More recent concerns have developed over the Khan network in Pakistan, a clandestine nuclear suppliers' network that can only have assisted nuclear proliferation at the global level (see Kampani, 2002).

And of course, as with North Korea, the charge of neglecting fundamental and pressing development needs at the expense of acquiring a hugely expensive and dangerous arsenal has not been lost on those who view nuclear weapons within a critical security framework and who advocate an emphasis on human security. Jennifer Bennet (2004: 41) and Ramesh Thakur (2000: 233) are among many observers who have both pointed in this context to the tragedy of expenditure on nuclear arsenals in the context of extreme poverty and under-development in both India and Pakistan.

If the nuclearization of India and Pakistan was not enough to disturb proponents of nuclear elimination, more recent political developments between the US and India, in particular, have served to raise fundamental concern about the commitment of these states to disarmament and the extent to which pressure might be continued to be brought on them to disarm. In light of the 'war on terrorism' it has become clear that any disapprobation shown by the US towards India and Pakistan after their nuclear tests has quickly evaporated against the need for allies in this campaign. Both states' flouting of their nuclear capabilities – and even the persistence of military rule in Pakistan – appear now to be unimportant in what has, for the US at least, eclipsed the danger of proliferation by these states. The most recent indicator of this has been the US agreement to provide nuclear materials and technology to India (see Boese, 2005a: 9). Aside from being inconsistent with the terms of the NPT, such an agreement appears to legitimate the fact of nuclear proliferation in South Asia, with all the risks and insecurities that this might bring to the people most likely to be affected by nuclear warfare. Perhaps most worryingly, this policy signals a US wish to alter international legal and non-proliferation norms. These include, it would seem, an emphasis on counter-proliferation (as opposed to non-proliferation), whereby the acquisition of nuclear weapons is seen as acceptable in some states, but clearly to be denied to others. Such a stance, together with the continued possession of nuclear weapons by the nuclear weapon states, will do nothing, however, to reduce the risk of nuclear dangers in the Asia-Pacific.

Perpetuating nuclear weapons and a nuclear weapons culture: the US, Russia and China

The instances of proliferation outlined above are unlikely to be resolved in the long term without substantial change on the part of the nuclear weapon states themselves. One of the key points made by those arguing for the elimination of nuclear weapons is that the retention of these weapons by a select group of states acts as an incentive to others to acquire them also. As the Canberra Commission has noted:

> Nuclear weapons are held by a handful of states which insist that these weapons provide unique security benefits, and yet reserve uniquely to themselves the right to own them. This situation is highly discriminatory and thus unstable; it cannot be sustained. The possession of nuclear weapons by any state is a constant stimulus to other states to acquire them. (*Canberra Commission on the Elimination of Nuclear Weapons*, 1996)

Among these handful of states are the US, Russia and China, which between them currently hold between 20,000 and 30,000 nuclear warheads, well over 95% of the world's total stockpiles. It must be noted that recent arms control agreements between the US and Russia promise to bring these numbers down significantly, and that they in any case represent a substantial lowering of totals from the height of the Cold War. Nevertheless even the most ambitious of these agreements, the Moscow Treaty of 2002 will still allow the US and Russia to deploy up to 2,200 strategic warheads each, and the number of tactical warheads may not be diminished greatly. More worryingly, despite a legal obligation under the NPT to move to complete nuclear disarmament, and despite 'unequivocal' pledges made at the 2000 NPT Review Conference to eliminate their nuclear arsenals, none of these states appears willing to do this.

The retention of nuclear arsenals by these states at once retains the danger of an actual nuclear strike, feeds claims of inequality in international security politics, and prevents achieving a climate of compliance that might deter would-be proliferators. Beyond this, however, there have been some distinctly dangerous trends in the evolution of strategic doctrine in these states.

Perhaps most illustrative here is the US Nuclear Posture Review of 2002 which reiterated the high salience of nuclear weapons in US security policy and openly listed eight states, some of them non-nuclear states, against which it would be prepared to launch a nuclear attack if deemed necessary for US interests and security. This stance has subsequently been compounded by a number of other decisions: rejecting of arms control agreements made at earlier meetings, plans for developing a new generation of 'mini-nukes' and displaying a general rejection of international law at a number of different but nevertheless related levels. One prominent critic of these trends, Jack Mendelsohn (2005: 8) has concluded that this shows 'how poorly served we have been by what passes for strategic thinking in the twenty first century'.

Russia, for its part, while it has not openly rejected treaties in quite the same way, has done little to reduce the centrality of nuclear weapons in its strategic doctrines (Sokov, 2002). Indeed some fear that Russia is affirming nuclear options to a greater extent than it did at the end of the Cold War, at least in part because of the deterioration of its conventional forces (see Rogers, 2000: 56), but possibly also because of unwillingness to discard what continue to be seen as symbols of great power status. China is likely to modernize its nuclear weapons capability, fuelled by an unsurprising calculation that its forces are susceptible to US ballistic missile defence plans. Despite this, its white paper on arms control (*White Paper*, 2005) – while still lukewarm about the idea of ballistic missile defence – was distinctly more conciliatory in tone than an earlier 1995 document, reaffirming a wish for a peaceful neighbourhood in the Asia-Pacific region, strong support for nuclear disarmament (even though this was aimed more at the US and Russia than at itself), support for the CTBT (although China itself has yet to ratify that Treaty), and a recommitment to a 'no-first-use' of nuclear weapons policy.[7] Additionally, China appears to have reformed its previous controversial policies of exporting WMD materials and technology (Lieggi, 2005). While all this reflects a reasonably good report card, it also remains clear that China will not move towards elimination of its arsenal unless there is a substantial change in US and Russian policies.

There had been hopes that the Review Conference of the NPT, held in New York in May 2005 might be able to take nuclear arms control and disarmament forwards. High on the agenda was concern about the withdrawal of North Korea from the regime, but of equal concern for many states was the lack of progress on disarmament shown by the nuclear weapon states. Not surprisingly, the Conference was not able to make any progress on any of these issues, leaving prospects for reducing nuclear dangers in the Asia-Pacific low (Boese, 2005b; Johnson, 2005). Two states in the region, Australia and Indonesia formed part of the Seven-Nation Initiative, designed to further the stalled arms control agenda by taking specific proposals to the United Nations World Summit in September 2005. As with the NPT meeting however, this was also resisted strongly by the US, and in the end, was not able to have any impact on that summit.

Conclusion

In the early part of the twenty-first century, it is difficult to escape the conclusion that the placement and nature of nuclear weapons in the Asia-Pacific remains dangerous and that there has been little real change in the strategic mindsets that continue to rely on a weapon paradoxically of little military value but overwhelmingly inimical to the security of human beings.

There are grounds for arguing that in some ways the situation is more dangerous than during the Cold War, given the proliferation of nuclear weapons in India and Pakistan and most recently to North Korea. At the same time, there have been some important initiatives emanating from the region: the Canberra Commission report and the Japanese-sponsored *Tokyo Forum Report, Facing Nuclear Dangers,* were attempts to shift the status quo away from nuclear deployment and towards non-proliferation and disarmament. Additionally, it should be noted that the region is home to two very important Nuclear Weapon Free Zones (NWFZ): the South Pacific NWFZ, established by the Rarotonga Treaty in 1985, and the Association of Southeast Asian Nations (ASEAN) states' NWFZ, a result of the Treaty of 1996 which declared the ASEAN territory free of nuclear weapons. These play an important role in putting restraints on the acquisition, deployment or use of nuclear weapons. It may be that a new, broad-based initiative from the region can kick-start sentiments of disarmament and an emphasis on human security, but it is also clear that much will depend on the decisions of the large nuclear weapon states involved in the region, especially the United States.

The more far-reaching issue here is that until the possession and threat of use of nuclear weapons – the broad perpetuation of a nuclear weapons culture – is widely affirmed as a threat to humanity, bringing with it dangers and insecurity in proportions far greater than any possible security that can be derived from such weapons, it is unlikely that major change can occur. We are in urgent need of an informed critical security studies project that explicitly tackles the question of nuclear weapons at a global level, and of which this chapter represents only a very small beginning.

Notes

1 The following section draws from an earlier work by Marianne Hanson (2000).

2 For excellent analyses of the dilemmas inherent in nuclear deterrence and why moral assessments were almost always omitted, see the following selection of works: Blake and Pole (1983), McGwire (1985/6), Lee (1993) and Payne (2001).

3 For a philosophical analysis of the impact that nuclear policies can have on individuals and society, see Kavka (1987: 101–16).

4 For recent commentary on Herz's analysis, see Stirk (2005).

5 For extensive analysis of these developments, see Center for Nonproliferation Studies (2006).

6 For coverage of the motivations and implications of the 1998 tests, see Johnson (1998), Paul (1998) and Thakur (1998).

7 China's commitment to a 'no-first-use' policy is especially important in relation to the China–Taiwan dispute, an issue that appears to have been de-linked from nuclear calculations.

12

US hegemony, the 'war on terror' and security in the Asia-Pacific

Matt McDonald

Any survey of the processes, dynamics or futures of security in the Asia-Pacific would clearly be incomplete without engagement with the role played by the United States. Indeed, US hegemony[1] has been the defining feature of East Asian security architecture and interaction since the Second World War. And according to traditional accounts, particularly American analysts writing about the region, the United States has performed and continues to perform the role of security guarantor in an unstable and dangerous regional environment (Mastanduno, 2003; Hoge, 2004; Christensen, 2003; Ikenberry and Mastanduno, 2003). To be sure, such accounts of the US role are also to be found within the Asia-Pacific itself, not least of all from political leaders of smaller states (such as Singapore, South Korea and Australia) concerned about future prospects for large-scale violence. But all of these accounts or concerns tend to be built on assumptions about the likelihood of conflict without US involvement, or about the impossibility for alternative security orders to develop. Most importantly, such accounts tend to fail to ask the most necessary questions about US hegemony as a 'stabilizing' security force, such as whom does the US render secure (individuals and/or political regimes); from what types of threats and from which actors? At the height of the US-led 'war on terror' and an interventionist[2] US foreign policy, asking such fundamental questions about the US foreign and security policy agenda could hardly be more important.

This chapter constitutes a necessarily partial and selective attempt to address some of these questions by analysing the scope and consequences of the US-led 'war on terror'. First, it addresses the 'war on terror's' implications for democracy and human rights, arguing that it has legitimated political oppression and undermined democratization processes in some states in the region, particularly in Southeast Asia. Second, it addresses the implications of the 'war on terror' and associated 'Bush doctrine' for regional militarization and militarism.[3] I argue here that the US response to the 2001 terrorist attacks encourages violent responses to the resolution of political issues and contributes to broader dynamics of militarization, particularly in Northeast Asia. Both of these implications clearly undermine individual wellbeing in the region by exposing individuals to limits on political and civil freedoms and/or through increasing the possibility for large-scale violence. Further, both are inimical to the US' self-professed goals of combating terrorism and contributing to regional stability and security.

This chapter proceeds in four sections. First, it outlines the links between the 'war on terror', US foreign policy (during the Bush administration) generally and US hegemony, before outlining the ways in which these policies, interests and dynamics have played out in relations with the Asia-Pacific since 2001. The second and third sections outline the threat posed by the US-led 'war on terror' for human rights, democracy and prospects for organized violence. The final section reflects generally on the extent to which the United States might be viewed as a source of security and stability for the region. It concludes by highlighting possibilities for alternative security orders to emerge in the region which further (rather than prevent or undermine) individual emancipation.

A renewed interest: the United States and the Asia-Pacific

While focusing in this chapter on the implications of the 'war on terror', it is important to be clear about the relationship between the US-led 'war on terror', US foreign and security policy and US hegemony. Clearly, US hegemony pre-dated 9/11, while proponents and elements of a neo-conservative foreign and security policy agenda under Bush were evident prior to the terrorist attacks of 2001. But the United States' response to these attacks has illustrated the extent of its power on the one hand and its central principles and assumptions about global politics, America's role in the world, and the ways in which that power should be employed on the other.

The events of 9/11 created a context in which the United States was both willing and able to actively pursue an interventionist foreign policy agenda, one captured most completely in the 2002 National Security Strategy with its commitment to pre-eminence, pre-emption and unilateralism: the so-called 'Bush doctrine' (Bush, 2002). In the post-9/11 period, the United States government was enabled in the pursuit of this foreign policy agenda generally, and the 'war on terror' specifically, by three factors. The first was the pre-existing state of American hegemony, particularly the United States' material power resources that allowed the government to pursue such foreign policy imperatives. The second was the support accorded to a hitherto relatively unpopular administration by its domestic population in responding to terrorism aggressively and by whatever means necessary. Of course, the administration was central to creating this support, not least of all through portraying a military response to terrorism as an important (even the most important) means of redressing the terrorist threat (Jackson, 2005). Finally, the United States was enabled in its pursuit of the 'war on terror' (at least until the divisive debate over intervention in Iraq in 2003) by the goodwill felt towards the United States throughout much of the world after the tragic events of 9/11, including in the Asia-Pacific (Acharya, 2005b: 206–10). These dynamics provided a context in which the United States could, in the words of neo-conservative Max Boot (2003), 'embrace its imperial role' and reassert its role in the Asia-Pacific.

American interest in the Asia-Pacific, linked to its perception of the strategic importance of the region, certainly increased dramatically after 2001. For some analysts, this increased interest and involvement represented the major change in US foreign policy to the region, with the central determinants or commitments of policy (deterring Chinese hegemonic ambitions and attempting to prevent the emergence of a nuclear-capable North Korea, for example) remaining intact (Acharya and Tan, 2004: xvi; Limaye, 2004). Following 9/11, however, the focus in public statements on foreign policy did change, with the Bush administration linking (or more accurately conflating) the imperative of responding aggressively to terrorism with the threat posed by 'rogue states' such as North Korea, and emphasizing the threats posed by terrorist and militant groups in the region, particularly Southeast Asia. Indeed, Southeast Asia would become the 'second front' in the 'war on terror' (Gershman, 2002).

The US pursued its 'war on terror' in the Asia-Pacific in a number of ways. First, as was the case in much of the world, the United States pushed for strong support from states in the region for global counter-terror campaigns in Afghanistan and Iraq, requesting at least diplomatic support, and preferably direct involvement. Second, the US commitment to confronting the terrorist threat posed by Al-Qaeda and associated fundamentalist Islamic terrorist organizations in the region (such as *Jemaah Islamiah* (JI), responsible for the 2002 terrorist bombings on the Indonesian island of Bali) involved an increase in the American military presence in the region, particularly in the Philippines and Singapore, as well as an increase in financial support for counter-terrorist action. This dimension of the 'war on terror' in the region has had particularly significant implications for human rights and democracy, to be discussed.

Third, the United States directly encouraged regional cooperation on terrorist responses, launching regional workshops on terrorism through the ASEAN Regional Forum (ARF), for example, and even turning the 2001 and 2003 APEC (Asia-Pacific Economic Cooperation) meetings (to the irritation of some regional leaders) into forums on the 'war on terror' (Limaye, 2004;

Camroux and Okfen, 2004: 165). As such, while the United States continued to favour 'hub and spoke' bilateralism in the region, and while its approach to international cooperation has been underpinned by a willingness to 'go it alone' if other states and institutions are unwilling to support the US agenda, it has worked through and with multilateral forums when institutions and regional cooperative mechanisms are seen as furthering American interests in the 'war on terror'.

While some of the most important implications of this approach to the region will be addressed in detail below, it is worth noting that in the wake of 9/11 the US was immediately fairly successful in building stronger relations with China and strengthening (somewhat neglected) relations with traditional friends and allies such as Australia and South Korea (Mastanduno, 2003: 151; Limaye, 2004: 206–7). In terms of general government-to-government relations, however, and before even discussing the disjuncture between regime and individual security evident in the prosecution of the 'war on terror', the administration's approach has strained some regional relations. The US-led 'war on terror', particularly its focus on Islamic fundamentalism and military incursions in predominantly Islamic states, has created problems with states such as Indonesia and Malaysia. These states, with the largest Islamic populations in the region (the former in the world), have been caught between being sensitive to the concerns of their domestic populations, the majority of whom were opposed to intervention in Afghanistan much less Iraq, and being seen to support the United States wholeheartedly in its pursuit of the 'war on terror' (Capie, 2004). This is obviously particularly important in a context in which the US administration views any opposition to its approach as evidence of support for the terrorists' cause. The result has been oscillation in both states, particularly Malaysia, between support for the American cause and harsh criticism of the manner in which the US has sought to confront the terrorist threat (Mak, 2004).

The US approach to the 'war on terror' has created other problems familiar to traditional (statist) accounts of security. Over time, the increased US military presence in Southeast Asia, combined with the renewed commitment to missile defence, has raised concerns in China that the 'war on terror' is a front for a more aggressive US policy of containment (Acharya, 2002: 196–7; Yuan, 2005: 115–17). Meanwhile, the US' increasingly hard-line approach to North Korea (with its tenuous link to the broader 'war on terror') raised serious concerns in a range of Northeast Asian states who viewed engagement as the best means of preventing a threatening, nuclear-capable North Korea from emerging, concerns that have been borne out with North Korea's nuclear test in 2006. The worry here is that the US government's approach to North Korea and the containment of China will become something of a self-fulfilling prophecy, *creating* hard-line and threatening responses on the part of those states that feel targeted by US military power. This concern is at once familiar to traditional strategic scholars of international relations in the form of the security dilemma (Herz, 1950; Jervis, 1976) and to critics of traditional approaches to international relations who argue that fear of 'the other' ultimately underpinning such perspectives creates conditions for militarism, violence and war (Ashley, 1989).

A necessary sacrifice? Counter-terrorism, human rights and democracy

The relationship between security and human rights has been a significant issue of debate in international relations literature, although this has been particularly pronounced in the context of the global 'war on terror'. In this context, serious concerns have been raised about a gamut of responses to the terrorist threat, from the 'collateral damage' (i.e. thousands of civilian deaths) caused by military campaigns in Afghanistan and Iraq to anti-terror legislation in a range of states (especially liberal democracies) with detrimental implications for civil liberties and political rights (Wheeler, 2002; Hocking, 2004). While the dichotomy between security and human rights is clearly problematic, not least of all because the conception of security advocated here necessarily entails the promotion of human rights, this distinction between security and human rights still captures the way in which a range of political leaders, especially in the Asia-Pacific, think about security in international politics and specifically the way such states think about the need to confront the threat posed by terrorism.[4]

In the Asia-Pacific and particularly Southeast Asia, a pre-existing tendency to justify oppressive rule through a claim of prioritizing economic over civil and political rights (linked to the so-called 'Asian values' debate) has merged with the new global imperative of redressing the terror threat to significantly undermine prospects for the emergence of mature democracies and allowed some governments in the region greater scope to repress domestic populations. The 'war on terror' has undermined human rights and democratization in three central ways. First, it has served to legitimate a crackdown on political opposition, both through the emulation of the United States' example and through the general prioritization of terrorism as a security threat in global politics that renders all other concerns (including individual welfare) secondary. Existing opposition to the human rights–security dichotomy within the Asia-Pacific has been marginalized by the hegemonic discourse of the 'war on terror', with its 'common sense' which suggests the need to sacrifice some human rights in the pursuit of security from terrorism. Second, the 'war on terror' has entailed direct material support (through training and financial aid) for organizations implicated in some of the worst examples of human rights abuses in the region, and for violent responses to internal dissidence generally. Finally, the 'war on terror' has limited the role of human rights promotion by forces external to the region and particularly by the United States, even to the point of promoting the types of hard-line responses reminiscent of the region's authoritarian regimes of the 1970s and 1980s.

Many of the states of the Asia-Pacific, and particularly Southeast Asia, have proven only too willing to allow the United States' concern with, and approach to, counter-terrorism to inform their own counter-terrorism initiatives. While some of this eagerness can be understood as an attempt to redress the threat of terrorism, much of it also indicates a willingness to use the anti-terror imperative as a cover for darker political objectives relating to the marginalization of domestic dissent. This has been particularly apparent in China and Malaysia. In China, the government's own 'war on terror' has focused significantly on Uighur separatists in the northwest province of Xinjiang, which separatists refer to as 'Eastern Turkmenistan' (Xinjiang, 2002). According to Amnesty International, since 9/11 'China has repackaged its repression of Uighurs as a fight against "terrorism" despite official claims that not one incident of explosion or assassination has taken place in the region in the last few years' (Amnesty International, 2004). And although initially expressing concerns about this, the United States agreed in 2002 to push for the United Nations Security Council to label the East Turkestan Islamic Movement (ETIM) a 'terrorist organisation', in what was widely perceived as a *quid pro quo* for Chinese support in the broader 'war on terror' (Lam, 2002).

The Malaysian government has also proved eager to define political repression as part of the 'war on terror', introducing a series of restrictive measures under an Internal Security Act and arresting members of the main opposition party – the *Parti Islam se-Malaysia* – for suspected terrorist activity (Collins, 2003: 201–9). It is significant to note here that the Malaysian justice minister has argued that the Internal Security Act is both accepted by the United States as a legitimate response to the terrorist threat and mirrors the provisions of the (controversial) USA Patriot Act (Capie, 2004: 230–3). Indeed, Rosemary Foot (2005: 423) has argued that the United States has 'done untold damage' not only to the human rights of those affected by restrictive domestic laws and detention in Guantanamo Bay, but also, because of the extent of emulation of its actions internationally, 'to the human rights regime itself'.

The 'war on terror' has also seen the United States working directly with militaries and counter-terror organizations that have been implicated in human rights abuses and have been central to cycles of violence within states. There are also broader concerns here about promoting the importance of the military, especially in a (difficult) period of democratization *from* military-based political systems. Both of these dynamics are particularly evident in Indonesia, where the US government has circumvented congressional restraints on cooperation with the military to provide millions of dollars in aid and logistical support for counter-terror operations, despite criticism from analysts and human rights non-governmental organizations (NGOs) (Simon, 2004: 70; Foot, 2004: 50–4). This criticism has focused on the implications support for the military has for an already difficult transition to democracy; on the lack of accountability of the Indonesian military (TNI) generally, and counter-terrorist units (such as *Kopassus*) specifically; and their role in a range of human rights abuses in separatist struggles in provinces such as Aceh (Gershman, 2002; Manning, 2003; Amnesty International, 2005; Ojendal, 2004: 527). The Bush administration's push to 'normalise' military-to-military relations with Indonesia (Foot, 2004: 50–4), suspended since 1999, speaks significantly to the downgrading of human rights concerns in US foreign policy under the 'war on terror', discussed below. As Alex Bellamy and Bryn Hughes argue in their contribution to this volume, such assistance risks ignoring the ways in which militaries in the region have historically been the source of, rather than the agent for redressing, their citizens' suffering and insecurity.

Finally, the US-led 'war on terror' has had negative implications for human rights in limiting international pressure on states in the region to redress human rights problems. This is particularly regressive given that (particularly civil and political) human rights have limited resonance in the Asia-Pacific context, especially among political leaders, and in nascent democracies in the region domestic civil society forces are comparatively weak. Having been consistently criticized by Washington for its approach to human rights prior to 9/11, for example, the Malaysian government has subsequently been lauded by the Bush administration as a model Islamic state. US Assistant Secretary of State James Kelly, for example, described Malaysia as a 'beacon of stability in the region' (cited in Foot, 2004: 55). Indeed on returning from the US after a visit in 2002, Prime Minister Mahatir Mohammed noted that discussions had focused almost exclusively on counter-terrorism, and that President Bush 'did not raise anything about democracy or human rights in Malaysia' (cited in Manning, 2003). While a return to the type of 'megaphone diplomacy' that has at times characterized the US government's promotion of human rights in the region should not necessarily be desired, a failure to promote human rights because of the strategic importance of a particular state or actor both downgrades human rights as important for their own sake and raises questions about the extent to which the United States is really as committed to the global promotion of democracy and human rights as it claims.

These implications of the 'war on terror', and particularly the US' pursuit of the 'war on terror', are problematic for two central reasons. First, and most obviously, they are ethically problematic. The justification of repressive action and rule on the basis of redressing the terrorist threat is in many cases (particularly in China and Malaysia) no more than a justification. It also serves to present security and human rights as an either/or proposition, rather than as inexorably intertwined. From a critical security perspective, security understood as emancipation specifically *requires* a central concern with the human rights of the most vulnerable: not their further marginalization or oppression in the name of security (Booth, 1991; Collins, 2003: 208–11; Burke, 2001b).

Second, the above implications of the 'war on terror' are strategically problematic, even counterproductive. As Adam Roberts (2005: 126) has argued, historically counter-terrorism has been successful when carried out in a manner consistent with human rights norms and rules, when not relying exclusively or even primarily on military means, and when terrorists are relegated 'to a status of near-irrelevance as life moves on, long-standing grievances are addressed, and peoples can see that a grim terrorist war of attrition is achieving little and damaging their own societies'. These lessons of history appear not to have been learnt or applied in the Asia-Pacific branch of the US-led 'war on terror', as a range of analysts have argued (Wright-Neville, 2004; Rogers, 2004). This is particularly evident in the case of the Philippines, where the commitment of over $US 100 million in US military aid and 1200 US troops to a military campaign against the Abu Sayyaf separatist group since early 2002 has achieved minimal success in either eradicating the group or preventing further violent incidents (Acharya, 2005b: 208; Capie, 2004: 233). Steven Rogers (2004) argues that in this case, the United States has failed to appreciate the difference between terrorists and separatists, or the political environment in which violence becomes possible. Certainly, the consistent failure, both within the region and globally, to address the complex political, social and economic contexts that give rise to violent extremists limits the extent to which the 'war on terror' can ever be successful.

The 'war on terror', militarism and militarization

As noted, the US-led 'war on terror' has prioritized military responses to the threat of terrorism, a prioritization reflected in the Asia-Pacific region. Here, two implications of the 'war on terror' for processes and dynamics of militarism and militarization are noted. The first concerns the Bush administration's interpretation of the doctrine of pre-emption elaborated in the National Security Strategy in 2002, which poses significant problems in the region in terms of worsening regional tensions and (again) creating possibilities for emulation. Second, the legitimization of militarism and militarization through the 'war on terror', evident in the attempt to reinterpret (Article 9) constitutional limits on the development and use of military force in Japan, decreases the possibility for regional cooperation and increases the likelihood of conflict. Clearly these dynamics have not been *caused* by the 'war on terror': pre-emption was certainly advocated by elements of the Bush administration prior to the 2001 terrorist attacks, while Japanese militarization and the government's 'reinterpretation' of Article 9 similarly pre-dated the 'war on terror'. Nevertheless, the 'war on terror' has had important implications in legitimating and accelerating these dynamics.

The US commitment to the doctrine of pre-emption was most fully articulated in the US National Security Strategy of September 2002, although of particular concern here has been the willingness of the administration to conflate pre-emption with preventative war: most notably in Iraq.[5] In the National Security Strategy, the right of pre-emptive war was claimed as a response to the threat posed by terrorists and particularly by 'axis of evil' states (Iran, Iraq and North Korea) seeking to develop weapons of mass destruction (WMDs), sponsor terrorists, or willing and able to provide terrorists with WMDs (Bush, 2002). The linkage of the right to use force against threats 'before they are fully formed' to rogue states and the 'war on terror', and the blurring of the important distinction between pre-emption and prevention, has had important implications for regional security. Most obviously, it signalled a hard-line, confrontational approach to the North Korean regime on the part of the US, with associated effects for security and stability in Northeast Asia. Second, it has raised the spectre of 'emulation': the potential for other states in the region to apply this doctrine to their own conception of security threats. In particular, both Australia and Japan have invoked pre-emption as a policy option against future regional 'threats' since 2002.

The US' elaboration of pre-emption as part of a hard-line approach to North Korea has, as Roland Bleiker argues in his chapter and elsewhere (Bleiker, 2003), failed to halt the regime's nuclear ambitions or redress the suffering of North Korea's citizens. Indeed to the extent that it has had any effect on North Korea's approach, it appears to have been to *create* a more hard-line response on the part of North Korea and an open acknowledgement of its WMD ambitions/programme in response to American accusations. This in turn has created alarm within the region, particularly among South Korea, Japan and China who have declared a preference for negotiation and peaceful resolution in the face of threats emanating from hard-liners in the Bush administration (Moon and Bae, 2005: 53–5).

The US' doctrine (and interpretation) of pre-emption has also established a precedent that some regional allies have been willing to emulate, at least rhetorically. Soon after 88 Australians had been killed in the Bali bombings in late 2002, Prime Minister John Howard declared that if confronted with evidence that terrorists were planning an attack on Australians in another country, he would be willing to launch a pre-emptive strike. The comment raised a series of objections and criticisms from regional leaders, who rejected what they saw as an unnecessary, insensitive and even imperialistic attempt to apply the Bush doctrine to the Southeast Asian struggle against terrorism (Acharya, 2005b: 213–5). The Japanese Defence Minister, meanwhile, argued in early 2003 that Japan would consider a pre-emptive strike against North Korea if faced with an immediate nuclear threat (Acharya, 2005b: 218). While the latter (Japanese) invocation of pre-emption is better viewed as something of an aberration in this case rather than as an indication of a broader security world-view (as is the case in Australia), in both cases such statements have been enabled by the context of the Bush doctrine and associated 'war on terror'. And in both cases, these statements have produced an increase in regional tensions, undermining the prospect of cooperative approaches to a range of security, political and economic issues.[6]

In recent years, and related to the above articulation of pre-emption, the constitutionally imposed limitation on external Japanese military action has been the subject of concerted political debate.[7] This debate began in earnest during the (first) Gulf War, when the Japanese government failed to commit troops to the international coalition. This decision subsequently loomed in discussions about whether Japan should contribute (and if so in what form) to the 'war on terror' in Afghanistan and later Iraq. As Christopher Hughes (2004: 431) argues, 'Japanese policy-makers were concerned that they would face *gaiatsu* (external pressure), similar to the time of the Gulf War, from its US ally to provide a human and military contribution to the international coalition, and that failure to respond could again jeopardise the political basis of the Japan-US alliance'. This concern appeared well-founded in that it was articulated by other political leaders in the region and internationally,[8] consistent with comments in the US administration about what type of ally it hoped for in Japan,[9] while President Bush's 'you're with us or against us' position on participation in the 'war on terror' left little room for ambivalence or inactivity. Japan's eventual participation and deployment of military personnel in both Afghanistan and Iraq has signalled a broader commitment to (or at least precedent for) involvement in external military operations and appears to have reinforced a broader shift towards Japan becoming a 'normal' security state. While potentially allowing Japan to contribute militarily to future humanitarian or peacekeeping missions, the linkage of such a shift to the weakening of the Japanese peace movement, a more confrontational approach to North Korea and to the specific example of intervention in Iraq should give serious pause to those who would see the erosion of Article 9 as a potentially normatively progressive move (Tanter, 2005). Given the regional climate in part created by the 'war on terror', militarization carries the inherent risks of large-scale violence in a crisis.

Towards alternative security futures

To what extent does US hegemony generally, and the pursuit of the 'war on terror' specifically, further peace and security in the Asia-Pacific region? There is little doubt that the US presence is desired by a range of states in the region (particularly those fearing Chinese hegemonic ambitions), while many security analysts portray the US presence as the only factor preventing the outbreak of large-scale war in Northeast Asia. Further, there is little doubt that terrorism and politically motivated small-scale violence pose a threat to state and individual security in the region, particularly in Southeast Asia. But defences of US hegemony are based on a series of assumptions about an anarchic and unsafe regional environment made stable by the US presence, assumptions which must appear questionable in the face of the Bush administration's role in raising Chinese concerns of US containment or encirclement; promoting Japanese militarization; and encouraging a more confrontational (and nuclear-capable) North Korea. And acknowledging the threat of terrorism to both state and individual welfare should not lead us to blindly accept the argument that an increased willingness and capacity to use military force against this threat serves to either enhance individual or indeed regime security. Ultimately, under the Bush administration generally, and through the 'war on terror' specifically, the US presence has undermined rather than enhanced the security of people in the Asia-Pacific.

Despite these limitations, indeed in part because of them, there are immanent possibilities for the emergence of alternative security futures in the region, and for the realization of security for the most vulnerable. The US approach to the 'war on terror' in the Asia-Pacific has been contested both domestically and in the region. International NGOs such as Amnesty International and Human Rights Watch have pointed to the danger of the 'war on terror' legitimating political oppression and human rights abuses both in the Asia-Pacific and in states such as Pakistan, Egypt, Russia and Uzbekistan (Human Rights Watch, 2002; Amnesty International, 2004). International criticism of the US anti-terror approach certainly reached a high point with its intervention in Iraq in 2003. The concerns expressed then about the likelihood of violence and instability characterizing Iraq's immediate future have sadly been borne out, with (at the time of writing) at least 55,000 civilians killed there since the military campaign began (Iraq bodycount.org, 2007). Within the US, both NGOs and members of Congress have voiced concerns about US cooperation with states in the Asia-Pacific with poor human rights records, and have attempted to tie human rights conditions to US bilateral military cooperation (Foot, 2005: 424). These critical voices have ensured that even while downgraded, concerns for human rights and democratization in interactions with states cooperating in the 'war on terror' have not disappeared entirely from US foreign policy (Foot, 2004).

At the regional level, some states have demonstrated a willingness at times to buck the trend of increased militarized vigilance, or at least increased US military presence, in the face of the terrorist threat. In 2004 both the Malaysian and Indonesian governments rejected a US offer to allow its military to patrol the Malacca Strait, based on fears that Islamic fanaticism would be fuelled rather than redressed by the US presence. Indeed Indonesia's chief foreign affairs spokesman argued that 'you cannot arm yourselves to the teeth and expect that will lead of itself to a sense of security. You have to work with the region to share in a sense of security' (Guerin, 2005). Arguably, such a perspective has informed the Indonesian government's pursuit of a peace agreement with separatists in Aceh in mid-2005. Senior figures in the Philippine government were also strongly critical of US military involvement in the campaign against the Abu Sayyaf group. The foreign affairs spokesperson resigned in protest over the issue, while the Vice President echoed the Indonesian foreign affairs spokesperson in arguing that the US approach would breed rather than redress animosity among its Islamic population (Acharya, 2005b: 209; Capie, 2004: 236).

And although civil society forces in some states in the region remain weak (and potentially weakened further by the 'war on terror'), human rights groups, minor political parties and the sheer force of public opinion have constrained the room to move of governments in a number of states in the region, despite US pressure. Regional human rights NGOs and networks such as the Asian Human Rights Commission and the Asia-Pacific Human Rights Centre have been particularly vocal about human rights abuses in the 'war on terror'. Minor political parties in Australia, Indonesia and Japan, for example, have been critical of their governments' support for the American counter-terror agenda for both normative and pragmatic reasons (McDonald, 2005c: 311–15; Jakarta Post, 2003; McCurry, 2004). These voices constitute a counter-hegemonic discourse, questioning the commonsense of a campaign against terrorism necessitating some suspension of human rights and civil liberties. Such opposition to the 'war on terror', combined with the continued occurrence of civil unrest and violence in regional 'trouble-spots', has arguably pushed the Bush administration further towards advocating 'greater political freedom and the nurturing of civil society as a component of its wider counterterrorist agenda' (Wright-Neville, 2004). This also highlights the fact that there are voices in the region questioning taken-for-granted assumptions about the US as regional security provider, even providing an important basis for the emergence of security practices in the region in which human rights are part of (rather than inimical to) the realization of security.

Regionalism and increased multilateral cooperation in the Asia-Pacific also provide some basis for optimism about normatively progressive security futures in the region. Movements in this direction could be related to the 'war on terror' and US hegemony in two ways. First, regionalism and regional security cooperation may be furthered in the region as a *reaction* to the American 'unilateral' agenda (Beeson, 2003; Ojendal, 2004). This was arguably evident in the cooperative efforts of China, Japan and South Korea to pursue a conciliatory approach to North Korean nuclear ambitions, and in the holding of the inaugural East Asia Summit in December 2005: the first meeting of Asia-Pacific heads of government that has excluded the US. Second, some argue that the (albeit piecemeal) US engagement with multilateral institutions legitimizes these mechanisms and provides a basis for regional cooperation. In this context, even limited attempts to create regional agreements on counter-terrorism or to work through institutions such as APEC might be viewed as serving to institutionalize cooperation as the basis for addressing regional security threats.[10]

Increased regionalism in security terms has both normative possibilities and limitations. There are limits to the extent to which 'deeper' multilateralism can be achieved and even questions about whether it is to be desired. For some, the absence of a shared regional identity and the continued commitment to sovereignty defined as non-intervention make the prospects for realizing a mature security community in the Asia-Pacific region highly unlikely (Mastanduno, 2003). For others, the elite-driven nature of regionalization and regional cooperation in the Asia-Pacific raises questions about the extent to which further regionalization is even desirable in terms of redressing individual insecurity (Lawson, 2005).

These problems or limitations, along with the traditional emphasis in the region on regime rather than individual or human security (Burke, 2001a), clearly pre-date 9/11 and the 'war on terror'. Yet regional security cooperation does have progressive potential. Such cooperation is increasingly occurring through track-two and track-three mechanisms, which involve an expansion of the number of voices heard in mainstream security debates and the number of issues raised and addressed in regional (security) forums.[11] More fundamentally, regional security cooperation creates a context in which conflict between states becomes less likely and in which security can be thought about in absolute rather than relative terms. The emergence and continued institutionalization of a pluralistic security community (in which members resolve disputes without recourse to violence), for example (Acharya, 2001), would be a positive step in this direction, even while a long way from the type of political community that would best allow for the realization of individual emancipation.

Conclusion

This chapter has emphasized the costs of the US prosecution of the 'war on terror' for the security of the most vulnerable people in the region, pointing not only to the disjuncture between the security of states/regimes and those of individuals, but also to the ways in which the US approach has been inimical to the goals it has set itself in the prosecution of the 'war on terror' and in advancing regional security more broadly. In this latter context, this chapter shares some criticisms advanced by traditional realist and neo-realist scholars of security, who have argued that elements of the US (neo-conservative) approach risk destabilizing the region and creating conditions conducive to nuclear proliferation, interstate war or terrorism (Hoge, 2004; Christensen, 2003). Such convergence between realist and critical approaches to security is perhaps intuitively surprising, although it should be noted that the reasons for defining the threat of conflict as a security threat are fundamentally different. While the former views violent conflict as one of a number of ways in which individual lives are threatened, the latter views this threat in terms of prospects for further 'instability', 'spill-over' and the general disruption of the regional status quo. In short, an emancipatory approach is predicated upon an ethical reorientation that is fundamentally foreign, indeed threatening, to both realist and what might be termed neo-conservative approaches to security: a commitment to the prioritization of the needs of the most vulnerable in global politics, and a focus on their emancipation. This critical, emancipatory approach involves asking how the contemporary world order came about, who is benefiting from it, and whether it is worth preserving.

As Ken Booth (2005c: 182–3) and Richard Wyn Jones (2005: 229–32) argue, individual emancipation should be viewed as progress rather than an end-point, an idea that allows us to focus on the always immanent possibilities for progressive change while recognizing that scholars should avoid prescribing alternative (utopian) security orders that are neither developed indigenously nor practically realizable in an immediate sense. At a minimum and in the contexts outlined above, emancipation may be defined in terms of processes that involve a diffusion of power (away from the centralized power of state regimes), such that more voices speaking security, including most importantly those articulating alternative visions for the future, may be heard. Such possibilities are evident in the region, even while clearly circumscribed by a US-led 'war on terror' that legitimates and even encourages the suspension of human rights concerns in the name of state security, and reinforces the primacy of regime security through militarized vigilance.

NOTES

1 Hegemony is used here both to refer to the preponderant material power capabilities of the United States, and (in a Gramscian sense) in terms of its capacity to position particular responses to terrorism, most notably the inevitability of sacrificing some human rights concerns in the pursuit of the 'war on terror', as 'commonsense'.

2 'Interventionist' refers here to the willingness of the United States to promote its interests more forcefully in the international arena, including through increased interference in domestic politics in other states. In this context this willingness is linked to a neo-conservative political agenda and has manifested itself most clearly in the pursuit of regime change. See Kristol (1983).

3 Militarization and militarism refer respectively to the development or growth of military capacity and the primacy given to military means of responding to political issues.

4 Indonesian President Yudhoyono argued after the 2003 bombing of a hotel in Jakarta that 'those who criticise about human rights being breached must understand that all bombing victims are more important than any human rights issue' (cited in Foot, 2005: 421).

5 Pre-emption refers to a defensive response to an immediate threat, while preventative war refers to an offensive act against a hypothetical future threat. See Freedman (2004: 85–9).

6 Australia's position on pre-emption, for example, almost prevented its attendance at meetings to discuss the establishment of a regional trade bloc in Southeast Asia. See McDonald (2005b: 163–4).

7 Article 9 of Japan's 1946 constitution dictates that 'the Japanese people forever renounce war as a sovereign right of the nation and the threat or use of force as a means of settling international disputes', although under the constitution Japan retains the right of self-defence.

8 As Anthony Burke notes in his chapter, this concern was noted by Australian Foreign Minister Alexander Downer in March 2004.

9 US Deputy of State Richard Armitage (cited in Tanter, 2005: 162) argued in late 2003 that 'we are trying to develop a kind of relationship with Japan that we enjoy with Great Britain'.

10 Archarya and Tan (2004: xvi–xvii), for example, argue that 'a la carte multilateralism is better than no multilateralism at all'. See also Capie (2004: 238–40).

11 Among the most prominent here has been the Council for Security Cooperation in the Asia-Pacific (CSCAP), which in 1996 advocated the adoption of 'comprehensive security' as the organizing security principle for the region. See, for example, Camilleri (2005).

Part III

Futures

13

Dealing with a nuclear North Korea: conventional and alternative security scenarios

Roland Bleiker

DEALING WITH North Korea is perhaps one of the most difficult security challenges in global politics today.[1] Totalitarian and reclusive, ideologically isolated and economically ruined, it is the inherent 'other' in a globalized and neo-liberal world order. And yet, North Korea keeps surviving, not least because its leaders periodically rely on threats, such as nuclear brinkmanship, to gain concessions from the international community. The latest such attempt began in the autumn of 2002, when Pyongyang admitted to a secret nuclear weapons programme and subsequently withdrew from the nuclear Non-Proliferation Treaty (NPT). From that point the situation rapidly deteriorated. By early 2003 both the US and North Korea were threatening each other with outright war. The situation became even more tense in October 2006, when the United Nations Security Council unanimously decided on tough sanctions in response to Pyongyang's announcement that it had successfully completed its first nuclear test. Even China, one of Pyongyang's very few remaining supporters, was highly alarmed by North Korea's move, labelling the test 'flagrant and brazen' and calling immediately for punitive actions (Kahn, 2006). North Korea's demonstrated nuclear ambition does, indeed, substantially increase the risk of a nuclear arms race in the region and an escalation of the security situation with possible global consequences.

Finding ethical and politically acceptable ways of dealing with North Korea is neither obvious nor easy. The debates are correspondingly polarized. On one end of the spectrum are advocates of a hard-line policy towards the North, which relies on the projection of military threats and aims to undermine the authoritarian regime as fast as possible, leading to a quick disintegration and subsequent absorption (Eberstadt, 1997; Hunter, 1999; Rice, 2000). The second approach favours engaging North Korea in political, economic and cultural interactions. It is based on what is often called the 'soft-landing scenario', which seeks a gradual integration of North Korea into the world community (Harrison, 1997; Snyder, 1998). With the re-emergence of major tensions over North Korea's nuclear programme, the front-lines of these debates became even more polarized. Some believe that a firmer stance towards North Korea, as currently advocated by the US administration, was long overdue and is, indeed, essential for dealing with the challenges ahead (Cha, 2002a; Miles, 2002: 38–9). Others stress that precisely at such a moment of crisis it is crucial to hold on to the more tolerant approach favoured by the subsequent South Korean presidents Kim Dae-jung and Roh Moo-hyun (Harrison, 2001; Dujarric, 2001; Moon, 2001a; Wolfsthal, 2006).

The task of this chapter is to discuss these opposing approaches, using the US and South Korean positions as key points of reference. The fact that there is a relatively significant difference between these two close allies is new and rather unusual. During the Clinton administration Washington was highly supportive of South Korea's engagement policy, taking a number of additional steps, such as lifting restrictions on investment in and trade with North Korea. The inauguration of George W. Bush in 2002 marked a dramatic shift towards a more confrontational US policy to Korea. The new, more hawkish approach, viewed the North as an 'evil' rogue state that could only be contained through an aggressive military posture. This change in attitude posed serious difficulties for Kim Dae-jung's engagement policy, which had already come under challenge within South Korea. But the presidential election of 2002 produced a winner, Roh Moo-hyun, who strongly believed in the need to continue his predecessor's approach. A significant policy rift thus emerged between Washington and Seoul, not least because Roh won the election in the context of a nationwide wave of anti-Americanism (Weisman, 2003).

I identify various problematic elements in the confrontational approach and argue for the need to embrace an engagement policy. The latter has the best chance of easing tensions on the peninsula, for it promotes various interactions between North and South. Particularly crucial here are those interactions that engender face-to-face encounters among average citizens across the dividing line. Over time, such contacts can help to reduce the high levels of mutual antagonism and distrust that have fuelled conflict on the peninsula for half a century.

But the engagement approach, as currently practised, also displays more parallels with the confrontational policy than it seems at first sight. Given that the key leitmotif of normalizing political interactions on the peninsula is integrating North Korea into the world community, the idea is still one of absorption – not by force, but by gradual integration. Peace, in other words, can only occur if the North reforms its political system and acquires the democratic and neo-liberal values that prevail in the South. While desirable on numerous accounts, such an approach can also lead to a more aggressive stance by North Korea, whose primarily goal is state survival.

I thus argue for a more nuanced promotion of engagement, one that accepts North Korea as it is – thus taking into account how Pyongyang is likely to react to different policy initiatives from South Korea and the US. Advancing such an approach, which entails components of an ethics of difference, is not to abandon military-based defence. Nor is it to legitimize the highly repressive political regime in Pyongyang, whose brinkmanship tactics pose grave risks to world peace. Rather, the point is to understand the complex political and psychological dynamics that are at play in Korea – and extract from them critical but at the same time tangible suggestions about how to best promote peace on the peninsula.

A critical approach to Korean security

Before engaging debates about how to deal with the government in Pyongyang it is important to stress that advancing a critical approach to East Asian security issues is to challenge the manner in which North Korea has conventionally been represented in prevailing policy and media discourses. Journalists, academics and policy-makers alike tend to stress that the 'hermit-kingdom' of North Korea is so secretive that it is virtually impossible to obtain objective information about its policy formation. 'We are completely ignorant of what is happening in that part of Korea', summarizes one observer (Lee, 1995: 119).[2] Economists emphasize similar themes, stressing, for instance, that the North is a 'statistical wasteland' (Derenberger, 1988: 243). North Korea is, indeed, one of the world's most secluded states. Much about the decision-making that occurs is impossible to retrace. But more details about North Korea are becoming known to the outside world. There are increasingly numerous and detailed studies on society and politics, including Pyongyang's foreign policy and negotiating behaviour. Moreover, as a result of the famines that followed the floods of 1995 various representatives of foreign humanitarian organizations took up residence in North Korea. Hazel Smith points out that many of the non-governmental organizations (NGOs) active in the North have been able to get access to significant information about the country, often with collaboration from government authorities. But the reports that document these experiences and insights seem to have little impact in the West (Smith, 1999, 2000: 603). Bruce Cumings (2000: 152), likewise, argues that a wealth of information is now available about many crucial aspects of North Korea's history, but it is hardly ever consulted by Western policy analysts.

At the same time as perpetuating the image of an unknowable hermit kingdom, many influential academic and policy approaches towards North Korea advance strong claims to objectivity. This practice is as widespread as it is paradoxical. Consider a South Korean report on human rights in North Korea. The authors readily admit that there is a 'lack of verifiable or corroborating evidence'. But that does not prevent them from stressing that their study is 'based on facts' (Suh and Suh, 2001). This tendency is particularly fateful in the domain of foreign and security policy. Look at how the otherwise very nuanced Perry Report, commissioned by President Clinton, insisted that the US should deal with North Korea 'as it is, not as we might wish it to be'. It advocated a 'realistic view of the DPRK, a hardheaded understanding of military realities' (Perry, 1999; see also Choi, 1999).

Strategic 'reality' in Korea is the reality seen through the lenses of the strategic studies paradigm. This paradigm filters or selects information in a way that sets limits to what can and cannot be recognized as 'real' and 'realistic'. The policy perspectives that are based on realist ideology can thus be presented as 'hard-headed' understandings of 'military realities', even though (or, precisely because) next to nothing is known (or being acknowledged) about the actual realities of North Korea. But because the realist ideology is articulated from the privileged position of the state, any opposing perspective can relatively easily be dismissed as unreasonable or unrealistic. Realist approaches to foreign policy have been around for so long and have become so influential that their political origin appears more and more real until the ensuing world-views, and the conflicts they generate, seem inevitable, even natural.

A critical approach to Korean security must challenge the equation of realist ideology with objectivity and commonsense. A major purpose of this chapter is thus to question their taken-for-granted nature. One must problematize prevailing approaches, particularly if they legitimize themselves through an uncritical reference to 'reality'. A critical approach asks: Whose reality? For what purpose? In whose interest? With which consequences?

US foreign policy and the failure of the confrontational approach

The political and ethical dilemmas of how to engage North Korea are as difficult as they are open-ended. The respective debates are, in essence, dominated by two opposing approaches.

The first approach advocates a hard-line policy towards North Korea, which is aimed at undermining the authoritarian regime as fast as possible, leading to a quick collapse and subsequent unification. 'If the North Korean regime is irredeemable', Marcus Noland (2000: 8) asks, 'should not the rest of the world act to hasten its demise?' Withdrawing support would, undoubtedly, worsen the economic situation in the North and precipitate yet another famine. But is this not the price to pay for the promotion of a more just political order? Providing Pyongyang with trade possibilities and humanitarian aid would, according to this logic, not only sustain a dictatorial and dangerous regime but also prolong the suffering of the North Korean people. The longer the peninsula is divided, Nicolas Eberstadt stresses, the bigger the economic chasm between North and South will grow. This, in turn, will render eventual unification more expensive and more difficult (Eberstadt, 1997: 82). Consider some of the immediate practical dilemmas. Several NGOs that provided humanitarian aid, such as Oxfam, left North Korea because they were prevented from adequately monitoring and evaluating the impact of their aid, which they feared did not reach the most vulnerable part of the population. Most explicit in its critique was Médecins Sans Frontières, which also protested against the existence of alleged concentration camps that hold people who were caught foraging for food across the border in China (Noland, 2000: 183). If humanitarian assistance is channelled directly through the repressive regime, a representative of the organization argued, then it 'has become part of the system of oppression' (Terry, 2001).

The confrontational approach is best exemplified by the current US foreign policy towards North Korea. A brief summary of the two nuclear crises that haunted the peninsula in the last decade is necessary to understand the historical context of this position. Tensions rose in 1993 when North Korea threatened to withdraw from the NPT. William Perry (2002: 121), then US secretary of defense, considered the subsequent crisis the only time during his tenure when he 'believed that the US was in serious danger of a major war'. An agreement, signed in October 1994, managed to avert an open conflict. Pyongyang consented to freeze its nuclear programme in return for a number of US, South Korean and Japanese promises, including aid, heating oil and the eventual construction of two light-water nuclear reactors that would provide North Korea with energy sources.

By early 2002 this so called Agreed Framework started to break down. Intelligence reports indicated that North Korea was secretly enriching uranium, in direct violation of the agreement. Rather than trying to address this challenge in the context of the existing security framework, the new US president, George W. Bush, adopted a more confrontational policy. In his first State of the Union address he singled out North Korea as one of three 'rogue' states belonging to an 'axis of evil'. Soon afterwards, the Defense Department, in a report to Congress, included North Korea in a group of seven nations that were potential targets of pre-emptive nuclear strikes. Pyongyang reacted in an angry manner, warning that it would abandon the agreed freeze of its nuclear weapons programme, which it subsequently did. The situation then rapidly deteriorated. The crisis further intensified in October 2006, when North Korea publicly announced that it had successfully conducted its first nuclear test at an underground site in Gilju, Hamgyong province.

One can argue about who is to blame for the re-emergence of a crisis situation on the Korean peninsula. North Korea certainly deserves a fair share of the responsibility. The dangers of its nuclear brinkmanship are evident and much discussed. Miscalculations or a sudden escalation could precipitate a human disaster at any moment. Equally dangerous, although much less evident, are the confrontational and militaristic attitudes with which some of the key regional and global players seek to contain the volatile situation. Particularly problematic is Washington's inability to see North Korea as anything but a threatening 'rogue state', which seriously hinders both an adequate understanding and possible resolution of the conflict. Very few policy-makers, security analysts and journalists ever make the effort to imagine how threats are perceived from the North Korean perspective, and how these perceptions are part of an interactive security dilemma in which the West is as much implicated as the vilified regime in Pyongyang. Particularly significant is the current policy of pre-emptive strikes against rogue states, for it reinforces half a century of American nuclear threats towards North Korea.

Issues of responsibility are, of course, open to debate. Less debatable, though, is the fact that conventional security approaches, based on deterrence and the projection of military threats, have clearly not been able to solve the security dilemmas on the Korean peninsula. Tensions are as high as ever and North Korea, having withdrawn from the NPT, has now tested a nuclear weapon and is openly pursuing a nuclear weapons programme. The confrontational approach has been equally unsuccessful in bringing about change within North Korea or improving its human rights record. The regime is as stable and as authoritarian as ever.

Historical evidence suggests that the key policy options of conventional approaches – military threats and economic sanctions – have only limited chances for success in Korea. Ever since the latest crisis emerged, officials in Washington stressed on numerous times that 'no military option's been taken off the table' (Dao, 2003a; Green, 2003). This approach has been underlined by some of Washington's allies. Australia's prime minister, John Howard, reiterated in response to Pyongyang's nuclear test in 2006 that 'all options are on the table', including military action (*The Australian*, 2006). Washington then pushed strongly for a United Nations Security Council resolution that would authorize the use of military power to enforce sanctions against Pyongyang – an option that had to be dropped only because of opposition by China and Russia.

The US has, of course, threatened and used military power quite frequently to achieve political goals, most recently in Afghanistan and Iraq. Such actions are aimed at either pressuring a regime to change its behaviour or at actually removing it from power altogether. But strategic experts largely agree that a military solution to the nuclear crisis in Korea is highly problematic. One of the world's biggest cities, Seoul, is only 50 km away from the (heavily militarized) demilitarized zone. Even if pre-emptive strikes were to neutralize North Korea's growing nuclear arsenal, they would not be able to destroy all its conventional weapons. The latter alone could easily trigger a second Korean war with disastrous consequences on all sides. Intensifying threats against North Korea would also provide its regime with a welcoming source of legitimacy. The result may be a population rallying around its threatened government, no matter how despotic it is.

The second conventional option is economic sanctions, which the United Nations Security Council pronounced in a unanimously accepted resolution on 14 October 2006. Taken in direct response to Pyongyang's nuclear test, these sanctions are the most far-reaching ones imposed against North Korea since the end of the war in 1953. They include not only a blockade of any material that could be used to produce nuclear, biological and chemical weapons, but also a ban on international travel and a freeze of assets held by people associated with Pyongyang's contentious weapons programmes. The resolution also provides the authorization to inspect cargo that goes into and out of North Korea (Hoge, 2006).

The problem with sanctions is that they have historically been of very limited use. Only in rare cases, such as Libya and Sudan, did they pressure rogue states into adopting 'compliant' or 'partly compliant' behaviour. Miroslav Nincic (2005) stresses that failure is the norm, as in the cases of Iran, Iraq, Yugoslavia, Afghanistan and – at least so far – North Korea. In fact, Nincic goes as far as stressing that comprehensive economic sanctions often had a counterproductive effect, leading to a modification of a regime's ideology and economy that actually ended up strengthening its grip on power. The new regime of far-reaching sanctions against North Korea is thus unlikely to diffuse tensions or generate genuine change. The most likely result is more belligerence from the rulers in Pyongyang and more suffering for North Korea's population, which already faces famine conditions.

Negotiations with North Korea are thus necessary, even from a confrontational perspective. The Bush administration is, indeed, well aware of this imperative. All top US officials publicly stressed one common theme: that 'there is no reason why discussion about confidence-building measures cannot take place with Pyongyang' (Hubbard, 2002). Even the reaction to Pyongyang's nuclear test of October 2006 was remarkably focused on dialogue. President Bush stressed on numerous occasions that 'diplomacy hasn't run its course' (Stolberg, 2006). At the very same time, though, the projection of threats towards Pyongyang was carefully maintained, even intensified. The message was clear: a nuclear North Korea would not be tolerated.

'Hawk engagement' has emerged as a term to describe the new and much tougher US stance (Cha, 2002a). Like Pyongyang, Washington explicitly threatens the opponent it allegedly wants to engage in dialogue. It advances policies that intentionally create a crisis in order to win concessions from its arch-enemy. The assumption behind this approach is that including North Korea in an 'axis of evil' does not necessarily preclude the possibility of engaging it in dialogue. Indeed, the assumption is that threats will induce dialogue. William Safire (2003) expresses this strategy in blunt but entirely appropriate words: 'We make clear to weapons traders in the North that their illicit nuclear production is vulnerable to air attack from a nation soon to show its disarmament bona fides in Baghdad. . . . That readiness will bring about what diplomats call "fruitful, regional, multilateral negotiation."'

There are various reasons why the confrontational approach has not worked. Despite playing lip service to the idea of negotiations, a hard-line approach forecloses all options other than those based on military means. 'The opposition between good and evil is not negotiable', Allan Bloom already noted at the time of Ronald Reagan's presidency. It is a question of principles, and thus 'a cause of war' (Bloom, 1987: 142). Expressed in other words, the rhetoric of evil moves the phenomenon of rogue states into the realm of irrationality. Evil is in essence a term of condemnation for a phenomenon that can neither be fully comprehended nor addressed, except through militaristic forms of power politics. This is why various commentators believe that the rhetoric of evil is an 'analytical cul de sac' that prevents, rather than encourages understanding. They go as far as arguing that a rhetoric of evil entails an 'evasion of accountability', for the normative connotations of the term inevitably lead to policy positions that 'deny negotiations and compromise' (Klusmeyer and Suhrke, 2002: 27, 29, 35–7; Euben, 2002: 4; Henningsen, 2002). Indeed, how is it possible to negotiate with evil without being implicated in it, without getting sucked into its problematic vortex?

Engaging North Korea: South Korea and the Sunshine Policy

There are alternatives to confrontation. A second, opposing approach advocates a gradual rapprochement between the two sides. This so-called soft-landing strategy assumes that engagement is the best opportunity to prevent a military escalation and a sudden collapse of the North Korean regime. The latter alone, proponents of rapprochement stress, could create a major crisis, including large-scale refugee movements or a civil war. Most humanitarian organizations, for instance, stayed behind in North Korea, believing that the possibility of providing humanitarian assistance and development cooperation is essential, even if the conditions of engagement are far from ideal (Smith, 2002: 14–15). Withdrawing aid, they fear, would only heighten the danger of a confrontation and worsen the situation of the populace but not necessarily bring about change for the better. Underlying the logic of this position is the recognition that there are 'few if any examples of authoritarian governments being brought down by famine conditions' (Savage and Team, 2002: 155).

South Korea has become the most explicit and outspoken proponent of an engagement policy with the North. Starting with his inaugural speech in February 1998, South Korea's president, Kim Dae-jung, called for a new approach towards the North. Termed 'Sunshine Policy', Kim's initiative revolved around moving from a deeply entrenched politics of containment towards a more active engagement that promotes 'reconciliation and co-operation between the South and North' (Young, 1998: 23; see also Moon and Steinberg, 1999). The most spectacular result of this policy was the unprecedented summit meeting between the two Korean heads of state in June 2000. But far more important, even though less dramatic, is that Kim's engagement policy generated various forms of low-level cross border exchanges, from tourist visits, cultural and sports engagements to family reunions. Particularly significant was the increase in cross border economic activities, which had been all but non-existent until recently. This changed with the introduction of the Sunshine Policy, which was based on the assumption that increased economic cooperation would eventually engender common interest and understanding. As a result, a key policy leitmotif became 'economy first, politics later' (Moon, 2001b: 283, 184, 186; Kim, 1994).

It is not the point of this chapter to elaborate on the implications of the Sunshine Policy in detail. Suffice it to stress that the key significance of these new cross border interactions is their promotion of face-to-face contacts between average Korean people. Such contacts are perhaps the best way out of the current security dilemmas, for they have the potential to dismantle the antagonistic threat images that continue to fuel the Korean conflict. Compromise needs confidence, and the emergence of confidence requires personal encounters that can build trust over time. This is why the most radical but often underestimated element of the Sunshine Policy is its attempt to loosen state control over security by promoting more interaction, communication and information exchange between the two parts of the divided peninsula.

The potential and limits of integration and normalization

All eight South Korean governments since 1948 were driven by the 'strategic goal of hegemonic unification', stresses Koh Byung Chul. They all advocated, either through the hard- or the soft-landing scenario, an approach to unification 'in which either the South Korean system, or a system embodying democratic values, prevails over the North Korean system' (Koh, 2001: 249). This does not, of course, mean that Seoul's position on the issue of unification has remained static. In the immediate post-war period an absorption of the North was accepted as a normal objective. It was only with Rhee Syngman's fall from power in 1960 that violence was explicitly renounced as a means of 'restoring the northern area' (Koh, 2001: 249; Moon, 1996: 32). During Park Chung Hee's long governing period, from 1961 to 1979, North Korea was seen as being occupied by an illegal regime that was so alien in its ideology it could not even be counted as part of the Korean nation (Shin, 1998: 152). Even during the subsequent presidential reigns of Chun Doo Hwan, Roh Tae Woo and Kim Young Sam, unification by absorption was never explicitly ruled out. South Korean school textbooks, for instance, continued to call, either implicitly or explicitly, for unification by 'having the South drive out the Communists and transform the North in a way that confirmed the South's superiority' (Hart, 1999: 79). The first president to explicitly revoke this model was Kim Dae-jung (cited in Young, 1998: 23), who declared in his inaugural speech in 1998 that 'we do not have any intention to undermine or absorb North Korea'. He repeated this promise several times afterwards (Kim D., 2002: 28; South Korea Ministry of National Defense, 2000). The US then endorsed this position, even under the more confrontational Bush administration. Secretary of State Colin Powell (cited in Kim Y., 2002), for instance, declared in November 2002 that 'we have no intention to impose our sovereignty upon their sovereignty'.

The more tolerant South Korean position of the last few years suggests a willingness to normalize relations with North Korea and integrate it into the world community. But integration and normalization are terms that indicate processes of adjustment to one standard norm; a desire to erase difference in favour of a single identity practice. The immediate objective of engagement, as articulated by the Sunshine Policy, may well be to avoid an open conflict or a sudden collapse of North Korea, but the underlying rationale remains a desire to annihilate the other side. The purpose is 'to win without fighting', as expressed by Lim Dong-won (2002), one of the key architects of the Sunshine Policy. Consider various versions of South Korea's defence white papers. They call for a peaceful construction of a unified nation, but one that is carried out on South Korean terms. The communist identity that has permeated the North for over half a century is to be eradicated, for 'an environment should be created in which the North can transform into an open society with a free market economy' (South Korea Ministry of National Defense, 2000: 94). A similar argument is advanced by Moon Chung-in (2001a: 188), one of South Korea's most influential political commentators and advocates of the Sunshine Policy. He too argues that the North 'should be more actively brought into the world society so that it can turn into a normal state'. Normalization, Moon adds, entails acquiring a market economy and a democratic system.

Few commentators – including the author of this chapter – would chose to opt for a North Korean governing style over the principles of democracy. But this is beside the point, for an adequate security policy must start with existing realities, with the fact that North Korea does exist and will so for the foreseeable future. The tactical elements of engagement may seem more tolerant than those of hard-line approaches. The ideal model may have shifted from an immediate and military-based absorption of the North towards a more contained and controllable collapse scenario, but the fundamental strategic goal remains strikingly similar: to annihilate the arch-enemy and strip away its sense of identity. It is still a 'long-term absorption theory', as one commentator put it (Kim, 2001: 21).

South Korea's approach to the promotion of engagement strongly resembles West Germany's Ostpolitik, which successfully managed to prepare unification through the promotion of communication and face-to-face encounters across the dividing line. But Ostpolitik not only took decades to unfold, it was also based on a process of normalization that foresaw, explicitly or implicitly, that a capitalist form of identity would eventually prevail over a communist one. The soft-landing scenario in Korea operates on a similar premise: that peace and unification would emerge only when North Korea opens up and embraces the values and virtues of democracy and market economics. The outcome remains a gradual and controllable collapse and absorption of North Korea. It is thus not surprising that Pyongyang has opposed from early on not only an application of Ostpolitik, but also the very term 'normalization' (see Pfenning, 1995: 51; Polomka, 1986: 13). Pyongyang's fears substantially grew when it became clear that Ostpolitik contributed to the downfall of the East German regime and its subsequent absorption by West Germany. Mistrust towards the Sunshine Policy has thus been manifested at various levels, formal and informal. For instance, North Korean participants at one of the joint North–South conferences that took place in the wake of the summit meeting of June 2000 stressed that they mistrusted the Sunshine Policy despite its advocacy of 'co-operation, peace and co-existence'. The 'real implication' behind this 'superficial message', so the argument goes, is a 'policy aimed at long-term systemic change, . . . bringing about unification by absorption'.[3] Whether or not this perception is justified remains open to debate, but that does not change its deeply seated existence and the political challenges that emerge from it. As a result, one needs to deal with Pyongyang's fear of absorption and of the outside world in general. And one needs to anticipate and minimize the spectre of violence that inevitably accompanies this fear.

Conclusion: towards 'Concrete Utopias'[4]

A reduction of tension in Korea can only emerge if security policies accept the existence of North Korea and deal with the government in Pyongyang as realistically as possible. Of course, this does not mean one has to rely on realist ideology in the formulation of foreign policy. Realist understandings of military realities, which revolve by and large around the principle of deterrence, have clearly not worked in Korea. The projection of military might, including the explicit threat of pre-emptive nuclear strikes against North Korea, has proven counterproductive. It has driven Pyongyang out of the security arrangement that had been carefully established in the wake of the Perry Report and the Sunshine Policy. Former US Secretary of State Madeleine Albright stressed that during the two terms of Clinton administration there was neither a North Korean weapons test nor new plutonium production. Albright's statement is, of course, politically motivated. But this does not detract from her argument that 'through our policy of constructive engagement, the world was safer. President Bush chose a different path, and the results are evident for all to see' (Stolberg, 2006).

The confrontational approach offers no lasting solution. Given the past patterns, and North Korea's highly predictable foreign policy behaviour, no amount of threat will convince Pyongyang to abandon its nuclear programme. On the contrary, a confrontational approach is likely to increase North Korea's perceived need for a nuclear-based defence. A good recent illustration is the new, more hard-line approach favoured by the US administration since the presidential inauguration of George W. Bush. The policy of hawk engagement has rendered the situation in Korea more volatile than it already was, triggering a new nuclear crisis. Best exemplified by realist Cold War policies, the confrontational approach defines safety and security with reference to the task of warding off an external threat. The result of this inside/outside pattern, which still dominates US foreign policy, is a highly problematic culture of insecurity according to which the constitution of an enemy – and antagonistic other – is required to feel safe and secure. That conflict emerges from such an attitude is self-evident, but largely obscured in practice. The prevailing and deeply entrenched realist security discourse makes it possible for each side to put all blame for the recurring crises on the vilified other – in this case North Korea – without having to acknowledge and deal with the deeper-seated and interactive nature of security dilemmas.

Bringing North Korea back to the negotiation table, and integrating it into a comprehensive security framework, is the best way to achieve stability on the peninsula. Of course, any security arrangement with North Korea will have to deal with the deep-seated levels of mutual hatred and distrust. There will always be the suspicion that North Korea may 'cheat' and continue to pursue a nuclear programme in secret. But no mater how problematic and porous it may be, any security arrangement and negotiation strategy is better than the present situation, where North Korea is openly pursuing a nuclear weapons programme that could further destabilize the entire region.

I have thus argued in favour of an engagement policy, as currently practised by the South Korean government and most great powers involved in Korea. The so-called Sunshine Policy officially eschews an absorption of the North. Instead it advocates a gradual rapprochement and eventual normalization of political relations on the peninsula. The ensuing promotion of dialogue and face-to-face encounters has the potential to dismantle at least some of the antagonistic attitudes that have fuelled conflict in Korea for decades.

South Korea's Sunshine Policy is, of course, not beyond contention. There has, indeed, always been opposition to it within South Korea. This opposition has intensified in the wake of North Korea's first nuclear test in 2006. Conservative segments of the political spectrum in particular called for an end of tolerance towards North Korea. Others see the very crisis as confirming the need for engagement. Former president, Kim Dae-jung, for instance, still holds on to his initiative, stressing that 'it's clear that the Sunshine Policy has succeeded between the two Koreas, and it could have been more successful were it not for the bad relations between North Korea and the United States' (Choe Sang-Hun, 2006).

There are conceptual challenges to the Sunshine Policy as well. Engagement should be supplemented with an ethics of difference: an attempt to understand what the world looks like from Pyongyang. Doing so, it must be stressed, is not to legitimize North Korean foreign policy decisions or to endorse its authoritarian governing style. Imagining the other does not mean one needs to agree with or become implicated in its world-view. Rather, the point is to understand the interactive dynamics entailed in security dilemmas. Washington's inability to see North Korea as anything but a threatening 'rogue state' seriously hinders both an adequate understanding and possible resolution of the conflict. By contrast, an approach that tries to understand why North Korea acts the way it does can help us anticipate the impact of policy choices. Such an approach is all the more compelling because several scholarly works now demonstrate that – contrary to the popularly held beliefs – North Korea acts and negotiates by and large in a rational manner. It deals with threats and opportunities not much differently than other states (Snyder, 1999; Downs, 1999; Sigal, 1998). Its actions and reactions are thus to a certain extent predictable, as long as one makes the effort to understand what the world looks like from Pyongyang. Any policy that takes such factors into account is better attuned than the confrontational approach that simply rehearses the stereotypical image of an irrational and threatening rogue state.

The first and undoubtedly most striking feature to notice from Pyongyang would be the long and unbroken period of American nuclear hegemony in Asia. Equally obvious and understandable is that this hegemonic practice must have been – and indeed was – interpreted as a clear threat to North Korea's security. Faced with a sudden intensification of American nuclear threats since it is hardly surprising that Pyongyang reacted angrily and called Washington officials 'nuclear lunatics' (Kim J., 2002) particularly since Washington continuously refuses to sign a non-aggression pact, which has been one of North Korea's key – and seemingly reasonable – demands for decades (Oberdorfer, 1998: 364). Nor is it surprising that Pyongyang is reluctant to give up its nuclear option, for it could serve as a credible deterrent against a US attack. 'Nuclear threat has always bred nuclear defense', Gavan McCormack (2004: 5) stresses. Indeed, the desire for such a deterrent only mirrors the attitude and behaviour of the US.

Declassified intelligence documents, which became available after the collapse of communist regimes in Eastern Europe, do indeed reveal that from the 1980s North Korea perceived itself as increasingly weak and vulnerable to external attacks (Suh, 1995). While the first nuclear crisis unfolded, Kim Il Sung talked about this dilemma to Cambodia's head of state, Norodom Sihanouk. He put it this way: 'They want to take off our shirt, our coat and now our trousers, and after that we will be nude, absolutely naked' (cited in Oberdorfer, 1998: 311; see also Mazarr, 1995: 100–1). As a result of this increasing vulnerability, the prime objective of the government in Pyongyang has moved, as many commentators now recognize, from forcefully unifying the peninsula to the simple task of regime-survival (Cha, 2002b: 216–19; Cha and Kang, 2003). But very few Western decision-makers have the sensitivity to recognize these factors and take them into account when formulating their policies. Donald Gregg (2002) is one of the rare senior American diplomats who acknowledges that 'the US scares North Korea'. But even he could make such an admission in public only once he had retired from all official functions.

Advancing a more tolerant and nuanced policy of engagement, one that integrates an ethics of difference, is essential not only to attenuate the present culture of insecurity, but also, and perhaps even more importantly, to prepare for the conflicts that could emerge with a possible collapse of North Korea. Most political commentators, but also most key decision-makers, acknowledge that such an uncontrolled collapse of North Korea could be highly problematic, precipitating anything from a civil war to a major refugee crisis. The soft-landing scenario is geared precisely towards avoiding an uncontrolled collapse of the North. But whether or not this approach can actually prevent a sudden disintegration of the North Korean system is an entirely different question. So far predictions of imminent collapse have been proven wrong (most notably Foster-Carter, 1998). Most commentators recognize that North Korean is relatively stable, despite famine conditions and a highly anachronistic political and economic ideology. While displaying a remarkable degree of stability, a collapse of the North Korean political system cannot be excluded. The disintegration of the present system seems merely a matter of time. In an age of globalization and neo-liberal economics, an authoritarian regime based on a self-reliant communist ideology is unlikely to survive in the long run.

Thinking ahead to what will be after the demise of North Korea should be a central concern of an adequate security framework for the peninsula. Major problems will undoubtedly emerge, particularly if policies of engagement and normalization put all hope in the soft-landing scenario, and even more so if the latter continues to be dominated by a long-term absorption model that fails to accommodate different identity practices.

An ethics of difference ought to be an essential element of a long-term security strategy, for the antagonistic identity constructs that emerged with the division of the peninsula will undoubtedly survive and pose problems long after the demise of North Korea. Here too the German precedent is highly revealing. Major identity differences still exist between East and West, even more than a dozen years after unification. These differences, which had been formed during the period of national division and which have to do with people's understanding of themselves, cannot easily be overcome, even in the context of a politically unified and ethnically homogeneous society. And these differences continue to pose a variety of psychological, social, political and economic difficulties. But the respective problems that Germany experienced are likely to pale in comparison to what awaits Korea. The two German states never fought a war against each other and the hostilities that nevertheless existed could be substantially reduced during two decades of Ostpolitik. Both of these mitigating factors are absent in Korea, where a three-year war devastated the peninsula. The memory of this traumatic event continues to shape virtually all aspects of politics on the peninsula. Given these highly problematic residues, and the almost total lack of interaction between the two divided parts, identity constructs in Korea are far more entrenched, hostile and volatile than they ever were in Germany.

Dealing with the residues of these problematic habits is essential for successfully facing the two main spectres that haunt the peninsula: the spectre of a military escalation, even of outright war, and the spectre of a North Korean collapse, which could easily destabilize the Northeast Asian region.

Notes

1 This chapter draws and expands upon research first presented in Bleiker (2005).
2 See also Eberstadt (1998: 541), Moon and Takesada (2001: 357) and Kim (1999: 579–80).
3 This is a quote from Baek Yong Cheol (cited in Nam-Buk-Haewae dongpo hakja tongil hoeui, 1999), a Southern delegate, representing the position of Northerners.
4 Wyn Jones (2005: 229–32).

14

Security as enslavement, security as emancipation: gendered legacies and feminist futures in the Asia-Pacific

Katrina Lee-Koo

THE VIOLENCE AND vastness of gendered insecurities in the Asia-Pacific remains confronting, and crosses the spectrum of insecurities seen worldwide. While many of these insecurities, like poverty, lack of access to political power or the spread of HIV/AIDS are not specific to gender, or indeed the Asia-Pacific, they do affect different women and men in the Asia-Pacific in different ways. Alternatively there are violences which are more likely to confront women and in recent decades have become prevalent in, or more associated with, the Asia-Pacific. These include cases of sexual slavery, trafficking in women, the feminization of labour, militarized prostitution, migration for domestic work and lack of post-conflict 'truth and reconciliation' for wartime experiences. These insecurities are implicated by statistics which claim, for instance, that over 225,000 women and girls are trafficked throughout the Southeast Asian region each year (Flamm, 2003); that the total number of prostitutes in India is close to eight million (Coalition Against Trafficking, 2006); and that around the military bases in Korea there are 18,000 registered and 9,000 unregistered prostitutes (Coalition Against Trafficking, 2006). Yet knowledge of this darker underbelly of 'international relations' remains removed from the states' agenda of national security and the academic field of security studies.

The recent proliferation of texts, articles and debates within the field of security studies and the Asia-Pacific seldom mention these experiences. Even though the number of those rendered insecure by these experiences stretch far into the hundreds of thousands, traditional security studies remains preoccupied with a more 'conventional' agenda. Particularly now, amidst fears of regional terrorism, the literature and focus of security in the Asia-Pacific reflects a return to a more familiar security agenda. Consequently, the literature emerging from traditional security studies is dominated by issues like the spread of terrorist cells in the Asia-Pacific, the potential threat of failed states, the growing power of China, and the opportunities of multilateral approaches to addressing these security threats.[1] Similarly, this agenda has justifiably caught the attention of scholars thinking critically about security who see new perils, not just in these threats, but also in the policies designed to combat them (see McDonald, 2005c).

Consequently, just as the Cold War framed the Asia-Pacific in a geopolitical security microcosm of the broader East/West ideological conflict, the post-9/11 period has redesigned the region within a broader 'war on terror' context. This renders issues of gendered insecurity virtually invisible within the field of security studies. It slams shut the theoretical and discursive explorations of 'critical security' that were opened in the period after the Cold War by feminists examining the relationships between gender, gendered practices and security (Tickner, 1992; Pettman, 1996). Despite valuable steps forward in the post-Beijing decade,[2] feminists, after 9/11, are finding their foundations within the field of security studies rapidly turning to quicksand. While excellent research is taking place in more 'gender-friendly' disciplines and discourses, 'the mainstream international policy debates on some of the most pressing and contested issues of our time . . . are not being systematically informed by the knowledge that is being generated through gender research and scholarship' (UNRISD, 2005: xv). Instead, both the implications of traditional security theorizing on gendered identities and more gender specific insecurities are being exiled to the periphery of global politics. The failure of security studies to recognize the full range of insecurities which plague the Asia-Pacific reflects a theoretical and disciplinary blindness of both its gendered nature and the gendered consequences of its theorizing.

In arguing that a gendered analysis needs to constitute a fundamental part of thinking about security in the Asia-Pacific, this chapter examines the challenges faced by feminists working in the Asia-Pacific and the opportunities open to them to negotiate space and voice within security studies. This chapter recognizes the excellent work by feminists in other academic disciplines and draws upon this to examine why the field of security studies has remained resistant to sustained feminist interventions. Furthermore, it highlights the contributions of feminist insights to a theory of security. To this end, this chapter has three main concerns. The first investigates the conceptual power of what I shall refer to as traditional security and traditional security studies as it has been developed in its positivist-empiricist framework. It argues that this conceptualization of security, with its primary focus on militarized state-based security and limited debates on the role of broader political, economic, societal and environmental based threats (Buzan, 1991: 116–34), exhibits an 'un-naturalness' with regard to everyday life and lacks a genuine organic derivation which is detrimental not just to women, but to the human interest more broadly. The second section examines feminist critiques of traditional security and argues that feminist theorizing has made significant epistemological and ontological contributions to the *post*-positivist theorizing of security. The subsequent possibilities of secure and feminist futures will be the focus of the final section of this chapter. It will explore particularly the emancipatory project of critical theory and the possibilities of transposing it into a feminist context in the Asia-Pacific.

Security: all for one and one for all?

Dominant approaches to thinking about security in the Asia-Pacific today do injustice to the complexities of such a diverse region. However broadly or narrowly defined, the Asia-Pacific is a region which encompasses a variety of identities, histories, forms of political organization, socio-economic-cultural contexts, languages and religions. Representing this complexity, however, is a conceptualization of security which craves (though never attains) graphic simplicity. In fact, that the study of security should be, primarily, about 'the threat, use and control of military force' (Walt, 1991: 212), with secondary debates on a broader agenda limited within a positivist framework (Buzan, 1991: 116–34), has remained steely static within the tradition in this diverse region. To question why this focus has remained steadfast despite the obvious insecurities outside of this framework, however, requires a complex engagement with the way in which security is theorized. While the security studies agenda is clearly deficient, it is not sufficient simply to 'add' the issue of sexual slavery or trafficking in women to the list of insecurities requiring research. Such a superficial solution fails to recognize the systemic and foundational nature of the neglect. Rather, it is the primacy of a certain *way* of theorizing security that requires examination (Tickner, 2004: 46). The positivist tradition in security studies which dominates mainstream theorizing of security encompasses both the realist and neoliberal approaches to state and regional security. While the subtleties and conflicts within these theories should not be overlooked (George, 1997), it must be remembered that the struggles within the positivist tradition do not offer alternative ways of conceptualizing security and insecurity but, at best, different versions of the same security problematic. According to this tradition, both security and insecurity are contingent upon a world based upon states pursuing economic, political and military power in an anarchical realm. Within this narrow range of possibilities terrorism, financial crises, regional nuclear proliferation and arms racing are of self-evident concern while an issue like militarized prostitution requires more complicated, if not impossible, intellectual leaps (Tickner, 2004: 46).

In establishing its agenda, the positivist approach to security, therefore, employs a number of pre-defined theoretical promises which mobilize both its power and its appeal. First, these promises are of a universal world 'out there' independent of the observer. The implication here is that there is one world, which can be observed by anybody who possesses the 'correct' analytical skills to do so. Second, therefore, positivism offers a static way of understanding the world which remains constant over time and place. While focus may shift from nuclear weapons to terrorism or from global East/West conflict to regionalized or localized conflict, the ways in which the security theorist views, analyses and solves these problems remain true and static. Third, these 'common sense truths' offer security studies a clear research agenda and intellectual coherence. The appeal of positivist security therefore is its offer of clarity. From this, a tradition has evolved whereby security has a single, universal truth, which can be readily identified and translated into a clearly defined policy agenda.

Positivist security therefore offers an appealing sterility. Yet it is also dangerous. Maintaining this sterility requires an abstraction which divorces the concept of security from the cacophony of concerns at the ground level of human interaction. Consequently, boundaries have been introduced into the conceptualization of security to separate it from the dirty, organic politics of the everyday. These boundaries include the demarcations between self and other; inside and outside; order and anarchy; and private and public (Campbell, 1998). Similarly, layers of political (and indeed scientific) technology have seen security move away from the beating of human hearts. In this sense, Burke (2001b: xxxiv) describes security as a political technology working 'as a network of practices and techniques which produce and manipulate bodies, identities, societies, spaces and flows'. These layers of political technology have been reified, synthesized and valorized over time. And in their abstraction from 'ordinary human experiences' security has become, in an apparently logical evolution, committed to an aggressive use of state power and even 'rational' acts of violence in pursuit of its aims (Walker, 1997: 75).

See no, speak no, hear no insecurity

Such an ethic of security fails men and women alike. Despite its intentions to create the structural stability from which human wellbeing may be enabled, traditional conceptualizations of security remain blind to much of the region's insecurity and silent on the suffering of, particularly, society's most wretched. In doing so, traditional security's role can, in fact, be more active and insidious. Far from a passive 'failure to speak and see', traditional security can be implicated in an active process of silenc*ing* and blind*ing* those who would be insecure. This happens both on the conceptual and the everyday level and has graphic consequences for women.

First, the traditional security project silences other ways of imagining security by declaring them illegitimate, irrelevant or 'wrong'. Consequently, with limited access to 'legitimate' political power, women who imagine security in different ways are silenced within the traditional security discourse. For instance, Okinawa feminists have long claimed that the US–Japan Security Treaty (which sees the establishment of US military bases in Okinawa) is actually a source of *in*security for many local Japanese women. They argue that the cases of sexualized violence perpetrated by visiting US soldiers and the proliferation of the prostitution industry create a different experience of security than that anticipated under the Treaty (Enloe, 2004: Chapter 8). Together with feminists from Korea, the Philippines and Puerto Rico, these women highlight the direct link between state sponsoring of US military bases and human insecurities brought on by assaults against civilians, the militarization of their society and culture, and environmental contaminations (Kirk and Okazawa-Rey, 2004: 59–64). While the work of women's groups and feminist scholars have persistently argued that peace and human security should be valued over militarism and strategic security, it has unsuccessfully challenged the statist/ regional security logic put forward by the tradition. The reason for this failure is the incapacity for positivist security to acknowledge the complex politics which sees a state security project simultaneously become the source of *insecurity* for some citizens of that state (Booth, 1991: 318). The response therefore, in deference to the universal security model, is to silence feminist claims to insecurity as 'illegitimate' or irrelevant.

Similarly, the traditional security studies agenda blinds us to the insecurities outside the ontological premises of the tradition even when these insecurities are a direct consequence of the tradition's theorizing. This is evidenced by the vast (yet neglected) insecurities which can be directly traced back to the securitizing practices of the tradition. The experiences of women in South Asian sweatshops, the trafficking of women throughout Southeast Asia and the spread of AIDS in the Pacific are all sources of insecurity which have at least some antecedents in the state's securitizing processes (Alker, 2005: 191). For example, Jean Enriquez (2003), writing for the Coalition Against Trafficking in Women – Asia-Pacific (CATW-AP) explains that neo-liberal policies designed to enhance the state's economic security, actually create insecurities for women in the Philippines. She argues that

> the neo-liberal paradigm has never seen the differential status and valuation of work of women and men in both the market and non-market economy. The dominant economic model is blind to the inequality of decision-making powers

> and patterns of expending within the household. It is oblivious to the reality that women historically ha[ve] been serving as safety nets of structural adjustment measures designed to promote globalization.

More generally, the United Nations Research Institute for Social Development (UNRISD) explains: 'Under conditions of economic hardship, low-income women became increasingly visible as economic actors outside the household sphere, as casual agricultural labourers, in the overcrowded urban informal economy, and as migrants' (UNRISD, 2005: xx). Many of these situations render women physically and economically insecure in an informal economy unregulated by any form of labour legislation. In Indonesia, for example 77 per cent of women in non-agricultural employment work within the informal economy (UNRISD, 2005: 77). Traditional security is blind to the manner in which women's insecurity contributes to the state's economic security agenda. Yet, while links between neo-liberal security practices and gendered insecurities are not rendered visible by traditional security theorizing, it can be revealed through the critique undertaken by critical feminist scholars.

A critical feminist approach to security studies

While critical theory more generally has a long philosophical tradition, the investment of key ideas into the field of security studies is recent (Wyn Jones, 1999). Critical security studies, as this volume demonstrates, is not a single platform,[3] but it does have some core concerns and commitments to conceptually engaging security within a post-positivist framework (see Booth, 2005a: 11–12). Central to the development and application of critical security studies has been feminist scholarship. The work of critical feminists has both pioneered and advanced critical interrogations of security at every level of traditional security's analysis (Tickner, 2001: 48). Critical feminists challenge not just traditional security's agenda but also its ways of theorizing, the foundational assumptions of its theory (particularly with regards to identity) and the discursive and representational politics which attend the international politics of security.

Key advances in feminist theorizing become relevant for the critical feminist security studies project. The first is feminist theorizing of identity politics, particularly gendered identity constructions and practices, at the individual, state and international level. For critical feminists these identities, socially constructed and reproduced in individuals and structures, constitute a world which is shaped by gendered meanings (Sheehan, 2005: 117). These subjective identities, 'through which we know and see the world' (Jones, 1996: 406) therefore influence each individual's experience within the politics of security. Critical feminists argue that the experiences of women in the international politics of security can be dramatically different from men (see Enloe, 1990). Similarly, they can also be different *between* women in the same geographical region because of the multiple identities of race, age, religion, ethnicity and socio-economic context (Yuval-Davis, 1997). For example, examinations into the experiences of women prostitutes in Thailand expose the extent to which nationality and ethnicity can play important roles in the levels of insecurity, abuse, treatment and protection of prostitutes (Pettman, 1997: 101–2). Jeffrey (2002: 149) argues that in post-financial crisis Thailand, Burmese and Chinese women who have been trafficked into Thailand as sex slaves are treated by the government as the 'real victims' while Thai prostitutes are dismissed as 'material girls who deserve to suffer for their folly'. Similarly, in Japan, there is a marked distinction between 'respectable' Japanese women who live near US military bases and warrant protection from abuse and 'unworthy' Japanese women who 'work' on the bases and are less deserving of protection (Enloe, 2004: 120). Beyond US military bases, Japan is confronting non-Japanese Asian migrant women who come to Japan for marriage or work in the 'entertainment' industry. These women are marked by eroticized and sexualized images of 'Otherness', often based on nationality, which enables a less active responsibility for their protection by the state and the local community (Yeoh *et al.*, 2002: 13). Consequently Asian identities within specific Asian countries can dramatically impact women's access to state-provided security.

At the state and regional level, gendered identities in the Asia Pacific have become further imbued in postcolonial and nationalist politics. The representation of gendered identities and the implications of this for women's actual bodies has been an important, if overlooked, source of gendered insecurities. For instance, colonial occupation has been represented in nationalist projects as heterosexual rape of the nation's (woman's) body which, in turn, requires a resurgent masculinity on behalf of the nation's men. In regional anti-colonial projects this metaphor has been realized on women's actual bodies. Historically, this was evident in the 1971 war of independence in Bangladesh (D'Costa, 2005: 227–47). More recently, East Timor's independence ballot of 1999 was accompanied by accounts of sexualized violence by the TNI (Tentara Nasional Indonesia (Indonesian Armed Forces)) against East Timorese women (Ball, 2002: 86). In this sense, women's bodies become both post/colonial battlefields and the site for nationalist imaginings by the home and foreign men.

In development and nationalism projects women's identities are similarly evoked. In the Philippines in the 1980s women who migrated out of their homeland to work and send money home were proclaimed the nation's 'new heroines' by the Aquino administration. More recently

President Gloria Macapagal-Arroyo similarly celebrated Filipinos working in Japan and sending remittances back into the national economy as national heroes (Suzuki, 2002: 99). Yet these women, while significant in the nation's economic security, are not similarly significant security referents themselves. Discursively they may be heroes but in practice they remain susceptible to discriminatory practices, violence and labour and human rights violations (UNIFEM, 2003). In Indonesia, statist discourses emerging from state-based programmes within the country represent women as the 'mothers of development'. For example, gendered identities played a significant part in the programme of transmigration which saw land-poor Javanese removed to outer islands with the dual purpose of alleviating unemployment/ poverty and creating 'cultural, economic and political uniformity across disparate "ethnic" groups' (Elmhirst, 2002: 79). This sees women needing to negotiate the expectation that they behave as 'good Indonesian women', central to the creation of an Indonesian space, with the imperatives for their personal security such as economic wellbeing and physical security. For instance one transmigrant woman told a researcher that 'she had learned to "hoe like a man" in order to feed her family; but her shame in failing to conform to a feminine ideal meant she did so at night so neighbours could not see' (Elmhirst, 2002: 82). Consequently, gendered identities mark men and women for particular roles in the nation-building and national security project. Yet, in doing so, it similarly limits their opportunities for security.

Outside of the region, the gendered legacies of colonialism have an ongoing impact upon the Asia-Pacific's relations with the 'West'. Born directly from the period of colonization, Jan Jindy Pettman (2005: 167–8) describes a 'neo-Orientalism' that, on both sides, seeks to replicate the boundaries and politics of difference between 'Asia' and the 'West'. This neo-Orientalism has more recently manifested itself in the idea of 'Asian values'. These 'Asian values' have been used by Western commentators and Asian elites alike to explain and propagate certain distinct cultural values and relationships specific to the region (Pettman, 2005: 168). Discursively, the concept of 'Asian values' has been used by political elites in the region to explain its economic successes of the 1980s and 1990s and have been simultaneously deployed in contrast to the 'West's' individualism and self-centred ambition. Yet for feminists, the deployment of 'Asian values', with its reported emphasis on family and community, replicates familiar gender constructions and relations (Pettman, 2005: 170). Attending the use of 'Asian values' as an identity marker, notions of women as the cultural markers and biological reproducers of their community have similarly been reinvigorated (Yuval-Davis, 1997: 32). Furthermore, with relation to the 'West', 'refiguring gender relations in Asian states becomes a way of recovering Asian masculinities in the face of previously hegemonic (including military) masculinity, as well as of marking changes and challenges within Asian-Western relations' (Pettman, 2005: 170). Simultaneously, Pettman (2005: 170) continues, 'these gender constructions naturalize the Asian woman and disguise actual Asian women's violent incorporation into their states' economic miracles, as labour made cheap, as global assembly workers, as labour migrants and as sex workers'. In revealing the possibilities of conflicting narratives under the *same* process and project of security, attention to identity politics specific to the region demonstrates the limitations of 'grand narratives' of security and similarly verbose claims to 'universal emancipation'. In cases throughout the Asia-Pacific the totalizing discourses which portray 'women of the region either as silent, domesticated housewives cloistered in the private sphere, or eroticized, exoticised objects of male desire' (Yeoh *et al.*, 2002: 2) profoundly influence women's lives without accurately reflecting their complexities.

Consequently, the second major contribution of feminist theorizing is recognition of the imprecision attending a universalized narrative of security. Feminists have revealed that for every 'grand narrative' of security there is a series of micro-narratives which may reveal vastly different experiences for groups and individuals involved in that project. Kim Huynh's (2004) work on the experiences of an 'ordinary woman' in mid-twentieth-century Vietnam demonstrates that neither the civilizing mission of the French, the nationalist mission of the communists, nor the liberating mission of the United States rendered her secure. In fact, these competing (though positivist) narratives of security had quite the opposite effect. Similarly, the 'grand narrative' of the 'Asian Miracle' does little to reflect the realities of gendered violence and oppression in the sweatshops, prostitution houses and families across Asia (Matsui, 1999). In the same vein the literature on the Asian financial crisis pays scant attention to the violent personalized insecurities suffered by gendered identities amidst the more prevalent state economic insecurity. In the aftermath of the crisis women disproportionately suffered from a lack of access to education, health care, employment and were increasingly victims of domestic violence as household tensions rose. Aslanbeigui and Summerfield (2000: 91) note that in Korea and Thailand women's services reported a dramatic increase in the number of reported cases of domestic violence in 1998 while it was estimated that in Jakarta two to four times as many women became sex workers in 1998 than 1997. Under the 'grand narrative' of Indonesia's transition to democracy in the aftermath of the Asian financial crisis, again, the experiences of women's insecurity was largely sidelined in the security studies literature. During the riots in mid-May in 1998 a large number of Indonesian women, many of Chinese origin, were systematically raped (Blackburn, 1999: 433). Caught amidst the economic fallout and broader violence, the attacks on women received little attention from either the national security apparatus of the state or security studies scholars. Consequently, the legacies and reasons for this violence were not incorporated into the theorizing about security during the move towards democracy in Indonesia. For feminists then, the intellectual and disciplinary boundaries established by traditional security studies are impediments to knowledge and understanding.

Critical feminists argue that these obstructions to knowledge can only be dismantled through a re-conceptualization of how we theorize security. For feminists, a richer understanding of security would accompany the validation of the voices and narratives of 'everyday women'. Far from the totalizing theory of security imposed from the inter/national level, 'everyday theorizing' is an organic approach which takes seriously the everyday experiences of men and women. Critical feminists argue that this enables a more sophisticated understanding of the causes of insecurity and the consequences of security practices for different identities. This organic approach 'takes the individual, situated in broader social structures, as its starting point' (Tickner, 2001: 48). Furthermore it considers every person's experience as a potential source of legitimate knowledge. It recognizes that both soldier and prostitute, trafficker and slave, and statesman and housewife are a product of, and embedded in, the power relationships, social and cultural constructions and knowledge claims inherent in the international politics of security. In this sense, everyone theorizes security, at their own individual level and beyond (Zalewski, 1996: 348). In doing so, critical feminists embrace the sometimes contradictory and conflicting voices and experiences of everyday politics as a source of knowledge useful in navigating new directions in international theory. A recognition of these multiple experiences and identities promotes, as Pettman (2005: 174) explains, 'more inclusive and emancipatory accounts of security, asking questions and seeking to learn from ordinary people's experiences of identity and security. This is a powerful corrective to more visible, elite, statist and militarized constructions of the identity-security nexus.'

Examining the possibilities of a feminist emancipatory project

In confronting the intellectual, disciplinary and theoretical boundaries of traditional security, a critical feminist approach inverts the foundational premises upon which traditional security is based. A critical feminist security is based upon a politics of inclusion rather than exclusion; a celebration of difference as diversity rather than a fear of difference as threat; it denaturalizes and dismantles socially constructed hierarchies of identity rather than reinforcing and reifying them; it breaks down intellectual boundaries as a path to integrated knowledge rather than relying upon artificial parameters and disciplinary constraints; it accepts alternative sources of knowledge as worthy of investigation in favour of a singular yet limited truth; and, finally, it focuses not upon states and the offensive use of (militarized) power but upon the diversity of the human experience and their pursuit of freedom. For critical feminists, a 'post-realist, post-positivist emancipatory notion of security offers the promise of maximizing the security and improving the lives of the whole of humankind' (Tickner, 2001: 47).

Embedded in critical feminist security theory is, consequently, an emancipatory goal. The possibilities of an emancipatory potential within security has been debated recently in the critical security studies literature. Most significantly evident in the work of Ken Booth (1991, 2005a–e) and Richard Wyn-Jones (1999, 2005), the emancipatory project of critical security studies owes its intellectual debts to the Frankfurt School of critical theory. Drawing from this, Booth (2005c: 181) describes emancipation as:

> The theory and practice of inventing humanity, with a view of freeing people, as individuals and collectivities, from contingent and structural oppressions. It is a discourse of human self-creation and the politics of trying to bring it about. . . . The concept of emancipation shapes strategies and tactics of resistance, offers a theory of progress for society, and gives a politics of hope for common humanity.

Booth's notion of emancipation therefore removes security's focus from the artificial structures of modern politics in recognition of the possibilities that those very structures may be the cause of individual oppression. This is not to say that Booth or critical scholars more generally eschew the state as a useful form of political organization but rather that it should not be considered the sole referent of security and that the pursuit towards security should be organically driven. Furthermore, in pursuit of emancipation, aggressive or violent behaviour would be considered abnormal and antithetical. Any attempt to 'create a virtuous circle of security and emancipation' (Booth, 2005c: 181) therefore should reject the argument that a secure end justifies a violent means.

Critics of the emancipatory project in security studies have emerged from across the theoretical spectrum. The emancipatory project has come under fire from those wary about setting up a 'rival good' to traditional security to those who reject the project for its perceived naivety and lack of 'real-world' application. For some, there is too much political baggage attending the concept of emancipation for it to be considered useful to a post-positivist security project. Emancipation's intellectual debts to both Marxism and liberalism (Wyn Jones, 2005: 216), theories which feminism has already had troubled engagements (Sylvester, 1996: 256), has given feminists reason to question the utility of a project which has not always respected diversity and the plurality of knowledge. Critics suggest that 'indelibly tainted by association with the meta-narratives of modernity,' the historical experience of emancipation is one that 'has become complicit in the suffering engendered by the practices and pathologies of modernism (broadly defined)' (Wyn Jones, 2005: 216). At the very least then one must be wary of the oppressive potential of a concept whose antecedents have been imbued in the political, economic and geographical colonizing projects of strong states for centuries.

It is not a revelation for critical feminists, however, that political concepts designed ostensibly for a 'universal good' might be, for some, the source of oppression. Any political concept claiming universality is destined to silence the experiences, imaginings and goals of those who deviate from the mainstream construction of knowledge. If we accept that 'theory is always for some one or for some purpose' (Cox, 1981: 182), then it is simultaneously *not* for others or for alternative goals. Therefore it reflects the ambitions only of those with the power to draft the agenda. Feminists have revealed the extent to which 'universalised concepts' born out of the Western European experience have been formulated for the ambitions of the sovereign (masculine) state by, for the most part, patriarchal thinkers (Pettman, 1996: 49). In this sense, emancipation is no different. Hoffman (2001: 52) argues that

> western political philosophy is patriarchal as a tradition, and even though the concept of emancipation is formulated in apparently universalistic terms, this patriarchy still characterises the rationalism of the Renaissance and the Enlightenment. . . . They betray notions of domination and subjugation which naturalise and normalise the subjection and oppression of women.

For critical feminists then, the peril of embedding emancipation into their security project is twofold. First, they must investigate whether emancipation can be coopted, rehabilitated or re-conceptualized in a manner that may be used to aid women in the processes of resisting the sources of their oppression and freeing themselves 'from those physical and human constraints which stop them carrying out what they would freely chose to do' (Booth, 1991: 319). Here, critical feminists face the same challenge faced throughout their political struggles: to deconstruct the gendered (which often simultaneously means oppressive) nature of the concept and to reconstruct it towards a feminist ethic that challenges *all* forms of domination of *all* women. This is not an impossible task. Booth argues that the historical domination of the concept of emancipation by 'Western ideas' need not render it useless. If the concept can be directed towards an inclusive emancipatory project in the human interest then 'what matters is not where ideas come from but how well they travel' (Booth, 2005c: 181). Similarly, Alker (2005: 190) argues that 'culturally sensitive concepts of emancipation can be linked to concretely researchable, equally sensitive conceptualisations of existential security in a post-hegemonic fashion'.

Second, critical feminists must also question whether emancipation is too totalizing a concept to reflect the myriad experiences of women in the world today. The suggestion that a 'universal' emancipatory project, particularly one that is 'Western' in design, can accommodate the experiences of *all* women, particularly non-Western women, can be fraught with danger. The key is to imagine a process of emancipation that does not establish an intellectually oppressive 'rival truth' for security. While not structurally oppressive in the form of state power and patriarchy, it is theoretically no better to force upon all women a universalized project of emancipation. Consequently, theorizing on emancipation must include the insights of an array of non-Western and postcolonial critical feminists working on issues of insecurity. While seduction by universalizing knowledge is ever present, the key to coopting the emancipatory project *for* women is to remain critically aware (and a little suspicious) of the processes of emancipation. Far from the claims of the 'timeless wisdom' of a concept (Buzan, 1996), a critical awareness demands that concepts and processes in international politics be fluid, dynamic, evolving and self-reflective. Furthermore, this must include a commitment to the idea that any kind of service directed towards some at the expense of others may not be good enough.

Yet, this is just the beginning of the process of establishing an emancipatory project *for* all women. A recognition of the potential for all forms of power to be oppressive, even power held by some women in relation to others, threatens at every turn to pervert the emancipatory project. Negotiating the power dynamic is complex terrain. While women may successfully imagine what it is that they should 'freely choose to do', realizing such a project requires certain levels of power. In some cases, those with the power to lobby for change and those oppressed by the status quo are not the same people. Speaking and acting *for* another's security requires trust. Traditional security offers many examples of the capacity for the state to abuse that trust. This is something that must be avoided in a critical feminist emancipatory project. Yet, rather than being paralysed by an anxiety regarding the assertion of hegemonic power, those with the 'power', the 'thinking space' and the ability to act surely cannot sit idly by while women continue to be oppressed. Sometimes empowering others can only come *after* you have acted on *behalf* of (and in association with) others in their own interests.

Postmodernists have a point when they suggest that this is a slippery slope. In some cases the security crisis is acute and readily apparent. There would be little protest from feminists about describing the violent experiences befalling many women trafficked through Asia as graphic forms of insecurity and antithetical to the human interest (Brown, 2000). The actions of feminists, international organizations and even states to abolish these practices would most likely warrant little in principle opposition from feminists. Yet, in deference to the recognition that one woman's oppression may be another woman's compromise in search of security, there is certainly enough historical evidence to argue that when the powerful act on behalf of the oppressed without full appreciation of the other's subjectivity, then the result can be consequences which, despite good intentions, are still profoundly oppressive. For example, the decision by women of the Philippines to leave their homeland for work or marriage in other countries creates anxiety amongst many Western feminists. However in situations where women are being mistreated or oppressed in their own country these are decisions, or gambles, made by women in pursuit of their own security. As Suzuki (2002: 103) points out, 'these decisions . . . make them neither heroines [n]or victims' as respective statist/ feminist discourses may imply. They are simply women making difficult choices about how they may become free. Yet, in many of these complex politics there remains moral, ethical and political dilemmas over these kinds of decisions. The key to negotiating these issues is calm honesty and dialogue.

A critical feminist security project must recognize and accommodate all these sites of anxiety and complexity if it is to be truly emancipatory. It must negotiate not only the power dynamics outside the emancipatory project, but also those within feminism(s). This process begins with dialogue. The tradition 'assumes' what security means. Feminists must not make the same mistake. To assume that emancipation means the same to all women will ultimately be problematic. The solution therefore is to simply ask women how they imagine themselves to be free. This grassroots epistemology is reminiscent of Cynthia Enloe's 'everyday voices' which reveals the complexities of international politics (Enloe, 2004). But a critical feminist emancipatory project could add to this with a two-way dialogue: an education which does not necessarily enforce certain truths but offers, into a level playing field, alternative knowledge(s) for consideration (Linklater, 2005). This means that we must treat the knowledge acquired from women's everyday experiences as analytically relevant if we are to understand the sources of insecurity befalling women in Asia. Ackerly and D'Costa (2005: 2) examine the problems created when poorer women become the 'face' rather than the 'voice' of criticism against gendered violence, arguing that '[s]uch a lack of critical respect re-enacts a colonial relationship in the realm of ideas'. A critical feminist security therefore does not render politically dispossessed women as objects of feminist theorizing and practice by others but rather as drivers in feminist emancipatory projects. If, after an exchange between feminists (and feminisms), what one woman 'freely chooses to do' is antithetical to another's own commitment to security then that must be respected. After all, emancipation is never a finished project, nor should it promise definitive answers.

If we accept that for women in the Asia-Pacific emancipation offers a path for re-engaging in the political not just for survival but for genuine security, how can this be translated into active agendas? While critics argue that such theoretical pipedreams raise 'unreal' expectation among the oppressed or that they have the potential to incite conflict (Ayoob, 1997: 128), critical feminists see clearings for post-hegemonic emancipatory projects. Within the feminist movement, often receiving little attention from mainstream politics or academia, the example has already been set. Gender studies has long been analysing ways in which gendered identities conspire, manipulate, resist and coopt ideas, structures, power and people to strategize for their own security. In response to the long neglect by the 'high politics' field of security studies, women and feminist groups in the Asia-Pacific region have developed their own security strategies. Groups like DAWN (Development Alternatives with Women for a New Era), CAPWIP (Centre for Asia-Pacific Women In Politics) and CATW-AP, while distinct, have all been instrumental in developing a grassroots emancipatory ethic for women in the Asia-Pacific. From household politics designed to stop domestic violence to mass mobilizations on the streets to organized groups lobbying state and international bodies, women in the region are engaging the emancipatory potential to address the security issues facing them (Matsui, 1999: 1–9). While there still remains important debate on the role of the state in such projects and the difficulties of negotiating complex identities and conflicting emancipatory ideals within these projects, there is simultaneously the suggestion that

> emancipatory politics can rely on no one single, universal formula but draw on multiple identifications and diverse strategies, sometimes working the ground 'locally', sometimes collapsing the personal and the political in opposing an exclusionary nation or the discriminatory practices of the state, and sometimes by drawing on transnational or global frameworks or discourses. (Yeoh *et al.*, 2002: 3)

This rich epistemology and ontology of security is already being practised by individual women, informal women's groups, transnational and non-governmental organisations (NGOs), and networks and regional bodies. These groups make significant impacts upon the human security of 'everyday women' in the Asia-Pacific and consequently have much insight to share with the academic discipline of security studies.

Conclusion

A critical feminist emancipatory project then is one that builds upon the critical theory-based project outlined by Booth, but is directed towards individual women as its particular (though theoretically transferable) referent. It brings with it particular feminist insights into identity politics and the gendered constructions of security studies, it focuses upon the particular insecurities faced by individual women, and it demonstrates the manner in which the construction of knowledge within the dominant discourse of security studies has marginalized or silenced these experiences. It seeks emancipation through an everyday theorizing of individual women's narratives and organic engagement with what it might mean *for them* to be free. It then collaborates to empower individual women to pursue their emancipation. It recognizes the possibilities of conflicting emancipatory goals but commits itself to negotiation and compromise. Because it does not take absolute security as its goal, it is prepared to compromise and sacrifice one's own position in order that others might also be free. Consequently, emancipation is not a zero-sum goal but rather an interrelated project capable of success only when it is achieved by all. Unlike realist security which purchases its power at the expense of others, critical feminist emancipation seeks security in collaboration with others, recognizing that 'I cannot be free if she is not free.' Adorno describes this as a world 'of distinctiveness without domination, with the distinct participating in each other' (cited in Wyn Jones, 2005: 233). Such an emancipatory community[4] recognizes similarities in the human condition but without hegemonic attempts at stifling or subordinating sites of diversity. It recognizes that there will always be multiple and sometimes fluid identities and that these identities can have differing understandings of, and relationships with, the structures, processes and identities around them. Yet if there is a simultaneous commitment to the emancipatory project, then there is the opportunity for everyone to be free.

Notes

1 See, for example, the recently launched journal *Asian Security*, 1(1) (2005).

2 UNRISD (2005: xix) reports that during the 1990s there were 'remarkable achievements . . . in bringing issues of sexual and reproductive health and rights, violence against women, and inequality of power in gender relations to the centre of global and national debates'.

3 This point is evident in the collection of essays put forth in the pioneering work edited by Krause and Williams (1997).

4 Booth (2005f: 109) describes an emancipatory community as one which 'in recognizing the right of individuals to express themselves through multiple identifiers of difference will, above all, celebrate human equality'.

Conclusion: emancipating security in the Asia-Pacific?

Simon Dalby

Asia-Pacific lessons?

THE CHAPTERS IN this volume tell various stories about security and states in the Asia-Pacific, and about human security or insecurity in a diverse region. Indeed how one might understand this diversity as a region at all is an implicit question in all, and an explicit question in some, of these texts. But clearly lumping these states together and then comparing the diverse experiences of security, and the possibilities of what is now frequently simply called human security, is a worthwhile comparative exercise. Especially so as the contrast between the practices of the 'West' or perhaps more precisely the OECD (Organization for Economic Cooperation and Development) states, and Asia, are at times apparently quite dramatic (Ruland, 2005). Not least the comparison with Europe in particular where agendas of human security and regional integration are, as Julie Gilson suggests in her chapter, sharply at odds with the fairly rigid notions of territorial sovereignty widespread among Asian elites as the starting point for discussions of security.

The exclusion of effective civil society actors, where they exist in the region, from discussions of security speaks to a very state-centric focus in the discussion of security. These limitations also point to the crucial questions of the ability of states to function and maintain a legitimacy that is widely respected by their populations. In so far as human rights activists and indigenous spokespeople are likely to be advocates for greater autonomy for peoples understood as ethnic minorities, then their activities can easily be understood as undermining the operation of state sovereignty. In the Indonesian case, not just with the East Timor secession and the struggles in Aceh, the state looks more like a latter day empire than a formation that fits the classic Westphalian definitions of a nation-state with at least some suggestion of a relatively homogeneous population within its boundaries. Thus the postcolonial boundaries are once again a matter of debate, and their effectiveness at demarcating functional political entities is also in question. This is not the only cause of insecurity within the region, but it is an important matter in terms of the use of political violence. It once again raises the crucial question of who and what agencies can provide security and against what threats to which identity. Because as many of the chapters in this volume make clear, many of the cases of insecurity actually have little to do with external territorial threats to state integrity.

The exclusion of discussions of human rights and human security in many (but not all) Asia-Pacific states might suggest a parochialism to the arguments about humanitarian intervention – except that the case of East Timor suggests that this debate is in fact very relevant in the region despite the suggestion that it is a Eurocentric preoccupation. More important however is the challenge mounted by critical security studies to the assumption that the contemporary state system actually provides security to its peoples. Insurgencies, not only in Indonesia but also in Thailand, Burma and the Philippines, suggest the importance of 'domestic' political violence as a cause of numerous insecurities. The nuclear standoff on the Korean peninsula reminds the reader forcefully of the overarching danger of military confrontations where weapons of mass destruction (WMD) really do exist and the practitioners of statecraft have given no indication that they will not use these devices in a situation of overt warfare. Because the human security of much of the population of the Korean peninsula is tied into this relic of the Cold War, nuclear bombs and the possibilities of extremely violent combat near population centres remain a substantial risk there.

Elsewhere the shadow of the mushroom cloud looms over political relations between Japan, China and the United States in particular. Traditional security considerations are alive and well in the Asia-Pacific where nuclear weapons remain very much on the political agenda. The more important argument here may be the one so eloquently summarized by Marianne Hanson in her challenge to the persistence of nuclear weapons culture, which suggests that any critical security project needs to tackle the assumptions at the heart of nuclearism. While the other chapters deal with numerous other issues related to security, the persistence of nuclear weapons and security thinking that makes possible their development and deployment remains a priority concern for all concerned about humanity and security. Because the willingness on the part of the most powerful states to build and contemplate using these devices emphasizes one of the most important concerns of those critical of conventional formulations of security, the practice of violence by the rich and powerful to maintain an order that keeps them that way. But while this is easy to conceptualize as a generality, how one might do critical analysis or advocacy for a better future is not so easy to specify, especially in this region.

The case study chapters in this volume offer a series of analyses that pose questions about the nature of critical security studies, and the possibilities of a human security agenda, and do so in a region, if such there is as Gilson notes, where both the academic exercise of critical security studies and the practice of human security are with some notable exceptions relatively rare. Being the 'hard case' should provide some practical lessons concerning the conceptualizations in the larger discussions, and the rest of this conclusion sketches out some of the lessons that can be drawn. Mostly it does so by considering the dilemmas and difficulties under three loose headings: first, the geopolitical context and the political economy; second, identity and security; and third, the relationships between human security as a political desideratum of emancipation and critical security studies as an intellectual project.

Geopolitical economy

The Asia-Pacific is in many ways, as these chapters suggest, the hard case for any attempt to muster either a human security agenda or critical security studies analyses. In part this is a legacy of decolonization which left states with boundary disputes and legitimacy issues unsettled. Simply establishing effective territorial rule – an essential attribute of territorial sovereignty – is not easy in many cases. The implication in some of the chapters in this volume is that the practitioners of statecraft have to deal with these matters first prior to dealing with other matters; Alex Bellamy and Bryn Hughes, Yongjin Zhang, and Katrina Lee-Koo explicitly cite Mohammed Ayoob's (1995) discussions of subaltern realism and his argument that states have to be consolidated in the South first before other matters can be attended to, to make this point. This raises the question of historical analogy and whether, following Charles Tilly's (1990) much cited arguments, the violence is inevitable in the process of state-making, whether violence does make states just as states make violence. In which case the answer to those who argue for human security in the face of state violence is simply to be patient! The people Hazel Lang investigates in her chapter on Myanmar are thus understood as the victims of an inevitable political evolution of modern states which will become peaceful eventually. The counter-argument is that the final arrangement of states in the region has yet to be arrived at as secessionist struggles in Aceh and Papua suggest. All of which implicitly suggests a political telos, a working out of an ideal form following which violence will be resolved.

But the sheer diversity of state forms and the dynamics of contemporary politics suggest that such thinking is misplaced. The diversity of cultures and political systems in the region discussed in this volume suggest clearly that there is no single mode of state-building, no single template that requires the subjugations of minorities prior to the construction of security for a nation-state. Where elites are imposing their order on recalcitrant ethnic minorities or forcing compliance with a national identity, the excuse of state-making reveals itself as just that: an invocation of security to provide an excuse for harsh repression. When coupled to the destruction of forests and the wholesale looting of resources in the peripheries of states, a theme Lorraine Elliott discusses, then the parallel question of development as violence is unavoidable. This isn't surprising given that development is all about rapid, frequently forced, change. Burma and Thailand, as the chapters dealing with them in this volume suggest, clearly present many of these difficulties.

The now apparently annual problem of pollution from fires in Indonesia as a result of the burning of forest to clear land is only the most obvious manifestation of the dramatic conversion of environment and the related displacement of traditional modes of existence in the expansion of global capitalism. Elliott's emphasis on this point is important in making clear the importance of political economy in understanding human insecurity. Resource extractions are part of the transformations wrought by modernity, part of a strategy of what is at times a desperate development stripping forests to sell the timber for immediate cash with little thought for long-term possibilities. These disruptions are part of the larger patterns of resource exploitation in the rural peripheries of the world economy, a shadow ecology reducing human security far from where the benefits occur (Dauvergne, 1997). This reinforces the crucial point in Mark Beeson's chapter that the global political economy has many deleterious security consequences in the peripheries; political economy is related to international institutions which act to maintain the current order much more than they challenge its inequities and insecurities.

This discussion also poses the questions of sustainable development strategies and the security implications for the region given its growing dependence on petroleum imports from outside the region. While Brunei and Indonesia have petroleum resources and others may yet be discovered, the growing appetite for gasoline and other petroleum products in the region is not being seriously reconsidered. Even in Singapore which prides itself, and not without good reason, on being a garden city, the affluence of the city state is dependent on petroleum supplies. Notably absent in its cityscape are solar collectors which could, given its tropical location, provide considerable water heating and some electricity generation capabilities. While water collection and recycling are gaining attention, energy security is not an integral part of the state's planning for long-term security. The implicit developmentalist assumption is that resources will come from some periphery somewhere; the disruptions, insecurities and related resistance in those peripheries is something beyond the scope of conventional security discussions (Jung, 2003).

If one links the discussion of environmental disruption together with the question of the provision of human security as something done by developed states to those who are suffering as a result of not being developed, as frequently happens in discussions of human security, the dilemmas facing critical analysis are especially clear. If the affluence that allows for international movements and international administration to impose forms of human security is dependent on a political economy that drastically disrupts those peripheries to provide the wealth in the first place, then one is facing a contradiction that suggests a more fundamental rethink of both development and security is overdue. This point may have many parallels in other matters of insecurity but it is perhaps clearest when matters of global change and environmental insecurity are the focus (Dalby, 2002).

This mode of thinking also focuses on the territorial organization of power and the important point that there is more than one form of sovereignty in operation (Agnew, 2005). Territorial integrity and formal norms of non-intervention are at the heart of the United Nations system, but states and international financial institutions have very varied influence across those borders. The non-intervention norm that is key to the Association of Southeast Asian Nations (ASEAN) arrangements is of course a re-affirmation of the non-intervention norm that has long been a crucial part of the United Nations system. This 'global covenant' that Bob Jackson suggests is tentatively in place, and the norm of territorial integrity and stable boundaries that Mark Zacher focuses on as a crucial innovation in the world political map, in combination suggest that few states now face an external existential threat (Jackson 2000; Zacher, 2001). This covenant suggests clearly that wars to annihilate other states and incorporate their populations and territories as a result of aggression are a thing of the past. The end of territorial aggrandizement is the trade off for the establishment of the permanent administrative arrangements of the contemporary state system. Despite the fact that these boundaries frequently may make little practical sense on the ground, especially in 'postcolonial' Africa, this 'covenant' is now widely accepted.

The assumption that territorial ambition is such a powerful *casus belli* has permeated international understanding to such an extent that by the beginning of the twenty-first century it is widely accepted that, even when secessionist states are recognized, they will be established within the territorial boundaries of prior non-sovereign administrative units. The long-delayed independence of East Timor appears to confirm this norm once again, although the violence unloosed by militias and the Indonesian military in 1999 suggest a reluctance to recognize this state as a legitimate part of the geopolitical order in the region. While there are unresolved territorial disputes, and the issue of the status of Taiwan is a constant irritant in many quarters, for the most part few commentators think that major wars of aggression for territorial change are likely in the region any time soon (Alagappa, 2003a).

The irony is that just as boundaries are fixed and wars to settle such matters increasingly becoming a thing of the past, 'global' problems of economics, disease and environment seem to be flowing across those boundaries with increasing speed – meaning that populations in these states face all sorts of insecurities. The response in part is the discourse of human security which is usually implicitly critical of the failure of many new states to provide for the wellbeing and safety of all their peoples. The assumption here is that states are competent to provide modern medical services, political rights, protection from violence and ensure livelihoods for their populations. Membership in the United Nations supposedly brings with it all these responsibilities in exchange for recognition of sovereignty; development and modernity are part and parcel of the global covenant, but many states are simply incapable of doing what the theory suggests they ought to. The parallel assumption – that forms of international administration can competently do what states can't – also needs more critical evaluation than the advocates of peace-keeping, nation-building and other forms of intervention are usually willing to provide (Bain, 2006).

The ambiguous role of the United States in terms of interventions in the region is featured in a number of chapters in this volume. This is especially important in McDonald's discussion of security after 11 September 2001 where local elites have been quick to align themselves with the United States in its global 'war on terror'. Designating secessionist movements as terrorists is not a very original strategy, but clearly one that may bring American aid and troops to one's neighbourhood. Suggesting that each and every insurgency is part of a master plan by Al-Qaeda is clearly not credible. However the proliferation of internet connections which allow techniques for bomb-making and tactical innovations to be learnt quickly and easily, and the increased media visibility of terrorist actions, clearly gives rise to rapid learning and copycat activities which in turn give the impression of a common struggle to both insurgents and states tackling their violence. Once again the importance of critical academic analysis is to disaggregate these movements, understand their specificity and try to explain their origins. Alas, as is the case in so many secessionist struggles that turn violent, the links to criminality easily develop when the need to provide funds, food and provisions for a long struggle engage activists in larger matters of political economy.

All of which confirms a point Ken Booth (2005d) makes in his summation of the scholarly task of critical security studies; the need to focus on the structural conditions that may lead to the crises where security is invoked and violence practised. Avoiding such crises by focusing on antecedent causes is key to a long-term project for human security. But it emphasizes the difference between a critical approach and a problem-solving approach which focuses on the immediate and takes the context for granted. Precisely the opposite is of concern to critics: the long-term structural construction of institutions that deal with matters in crisis mode is of concern because military action is at least conventionally understood as crisis mode – the last resort when all else fails.

In so far as international relations remains an American-dominated intellectual discourse its role in facilitating contemporary modes of hegemony cannot be ignored by self-proclaimed critical scholars. The difficulties of this are both considerable and very ironic in Yongjin Zhang's analysis where Chinese security specialists seem to be quite willing to take on board American notions of national interest and international rivalry as the new terms of security thinking, in contrast to reinventing their Marxist roots to look to more comprehensive understandings of vulnerability and violence in a global political economy. Taking states for granted is of course precisely what allows realist discourse to operate within its claims to be a 'problem-solving' practice. Once again there is a remarkable disjunction between discussions of globalization and global integration in economic terms and a reconstruction of state boundaries in security discourse.

One of the striking contradictions in the discussion of Asia-Pacific security matters is the key point about economic and military security being increasingly at odds with one another. Economic integration and security practices in the region frequently have oddly discrepant geographies. Australia has been trying to shore up military alliances with the United States against all sorts of vaguely specified Asian threats, while at the same time engaging in increased trade with the only states in Asia that could conceivably actually mount a threat to Australian shores. The ongoing discussion of possible Chinese military threats to American interests takes places as exports from China continue to supply many of the basic consumer items sold in American stores. The prospect of the American air force planning to destroy Wal-Mart supply chains suggests that something is seriously amiss in how threats are conceived in the contemporary world.

Identity and security

The success of the expansion of modernity, which frequently disrupts peoples at its margins, has the ironic result of taking its success and its categories for granted, rarely more so than in the popular expansion of claims to rights and entitlements that modern political actors articulate so frequently in international campaigns, and the advocacy of all sorts of interventions in numerous places which require such actions to fix their lack of appropriate global behaviours (Mutua, 2001). 'Cultures that probably represent the majority of the people on earth lack words or concepts equivalent to the notion of "a right". In these cultures, the western notion of rights contradicts their sensibilities and notions of responsibilities for communal or cosmic solidarity' (Esteva and Prakesh, 1998: 130). Instead the global frequently provides an abstraction that suggests a universality, while simultaneously transcending the particularities of specific states. Civil rights are now human rights enshrined in a global United Nations charter that applies to all humans, because the assumption is simply that all people living within the boundary of a sovereign state are citizens of that state and the bearer of such rights whether they understand that 'fact' or not!

The difficulty with arguments about such linked autonomies is at the heart of both human security and critical security studies. Ethnocentrism is unavoidable here, but recognizing it as such and thinking through the practicalities of action in particular cases focused on the ethical relations involved is, it seems, essential for a human security agenda that does not simply repeat the difficulties of colonial administration from the past. And of course that is frequently precisely what state-building development projects do (Scott, 1998). The point here is that there is no simple solution, nor any right answer to these political difficulties, a case made well in Katrina Lee-Koo's discussion of emancipation. Her discussion of 'Asian values' also poses the question of ethnocentrism before suggesting, at least implicitly, that regardless of whether this is the case, emancipating women is a political desideratum. But Lee-Koo is careful to suggest multiple emancipatory practices rather than a singular formulaic agenda. What she doesn't do is suggest that the transformative forces of modernization in the last few generations have been such that ethnocentrism is at least much less of a criticism than it might once have been, given the widespread adoption of economic growth with all the trappings of modern cultural aspiration that come with it in Asia. Although that said, the disastrous adoption of earlier versions of modernity by a militarist Japan is an object lesson on imitation and disaster that still resonates in the region.

As the chapters in this volume make clear, the sheer geographical diversity of the Asia-Pacific region make any single approach to all this impossible; context-specific analyses and advocacy are necessary to make a difference for 'real people in real places' to use Ken Booth's (2005d: 276) phrasing. This suggests, in addition to culturally and historically sensitive analyses, that academic analysis based in political science modes of doing security studies that take the state for granted as the starting point for analysis is not enough. Clearly sociologists, anthropologists, historians, economists and geographers may have much to say about the human fate that is relevant to a discussion of security that deals with non-state entities, especially those targeted by state violence. The necessity of such interdisciplinary endeavours is an obvious conclusion that can be drawn from the analyses in this volume; it is a clear implication from See Seng Tan's discussion of two forms of essentialism in Singapore and likewise a necessity for tackling the identity politics, and recognizing it as such, that Anthony Burke analyses in the Australian case.

Security, with the presupposition of enmity and the near inevitability of state rivalry leading to conflict, produces strange effects when viewed through different prisms, in this case a political economy lens on economic change and interdependence. It is not at all clear why China would choose to try to fight the United States, its best export market and the key to the economic growth which now legitimizes the ruling party. But military contingency planning is all about making precisely such scenarios, in the words of the motto of the Institute for Defense and Strategic Studies in Singapore, one of the leading think tanks on security in the Asia-Pacific, one needs to 'ponder the improbable'. But in so far as this strategic mode of thinking perpetuates the possibilities of conflict and leads to war preparation then it reproduces precisely the forms of conduct that it ostensibly protects against.

It is precisely the logic of realism with its key specification of competing autonomous units that provides the irony of ASEAN as a practice that facilitates the suppression of dissent. While it has frequently been external threats that provide the pretext for internal repression, ironically in this case the mutual agreement to non-interference has allowed internal violence without the danger of international destabilization. There is a larger irony for the agendas of human security and critical security studies in that the non-intervention agreements run very close to the United Nations conventions. Here is the larger pattern which the critical security analyses have to confront. Where state elites have a compact, the possibilities of cross border interventions are precluded. This is of course precisely what the United Nations system was set up to try to accomplish, it being first and foremost a war prevention system. But this allows violence within with no check on the misdeeds of a state against the population that it supposedly protects. It also allows, as Sara Davies documents, for the specification of refugees and displaced people as illegal migrants making them doubly vulnerable in the state system. Hence, in part, the argument for intervention in the case of the International Commission on Intervention and State Sovereignty (2001) and the 'responsibility to protect' as a suggested mode of posing the limits to membership in the society of states. Nonetheless even in this case, as the debate over the behaviour of the military in Myanmar and its inclusion in the activities of ASEAN suggests, these non-intervention conventions have their limits when state behaviour is so violent as to demand censure. Once again, as the case of refugees and migration suggests, states are the threat to people in need of security.

Most such discussions operate in a geopolitical specification of the world into wild zones and tame zones, security being about deterring or reducing the dangers from the periphery to the core. The converse isn't considered a danger; the disruptions in the periphery are after all development, necessary changes that will ensure security based on affluence eventually. That indigenous peoples might need or prefer a version of security without development, or at least a different mode of incorporation into the world economy, simply cannot be considered given the specification of threats and order subject to these threats. This point suggests that most of the discussions of security are about the provision of security for modernity, lack of modernity being the problem. But this raises the crucial question of how human security is to be provided and by whom in many of the places where it is currently lacking.

The Clausewitzian mode of thinking – of war as politics by other means – has had considerable purchase in security studies over the last few generations, but the persistence of states of emergencies and the military standoff of the Cold War, not to mention the use of military forces for political purposes in many places, suggests that the simple division between war and peace and the assumptions of peacetime as normal are no longer useful assumptions. Formal declarations of war are frequently now a thing of the past; most military actions are now undertaken without such rituals. Hence the focus on security as the dominant formulation for state activity, one that encompasses more than a strictly wartime situation and extends extraordinary powers so that they have long since become the norm. Indeed precisely this norm, and the connection between the security forces of industrial states in particular, with the discourse of strategic studies as part of this approach to the world as a threatening place, is part and parcel of American hegemony in the global system (Klein, 1994). This point is crucial to placing critical security studies in appropriate intellectual and political context. It is both a critique of political practices and, in a more Foucauldian mode (Foucault, 2003), sometimes an engagement with the modes of knowing that specify the world as a venue in which security is an appropriate practice for the designation of dangers and threats.

This is only most obviously a task for those identified as post-structuralist, with their focus on the ontological givens of political discourse, and their insistence on critique as the practice of explaining both how those categories come to dominate discussion and how they might be tackled and changed. What is frequently most difficult in challenging security is precisely the designation of a situation as a danger to political order requiring security measures. But it also has to be remembered that not all claims to the necessity for the application of emergency powers work; threats are not always credible and securitization may fail. But implicit in much of this discussion, and explicit in many places in the chapters of this volume, is the invocation of a political *identity* as under threat. This point is crucial in focusing on the taken for granted that needs to be secured, because once analysis focuses on this it becomes clear that the process of declaring something beyond politics, a matter of survival, an existential threat, or a pressing necessity that requires emergency powers, is a very political process indeed (Buzan *et al.*, 1998).

This in turn raises the prospect that identity is ultimately more important than security, as Tony Burke argues in the politics of the Howard administration in Australia. In the case of Korea clearly the identity of the US as a superpower is maintained in the practices of confrontation. So too, precisely by the refusal to enquire into the dynamics of confrontation, and instead attribute hostile intentions to the antagonist, rendered as a separate autonomous entity, rather than as a party to an ongoing relationship, are the interpretations of threat rehearsed and the rituals of technological war preparation maintained. Because in Burke's terms the identities of the realist practitioners are at stake too in the confrontation in Korea. So also, as McDonald notes, are they being reproduced in the specification of the struggles with Al-Qaeda as a matter of warfare rather than as a matter of policing and diplomacy.

Given the importance of the military as an organization, in some cases effectively the state mechanism as in Myanmar, the assumption of war as unusual, of peace as the norm and its violation for reasons of state as the exception is not necessarily a useful mode of thinking in the Asia-Pacific context. The invocation of threats to national identity and the use of political polarization and violent oppression of those marginalized in the process is a mode of conduct all too familiar to those watching the Indonesian military in particular as Edward Aspinall and Richard Chauvel remind us. Critical security studies here might well find itself in clear agreement with those in the US and Britain who have advocated institutional reform among militaries as a way to reduce violence and human rights abuses by the forces of state violence. As Alex Bellamy and Bryn Hughes point out, professionalization and the removal of military organizations from routine economic activities suggests a modern military dedicated to security of state, but not one involved in routine matters of economics or public administration. This in turn should provide the military with fewer temptations to use its powers in nefarious ways that affect the local population. This is of course an extension of the long-running liberal aspiration to banish warfare from politics, to reduce violence and promote trade as the means of maximizing human happiness in a world of material scarcity. Human security advocates are firmly within this intellectual tradition; critical security analysts, in so far as they draw on political economy analyses influenced by Marx and the Frankfurt School, or Coxian theory, are not. But the aspirations are nonetheless similar.

Human security and critical security studies

The theoretical question raised by the contributors to this volume suggests that critical security studies, as formulated in the Welsh school of Ken Booth (1991) and Richard Wyn Jones (1999) at least, links critical security analyses closely with advocacy of human security. This is implied by a language of emancipation in the case of critical security studies and more generally in the human security literature in terms of freedom from fear, violence, need and so on. Human security has the advantage of being understood in terms of advocacy plain and simply. In its various articulations, human security promises freedom from want, fear and political violence (Hampson, 2002; Dodds and Pippard, 2005; *Human Security Report*, 2005). While this agenda is agreed upon widely, there is much less consensus on the tools to be used so these aspirations can be implemented in many parts of the world. These difficulties with implementation, and the crucial question of when interventions across state boundaries might be judged to be legitimate in the face of the conflicting norm of state sovereignty, suggest the need for much more careful thinking all round. While the theoretical background in Frankfurt School critical theory, via Robert Cox's political economy in some cases, or more directly from social theory in others, is not directly congruent with the intellectual sources that try to extend security towards new referent objects far from the traditional purview of national security, nonetheless the end point of both is loosely similar.

This raises the key question of whether the analytical approaches in critical security studies are compatible with the policy agendas of human security. There are few regions where such a juxtaposition might be more usefully examined than the Asia-Pacific, precisely because it presents the 'hard case', a set of circumstances perhaps least likely to be amenable to critical security studies-inspired examination, and a region far removed – at least at first glance – from policies of human security. Hazel Lang's analysis of the difficulties facing displaced people in the ongoing violence of Myanmar's counter-insurgency campaign highlights the violence that needs to be addressed, while also pointing out the difficulties of implementing human security policies in regimes that are much less concerned with individual welfare than with asserting a sometimes tenuous political control in remote regions.

Critical social theory of the Frankfurt variety is not obviously theoretically in line with a policy agenda extending national security into realms of domestic jurisdiction. It might however be more easily reconciled with discussions of social security and the responsibilities of states to provide for the basic welfare of their inhabitants. Some claim to universal human rights and some notion of basic entitlements are in common too as end points. But the origins of critical theory in arguments about the violence of capitalist states, their role in maintaining the inherent inequities of its economic system and perpetuating divided polities are in sharp contrast with the universal liberal aspirations implicit in most of the human security agendas. While China still officially embraces some version of Marxist thinking, it has long since in practice conceded that economic innovation is best conducted by capitalism, and the growing disparities of wealth in that state are clearly not the kind of society that socialists concerned with equity ever envisioned. In doing so critical scholarship interested in the larger transformations of our time gets short shrift in the concern for national economic growth.

Given the violence caught up with security, and the failure of security to deliver what it promises, critical security studies as a series of academic endeavours has the considerable advantage of explicitly putting security itself in doubt, of insisting that its promises and supposed operations be put under radical scrutiny. At least this is sometimes the case, but there remain tensions at the heart of the enterprise given that emancipation is so frequently invoked and expressed in clearly modern terms which are sometimes in danger of linking up with neo-liberal variants of freedom understood in terms of material affluence. Not least this is the case when states are explicitly focused upon as the source of numerous insecurities. Understood in these terms critical security studies is both analysis and advocacy. In this it is in the same situation as the realist camp it criticizes which also aspires to provide security by its technical knowledges and practices focused on states and their boundaries.

Thus the question for critical security studies is whether its analyses of the structural causes of violence and its attempts to probe beyond the immediate problem-solving formulations that lead to immediate policy advice, come unstuck when it moves from analyses to advocacy. This is especially so when the agents to whom policy advice is usually given are states – frequently the source of insecurity in the first place. Here the dangers of implicit liberal categories whether autonomous states or autonomous individuals are especially important. If human security is understood as providing freedom from fear, want and violence to individuals then the danger is that the social networks, communities and societies that those people form is underplayed. The causal connections to the larger global economy, the arms trade, and geopolitical linkages into the larger system are always in danger of being underplayed in the immediate need to 'do something' when violence and disaster strike in a particular place. The geographical vocabulary that specifies disaster as happening in one place, be it East Timor, Myanmar or anywhere else, can reinforce the assumption of indigenous causes of insecurity while downplaying the connections to the larger global political economy where those connections may be both causal factors, and ones that can be dealt with in an anticipatory manner. Focusing on these linkages, the connections and causations, as for instance the campaign against blood diamonds, and the attempts to remove illegally mined and harvested natural resources from international markets tries to do, suggests a more comprehensive, and a more 'critical' approach to these matters (le Billon, 2005). This is about more than autonomous entities, whether states or individuals; collectivities, connections and responsibilities are linked directly. Policy innovations are about much more than 'interventions' and state actions too; they are about constructing sustainable and just modes of conduct, not just about coercive prevention and negative sanctions that is so frequently central to security policies designed to forcibly produce 'good' behaviour.

Invoking the term security thus brings dilemmas, ironies and difficulties to the fore immediately, so much so that critical thinking is compelled to continue to contest its conceptualizations (Dalby, 1997; Smith, S., 2005). The term itself seems an inescapable part of the practice of modernity. As such scholars of war, violence and politics have little choice but to confront it and address the term in all its many facets. But to do so is never easy as all the chapters in this volume suggest in their various ways. It is particularly difficult because security so frequently promises what it can't deliver. While suggesting safety, it frequently brings violence; while implying the benefits of peace, it conjures a prior condition of danger; while suggesting permanence and protection, its practices frequently remind the supposed beneficiaries of the painful contingencies of human existence.

Following Tony Burke's (2007) analysis in *Beyond Security, Ethics and Violence* we can think about security as metaphysical, or more specifically the metaphysics of domination, and then ask if critical security studies is about emancipating security from this straightjacket. Can security be so emancipated? The chapters in this volume suggest that this is unlikely. Indeed most of them implicitly operate within a mode of analysis that suggests extending security to operate in other modes, and in particular shifting the referent object from states to people, or individuals in particular, rather than to other social collectivities. This perpetuates modes of thinking which take protection and spatial autonomy, the key to liberal formulations of security for granted, while simultaneously attempting to transcend them in the invocation of universal aspirations to security (Dalby, 2005). Such difficulties are not easy to deal with, but a critical sensibility constantly reminds one that they are there, rather than fixing on a correct metaphysical position and imposing this on the object of analysis. In this sense critical approaches also suggest a focus on the social production of insecurity rather than an external imposition of policy to transform conduct judged to be inappropriate. The links between the formulation of human security in the United Nations Development Report in 1994, which got so much of the human security discussion moving, with its forward-looking preventative ethos, and a more critical political economy approach deserve elaboration beyond what is hinted at in the chapters of this volume.

In so far as critical security studies focuses on the specific causes of insecurity, refusing to assume that states do actually provide security, it is on safe ground. It shares the assumption of sub-optimal state performance and the desire to formulate strategies to tackle this condition. As such both point to the central contradiction of our times; the agents of security provision end up not providing what their efforts promise. It remains to be seen whether the human security agenda in some form may do better. Ironically it might just succeed best by insisting that key matters of health and safety not be dealt with as security issues at all. The example of China's volte-face on SARS and its decision to invoke health rather than sovereignty and national security as the appropriate way of dealing with the disease is immensely suggestive, not least because of the shift in operating premises from national concern to one of a common humanity facing disease.

In so far as critical security studies is anything, it is primarily an academic project, one designed to challenge conventional practices of security as done by states. Its task can be understood as being a critical enterprise in Robert Cox's terms, one that seeks the larger contexts to understand how things came to be as they are, rather than to work with things as they are to manipulate them for immediate ends. The problem-solving approach of policy-makers and their academic advisors in contrast takes the context as given rather than that which is to be investigated. In the world of nuclear armed rivals, and the Cold War in particular, security studies was an explicitly instrumental practice. The remnants of this remain clear in the standoff over North Korea where ideological animosities remain in addition to huge suspicions concerning the 'other' side. But it is interesting to note that even in Roland Bleiker's analysis, sympathetic as it is to the limits of realist approaches, the problem is still posed in terms of how the rest of the world will manage North Korea rather than in any other register. The question of whether North Korea cheated in the agreements of the 1990s is raised, but not whether the United States lived up to its obligations. The crucial point is made that the US has refused to countenance a non-aggression treaty with the implicit recognition of the legitimacy of the North

Korean regime that this would imply. Force is key here, not security despite the language.

But clearly reading the chapters in this volume shows that there is much more to critical security studies as an intellectual enterprise than such instrumentalities. Since its emergence under the name critical security studies, the debate has drawn on other intellectual sources driving a broader series of modes of critique (Krause and Williams, 1997). It would be all too easy at this stage to enter into the current name-calling exercise that passes as a discussion of method in the field of international relations, but the debate about constructivism and post-structuralism, neo-realism and institutionalism is only partly germane to either critical security studies or the discussion of human security, given the continued focus in international relations on state to state arrangements and conflicts, rather than a more encompassing understanding of either politics or security as about much more than this. Indeed it is not too much of a stretch to suggest that some of the limitations of the international relations enterprise are precisely due to this narrowing of the discussion of politics in a way that facilitates the operation of political power exercised by elites. Here policy-makers and civil servants charged with long-term thinking for their states, could benefit considerably by working with critical intellectuals to think about how human security agendas can be facilitated by ensuring that there is much more to policy than the short-term priorities of political elites. This is undoubtedly going to be a fraught enterprise in many places, but the scale of global transformations, both in the natural world and the global political economy, demands that security be understood in innovative ways that looks beyond the short-term rivalries of states, or the short-term implementation of modernization.

The chapters in this volume show both the diversity of approaches under the label of critical security studies and the diversity of situations in need of analysis in the Asia-Pacific region. They suggest that the plurality of intellectual approaches under the label critical security studies is unavoidable. Such methodological pluralism may offend those who think intellectual enquiry within the social sciences needs to be conducted in a more rigorous or systematic manner, but the whole point of critical thinking is to challenge the instrumentalisms of conventional analysis given the violence they so frequently involve.

Both the advocates of human security and those approaching matters with some notion of critique as an appropriate scholarly practice have in common a concern to improve the lot of humanity in specific places. They also share a recognition that security is in many ways far too important to leave to states alone, especially so when states both claim a monopoly of the legitimate use of force and then proceed to use that supposed monopoly to endanger their own, and others' populations. But this does not necessarily make it at all clear how to proceed with either analysis or advocacy. It is perhaps even more difficult to suggest appropriate modes of combining both, but it is clear from the voices in the chapters in this volume that any critical security studies project worth its name has the self-imposed obligation to try.

REFERENCES

AAP (Australian Associated Press) (2003) 10 July, available at: www.aap.com.au

AAP (2005a) 'Detainees driven to suicide, say advocates', *Sydney Morning Herald*, 11 September

AAP (2005b) 'Politicians "stoking anti-Muslim hysteria"', *Sydney Morning Herald*, 11 September

ABC News Online (1999) 'UN to withdraw from East Timor', 8 September

ABC News Online (2004) 'Minister tells Muslims: accept Aussie values or "clear off"', 24 August

ABC News Online (2005) 'Govt accused of anti-terror law diversion tactic,' 9 September

Abernathy, David B. (2000) *Global Dominance: European Overseas Empires, 1415–1980*, New Haven, NJ: Yale University Press

Acharya, Amitav (1997) 'Ideas, identity, and institution-building: from the "ASEAN way" to the "Asia-Pacific way"?', *Pacific-Review,* 10:3, 319–46

Acharya, Amitav (1999) 'A concert of Asia?', *Survival,* Autumn, 41:3, 84–101

Acharya, Amitav (2000) *Constructing a Security Community in South East Asia: ASEAN and the Problem of Regional Order*, London: Routledge

Acharya, Amitav (2001) *Constructing a Security Community in Southeast Asia*, London: Routledge

Acharya, Amitav (2002) 'State-society relations: Asian and World Order after September 11', in K. Booth and T. Dunne (eds) *Worlds in Collision: Terror and the Future of Global Order*, New York: Palgrave

Acharya, Amitav (2003) 'Will Asia's past be its future?', *International-Security*, Winter, 28:3, 149–64

Acharya, Amitav (2003a) 'Regional institutions and Asian security order: norms, power, and prospects for peaceful change', in Muthiah Alagappa (ed.), *Asian Security Order: Instrumental and Normative Features*, Stanford: Stanford University Press.

Acharya, Amitav (2003b) 'Democratization and the prospects of participatory regionalism in Southeast Asia', *Third World Quarterly*, 24, 375–90

Acharya, Amitav (2004) 'A holistic paradigm', *Security Dialogue*, 35:3, 355–6

Acharya, Amitav (2005a) 'Issues for an ASEAN Charter', *IDSS Commentaries*, 71

Acharya, Amitav (2005b) 'The Bush doctrine and Asian regional order', in M. Gurtov and P. Van Ness (eds), *Confronting the Bush Doctrine: Critical Views from the Asia-Pacific*, New York: Routledge

Acharya, Amitav and See Seng Tan (2004) 'Introduction', in S. Tan and A. Acharya (eds), *Asia-Pacific Security Cooperation*, New York: M.E. Sharpe

Ackerly, Brooke A. and Bina D'Costa (2005) 'Transnational feminism: political strategies and theoretical resources', *Working Paper*, March, 1, Canberra: RSPAS

Adler, Emanuel (1997) 'Imagined (security) communities: cognitive regions in international relations', *Millennium*, 26, 249–77

Adler, Emanuel (2005) *Communitarian International Relations: The Epistemic Foundations of International Relations*, London and New York: Routledge

Adler, Emanuel and Barnett, Michael (eds) (1998) *Security Communities*, Cambridge: Cambridge University Press

AFP (1999) 'Britain says Indonesia must secure E Timor or accept help', *Sydney Morning Herald*, 8 September

Agence-France Press (2000) 'Biologists issue warning over deforestation in Indo-China', 24 March

Agence-France Press (2005) 'Jakara rejects US demand for military suspensions', 22 November.

Agence-France Press (2005) 'ASEAN troops in Indonesia's tsunami-hit Aceh to remain', 17 January

Agnew, John (2005) 'Sovereignty regimes: territoriality and state authority in contemporary world politics', *Annals of the Association of American Geographers*, 95, 437–61

Agnew, Jonathan and Stuart Corbridge (1995) *Mastering Space: Hegemony, Territory and International Political Economy*, London: Routledge

Alagappa, Muthiah (1988) 'Comprehensive security: interpretations in ASEAN countries', in R. A. Scalapino, S. Sato, J. Wanandi and S.J. Han (eds), *Asian Security Issues: Regional and Global*, Berkeley, CA: Institute of East Asian Studies, University of California Press

Alagappa, Muthiah (ed.) (1998) *Asian Security Practice: Material and Ideational Influences*, Stanford, CA: Stanford University Press

Alagappa, Muthiah (1998) 'Asian practice of security: key features and explanations, in Muthiah Alagappa (ed.), *Asian Security Practice: Material and Ideational Influences*, Stanford, CA: Stanford University Press

Alagappa, Muthiah (2003) 'Managing Asian security: competition, cooperation, and evolutionary change', in Muthiah Alagappa (ed.), *Asian Security Order: Instrumental and Normative Features*, Stanford, CA: Stanford University Press

Alexander, Michael (1999) 'Refugee status determination conducted by UNHCR', *International Journal of Refugee Law*, 11:2, 251–89

Alker, Hayward (2005) 'Emancipation in the critical security studies project',in K. Booth (ed.), *Critical Security Studies and World Politics*, Boulder, CO: Lynne Rienner

Allard, Tom (2004) 'Going to war secured US alliance, says Downer' , *Sydney Morning Herald*, 3 March

Allen, Richard (1970) *A Short Introduction to the History and Politics of Southeast Asia*, New York: Oxford University Press

Allon, Fiona (1997) 'Home as cultural translation: John Howard's Earlwood', *Communal/Plural*, 4, 1–25

Amnesty International (1998) 'ASEAN Regional Forum: Human Rights integral to regional security', *Amnesty International* available at: <http://web.amnesty.org/library/index/ENGIOR640011998?open&of=ENG.312>, accessed 26 July 2005

Amnesty International (2004) 'China exploits international "war on terror" to repress Uighurs', *Amnesty International* August, available at: <http://web.amnesty.org/wire/August2004/China>, accessed 18 September

Amnesty International (2005) 'Indonesia, 2004' , in *Amnesty International Report*, available at: <http://web.amnesty.org/report2005/idn-summary-eng>, accessed 18 September 2005

Amnesty International (2005) 'The death penalty worldwide: developments in 2004', *Amnesty International*, 5 April, available at: http://web.amnesty.org/library/Index/ENGACT500012005

Analisa (2004) 29 April, available at: http://www.analisadaily.com/

Anderson, Benedict (1999) 'Indonesian nationalism today and in the future', *New Left Review*, 235: 3–17

Anon (1999) 'Indonesia loses 4 billion in lost revenue every year', *Jakarta Post*, 1 November

Antara News (2004) 'U.S. demands settlement of Timika case to recover Mily Ties', 22 November

Anwar, Dewi Fortuna (2003) 'Human security: an intractable problem in Asia', in Muthiah Alagappa (ed.), *Asian Security Order: Instrumental and Normative Features*, Stanford, CA: Stanford University Press

Arif, Mohamed (1995) 'Environmental politics of the OECD and their implications for ASEAN', in Kiichiro Fukasau and Joseph Tan (eds), *OECD and ASEAN Economies: The Challenge of Policy Coherence*, Paris: OECD

Armijo, Leslie Elliott (2002) 'The terms of the debate: what's democracy got to do with it?', in L. E. Armijo (ed.), *Debating the Global Financial Architecture*, Albany, NY: State University of New York Press

ASEAN (2005) ASEAN Security Community Plan of Action, available at: <html://www.aseansec.org/16826.htm>, 19 September

ASEAN-ISIS (1992) *The Environment and Human Rights in International Relations: An Agenda for ASEAN's Policy Approaches and Responses*, Memorandum 2, Jakarta: ASEAN-ISIS Secretariat

ASEAN-ISIS (1993a) *Confidence Building Measures in Southeast Asia*, Memorandum 5, Jakarta: ASEAN-ISIS Secretariat

ASEAN-ISIS (1993b) *Enhancing ASEAN Security Cooperation*, Memorandum 3, Jakarta: ASEAN-ISIS Secretariat

ASEAN Regional Forum (1997) 'Chairman's statement, 1994', reproduced in Takashi Inoguchi and Grant B. Stillman (eds), *Northeast Asian Regional Security: The Role of International Institutions*, Tokyo: United Nations University Press

ASEAN Regional Forum (1998) 'Statement of the Chairman of the Fifth ASEAN Regional Forum meeting', Manila, July

AEAN Regional Forum (2001) 'Concept and Principles of Preventive Diplomacy', Hanoi, July

ASEAN Secretariat (1994) *From Strength to Strength – ASEAN Function Cooperation: Retrospect and Prospect*, Jakarta: ASEAN Secretariat

ASEAN Secretariat (1997) *First ASEAN State of the Environment Report*, Jakarta: ASEAN Secretariat

ASEAN Secretariat (2001) *Second ASEAN State of the Environment Report*, Jakarta: ASEAN Secretariat

ASEAN Secretariat (2004) 'The ASEAN regional forum: a concept paper', in ASEAN Regional Forum, *Documents Series, 1994–2004*, Jakarta: ASEAN Secretariat

Ashley, Richard (1984) 'The Poverty of Neorealism', *International Organization* 38:2, 225–86

Ashley, Richard K. (1987) 'The geopolitics of geopolitical space: toward a critical social theory of international politics', *Alternatives*, 12: 403–34

Ashley, Richard K. (1988) 'Untying the sovereign state: a double reading of the anarchy problematique', *Millennium: Journal of International Studies*, 17, 227–62

Ashley, Richard K. (1989) 'Living on borderlines: man, poststructuralism and war', in J. Der Derian and M. Shapiro (eds), *International/Intertextual Relations*, Lexington, MA: Lexington Books

Aslanbeigui, Nahid and Gale Summerfield (2000) 'The Asian crisis, gender and the international financial architecture', *Feminist Economics*, 6:3, 81–103

Aspinall, Edward (2005) *The Helsinki Agreement: A More Promising Basis for Peace in Aceh?*, Washington, DC: East-West Center

Aspinall, Edward and Mark T. Berger (2001) 'The breakup of Indonesia? Nationalism and the contradictions of modernity in post-cold war Southeast Asia', *Third World Quarterly*, 22 :6, 1003–24

Aspinall, Edward and Greg Fealy (eds) (2003) *Local Power and Politics in Indonesia: Democratisation and Decentralisation*, Singapore: Institute of Southeast Asian Studies

Asian Development Bank (1997) *Emerging Asia: Changes and Challenges*, Manila: Asian Development Bank

Associated Press (2005) 'Lawmakers want ASEAN to suspend Myanmar', reprinted in *The Straits Times*, September 27, p. 10

Aung San, Suu Kyi (1991) *Freedom from Fear and Other Writings*, London: Penguin

The Australian (2006) 'Military action an option for North Korea: Howard', 13 October

Australia's National Security: A Defence Update (2003), Canberra: Department of Defence

Ayoob, Mohammed (1995) *The Third World Security Predicament: State Making, Regional Conflict and the International System*, Boulder, CO: Lynne Rienner

Ayoob, Mohammed (1997) 'Defining security: a subaltern realist perspective', in Keith Krause and Michael C. Williams (eds), *Critical Security Studies: Concepts and Cases*, London: University College London Press

Ayoob, Mohammed (2002) 'Inequality and theorizing in international relations: the case for subaltern realism', *International Studies Review*, 4 :3, 27–48

Bain, Will (2006) 'In praise of folly: international administration and the corruption of humanity', *International Affairs*, 82:3, 525–38

Baldwin, David A. (1997) 'The concept of security', *Review of International Studies*, 23, 5–26

Ball, Desmond (1998) 'Military acquisitions in the Asia-Pacific Region', in Michael E. Brown, Sean M. Lynn-Jones and Steven E. Miller (eds), *East Asian Security*, Cambridge, MA: MIT Press

Ball, Desmond (2000) *The Council for Security Cooperation in the Asia-Pacific (CSCAP): Its Record and Its Prospect*, Canberra Papers on Strategy and Defence 139, Canberra: Australian National University

Ball, Desmond (2002) 'The defence of East Timor: a recipe for disaster', *Pacifica Review*, 14:3, 175–89

Ball, Nicole (1998) *Spreading good practices in security sector reform: policy options for the British Government*, London: Saferworld

Bangkok Post (2004) 'Gunmen kill three, petrol station bombs expected to increase', 30 August

Barkenbus, Jack (2001) *APEC and the Environment: Civil Society in an Age of Globalisation*, Asia Pacific Issues, 51, Hawaii: East-West Center

Barker, Geoffrey (1999) 'Australia pushes US over Timor', *Australian Financial Review*, 8 September

Baudrillard, Jean (1988) 'Simulacra and simulations', in Mark Poster (ed.), *Selected Writings*, Oxford: Polity Press

BBC (2006) 'North Korea talks set to resume', *BBC Online*, 31 October, available at: http://news.bbc.co.uk/1/hi/world/asia-pacific/6102092.stm

Beeson, Mark (1998) 'Indonesia, the East Asian crisis and the commodification of the nation-state', *New Political Economy*, 3, 357–74

Beeson, Mark (2001) 'Globalisation, governance and the political-economy of public policy reform in East Asia', *Governance*, 14, 481–502

Beeson, Mark (2003) 'ASEAN plus three and the rise of reactionary regionalism', *Contemporary Southeast Asia* 25 :2, 251–68

Beeson, Mark (2004) 'The rise and fall (?) of the developmental state: the vicissitudes and implications of East Asian interventionism', in L. Low (ed.), *Developmental States: Relevant, Redundant or Reconfigured?*, New York: Nova Science Publishers

Beeson, Mark (2006a) *Regionalism and Globalisation in East Asia: Politics, Security and Economic Development*, Basingstoke: Palgrave

Beeson, Mark (2006b) 'Southeast Asia and the international financial institutions', in G. Rodan, K. Hewison and R. Robison (eds), *The Political Economy of South-East Asia: An Introduction*, Melbourne: Oxford University Press, 3rd edn

Beeson, Mark and Stephen Bell (2005a) 'Structures, institutions and agency in the models of capitalism debate' in N. Philips (ed.), *Globalising International Political Economy*, London: Palgrave

Beeson, Mark and Stephen Bell (2005b) *The G20 and the Politics of International Financial Sector Reform: Robust Regimes or Hegemonic Instability?*, CSGR Working Paper, 174, Warwick University

Beeson, Mark and Yan Islam (2005) 'Neoliberalism and East Asia: resisting the Washington Consensus', *Journal of Development Studies*, 41, 197–219

Beitz, Charles (1979) *Political Theory and International Relations*, Princeton, NJ: Princeton University Press

Bellamy, Alex J. (2004) *Security Communities and their Neighbours: Regional Fortresses or Global Integrators?* Basingstoke and New York: Palgrave Macmillan

Bellamy, Alex J. and Matt McDonald (2002) 'The utility of human security: Which humans? What security? A reply to Thomas and Tow', *Security Dialogue*, 33:3, 373–7

Bengwayan, Michael A. (2000) 'Deaths and illnesses from pollution in Asia increasing', *Earth Times*, 11 March, available at: <http://www.earthtimes.org/mar/environmentdeathsandillnessmar11_01.htm>

Bennet, Jennifer (2004) 'Globalization and human development: the case of India and Pakistan', in Ramesh Thakur and Edward Newman (eds), *Broadening Asia's Security Discourse and Agenda*, Tokyo: United Nations University Press

Berger, Mark T. (2004) 'Decolonizing Southeast Asia: nationalism, revolution and the cold war', in Mark Beeson (ed.), *Contemporary Southeast Asia: Regional Dynamics, National Differences*, Hampshire: Palgrave Macmillan

Berry, William E. (1986) 'The changing role of the Philippine military during martial law and the implications for the future', in Edward Olsen and Stephen Jurika, Jr (eds), *The Armed Forces in Contemporary Asian Societies*, Boulder, CO: Westview Press

Bilgin, Pinar (2002) 'Beyond statism in security studies? Human agency and security in the Middle East', *Review of International Affairs* 2:1, 100–18

Blackburn, Susan (1999) 'Gender violence and the Indonesian political transition', *Asian Studies Review*, 23:4, 431–46

Blake, Nigel and Kay Pole (eds) (1983) *Dangers of Deterrence: Philosophers on Nuclear Strategy*, London: Routledge

Bleiker, Roland (2003) 'A rogue is a rogue is a rogue: US foreign policy and the Korean nuclear crisis', *International Affairs*, 79:4, 719–37

Bleiker, Roland (2004) 'Alternatives to peacekeeping in Korea: the role of non-state actors and face-to-face encounters', *International Peacekeeping*, 11:1, 1–17

Bleiker, Roland (2005) *Divided Korea: Toward a Culture of Reconciliation*, Minneapolis, MN: University of Minnesota Press

Block, Fred (1990) *Postindustrial Possibilities: A Critique of Economic Discourse*, Berkeley, CA: University of California Press

Bloom, Allan (1987) *The Closing of the American Mind*, New York: Simon & Schuster

Boese, Wade (2005a) 'Suppliers weigh India nuclear cooperation', *Arms Control Today*, 35:9

Boese, Wade (2005b) 'Nations remain split on disarmament', *Arms Control Today*, 35:8

Boot, Max (2003) 'Imperialism', *Weekly Standard*, 6 May

Booth, Ken (1991) 'Security and Emancipation', *Review of International Studies*, 17:4, 313–26

Booth, Ken (1995) 'Human Wrongs and International Relations', *International Affairs*, Vol. 71, No. 1, pp. 103–126

Booth, Ken (1997) 'A reply to Wallace', *Review of International Studies*, 23:3, 371–77

Booth, Ken (1999) 'Three tyrannies', in Tim Dunne and J. Nicholas Wheeler (eds), *Human Rights in Global Politics*,Cambridge: Cambridge University Press

Booth, Ken (2005a) 'Critical Explorations', in Ken Booth (ed.), *Critical Security Studies and World Politics*, Boulder, CO: Lynne Rienner

Booth, Ken (2005b) 'Preface', in Ken Booth (ed.), *Critical Security Studies and World Politics*, Boulder, CO: Lynne Rienner

Booth, Ken (2005c) 'Emancipation' in Ken Booth (ed.), *Critical Security Studies and World Politics*, Boulder, CO: Lynne Rienner

Booth, Ken (2005d) 'Beyond critical security studies', in Ken Booth (ed.), *Critical Security Studies and World Politics*, Boulder, CO: Lynne Rienner

Booth, Ken (ed.) (2005e) *Critical Security Studies and World Politics*, Boulder, CO: Lynne Rienner

Booth, Ken (ed.) (2005f) 'Part 2: Community', in *Critical Security Studies and World Politics*, Boulder, CO: Lynne Rienner

Bourchier, David (1997) 'Totalitarianism and the "national personality": recent controversy about the philosophical basis of the Indonesian state', in Jim Schiller and Barbara Martin-Schiller (eds), *Imagining Indonesia: Cultural Politics and Political Culture*, Athens, OH: Ohio University Center for International Studies

Bourdieu, Pierre (1991) *Language and Symbolic Power*, Cambridge: Polity Press

Bowen, Clayton B. and Daniel Wolven (1999) 'Command and control challenges in South Asia', *The Nonproliferation Review*, (6:3, 25–35)

Bowornwathana, Bidhya (2001) 'Thailand: bureaucracy under coalition governments', in John P. Burns (ed.), *Civil Service Systems in Asia*, Cheltenham, UK: Edward Elgar

Brett, Judith (2003) *Australian Liberals and the Moral Middle Class*, Cambridge: Cambridge University Press

Brown, Chris (1994) 'Turtles all the way down: anti-foundationalism, critical theory and international relations', *Millennium*, 23:2, 53–76

Brown, Louise (2000) *Sex Slaves, The Trafficking of Women in Asia*, London: Virago

Bunbongkarn, Suchit (1988) 'The military and development for national security in Thailand', in J. Soedjati Djiwandono and Yong Mun Cheong (eds), *Soldiers and Stability in Southeast Asia*, Singapore: Institute of Southeast Asian Studies

Bundongkorn, Suchit (1999) 'Thailand's successful reforms', *Journal of Democracy*, 10:4, 54–68

Burchill, Scott (2002) 'Indefensible breach of privacy,' *The Australian*, 13 February

Burchill, Scott (2004) 'The trouble with the alliance,' *The Age*, 3 May

Burke, Anthony (2001a) 'Caught between national and human security: knowledge and power in post-crisis Asia', *Pacifica Review*, 13:3, 215–39

Burke, Anthony (2001b) *In Fear of Security: Australia's Invasion Anxiety*, Sydney: Pluto Press Australia

Burke, Anthony (2002) 'Aporias of security', *Alternatives: Global, Local, Political*, 27:1, 1–28

Burke, Anthony (2007) *Beyond Security, Ethics and Violence: War Against the Other*, London: Routledge

Bush, President George W. (2002) 'The national security strategy of the United States of America', available at: <http://www.whitehouse.gov/nsc/nss.html>,accessed 12 September 2005

Busse, N. (1999) 'Constructivism and southeast Asian security', *The Pacific Review*, 12:1, 39–60

Butfoy, Andrew (1999) 'The future of nuclear strategy', in Craig Snyder (ed.), *Contemporary Security and Strategy*, Basingstoke: Macmillan

Butler, Judith (1993) *Bodies That Matter: On the Discursive Limits of 'Sex'*, London and New York: Routledge

Butler, Lee (2000) 'At the end of a journey: the risks of cold war thinking in a new era', in John Baylis and Robert O'Neill (eds), *Alternative Nuclear Futures: the Role of Nuclear Weapons in the Post-Cold War World*, Oxford: Oxford University Press

Button, James (2005) 'Faces in a peak hour crowd', *Sydney Morning Herald*, 14 July

Buzan, Barry (1991) *People, States and Fear: An Agenda for International Security Studies in the Post-Cold War Era*, New York: Harvester Wheatsheaf, 2nd edn

Buzan, Barry (1996) 'The timeless wisdom of realism?', in Steve Smith, Ken Booth and Marysia Zalewski (eds), *International Theory: Positivism and Beyond*, Cambridge: Cambridge University Press

Buzan, Barry, Ole Wæver and Jaap Wand de Wilde (1998) *Security: A New Framework for Analysis*, Boulder, CO: Lynne Rienner

Callahan, Mary P. (2001) 'Burma: soldiers as state builders', in Muttiah Alagappa (ed.), *Coercion and Governance: The Declining Role of the Military in Asia*, Stanford, CA: Stanford University Press

Callahan, Mary P. (2004) *Making Enemies: War and State Building in Burma*, Singapore: National University of Singapore Press

Camilleri, Joseph (2004) 'The Howard years: cultural ambivalence and political dogma', *Borderlands*, 3:3

Camilleri, Joseph (2005) 'East Asia's emerging regionalism: tensions and potential in design and architecture', *Global Change, Peace and Security*, 17, 253–61

Campbell, David (1998) *Writing Security: United States Foreign Policy and the Politics of Identity*, Minneapolis, MN: University of Minnesota Press, 2nd edn

Camroux, David and Nuria Okfen (2004) '9/11 and US-Asian relations: towards a "New World Order"?', *The Pacific Review*, 17:2, 163–77

Canberra Commission on the Elimination of Nuclear Weapons (1996) Canberra: Australian Government, Department of Foreign Affairs and Trade, available at: http://www.dfat.gov.au/cc/cchome.html

Capie, David (1995) 'Regional security in the Asia Pacific: a critical theoretical perspective', *AntePodium*, 4, available at: <http://www.vuw.ac.nz/pols/Journals/Antepodium/articles/capie-1995.aspx >

Capie, David (2004) 'Between a Hegemon and a hard place: the "war on terror" and Southeast Asian-US relations', *The Pacific Review*, 17:2, 223–48

Capie, David and Paul Evans (2002) *The Asia-Pacific Security Lexicon*, Singapore: Institute of Southeast Asian Studies

Center for Nonproliferation Studies (2006) *North Korea Special Collection*, Monterey, CA: Monterey Institute for International Studies, available at: http://www.cns.miis.edu/research/korea/index.htm

Cha, Victor D. (2002a) 'Korea's place in the axis', *Foreign Affairs*, 81:3, 79–92

Cha, Victor D. (2002b) 'North Korea's weapons of mass destruction: badges, shields, or swords?', *Political Science Quarterly*, 117:2, 209–30

Cha, Victor D. and David C. Kang (2003) *Nuclear North Korea: A Debate on Engagement Strategies*, New York: Columbia University Press

Chalk, Peter (2000) *Non-Military Security and Global Order*, Basingstoke: Macmillan

Chalk, Peter (1998) 'The international ethics of refugees: a case of internal or external political obligation?', *Australian Journal of International Affairs*, 52, 142–57

Chalmers, Malcolm (2000) 'Security sector reform in developing countries: an EU perspective', *Saferworld and the Conflict Prevention Network*, available at: <www.saferworld.co.uk/pubsecu.htm>

Chance, Matthew (2005) 'Britain's home gown terrorists', *CNN.com*, 14 July

Chang, Ha-Joon (2002) *Kicking Away the Ladder: Development Strategy in Historical Perspective*, London: Anthem Books

Chanto, Sisowath Doung (2005) 'The ASEAN regional forum: the emergence of "soft security": improving the functionality of the ASEAN security regime', available at: <http://www.fesny.org/docus/peacesec/the_asean_regional_forum_2.pdf>, accessed 29 July 2005

Chapman, John M. W., Reinhard Drifte and Ian T. M.Gow (1983) *Japan's Quest for Comprehensive Security: Defence, Diplomacy, Dependence*, London: Pinter

Chatelard, Gabrielle (2002) 'Jordan as a transit country: semi-protectionist immigration policies and their effects on Iraqi forced migrants', *New Issues in Refugee Research*, Working Paper 16, Geneva: UNHCR Policy Research Unit

Chauvel, Richard (2003) *Essays on West Papua: Volume One*, working paper 120, Melbourne: Monash Asia Institute.

Cheeseman, Graeme (1996) 'Back to "Forward Defence" and the Australian National Style', in Graeme Cheeseman and Robert Bruce (eds), *Discourses of Danger: Australian Defence and Security Thinking After the Cold War*, Sydney: Allen & Unwin

Cheeseman, Graeme (2005) 'Military forces and in/security', in Ken Booth (ed.), *Critical Security Studies and World Politics*, Boulder, CO: Lynne Rienner

Cheng, Yawen (2004) 'A new warring states era and China's foreign policy choice', *Global Fortnightly*, 22, 3–5

Chimni, B.S. (1998) 'The geopolitics of refugee studies: a view from the south', *Journal of Refugee Studies*, 11, 350–374

Choe, Sang-Hun (2006) 'South Korea grapples with competing pressures as it weighs its response to North Korea', *New York Times*, 13 October

Choi, Won-Ki (1999) 'Dealing with North Korea "as it is"', *Nautilus Institute Policy Forum Online*, available at: <http://www.nautilus.org/fora/security/9907K_Choi.html>, accessed 16 May 2006

Christensen, Thomas J. (2003) 'China, the US-Japan Alliance and the Security Dilemma in East Asia', in J. Ikenberry and M. Mastanduno (eds), *International Relations Theory and the Asia-Pacific*, New York: Columbia University Press

Christensen, Thomas (1996) 'Chinese Realpolitik', *Foreign Affairs* 75:5, 37–52

Clark, Ian (1999) *Globalisation and International Relations Theory*, Oxford: Oxford University Press

CNN (2005) 'Bush: Iraqi Democracy Making Progress' , *CNN* 13 December, available at: <http://edition.cnn.com/2005/POLITICS/12/12/bush.iraq/?section=cnn_topstories>

Coalition Against Trafficking in Women (Asia-Pacific) (2006) 'Facts and statistics', available at: <http://www.catw-ap.org/facts.htm>

Coates, David (2000) *Models of Capitalism*, Oxford: Polity Press

'Co-Chairman's report of the second ARF inter-sessional meeting on disaster relief', (1998) Bangkok, 18–20 February, in ASEAN Regional Forum, *Documents Series 1994–2004*, Jakarta: ASEAN Secretariat

Cohn, Carole (1987) 'Sex and death in the rational world of the defense intellectual', *Signs: Journal of Women in Culture and Society*, 12:4, 617–718

Collins, Alan (2003) *Security and Southeast Asia: Domestic, Regional and Global Issues*, Boulder, CO and London: Lynne Rienner

Collins, Lance and Warren Reed (2005) *Plunging Point*, Sydney: HarperCollins

Colman, Elizabeth (2005) '"Shared values" push for migrants', *The Weekend Australian*, August, 6–7, 10

Commission on Global Governance (1995) *Our Global Neighbourhood*, Oxford: Oxford University Press

Commission on Human Security (2003) *Human Security Now*, New York: Commission Secretariat

Commonwealth of Australia (1925) *House of Representatives, Hansard Parliamentary Debates*, 25 June

Commonwealth of Australia (1950) *House of Representatives, Hansard Parliamentary Debates*, 27 April

Commonwealth of Australia (2005) *Anti-Terrorism Bill, 2*

Contreras, Antonio P. (2002) 'Role of civil societies in transboundary common property resource governance in Southeast Asia', paper presented to the conference of the *International Association for the Study of Common Property*, Victoria Falls, Zimbabwe, June ,17–21

Cooper, Neil and Michael Pugh (2002) *Security Sector Transformation in Post-Conflict Societies*,London: CDS Working Paper 5

Cottey, Andrew, Timothy Edmunds and Anthony Forster (2002) *Democratic Control of the Military in Postcommunist Europe: Guarding the Guard*, Basingstoke: Palgrave

Cox, Robert (1981) 'Social forces, states and world orders', *Millennium*, 10:2, 162–55

Cox, Robert (1986) 'Social forces, states and world orders: beyond international relations theory' in Robert O. Keohane (ed.), *NeoRealism and its Critics*, New York: Columbia University Press

Cox, Robert (1987) *Production, Power and World Order: Social Forces in the Making of History*, New York: Columbia University Press

Cox, Robert (1999) 'Civil society at the turn of the millennium: prospects for an alternative world order', *Review of International Studies*, 25, 1–28

Creegan, Eric (2005) 'India, Pakistan, sign missile notification pact', *Arms Control Today*, 35:9

Crispin, Shawn W. (2004) 'Thailand's war zone', *Far Eastern Economic Review*, March, 167:10, 12–14

CSCAP (1995) *Asia Pacific Confidence and Security Building Measures*, Memorandum 2, Kuala Lumpur: CSCAP Secretariat

Cumings, Bruce (1997) 'Japan and Northeast Asia into the twenty-first century', in P.J. Katzenstein and T. Shiraishi (eds), *Network Power: Japan and Asia*, Ithaca, NY: Cornell University Press

Cumings, Bruce (2000) 'The last hermit', *New Left Review*, 6: 150–4

Cumings, Bruce (2004) *North Korea: Another Country*, New York: The New Press

Curtis, Gerald L. (1999) *The Logic of Japanese Politics: Leaders, Institutions and the Limits of Change*, New York: Columbia University Press

D'Costa, Bina (2005) 'Coming to terms with the past in Bangladesh: naming women's truths', in Luciana Ricciutelli, Angela Miles and Margaret H. McFadden (eds), *Feminist Politics, Activism and Vision: Local and Global Challenges*, London: Zed Books

Daily Telegraph (2005) 'Ban Muslim scarves', *Daily Telegraph*, 29 August

Dalby, Simon (1997) 'Contesting an essential concept: reading the dilemmas in contemporary security discourse', in Michael C. Williams and Keith Krause (eds), *Critical Security Studies: Concepts and Cases*, Minneapolis, MN: University of Minnesota Press

Dalby, Simon (2000) *Geopolitical Change and Contemporary Security Studies: Contextualizing the Human Security Agenda*, Working Paper 30, Vancouver: Institute of International Relations, University of British Columbia

Dalby, Simon (2002) *Environmental Security*, Minneapolis, MN: University of Minnesota Press

Dalby, Simon (2005) 'Political space: autonomy, liberalism and empire', *Alternatives: Global, Local, Political*, 30, 415-41

Daly, M.T. and M.I. Logan, (1998) *Reconstructing Asia: The Economic Miracle that Never Was, The Future That Is*, Melbourne: RMIT University Press

Dao, James (2003a) 'Bush administration defends its approach on North Korea', *New York Times*, 7 February,13

Dao, James (2003b) 'Bush urges Chinese president to press North Korea on arms', *New York Times*, 8 February, 10

Dauvergne, Peter (1997) *Shadows in the Forest: Japan and the Politics of Timber in South East Asia*, Cambridge: MIT Press

Davies, Sarah E. (2005) 'Legitimising Rejection: International Refugee Law in Southeast Asia', PhD thesis, University of Queensland

Deane, Phyllis (1978) *The Evolution of Economic Ideas*, Cambridge: Cambridge University Press

Deng, Yong (1999) 'Conception of national interests: realpolitik, liberal dilemma and possibility of change', in Deng, Yong and Fei-Ling Wang (eds), *In the Eyes of the Dragon – China Views the World*, Lanham, MD: Rowman & Littlefield

Deng, Yong and Thomas G. Moore (2004) 'China views globalization: towards a new great-power politics?', *Washington Quarterly*, 27:3, 117–36

Department of Foreign Affairs and Trade, Australia (2002) 'ARF (ASEAN Regional Forum), 31 July 2002', available at: <http://www.dfat.gov.au/arf/statements/arf9_chairman.html>, accessed 27 July, 2005

Department of Foreign Affairs and Trade, Australia (2003) *Advancing The National Interest: Australia's Foreign and Trade Policy White Paper*, Canberra: Commonwealth of Australia

Derenberger, Robert F. (1988) 'The Economies of China, North Korea, and Vietnam: a comparative study', in Robert A. Scalapino and Dalchoong Kim (eds), *Asian Communism: Continuity and Transition*, Berkeley, CA: Center for Korean Studies

Desker, Barry (2001) 'The future of the ASEAN regional forum', *Pacific Forum*, CSIS, Honolulu, Hawaii, 7 September,available at: <http://www.csis.org/pacfor/pac0136.pdf>

Devetak, Richard (2005) 'Critical theory', in Scott Burchill, Andrew Linklater, Richard Devetak, Matthew Paterson, Christian Reus-Smit and Jacqui True (eds),*Theories of International Relations*, London: Palgrave Macmillan

Dibb, Paul (1986) *Review of Australia's Defence Capabilities: Report to the Minister for Defence*, Canberra: AGPS

Dillon, Michael (1996) *The Politics of Security*,London: Routledge

Dimitrov, Radoslav S. (2002) 'Water, conflict and security: a conceptual minefield', *Society and Natural Resources*, 15:8, 677–91

Dinas, Nota (2000) 'Nota Dinas, Direktur Jenderal Kesbang dan Linmas, Ermaya Suradinata to Menteri Dalam Negeri', *Memorandum*, 9 June

Dodds, Felix and Tim Pippard (eds) (2005) *Human and Environmental Security: An Agenda for Change*, London: Earthscan

Dodson, Louise and Kerr, Joseph (2005) 'Terror redefines our freedom', *Sydney Morning Herald*, 6–7 August, 1

Doty, Roxanne Lynn (1993) 'Foreign policy as social construction: a post-positivist analysis of U.S. counterinsurgency policy in the Philippines', *International Studies Quarterly*, 37: 297–320

Doty, Roxanne Lynn (2000) 'Desire all the way down', *Review of International Studies* 26, 137–39

Downs, Chuck (1999) *Over the Line: North Korea's Negotiating Strategy*, Washington, DC: American Enterprise Institute

Doyle, Michael (2000) 'A more perfect union? The liberal peace and the challenge of globalisation', *Review of International Studies*, 26, 81–94

Dreyfus, Hubert L. and Paul Rabinow (1983) 'Introduction' , in H.L. Dreyfus and P. Rabinow (eds), *Michel Foucault: Beyond Structuralism and Hermeneutics*, Chicago, IL: University of Chicago Press, 2nd edn

Duffield, Mark (1999) 'NGO relief in war zones: towards an analysis of the new aid paradigm', *Third World Quarterly*, 18:3, 527–43

Duffield, Mark (2001) *Global Governance and the New Wars: The Merging of Development and Security*, London: Zed Books

Dujarric, Robert (2001) 'North Korea: risks and rewards of engagement' , *Journal of International Affairs*, 54:2, 465–87

Dupont, Alan (1995) 'Concepts of securit', in J. Rolfe (ed.), *Unresolved Futures: Comprehensive Security in the Asia-Pacific*, Wellington: Centre for Strategic Studies

Dupont, Alan (1998) *The Environment and Security in Pacific Asia*, Oxford: Oxford University Press

Dupont, Alan (2001) *East Asia Imperilled: Transnational Challenges to Security*, Cambridge: Cambridge University Press

Dupont, Alan (2002) 'Refugees and illegal migrants in the Asia-Pacific region', in William Maley *et al.* (eds), *Refugees and the Myth of the Borderless World*, Canberra: Dept of International Relations, RSPAS, ANU

Dupont, Alan (2006) 'Transnational security', in Robert Ayson and Desmond Ball (eds), *Strategy and Security in the Asia-Pacific*, Crows Nest: Allen & Unwin

Eberstadt, Nicholas (1997) 'Hastening Korean unification', *Foreign Affairs*, 76:2, 77–92

Eberstadt, Nicholas (1998) 'South Korea's economic crisis and the prospects for North-South relations: how much has really changed?', *Korea and World Affairs* XXII, 4, 539–49

Edwards, Nick (1997) 'China's economy hit with $54 billion in losses from pollution' Singapore: Reuters, available at: <www.icsea.or.id/sea-span>

Elliott, Lorraine (2002) 'Global environmental governance', in Rorden Wilkinson and Steve Hughes (eds), *Global Governance: Critical Perspectives*, London: Routledge

Elliott, Lorraine (2006) 'Cosmopolitan environmental harm conventions', *Global Society*, 20:3, 345–63

Elmhirst, Rebecca (2002) 'Negotiating land and livelihood: agency and identities in Indonesia's transmigration programme', in Brenda Yeoh, Peggy Teo and Shirlena Huang (eds), *Gender Politics in the Asia-Pacific Region*, London: Routledge

Elsham News (2002) Elsham News Service, April, available at: http://www.westpapua.ca/?q=en/node/324

Emmers, Ralf (2005) *Maritime Disputes in the South China Sea: strategic and diplomatic status quo*, working paper 87, Singapore: Institute of Defence and Strategic Studies

Emmerson, Donald K. (2000) 'Will Indonesia survive?', *Foreign Affairs*, 79:3, 95–106

Enloe, Cynthia (1990) *Bananas, Beaches and Bases: Making Feminist Sense of International Politics*, Berkeley, CA: University of California

Enloe, Cynthia (2004) *The Curious Feminist: Searching for Women in a New Age of Empire*, Berkeley, CA: University of California

Enriquez, Jean (2003) 'The Asian financial crisis and prostitution: a question of pragmatics and ideology', *Coalition Against Trafficking in Women – Asia-Pacific*, available at: http://www.catw-ap.org/index_old.htm

Environmental Investigation Agency/Telepak Indonesia (2005) *The last frontier*, London: Environmental Investigation Agency

Eriksson, Johan (1999a) 'Observers or advocates? On the political role of security analysts', *Cooperation and Conflict*, 34:3, 311–30

Eriksson, Johan (1999b) 'Debating the politics of security studies: response to Goldman, Waever and Williams', *Cooperation and Conflict*, 34:3, 345–52

Esteva, Gustavo and Madhu Suri Prakesh (1998) *Grassroots Post-Modernism: Remaking the Soil of Cultures*, London: Zed Books

Euben, Roxanne , L. (2002) 'Killing (for) politics: jihad, martyrdom, and political action', *Political Theory* 30:1, 4–35

Evans, Gareth and Bruce Grant (1995) *Australia's Foreign Relations in the World of the 1990s*, Melbourne: Melbourne University Press

Evans, Paul (1994) 'Building security: the Council for Security Cooperation in the Asia Pacific (CSCAP)', *The Pacific Review*, 7, 125–39

Evans, Paul M. (2004) 'Human security and East Asia: in the beginning', *Journal of East Asian Studies*, 4, 263–84

Flamm, Mikel (2003) 'Trafficking of women and children in Southeast Asia', *UN Chronicle*, 40:2

Foot, Rosemary (2004) 'Human rights and counter-terrorism', *Adelphi Paper*, 363, Oxford: Oxford University Press

Foot, Rosemary (2005) 'Collateral damage: human rights consequences of counterterrorist action in the Asia-Pacific', *International Affairs*, 81:2, 411–25

Foster-Carter, Aidan (1998) 'North Korea: all roads lead to collapse – all the more reason to engage Pyongyang', in Marcus Noland (ed.), *Economic Integration of the Korean Peninsula*, Washington, DC: Institute for International Economics

Foucault, Michel (1980) 'Questions on geography', in C. Gordon (ed.), *Power/ Knowledge: Selected Interviews and Other Writings 1972–1977*, New York: Pantheon

Foucault, Michel (2003) *Society Must be Defended*, New York: Picador

Freedman, Lawrence (2004) *Deterrence*, Cambridge: Polity

Ganesan, Nicholas (2000) 'ASEAN's relations with major external powers', *Contemporary Southeast Asia*, 22:2, 258–78

Ganesan, Nicholas (2001) 'Illegal fishing and illegal migration in Thailand's bilateral relations with Malaysia and Myanmar', in Andrew T.H. Tan and J.D. Ken Boutin (eds), *Non-Traditional Security Issues in Southeast Asia*, Singapore: Institute of Defence and Strategic Studies/Select Books

Ganesan, Nicholas (2001) 'Appraising democratic developments in postauthoritarian states: Thailand and Indonesia', *Asian Affairs: An American Review*, 28:1, 53–74

Garran, Robert (2004), *True Believer: John Howard, George Bush and the American Alliance*, Sydney: Allen & Unwin

Garrett, Banning (2001) 'China faces, debates the contradictions of globalization', *Asian Survey*, 41:3, 409–27

Garrett, Banning and Jonathan Adams (2004) *US-China Cooperation on the Problem of Failing States and Transnational Threats*, Special Report, 126, United States Institute of Peace, www.usip.org/pubs/specialreports/sr126.html

Gelber, Katharine and Matt McDonald (2006) 'Ethics and exclusion: representations of sovereignty in Australia's approach to asylum-seekers', *Review of International Studies*, 32 :2, 269–89

Geng, Lihua (2004) 'Understanding issues in non-traditional security and traditional security', *Journal of Liaoning University*, 32:6, 82–6

George, Jim (1997) 'Australia's global perspectives in the 1990s: a case of old realist wine in new (neo-Liberal) bottles?', in Richard Leaver (ed.), *Middling, Meddling and Muddling: Multilateralism and Australian Foreign Policy*, Sydney: Allen & Unwin

Germain, Randall and Michael Kenny (1998) 'Engaging Gramsci: international relations theory and the new Gramscians', *Review of International Studies*, 24, 3–21

Gershman, John (2002) 'Is Southeast Asia the Second Front?', *Foreign Affairs*, 81:4, 60–74

Ghee, Lim Teck and Mark Valencia (1990) 'Introduction', in Lim Teck Ghee and Mark J. Valencia (eds), *Conflict over Natural Resources in Southeast Asia and the Pacific*, Singapore: Oxford University Press

Gills, Barry K. (2000) 'American power, neo-liberal economic globalization and low intensity democracy: an unstable trinity', in M. Cox, G.J. Ikenberry and T. Inoguchi (eds), *American Democracy Promotion: Impulses, Strategies and Impacts*, Oxford: Oxford University Press

Gilpin, Robert (1987) *The Political Economy of International Relations*, Princeton, NJ: Princeton University Press

Gilson, Julie (2002) *Asia Meets Europe*, Cheltenham: Edward Elgar

Glosserman, Brad (2004) 'ASEAN Plus Three Leads the Way', available at: <www.csis.org/pacfor>, accessed 29 June 2005

Goh, Evelyn (2001) 'The hydro-politics of the Mekong River basin: regional cooperation and environmental security', in Andrew T.H. Tan and J.D. Ken Boutin (eds), *Non-Traditional Security Issues in Southeast Asia*, Singapore: Institute of Defence and Strategic Studies/Select Books

Goldstein, Avery (1997) 'Great expectations: interpreting China's arrival', *International Security*, 22:3, 36–73

Goldstein, Avery (2003) 'An emerging China's emerging grand strategy: a neo-Bismarckian turn?', in G. John Ikenberry and Michael Mastanduno (eds), *International Relations Theory and the Asia-Pacific*, New York: Columbia University Press

Goldstein, Judith (1988) 'Ideas, institutions, and American trade policy', *International Organization*, 42, 179–217

Goldstein, Judith, and Robert O. Keohane (1993) 'Ideas and foreign policy: an analytical framework', in J. Goldstein and R. O. Keohane, *Ideas and Foreign Policy: Beliefs, Institutions, and Political Change*, Ithaca, NY: Cornell University Press

Gomez, Edmond T. (ed.) (2002) *Political Business in East Asia*, London: Routledge

Green, Shane (2003) 'North Korea warns final showdown with US will be a nuclear one', *Sydney Morning Herald*, 8 February , available at: <http://www.smh.com.au/articles/2003/02/07/1044579932073.html>

Gregg, Donald (2002) Speech delivered at the Second Jeju Peace Forum, Jeju City, 12 April

Guerin, Bill (2005) 'The not so ugly Americans', *Asia Times*, 11 January

Guo Shuyong (2005) 'Critical theory in the studies of international relations: origins, ideas and influence', *World Economics and Politics*, 7, 7–14

Haacke, Jürgen (2003) *ASEAN's Diplomatic and Security Culture*, London and New York: Routledge

Haas, Peter M. (1992) 'Introduction: epistemic communities and international policy coordination', *International Organization*, 46, 1–35

Hage, Ghassan (1998) *White Nation*, Annandale: Pluto Press Australia

Hage, Ghassan (2003) *Against Paranoid Nationalism*, Annandale: Pluto Press Australia

Haggard, Stephan (1990) *Pathways from the Periphery: the Politics of Growth in the Newly Industrialising Countries*, Ithaca, NY: Cornell University Press

Haggard, Stephan (2000) *The Political Economy of the Asian Financial Crisis*, Washington, DC: Institute of International Economics

Halabi, Yakub (2004) 'The Expansion of Global Governance into the Third World: Altruism, Realism or Constructivism?', *International Studies Review*, 6, 21–48

Hall, Peter A. (1989) *The Political Power of Economic Ideas*, Princeton, NJ: Princeton University Press

Hall, Peter and David Soskice (2001) 'An introduction to the varieties of capitalism', in P. Hall and D. Soskice (eds), *Varieties of Capitalism: The Institutional Foundations of Comparative Advantage*, Oxford: Oxford University Press

Hall, Rodney Bruce (2003) 'The discursive demolition of the Asian development model', *International Studies Quarterly*, 47, 71–99

Hampson Fen (2002) *Madness in the Multitude: Human Security and World Disorder*, Oxford: Oxford University Press

Hans, Asha and Astri Suhrke (1997) 'Responsibility sharing', in James Hathaway (ed.), *Reconceiving International Refugee Law*, The Hague: Kluwer Law

Hanson, Marianne (2000) 'Human security and nuclear weapons', in William Tow, Ramesh Thakur and In-Taek Hyun (eds), *Asia's Emerging Regional Order: Reconciling Traditional and Human Security*, Tokyo: United Nations University Press

Hanson, Marianne (2002) 'Nuclear weapons as obstacles to international security', *International Relations*, 16:3, 361–79

Haque, M. Shamsul (2001) 'Environmental security in East Asia: a critical view', *Journal of Strategic Studies*, 24:4, 203–34

Harris, Stuart (1995) 'The economic aspects of security in the Asia-Pacific region', *Journal of Strategic Studies*, 18:3, 32–51

Harrison, Selig S. (1997) 'Promoting a soft landing in Korea', *Foreign Policy*, 106, 56–75

Harrison, Selig S. (2001) 'Time to leave Korea?', *Foreign Affairs*, 80:2, 62–78

Harrison, Selig S. (2005) 'Did North Korea cheat?', *Foreign Affairs*, 84:1, 99–110

Hart, Dennis (1999) 'Creating the national other: opposing images of nationalism in South and North Korean education', *Korean Studies*, 23, 68–93

Hasluck, Paul (1952) *The Government and the People 1939–41, Official History: Australia in the War of 1939–45*, IV: I, Canberra: The Australian War Memorial

Hathaway, James (1992) *The Law of Refugee Status*, Toronto: Butterworth

He Zhongyi (2004) 'The conceptualisation of security: from traditional to non-traditional', *World Economics and Politics*, 2, 63–6

Heginbotham, Eric and Richard J. Samuels (1998) 'Mercantile realism and Japanese foreign policy', *International Security*, 22:4, 171–203

Held, David (1997) 'Cosmopolitan democracy and the global order: a new agenda', in James Bohman and Matthias Lutz-Backmann (eds), *Perpetual Peace: Essays on Kant's Cosmopolitan Ideal*, Cambridge, MA: MIT Press

Hendrickson, D (1999) 'Key Issues in Security Sector Reform', Working Papers 1, The Conflict, Security and Development Group, Centre for Defence Studies, King's College, London

Henning, C. Randall (2002) *East Asian Financial Cooperation*, Washington, DC: Institute for International Economics

Henningsen, Manfred (2002) 'Totalitarismus und politische religion: über die modernen regime des terrors', *Merkur*, 56:5, 383–92

Heppner, Kevin (2005) 'Sovereignty, survival and resistance: contending perspectives on Karen internal displacement in Burma', Karen Human Rights Group (KHRG), Working Paper, March, available at: <http://www.khrg.org/papers/wp2005w1.htm>

Hernandez, Carolina G. (1994) *Track Two Diplomacy, Philippine Foreign Policy, and Regional Politics*, Manila: University of the Philippines

Heryanto, Ariel (1999) 'Where communism never dies. Violence, trauma and narration in the last Cold War capitalist authoritarian state', *International Journal of Cultural Studies*, 2:2, 147–77

Herz, John (1950) 'Idealist internationalism and the security dilemma', *World Politics*, 2:2, 157–80

Herz, John (1959) *International Politics in the Atomic Age*, New York: Columbia University Press

Hettne, Björn, Andras Inotai and Osvaldo Sunkel (eds) (1999) *Globalism and the New Regionalism*,London: Macmillan

Higgott, Richard (1994) 'Introduction: ideas, interests and identity in the Asia-Pacific', *The Pacific Review*, 7, 367–79

Higgott, Richard (2000) 'Contested globalization: the changing context and normative challenges', *Review of International Studies*, 26, 131–53

Hocking, Jenny (2003) 'Counter-terrorism and the criminalisation of politics: Australia's new security powers of detention, proscription and control', *Australian Journal of Politics and History*, 49:3, 55–373

Hocking, Jenny (2004) *Terror Laws: ASIO, Counter-terrorism and the Threat to Democracy*, Sydney: University of New South Wales Press

Hoge, James F. (2004) 'A global power shift in the making', *Foreign Affairs*, 83:4, 2–7

Hoge, Warren (2006) 'Security Council backs sanctions on North Korea', *New York Times*, 15 October

Homer-Dixon, Thomas F. (1991) 'On the threshold: environmental changes as causes of acute conflict', *International Security* 16:2, 76–116

Honna, Jun (1999) 'The Military and Democratisation in Indonesia: The Developing Civil-Military Discourse During the Late Soeharto Era', PhD dissertation

Honna, Jun (2003) *Military Politics and Democratization in Indonesia*, London: RoutledgeCurzon

Honneth, Axel (2001) 'Recognition or redistribution? changing perspectives on the moral order of society', *Theory, Culture and Society*, 18:2–3, 43–55

Hook, Glenn, Julie Gilson, Christopher Hughes and Hugo Dobson (2005) *Japan's International Relations*, London: Routledge, 2nd edn

Horkheimer, Max (2002) *Critical Theory: Selected Essays*, New York: Continuum

Howard, John (1997) 'The inaugural prime ministers on prime minister's lecture', Old Parliament House, Canberra, 3 September

Hu, Richard Weixing (2001) 'China in search of comprehensive security', in J.C. Hsiung (ed.), *Twenty-First Century World Order and the Asia Pacific*, New York: Palgrave

Hubbard, Thomas C. (2002) 'The US approach to the Korean Peninsula', speech delivered at the Second Jeju Peace Forum, Jeju city, 13 April

Hughes, Christopher W. (2004) 'Japan's security policy, the US-Japan alliance, and the "war on terror": incrementalism confirmed or radical leap?', *Australian Journal of International Affairs*, 58:4, 427–45

Human Rights Watch (2001) 'World Report 2000', available at: <http://www.hrw.org/wr2k1/asia/indonesia.html>

Human Rights Watch (2002) 'Anti-terror campaign cloaking human rights abuses', January, available at: <http://hrw.org/english/docs/2002/01/16/global3690.htm>

Human Rights Watch (2003) 'Aceh under martial law: inside the secret war', available at: <http://hrw.org/>

Human Rights Watch (2004) 'World Report 2003', available at: <http://www.hrw.org/wr2k3/asia7.html>

Human Rights Watch (2005) 'They came and destroyed our village again', available at: <http://hrw.org/reports/2005/burma0605/>, accessed June 2005

Human Security Centre, University of British Columbia, Canada (2005) *Human Security Report: War and Peace in the Twenty First Century* New York: Oxford University Press

Hunter, Helen-Louise (1999) *Kim Il-Song's North Korea*, Westport, CT: Praeger

Huntington, Samuel P. (1957) *The Soldier and the State: The Theory and Politics of Civil-Military Relations,*Cambridge, MA: Belknap Press of Harvard University Press

Hurrell, Andrew (1995) 'Explaining the resurgence of regionalism in world politics', *Review of International Studies*, 21, 331–58

Hurrell, Andrew (2001) 'Global inequality and international institutions', *Metaphilosophy*, 32: 34–57

Huxley, Tim (2001) 'Reforming Southeast Asia's security sectors', CSDG Working Paper, 4

Huynh, Kim (2004) 'Modernity and my mum: a literary exploration into the (extra)ordinary sacrifices and everyday resistance of a Vietnamese woman', *Frontiers: A Journal of Women's Studies*, 25:2, 1–25

Huysmans, Jef (2004) 'Minding exceptions: the politics of insecurity and liberal democracy', *Contemporary Political Theory*, 3: 321–41

Huysmans, Jef (2006) *The Politics of Insecurity: Fear, Migration and Asylum in the EU*, London: Routledge

Ikenberry, G. John and Michael Mastanduno (2003) 'Images of order in the Asia-Pacific and the role of the United States', in J. Ikenberry and M. Mastanduno (eds), *International Relations Theory and the Asia-Pacific*, New York: Columbia University Press

Independent Commission on Disarmament and Security Issues (1982) *Common Security: A Blueprint for Survival*, London: Pan

Information Office of the State Council (2000) *China's National Defence in 2000*, Beijing: Information Office of the State Council

Information Office of the State Council (2002) *China's National Defence in 2002*, Beijing: Information Office of the State Council

Information Office of the State Council (2004) *China's National Defence in 2004*, Beijing: Information Office of the State Council

International Campaign to Ban Landmines (ICBL) (2004) *Landmine Monitor Report, 2004: Burma*, available at: http://www.icbl.org/lm/2004/burma

International Commission on Intervention and State Sovereignty (2001) *The Responsibility to Protect*, Ottawa: IDRC

International Crisis Group (2005) *Aceh: A New Chance for Peace*, Crisis Group Asia, Briefing 40, 15 August

Iraq Body Count (2007) available at: <http://www.iraqbodycount.org/>, accessed 17 January 2007

Jackson, Richard (2005) *Writing the War on Terrorism: Language, Politics and Counter-terrorism*, Manchester: Manchester University Press

Jackson, Robert (2000) *The Global Covenant: Human Conduct in a World of States*, Oxford: Clarendon

Jakarta Post (1999) 'Indonesia loses 4 billion in lost revenue every year', *Jakarta Post*, 1 November

Jakarta Post (2003) 'Massive anti-war rally in Jakarta', *Jakarta Post*, 9 February

Jayasuriya, Kanishka (1994) 'Singapore: the politics of regional definition', *The Pacific Review*, 7: 411–420

JCAAD (Joint Committee on ASIO, ASIS and DSD) (2003) *Intelligence on Iraq's Weapons of Mass Destruction*, Canberra: Parliament of Australia

Jeffrey, Leslie Ann (2002) *Sex and Borders: Gender, National Identity, and Prostitution Policy in Thailand*,Vancouver: UBC Press

Jepperson, Ronald L. (1991) 'Institutions, institutional effects, and institutionalism', in Walter W. Powell and Paul J. DiMaggio (eds), *The New Institutionalism in Organizational Analysis*, Chicago: Chicago University Press

Jepperson, Ronald, Alexander Wendt and Peter Katzenstein (1996) 'Norms, identity and culture in national security', in Peter J. Katzenstein (ed.), *The Culture of National Security: Norms and Identity in World Politics*, New York: Columbia University Press

Jervis, Robert (1976) *Perception and Misperception in International Politics*, Princeton, NJ: Princeton University Press

Jha, Raghbendra (2005) 'Alleviating environmental degradation in the Asia Pacific region: international cooperation and the role of issue-linkage', in Barrie Stevens and Randall Holden (eds), *Regional Integration in the Asia Pacific: Issues and Prospects*, Paris: OECD

Job, Brian L. (2003) 'Track 2 diplomacy: ideational contribution to the evolving Asia security order', in Muthiah Alagappa (ed.), *Asian Security Order: Instrumental and Normative Features*, Stanford, CA: Stanford University Press

Johnson, Carol (1997) *Governing Change: From Keating to Howard*, St. Lucia: University of Queensland Press

Johnson, Chalmers (1987) 'Political institutions and economic performance: the government-business relationship in Japan, South Korea and Taiwan', in F. Deyo (ed.), *The Political Economy of the New Asian Industrialism*, Ithaca, NY: Cornell University Press

Johnson, Rebecca (1998) 'International implications of the India-Pakistan tests', *Disarmament Diplomacy*, 28

Johnson, Rebecca (2005) 'Politics and protection: why the 2005 NPT Review Conference failed', *Disarmament Diplomacy*, 80

Johnston, Alastair Iain (2003) 'Is China a status quo power?', *International Security* 27:4, 5–56

Johnston, Alastair Iain (2004) 'Beijing's security behaviour in the Asia-Pacific: is China a dissatisfied power?', in J.J. Suh, Peter J. Katzenstein and Allen Carlson (eds), *Rethinking Security in East Asia: Identity, Power and Efficiency*, Stanford, CA: Stanford University Press

Jones, Adam (1996) 'Does gender make the world go round? Feminist critiques of international relations', *Review of International Studies*, 22, 405–29

Jones, David Martin and Michael L. R. Smith (2002) 'ASEAN's imitation community', *Orbis*, 46, 93–109

Jones, David Martin and Michael L. R. Smith (2001a) 'Is there a Sovietology of South-East Asian studies?', *International Affairs*, 77, 843–65

Jones, David Martin and Michael L. R. Smith (2001b) 'The changing security agenda in Southeast Asia: globalization, new terror, and the delusions of regionalism', *Studies in Conflict and Terrorism*, 24: 271–88

Jones, David Martin (ed.) (2004) *Globalisation and the New Terror: The Asia Pacific Dimension*, Cheltenham: Edward Elgar

JSCDFAT (Joint Standing Committee on Defence, Foreign Affairs and Trade (2001) *A Report on Visits to Immigration Detention Centres*, Canberra: Parliament of Australia, June

Jung, Dietrich (ed.) (2003) *Shadow Globalization, Ethnic Conflicts and New Wars: A Political Economy of Intra-State War*, London: Routledge

Kabar-Irian (2000) 'Pesan Sidang Sinode Gereja Kristen Injili Di Tanah Papua', *Kabair-Irian*, 5 November, available at: <www.kabar-irian.com>

Kadir, Suzaina (2004) 'Mapping Muslim politics in Southeast Asia after September 11', *The Pacific Review*, June, 17:2

Kahn, Joseph (2006) 'North's test seen as failure for Korea policy China followed', *New York Times*, 9 October

Kammen, Douglas Kammen and Siddharth Chandra (1999) *A Tour of Duty: Changing Patterns of Military Politics in Indonesia in the 1990's*, Ithaca, NY: Cornell Southeast Asia Program Publications

Kampani, Gaurav (2002) 'Second Tier Proliferation: the case of Pakistan and North Korea', *The Nonproliferation Review*, 9:3, 107–116

Katsumata, Hiro (2003) 'The role of ASEAN Institutes of Strategic and International Studies in developing security cooperation in the Asia-Pacific region', *Asian Journal of Political Science*, 11, 93–111

Katzenstein, Peter J. (1996) *Cultural Norms and National Security: Police and Military in Postwar Japan*, Ithaca, NY: Cornell University Press

Katzenstein, Peter J. (1996) 'Introduction: alternative perspectives on national security', in Peter J. Kazenstein (ed.), *The Culture of National Security: Norms and Identity in World Politics*, New York: Columbia University Press

Kavka, Gregory V. (1987) 'Dilemmas of nuclear protest', in Gregory V. Kavka, *Moral Paradoxes of Nuclear Deterrence*, Cambridge: Cambridge University Press

Kent, Jonathan (2005) 'Malaysia's trouble with migrants', *BBC News*, available at: <http://newsvote.bbc.co.uk/mpapps/pagetools/print/news.bbc.co.uk/1/hi/world/asia-pacific>, accessed 7 June 2004

Keohane, Robert O. and Joseph Nye (1977) *Power and Interdependence: World Politics in Transition*, Boston, MA: Little, Brown

Keohane, Robert O., Nye, Joseph S. and Hoffmann, Stanley (eds.) (1993) *After the Cold War: International Institutions and State Strategies in Europe, 1989–1991*, Cambridge, MA: Harvard University Press

Kerin, John (2005) 'Howard to strengthen terror laws', *The Weekend Australian*, August, 6–7, 1

Kerr, Paul (2007) 'No progress at North Korea Talks', *Arms Control Today*, January/February

Kerr, Paul (2005) 'North Korea talks achieve breakthrough', *Arms Control Today*, 35:8

Kerr, Pauline, William Tow and Marianne Hanson (2003) 'The utility of the human security agenda for policy-makers', *Asian Journal of Political Science*, 11:2, 89–114

Kibreab, Gaim (2003) 'Displacement, host government' policies, and constraints on the construction of sustainable livelihoods', *International Social Science Journal*, 55, 57–67

Kim, Dae-jung (1994) *The Korean Problem: Nuclear Crisis, Democracy and Reunification*, Seoul: The Kim Dae-jung Peace Foundation

Kim, Dae-jung (2002) 'The South-North summit: a year in review', in Woo Keun-Min (ed.), *Building Common Peace and Prosperity in Northeast Asia*, Seoul: Yonsei University Press

Kim, Hyung-chan (1999) 'North Korea: a nation of tragedy', *Korea and World Affairs*, 13, 579–89

Kim, Ji-ho (2002) 'Pyongyang's Threat Puzzles Analysts Concerned about Inter-Korean relations', *Korea Herald*, March,15

Kim, Myongsob (2001) 'Reexamining Cold War History and the Korean Question', *Korea Journal*, 412, 5–27

Kim, Young-sae (2002) 'U.S. Says it Recognizes the North as "Sovereign"', *Yoong Ang Ilbo*, 19 November

Kirk, Gwyn and Margo Okazawa-Rey (2004) 'Women Opposing U.S. Militarism in East Asia', *Peace Review*, March, 59–64

Klein, Bradley S. (1994) *Strategic Studies and World Order*, Cambridge: Cambridge University Press

Klotz, Audie (1995) *Norms in International Relations: The Struggle Against Apartheid*, Ithaca, NY: Cornell University Press

Klusmeyer, Douglas and Astri Suhrke (2002) 'Comprehending "evil": challenges for law and policy', *Ethics and International Affairs*, 16:1, 27–42

Koh, Byung Chul (2001) 'The foreign and unification policies of the republic of Korea', in Kil Soong Hoom and Moon Chung-in (eds), *Understanding Korean Politics*, Albany, NY: SUNY

Kompas (2003) 29 April, available at: <http://www.kompas.com/>

Kraft, Herman J. S. (2000) *Unofficial Diplomacy in Southeast Asia: the Role of ASEAN-ISIS*, CANCAPS 23,Toronto, ON: Canadian Consortium on Asia-Pacific Security

Krasner, Stephen D. (1983) *International Regimes*, Ithaca, NY: Cornell University Press

Krasner, Stephen D. (1993) 'Westphalia and all that', in J. Goldstein and R. O. Keohane (eds), *Ideas and Foreign Policy: Beliefs, Institutions, and Political Change*, Ithaca, NY: Cornell University Press

Kratochwil, Freidrich (2000) 'How do norms matter?', in Michael Byers (ed.),*The Role of Law in International Politics*, Oxford: Oxford University Press

Krause, Keith (2004) 'Is human security "More than just a good idea"?', in Michael Brzoka and Peter J. Croll (eds), *Promoting Security: But How and For Whom?* Bonn: International Centre for Conversion

Krause, Keith (1998) 'Critical theory and security studies: the research programme of critical security studies', *Cooperation and Conflict*, 33:3, 298–333

Krause, Keith and Michael C. Williams (eds) (1997) *Critical Security Studies: Concepts and Cases*, Minneapolis, MN: University of Minnesota Press

Kristol, Irving (1983) *Reflections of a Neoconservative*, New York: Basic Books

Laksamana (2003) 27 April, available at: <www.laksamana.net>

Lam, W. (2002) 'China smashes terror bases', *CNN,World*, 13 September <http://edition.cnn.com/2002/WORLD/asiapcf/east/09/13/china.turkestan/>

Lambrecht, Curtis W. (2004) 'Oxymoronic development: the military as benefactor in the border regions of Burma', in Christopher R. Duncan (ed.), *Civilizing the Margins: Southeast Asian Government Policies for the Development of Minorities*, Christopher R. Duncan, Ithaca, NY: Cornell University Press

Lang, Hazel (2001) 'The repatriation predicament of Burmese refugees in Thailand', *UNHCR New Issues in Refugee Research Working Paper*, 46, Geneva: UNHCR

Lang, Hazel J. (2002) *Fear and Sanctuary: Burmese Refugees in Thailand*, Ithaca, NY: SEAP, Cornell University

Lanjouw, Steven, Graham Mortimer and Vicky Bamforth (2000) 'Internal displacement in Burma', *Disasters*, 24:3, 228–39

Latham, Robert (1997) *The Liberal Moment: Modernity, Security and the Making of Postwar International Order*, New York: Columbia University Press

Lawson, Stephanie (2005) 'Regional integration, development and social change in the Asia-Pacific: implications for human security and state responsibility', *Global Change, Peace and Security*, 17:2, 107–22 le Billon, Philippe (2005) *Fuelling War: Natural Resources and Armed Conflict* Oxford: Routledge/International Institute for Strategic Studies

Lee, Joon-Koo (1995) 'Reflections on Korean unification cost studies', in Kang Myoung-kyu and Helmut Wagner (eds), *Germany and Korea: Lessons in Unification*, Seoul: Seoul National University Press

Lee, Pak K. (2005) 'China's quest for oil security: oil (wars) in the pipeline?', *The Pacific Review*, 18:2, 265–301

Lee, Steven (1993) *Morality, Prudence and Nuclear Weapons*, Cambridge: Cambridge University Press

Leftwich, Adrian (2000) *States of Development: On the Primacy of Politics in Development*, Oxford: Polity Press

Leifer, Michael (2000) *Singapore's Foreign Policy: Coping with Vulnerability*, London and New York: Routledge

Leifer, Michael (1986) 'The role and paradox of ASEAN', in Michael Leifer (ed.), *The Balance of Power in East Asia*, New York: St Martin's Press

Leifer, Michael (1987) *ASEAN's Search for Regional Order*, Singapore: Faculty of Arts and Social Sciences, National University of Singapore

Lévinas, Emmanuel (trans. A. Lingis) (1981) *Otherwise Than Being or Beyond Essence*, The Hague: Martinus Nijhoff

Li, Nan (2001) *From Revolutionary Internationalism to Conservative Nationalism: The Chinese Military Discourse on National Security and Identity in the Post-Mao Era*, Peaceworks 39, Washington, DC: United States Institute of Peace

Lieggi, Stephanie (2005) *A Decade of Chinese Arms Control: a Survey of Progress Ahead of Bush's Visit to China*, Monterey, CA: Center for Nonproliferation Studies

Lim, Dong-won (2002) 'Promises and challenges of the sunshine policy', speech delivered at the Second Jeju Peace Forum, Jeju City, 12 April

Limaye, Satu (2004) 'Recalibration not transformation: US security policies in the Asia-Pacific', in See Seng Tan and Amitav Acharya (eds), *Asia-Pacific Security Cooperation*, New York: M.E. Sharpe

Linklater, Andrew (1998) 'Cosmopolitan citizenship', *Citizenship Studies*, 2:1, 23–41

Linklater, Andrew (2001) 'The changing contours of critical international relations theory', in Richard Wyn Jones (ed.), *Critical Theory and World Politics*, Boulder, CO: Lynne Rienner

Linklater, Andrew (2002) 'The problem of harm in world politics: implications for the sociology of states-systems', *International Affairs*, 22:3, 319–38

Linklater, Andrew (2005) 'Political community and human security', in Ken Booth (ed.), *Critical Security Studies and World Politics*, Boulder, CO: Lynne Rienner

Lintner, Bertil (2003) 'Myanmar/Burma', in Colin Mackerras (ed.), *Ethnicity in Asia*, London: Routledge

Lowry, Robert (1996) *The Armed Forces of Indonesia*, Sydney: Allen & Unwin

McBeth, John (2003) 'Elite force', *Far Eastern Economic Review*, 166:45, 13 November

McCormack, Gavan (2004) *Target North Korea: Pushing North Korea to the Brink of Nuclear Catastrophe*, New York: Nation Books

McCulloch, Lesley (2003) 'Greed: the silent force of the conflict in Aceh', *Programme on Humanitarian Policy and Conflict Research*, available at: <http://www.preventconflict.org/portal/main/greed.pdf>

McCurry, Justin (2004) 'Koizumi haunted by Aznar's fate', *The Guardian*, 23 March

McDonald, Hamish *et al.* (2002) *Masters of Terror: Indonesia's Military and Violence in East Timor in 1999*, Canberra Papers on Strategy and Defence,145, Canberra: Strategic and Defence Studies Centre, ANU

McDonald, Matt (2005a) 'Be alarmed? Australia's anti-terrorism kit and the politics of security', *Global Change, Peace and Security*, 17:2, 171–89

McDonald, Matt (2005b) 'Perspectives on Australian foreign policy, 2004', *Australian Journal of International Affairs*, 59:2, 153–68

McDonald, Matt (2005c) 'Constructing insecurity: Australian security discourse and policy post-2001', *International Relations*, 19:3, 297–320

McGibbon, Rodd (2004) *Secessionist Challenges in Aceh and Papua: Is Special Autonomy the Solution?* Washington, DC: East-West Center

McGwire, Michael (1985/6) 'Deterrence: the problem – not the solution', *International Affairs*, 62:1, 55–70

Mack, Andrew (2004) 'A signifier of shared values', *Security Dialogue*, 35:3, 366–7

McKenna, Thomas (1998) *Muslim Rulers and Rebels: Everyday Politics and Armed Separatism in the Southern Philippines*, Berkeley, CA: University of California Press

McRae, Dave (2002) 'A discourse on separatists', *Indonesia*, 74, 37–58

McSweeney, Bill (1999) *Security, Identity and Interests*, Cambridge: Cambridge University Press

Mak, J.N. (2004) 'Malaysian defense and security cooperation: coming out of the closet', in Tan and Acharya (eds), *Asia-Pacific Security Cooperation*, New York: M.E. Sharpe

Malik, J. Mohan (1993) 'Conflict patterns and security environment in the Asia Pacific Region – the post-cold war era', in Kevin Clements (ed.), *Peace and Security in the Asia Pacific Region*, Tokyo: United Nations University Press

Manilla Bulletin (2004) 'US aid prove government moving to maintain peace', 17 February

Manila Standard (2005) 'Terror suspects free on bail', 17 August

Manning, Kevin R. (2003) 'Securing democracy' , *The Irrawaddy*, 1 November

Mastanduno, Michael (2003) 'Incomplete hegemony: the United States and security order in Asia', in Muthiah Alagappa (ed.), *Asian Security Order: Instrumental and Normative Features*, Stanford, CA: Stanford University Press

Matsui, Yayori (1999) *Women in the New Asia: From Pain to Power*, Victoria: Spinifex Press

Mazarr, Michael J. (1995) 'Going just a little nuclear: nonproliferation lessons from North Korea', *International Security*, 20:2, 92–122

Mearsheimer, John J. (2001) *The Tragedy of Great Power Politics*, New York, W.W. Norton

Media Indonesia (2003), 27 November, available at: <http://www.mediaindo.co.id/>

Mendelsohn, Jack (2005) 'The muddle of US nuclear weapons strategy', *Arms Control Today*, 35:8

Michaelson, Christopher (2005) 'Anti-terrorism legislation in Australia: a proportionate response to the terrorism threat?', *Studies in Conflict and Terrorism*, 28: 321–39

Miles, James (2002) 'Waiting out North Korea', *Survival*, 44:2, 37–49

Millennium Ecosystem Assessment (2005) *Ecosystems and human well-being: synthesis*, Washington, DC: Island Press

Moertopo, Ali (1976) 'National resilience in Indonesia's foreign policy', in *The World's Problems and Ours*, Jakarta: Centre for Strategic and International Studies

Moon, Chung-in (1996) *Arms Control on the Korean Peninsula*, Seoul: Yonsei University Press

Moon, Chung-in (2001a) 'The Kim Dae Jung Government's Peace Policy towards North Korea', *Asian Perspective*, 25:2, 177–98

Moon, Chung-in (2001b) 'The sunshine policy and ending the cold war structure', in Moon Chung-in, Odd Arne Westad and Gyoo-hyoung Kahng (eds), *Ending the Cold War in Korea*, Seoul: Yonsei University Press

Moon, Chung-in and Chaesung Chun(2003) 'Sovereignty: dominance of the Westphalian concept and implications for regional security', in Muthiah Alagappa (ed.), *Asian Security Order: Instrumental and Normative Features*, Stanford, CA: Stanford University Press

Moon, Chung-in and David I. Steinberg (eds) (1999) *Kim Dae-jung Government and Sunshine Policy*, Seoul: Yonsei University Press

Moon, Chung-in and Hideshi Takesada (2001) 'North Korea: institutionalised military intervention', in Muthiah Alagappa (ed.), *Coercion and Governance: The Declining Political Role of the Military in Asia*, Stanford, CA: Stanford University Press

Moon, Chung-in and Fong-Yun Bae (2005) 'The Bush doctrine and the North Korean nuclear crisis', in Mel Gurtov and Peter Van Ness (eds), *Confronting the Bush Doctrine: Critical Views from the Asia-Pacific*, New York: Routledge

Morell, David (1986) 'Political dynamics of military power in Thailand', in Edward A. Olsen and Stephen Jurika, Jr (eds), *The Armed Forces in Contemporary Asian Societies*, Boulder, CO: Westview Press

Morrison, Charles E. (1998) 'The regional overview', in Charles E. Morrison (ed.), *Asia Pacific Security Outlook 1998*, Morrison, Tokyo: Japan Centre for International Exchange

Moulder, Francis V. (1977) *Japan, China and the Modern World Economy*, Cambridge: Cambridge University Press

Muntarbhorn, Vitit (1992) *The Status of Refugees in Asia*, Oxford: Clarendon Press

Murphy, Craig N. and Douglas R. Nelson (2001) 'International political economy: a tale of two heterodoxies', *British Journal of Politics and International Relations*, 3, 393–412

Mutimer, David (2000) *The Weapons State: Proliferation and the Framing of Security*, Boulder, CO: Lynne Reiner

Mutua, Makau (2001) 'Savages, victims, and saviors: the metaphor of human rights', *Harvard International Law Journal*, 42, 201–45

Myers, Norman (1989) 'Environment and security', *Foreign Policy*, 74, 23–41

Nadig, Aninia (2003) 'Forced migration and global processes: report of the eighth conference of the International Association for the Study of Forced Migration,

Chiang Mai, Thailand, 5–9 January 2003', *Journal of Refugee Studies*, 16, 361–75

Nam-Buk-Haewae dongpo hakja tongil hoeui: Nam-Buk daepyodanjang daehan interview (Unification Conference for North-South-Overseas Korean scholars: interviews with Southern and Northern delegates), 28 October 1999, *Donga Ilbo*, 23

Narine, Shaun (2002) *Explaining ASEAN: Regionalism in Southeast*,Boulder, CO: Lynne Rienner

Nesadurai, Helen E.S. (2005) 'Introduction: economic security, globalization and governance', *The Pacific Review*, 17, 459–84

Neufeld, Mark (2004) 'Pitfalls of emancipation and discourse of security: reflections on Canada's "Security with a Human Face"', *International Relations*, 18:1, 109–123

Neumann, Iver B. (1994) 'A region-building approach to northern Europe', *Review of International Studies*, 20, 51–74

Newman, Edward (2004) 'A normatively attractive but analytically weak concept', *Security Dialogue*, 35:3, 358–9

NGO Forum on Cambodia (2005) 'Review of the fishery conflict in Stung Treng', available at: <http://www.ngoforum.org.kh/Environment/Docs/review_of_the_fishery_ conflict_i.htm>, accessed 15 November 2005

Nincic, Miroslav (2005) *Renegade Regimes: Confronting Deviant Behavior in World Politics*, New York: Columbia University Press

Noda, Makito (1995) 'Research institutions in Singapore: from the perspective of Asia Pacific intellectual Exchange', in T. Yamamoto (ed.), *Emerging Civil Society in the Asia Pacific Community*, Singapore and Tokyo: ISEAS and Japan Center for International Exchange

Noland, Marcus (2000) *Avoiding the Apocalypse: The Future of the Two Koreas*, Washington, DC: Institute for International Economics

Noor, Farish A. (2005) 'Another ASEAN durbar?', *Daily Times*, 20 September

Nordstrom, Carolyn (2000) 'Shadows and sovereigns', *Theory, Culture and Society*, 17: 4, 35–54

The Nuclear Threat Initiative (2006) 'Country profiles: what are the global threats from weapons of mass destruction?', available at: <http://www.nti.org/e_research/profiles/index.html>

Oberdorfer, Don (1998) *The Two Koreas: A Contemporary History*, London: Warner Books

O'Connor Sutter, Valerie (1990) *The Indochinese Refugee Dilemma*, Baton Rouge, LA: Louisiana State University Press

Ojendal, Joakim (2004) 'Back to the future? Regionalism in South-East Asia under unilateral pressure', *International Affairs*, 80:3, 161–82

Ó Tuathail, Gearóid (1996) *Critical Geopolitics*, London: Routledge

O'Tuathail, Gearoid and John A. Agnew (1992) 'Geopolitics and discourse: practical geopolitical reasoning in American foreign policy', *Political Geography*, 11, 190–204

Ong, Keng Yong, H. E. (2005) 'Community building in ASEAN's social sector', available at: <html://www.aseansec.org/16324.htm>, accessed 18 October 2005

Paal, Douglas H. (2001) 'A policy agenda for achieving Korean reunification', in Nicholas Eberstadt and Richard J. Ellings (eds), *Korea's Future and the Great Powers*, Seattle, WA: University of Washington Press

Palmer, Norman (1990) *The New Regionalism in Asia and the Pacific*, Lexington, MA: Lexington Books

Palmujoki, Eero (2001) *Regionalism and Globalism in Southeast Asia*, London: Palgrave

Paris, Roland (2001) 'Human security: paradigm shift or hot air?' *International Security*, 26:2, 87–102

Pas-Ong, Suparb and Louis Lebel (2000) 'Political transformation and the environment in Southeast Asia', *Environment*, 48:8, 8–19

Pastika, Made (2002) 'Inspector General Drs Made M. Pastika', *Instruction*, 17 July

Paul, T.V. (1998) 'The systemic bases of India's challenge to the global nuclear order', *The Nonproliferation Review*, 6:1

Payne, Keith P. (2001) *The Fallacies of Cold War Deterrence and a New Direction*, Lexington, KT: University Press of Kentucky

Pearson, Donald (2002) 'Radical Islam in Indonesia: its potential impact on international Islamic terrorism', *Journal of Counterterrorism and Homeland Security International*, 8:2, 16–20

Pemberton, Gregory (1987) *All The Way: Australia's Road to Vietnam*, Sydney: Allen & Unwin

Peou, S. (2002) ' Realism and constructivism in southeast Asia today: a review essay', *The Pacific Review*, 15:1 119–38

Perry, William J. (2002) 'The United States and the Future of East Asian Security: Korea – Quo Vadis?', in Woo Keun-Min (ed.), *Building Common Peace and Prosperity in Northeast Asia*, Seoul: Yonsei University Press

Perry, William J. (1999) *Review of United States Policy Toward North Korea: Findings and Recommendations*, Washington, DC: US Department of State, available at: <http://www.state.gov/www/regions/eap/991012_northkorea_rpt.html>, accessed 18 May 2006

Persram, Nalini (1999) 'Coda: sovereignty, subjectivity, strategy', in J. Edkins, N. Persram and V. Pin-Fat (eds), *Sovereignty and Subjectivity*, Boulder, CO: Lynne Rienner

Pettman, Jan Jindy (1996) *Worlding Women: A Feminist International Politics*, NSW: Allen & Unwin

Pettman, Jan Jindy (2000) 'Body politics: international sex tourism', *Third World Quarterly*, 18:1, 93–108

Pettman, Jan Jindy (2005) 'Questions of identity: Australia and Asia', in Ken Booth (ed.), *Critical Security Studies and World Politics*, Boulder, CO: Lynne Rienner

Pfennig, Werner (1995) 'Steps towards normalization: a comparative look at divided nations', in Kang Myoung-kyu and Helmut Wagner (eds), *Germany and Korea: Lessons in Unification*, Seoul: Seoul National University Press

Phillips, Nicola (ed.) (2005) *International Political Economy*, Basingstoke: Palgrave

Pillsbury, Michael (2000) *China Debates the Future Security Environment*, Washington, DC: National Defence University Press
Polomka, Peter (1986) *The Two Koreas: Catalyst for Conflict in East Asia?*, Letchworth: International Institute for Strategic Studies
Press-Barnathan, Galia (2005) 'The changing incentives for security regionalization: from 11/9 to 9/11', *Cooperation and Conflict*, 40, 281–304
Price, Richard and Nina Tannenwald (1996) 'Norms and deterrence: the nuclear and chemical weapons taboos', in Peter Katzenstein (ed.), *The Culture of National Security: Norms and Identity in World Politics*, New York: Columbia University Press
Princen, Thomas (1994) 'NGOs: creating a niche in environmental diplomacy', in Thomas Princen and Matthias Finger (eds), *Environmental NGOs in World Politics: Linking the Local and the Global*, London: Routledge
Pugh, Michael (2004) 'Drowning not waving: boat people and humanitarianism at sea', *Journal of Refugee Studies*, 17:1, 50–69
Rachagan, S. Sothi (1987) 'Refugees and illegal immigrants: the Malaysian experience with Filipino and Vietnamese refugees', in John Ruggie (ed.), *Refugees: A Third World Dilemma*, New Brunswick, NJ: Rowman & Littlefield
Ramcharan, R. (2000) 'ASEAN and Non-Interference: A Principle Maintained', *Contemporary Southeast Asia*, 22:1, 60–88
Rapkin, David and Jonathan R. Strand (2003) 'Is East Asia under-represented in the International Monetary Fund?', *International Relations of the Asia-Pacific*, 3, 1–28
Ravenhill, John (2006) 'US economic relations with East Asia: from hegemony to complex interdependence?', in M. Beeson (ed.), *Bush and Asia: America's Evolving Relations with East Asia*, London: Routledge
Record, Jeffrey (2003) *Bounding the Global War on Terrorism*,Carlisle, PA.: Strategic Studies Institute, US Army War College
Reiss, Mitchell B., Robert L. Gallucci, and Richard L. Garwin (2005) 'Red-handed: the truth about North Korea's weapons program', *Foreign Affairs*, 84:2, 142–8
Ren Xiao (1999) 'Chinese international relations theory: a critique', in Lu Yi *et al.*, *Research on International Relations Theories in China's New Era*, Beijing: Shishi Press
Reus-Smit, Christian (2004) 'Blurred vision a symptom of unipolar disorder', *Sydney Morning Herald*, 14 May
Rice, Condoleezza (2000) 'Promoting the national interest', *Foreign Affairs*, 79:1, 45–62
Roberts, Adam (2005) 'The "War on Terror" in Historical Perspective', *Survival*, 47:2, 101–30
Roberts, Christopher (2005) 'The "ASEAN Charter": a crossroads for the region?', *IDSS Commentaries*, 60
Robinson, W.C. (1998) *Terms of Refuge: The Indochinese Exodus and the International Response*, London: Zed Books
Rogers, Paul (2000) *Losing Control: Global Security in the Twenty-First Century*, London: Pluto Press
Rogers, Steven (2004) 'Beyond the Abu Sayyaf', *Foreign Affairs*, 83:1, 15–20

Rolfe, Jim (1995) 'Preface', in J. Rolfe (ed.), *Unresolved Futures: Comprehensive Security in the Asia-Pacific*, Wellington: Centre for Strategic Studies

Rosero, Diego (former Senior Legal Officer, UNHCR Tokyo) (2003) 'Interview with the author', 27 August

Ruddock, Philip (2005) Transcript: Doorstop interview, Hyatt Regency, Adelaide, 1 August, available at: <http://www.ag.gov.au/agd/www/ministerruddock home.nsf>

Ruland, Jurgen (2005) 'The nature of South East Asian security challenges', *Security Dialogue*, 36, 545–63

Ryan, Alan (2000) *Primary Responsibilities and Primary Risks: Australian Defence Force Participation in the International Force for East Timor*, Canberra: Land Warfare Studies Centre

Sadoff, Claudia W. and David Grey (2002) 'Beyond the river: the benefits of cooperation on international rivers', *Water Policy*, 4:5, 389–403

Safire, William (2003) 'The Asian front', *New York Times*, 10 March, 19

Said, Edward W. (1993) *Culture and Imperialism*, New York: Alfred A. Knopf

Savage, Timothy and Nautilus Team (2002) 'NGO engagement with North Korea: dilemmas and lessons learned', *Asian Perspective*, 26:1, 151–67

Schofield, Matthew (2005) 'Bombers were "normal" Britons; officials fear homegrown terrorism', *Knight Ridder* Washington Bureau, 13 July

Schwarz, Adam (1994) *A Nation In Waiting: Indonesia In the 1990s*, Sydney: Allen & Unwin

Schweithelm, James (1998) *The Fire this Time: An Overview of Indonesia's Forest Fire in 1997/98*, Jakarta: WWF Indonesia Programme

Scott, James C. (1985) *Weapons of the Weak: Everyday Forms of Peasant Resistance*, New Haven, CT: Yale University Press

Scott, James C. (1998) *Seeing Like a State: How Certain Schemes to Improve the Human Condition Have Failed*, New Haven, NJ: Yale University Press

Segal, Gerald (1995) 'What is Asian about Asian security?', in J. Rolfe (ed.), *Unresolved Futures: Comprehensive Security in the Asia-Pacific*, Wellington: Centre for Strategic Studies

Segal, Gerald (1996) 'East Asia and the "constrainment" of China' , *International Security*, 20: 4, 107–35

Senate Legal and Constitutional Affairs Committee (2005) *Provisions of the Anti-Terrorism Bill (No. 2) 2005*, November

Serambi Indonesia (1999) 8 February, available at: <http://www.serambinews.com/>

Serambi Indonesia (2003) 6 October, available at: <http://www.serambinews.com/>

Serambi Indonesia (2004) 4 June, available at: <http://www.serambinews.com/>

Serambi Indonesia (2005) 15 August, available at: <http://www.serambinews.com/>

Selth, Andrew (2002) *Burma's Armed Forces: Power Without Glory*,Norwalk, CT: Eastbridge

Shambaugh, David (1996) 'Containment or engagement of China? Calculating Beijing's response', *International Security*, 21: 2, 180–209

Sheehan, Michael (2005) *International Security: An Analytical Survey*, Boulder, CO: Lynne Rienner

Shen, Jiru (2005) 'The Sino-Europe-US Triangle in the Strategic Adjustment of Great Power Relations', *Global Fortnightly*, 8: 1–4

Shepherd, Chris (2002) *The Trade of Elephants and Elephant Products in Myanmar*, TRAFFIC Online Report Series No. 5, Cambridge: TRAFFIC International

Shin, Eui-Soon (1997) 'Framework for environmental change in Asia', in Kent Butts (ed.), *Conference Report: Environmental Change and Regional Security*, Carlisle Barracks, PA: Centre for Strategic Leadership, US Army War College

Shin, Gi-Wook (1998) 'Nation, history and politics: South Korea', in Hyung Il Pai and Timothy R. Tangherlini (eds), *Nationalism and the Construction of Korean Identity*, Berkeley, CA: Institute of East Asian Studies

Shinn, James (ed.) (1996) *Weaving the Net: Conditional Engagement of China*, New York: Council on Foreign Relations

Shue, Henry (1980) *Basic Rights: Subsistence, Affluence and US Foreign Policy*, Princeton, NJ: Princeton University Press

Shue, Henry (1981) 'Exporting hazards', *Ethics*, 91:4, 579–606

Sigal, Leon V. (1998) *Disarming Strangers: Nuclear Diplomacy with North Korea*, Princeton, NJ: Princeton University Press

Sikkink, Kathryn (1991) *Ideas and Institutions: Developmentalism in Brazil and Argentina*, Ithaca, NY: Cornell University Press

Silverstein, Josef (1997) 'Fifty years of failure in Burma', in Michael E. Brown and Sumit Ganguly (eds), *Government Policies and Ethnic Relations in Asia and the Pacific*, Cambridge, MA: MIT Press

Simon, Sheldon W. (1995) 'The parallel tracks of Asian multilateralism', in M. W. Everett and M. A. Somerville (eds), *Multilateral Activities in South East Asia*, Washington, DC: National Defense University Press

Simon, Sheldon W. (2002) 'Evaluating track II approaches to security diplomacy in the Asia-Pacific: the CSCAP experience', *The Pacific Review*, 15, 167–200

Simon, Sheldon (2004) 'President Bush presses antiterror agenda in southeast Asia', *Comparative Connections*, 5:4

Smith, Hazel (1999) 'Opening up by default: North Korea, the Humanitarian Community and the Crisis' ,*The Pacific Review*, 12:3, 453–78

Smith, Hazel (2000) 'Bad, mad, sad or rational actor? Why the "securitization" paradigm makes for poor policy analysis of North Korea', *International Affairs*, 76:3, 593–617

Smith, Hazel (2002) *Overcoming Humanitarian Dilemmas in the DPRK*, Washington, DC: United States Institute of Peace

Smith, Martin T. (2005) 'Ethnic politics and regional development in Myanmar: the need for new approaches', in Kyaw Yin Hlaing, Robert H. Taylor and Tin Maung Maung Tan (eds), *Myanmar: Beyond Politics to Societal Imperatives*, Singapore: ISEAS

Smith, Steve (1997) 'Power and truth: a reply to William Wallace', *Review of International Studies*, 23: 507–16

Smith, Steve (1999) 'The increasing insecurity of security studies', *Contemporary Security Policy*, 20:3, 72–101

Smith, Steve (2000) 'Wendt's world', *Review of International Studies*, 26, 151–163

Smith, Steve (2005) 'The contested concept of security', in Ken Booth (ed.), *Critical Security Studies and World Politics*, Boulder, CO: Lynne Rienner

Snitwongse, Kusuma and Bunbongkarn, Suchit (2001) 'New security issues and their impact on ASEAN', in Simon S. C. Tay, Jesus P. Estanislao and Hadi Soesastro, *Reinventing ASEAN*, Singapore: Institute of Southeast Asian Studies

Snyder, Scott (1999) *Negotiating on the Edge: North Korean Negotiating Behavior* Washington, DC: United States Institute of Peace Press

Snyder, Scott (1998) 'Managing integration on the Korean peninsula: the positive and normative case for gradualism with or without integration', in Marcus Noland (ed.), *Economic Integration of the Korean Peninsula*, Washington, DC: Institute for International Economics

Soemitro (1992) *Tantangan dan Peluang 1993*, Jakarta: Pustaka Sinar Harapan

Soguk, Nevgat (1999) *States and Strangers: Refugees and Displacements of Statecraft*, Minneapolis, MN: University of Minnesota Press

Sokov, Nikolai (2002) 'Why do states rely on nuclear weapons? The case of Russia and Beyond', *The Nonproliferation Review*, 9:2, 101–11

Soontornpipet, Pichet (2002) 'Is a culture of accountability developing in Thailand?', available at: <http://cdi.anu.edu.au/CDIwebsite 1998–2004/thailand/thailand downloads/Culture%20of%20accoutability.pdf>

South, Ashley (2004) 'Political transition in Myanmar', *Contemporary Southeast Asia*, 26 :2, 233–55

South Korea Ministry of National Defense (2000) *Defense White Paper*, Seoul: Ministry of National Defense

Spender, Percy (1969) *Exercises in Diplomacy: The ANZUS Treaty and the Colombo Plan*, Sydney: Sydney University Press

Stamnes, Eli (2004) 'Critical security studies and the United Nations preventive deployment in Macedonia', *International Peacekeeping*, 11:1, 161–81

Stiglitz, Joseph E. (2002) *Globalization and Its Discontents*, New York: W.W. Norton

The Stimson Center (1997) *An American Legacy: Building a Nuclear Free World*, Washington, DC: The Henry L. Stimson Center, available at: <http//www.stimson.org/pubs.cfm?ID=176>

Stirk, Peter (2005) 'John H. Herz: realism and the fragility of the international order', *Review of International Studies*, 31:2, 285–306

Stolberg, Sheryl Gay (2006) 'For Bush, many questions on Iraq and Korea', *New York Times*,12 October

Straits Times (2005) 'Lawmakers want ASEAN to suspend Myanmar', *The Straits Times* 27 September, 10

Strange, Susan (1994) *States and Markets*, London: Pinter

Strange, Susan (1997) 'The future of global capitalism; or, will divergence persist forever?', in C. Crouch and W. Streeck (eds), *Political Economy of Modern Capitalism: Mapping Convergence and Diversity*, London: Sage

Struck, Doug (2003) 'North Korean threat erodes Japan's pacifism', *Guardian Weekly*, 28, 20 February

Stubbs, Richard (2002) 'ASEAN plus three: emerging Asian regionalism?', *Asian Survey*, 42, 440–55

Su Jingxiang *et al.* (2004) 'Six principal challenges to China's non-traditional security environment', available at: www.xinhuanet.com

Sudo, Sueo (2001) 'A reinvigorated version of Japan's comprehensive security: key to stability in the Asia Pacific', in James C. Hsuing (ed.), *Twenty-First Century World Order and the Asia Pacific: Value Change, Exigencies, and Power Alignment*, Hsuing, New York: Palgrave

Suh, Byung-Chul and Suh Jae-Jean (eds) (2001) *White Paper on Human Rights in North Korea*, Seoul: Korean Institute for National Unification

Suh, J.J., Peter J. Kazenstein and Allen Carlson (eds) (2004) *Rethinking Security in East Asia: Identity, Power and Efficiency*, Stanford, CA: Stanford University Press

Suh, Mark B.M. (1995) 'North Korea seen through the confidential documents of the former East Germany', in Kang Myoung-kyu and Helmut Wagner (eds), *Germany and Korea: Lessons in Unification*, Seoul: Seoul National University Press

Suhrke, Astri (1993) 'The "High Politics"of population movements: migration, state and civil society in southeast Asia', in Myron Weiner (ed.), *International Migration and Security*, San Francisco: Westview Press

Suhrke, Astri (1999) 'Human security and the interests of states', *Security Dialogue*, 30, 265–76

Suhrke, Astri (2003) 'Human security and the protection of refugees', in Edward Newman and Joanne van Selm (eds), *Refugees and Forced Displacement*, Tokyo: United Nations University Press

Sukma, Rizal (2004) *Security Operations in Aceh: Goals, Consequences and Lessons*, Washington, DC: East-West Center

Sun Geqin and Cui Hongjian (1996) *Containing China: Myth and Reality*, Beijing: China Yanshi Press

Suzuki, Nobue Suzuki (2002) 'Gendered surveillance and sexual violence in Filipina pre-migration experiences to Japan', in Brenda Yeoh, Peggy Teo and Shirlena Huang, *Gender Politics in the Asia-Pacific Region*, London: Routledge

Sylvester, Christine (1996) 'The contributions of feminist theory to international relations', in Steve Smith, Ken Booth and Marysia Zalewski (eds), *International Theory: Positivism and Beyond*, Cambridge: Cambridge University Press

Tan, See Seng (2001) *Human Security: Discourse, Statecraft, Emancipation*, Singapore: Institute of Defence and Strategic Studies

Tan, See Seng (2002) 'Human security: discourse, statecraft, emancipation', in D. Dickens (ed.), *The Human Face of Security: Asia-Pacific Perspectives*, Canberra Papers on Strategy and Defence , 144, Canberra: Strategic and Defence Studies Centre, Australian National University

Tan, See Seng (2005) 'Untying Leifer's discourse on order and power', *The Pacific Review*, 18, 71–93

Tan, See Seng and Ralph A. Cossa (2001) 'Rescuing realism from the realists: a theoretical note on East Asian security', in Sheldon W. Simon (ed.), *The Many Faces of Asian Security*, Lanham, MD: Rowman & Littlefield

Tan, See Seng *et al.* (2002) *A New Agenda for the ASEAN Regional Forum*, Monograph 4, Singapore: Institute of Defence and Strategic Studies

Tanter, Richard (2005) 'With eyes wide shut: Japan, Heisei militarization, and the Bush doctrine', in Mel Gurtov and Peter Van Ness (eds), *Confronting the Bush Doctrine: Critical Views from the Asia-Pacific*, New York: Routledge

Terada, Takashi (2003) 'Constructing an "East Asian" concept and growing regional identity: from EAEC to ASEAN+3', *Pacific Review*, 16, 251–77

Terry, Fiona (2001) 'Food aid to North Korea is propping up a Stalinist regime', *Guardian Weekly*, 21, 6 September

TBBC (2006) 'IDPs in Eastern Burma', available at: <http://www.tbbc.org/news>

Thailand Burma Border Consortium (TBBC) (2006) *Programme Report January – June 2006*

Thakur, Ramesh (1998) 'India in the world: neither rich, powerful nor principled', *Foreign Affairs*, 76:4

Thakur, Ramesh (2000) 'Human security regimes', in William Tow, Ramesh Thakur and In-Taek Hyun (eds), *Asia's Emerging Regional Order: Reconciling Traditional and Human Security*, Tokyo: United Nations University Press

Thakur, Ramesh (2004) 'A political worldview', *Security Dialogue*, 35 :3, 347–8

Thakur, Ramesh and Edward Newman (2004) 'Introduction: non-traditional security in Asia', in Ramesh Thakur and Edward Newman (eds), *Broadening Asia's Security Discourse and Agenda: Political, Social and Environmental Perspectives*, Tokyo: United Nations University Press

Thomas, Caroline (2000) *Global Governance, Development and Human Security*, London: Pluto Press

Thomas, Nicholas and William T. Tow (2002a) 'The utility of human security: sovereignty and humanitarian intervention', *Security Dialogue*, 33:2, 177–92

Thomas, Nicholas and William T. Tow (2002b) 'Gaining security by trashing the state? A reply to Bellamy and McDonald', *Security Dialogue*. 33:3, 379–82

Tickner, J. Ann (1992) *Gender in International Relations*, New York: Cambridge University Press

Tickner, J. Ann (2001) *Gendering World Politics*, New York: Columbia University Press

Tickner, J. Ann (2004) 'Feminist responses to international security studies', *Peace Review*, 16:1, 43–8

Tifa Irian (1999) 'Wapres: Tanpa Irian, Indonesia tidak Utuh', *Tifa Irian*, 20–31, December

Tilly, Charles (1984) *Big Structures, Large Processes, Huge Comparisons*, New York: Russell Sage Foundation

Tilly, Charles (1990) *Coercion, Capital, and European States, AD 990–1990*, Cambridge, MA: Blackwell

The Tokyo Forum Report: Facing Nuclear Dangers: An Action Plan for the 21st Century (1999) Tokyo: Ministry of Foreign Affairs,available at: <http://www.mofa.go.jp/policy/un/disarmament/forum/tokyo9907/index.html>

Tow, William T. (2000) 'Introduction', in William T. Tow, Ramesh Thakur and In-Taek Hyun (eds), *Asia's Emerging Regional Order: Reconciling Traditional and Human Security*, Tokyo: United Nations University Press

Tow, William T. (2001a) *Asia-Pacific Strategic Relations: Seeking Convergent Security*, Cambridge: Cambridge University Press

Tow, William T. (2001b) 'Alternative security models: implications for ASEAN', in Andrew T.H. Tan and J.D. Kenneth Boutin (eds), *Non-Traditional Security Issues in Southeast Asia*, Singapore: Select Publishing for Strategic Defence Studies

Tow, William T. and Russell Trood (2000) 'Linkages between traditional and human security', in William T. Tow, Ramesh Thakur and In-Taek Hyun (eds), *Asia's Emerging Regional Order: Reconciling Traditional and Human Security*, Tokyo: United Nations University Press

Turner, Stansfield (1999) *Caging the Genies: a Workable Solution for Nuclear, Chemical and Biological Weapons*, Boulder, CO: Westview Press

UNDP (1995) *Human Development Report, 1994*, New York: UNDP

UNDRP (2005) *Human Security Report, 2005*, New York: Oxford University Press

UNEP (2000) *Global Environmental Outlook 2000*, London: Earthscan

UNGA (1982) 'Summary records on 13 October', 33rd Session UNGA, 18 October

UNGA (1985) 'Report on UNHCR Assistance Activities in 1984–1985', 36th Session, UNGA, 5 August

UNHCR (1959a) 'UNHCR Deputy High Commissioner to Prime Minister for Foreign Affairs, Federation of Malaya', correspondence, 4 November

UNHCR (1959b) 'Report of Mr de Kemoularia's Visit to Malaya', memorandum, 13 November

UNHCR (1965) 'Report of the colloquium on legal aspects of refugee problems', memorandum,April

UNHCR (1969) 'Malaysia: attitude to convention', memorandum, 15 March

UNHCR (1977) *On Special Aspects of the 1951 Convention and 1967 Protocol relating to the status of refugees*, Geneva: UNHCR

UNHCR (1984a) 'Report on situation of the VNBP', Annual Review Meeting, 30 January

UNHCR (1984b) 'Set up of Afghan Mujahidin office in Kuala Lumpur', Report, 24 April

UNHCR (1993) *The State of the World's Refugees: The Challenge of Protection*, New York: Penguin

UNHCR (1996) *Handbook on Repatriation: International Protection*, Geneva: UNHCR

UNHCR (1999) 'Representative of the Secretary-General on internally displaced persons', Statement,16 April

UNHCR (2000) *The State of the World's Refugees*, New York: Oxford University Press

UNHCR (2003a) *UNHCR Global Report 2003*, Geneva: UNHCR

UNHCR (2003b) *Country Operations Plan: Malaysia*,Geneva: UNHCR

UNHCR (2004a) *Trends in Refugee Status Determination, 1 January-30 September 2004*, Geneva: UNHCR

UNHCR (2004b)*UNHCR Refugees by Numbers*, available at: <www.unhcr.ch/egi-bin/texts/basics>

UNIFEM (2003) 'Asia Pacific regional programme on empowering women migrant workers in Asia (2001–2003)' , available at: <http://www.unifem-eseasia.org/projects/migrantworkers.htm>

UNRISD (2005) *Gender Equality: Striving for Justice in an Unequal World*,France: UNRISD

UNSEC (1984) *Report of the UNHCR*, 30 May

UN Secretary General (2000) 'We the peoples: the role of the United Nations in the 21st century', New York: United Nations General Assembly

USCR (2002) *World Refugee Survey, 2002*,Washington, DC: USCR

USCR (2004) *World Refugee Survey, 2004*, Washintgon, DC: USCR

Vervoorn, Aat (1998) *ReOrient: Change in Asian Societies*, Oxford: Oxford University Press

Voice of America (2004) 'Thai government cracks down on southern violence as Monday's death toll shoots upward', Voice of America Press, 25 October

Wade, Robert (2001) 'The US role in the long Asian crisis of 1990–2000', in A. Lukanskas and F. Rivera-Batiz (eds), *The Political Economy of the East Asian Crisis and its Aftermath: Tigers in Distress*, Cheltenham: Edward Elgar

Wade, Robert (1996) 'Japan, the World Bank and the art of paradigm maintenance: the East Asian miracle in political perspective', *New Left Review*, 217, 3–36

Wain, Barry (1980) *The Refused: The Agony of the Indochina Refugees*, Hong Kong: Dow Jones Publishing

Wakim, Joseph (2005) 'New laws will be a red rag to terrorists', *Sydney Morning Herald*, 14 September

Walker, R. B. J. (1997) 'The subject of security', in Michael C. Williams and Keith Krause (eds), *Critical Security Studies: Concepts and Cases*, Minneapolis, MN: University of Minnesota Press

Wallace, William (1996) 'Truth and power, monks and technocrats: theory and practice in international relations', *Review of International Studies*, 22:3, 301–21

Wallace, William (1998) 'Conclusion: ideas and influence', in D. Stone, A. Denham and M. Garnett (eds), *Think-Tanks Across Nations: A Comparative Approach*, Manchester: Manchester University Press

Walt, Stephen M. (1991) 'The renaissance of security studies', *International Studies Quarterly*, 35:2, 211–39

Wanandi, Jusuf (1991) *Global Changes and Its Impact on the Asia-Pacific Region: An ASEAN View*,Jakarta: Centre for Strategic and International Studies

Wang Jian, Li Xiaoning, Qiao Liang and Wang Xianghui (2004) *The Coming of a New Era of Warring States*, Beijing: Xinua Publishing House

Wang Zhuxun (1999) 'Effects of Kosovo on global security', *Outlook Weekly*, 19 May

Warr, Carl Grundy and Elaine Wong Siew Yin (2002) 'Geographies of displacement: the Karenni and the Shan across the Myanmar-Thailand border', *Singapore Journal of Tropical Geography*, 23:1, 93–122

Weber, Cynthia (2001) *International Relations Theory: A Critical Introduction*, London and New York: Routledge

Weisman, Steven R. (2003) 'South Korea, once a solid ally, now poses problems for the US', *New York Times*, 2 January

Wheeler, Nicholas (2002) 'Dying for "enduring freedom": accepting responsibility for civilian casualties in the war against terrorism', *International Relations*, 16:2, 205–25

White Paper: China's Endeavours for Arms Control, Disarmament and Non-Proliferation (2005) Beijing: Information Office of the State Council of the People's Republic of China, available at: <http://www.chinadaily.com.cn/english/doc/2005-09/01/content_474248.htm>

Wickramasekera, Piri (2001) 'Labour migration in Asia: issues and challenges', in *International Migration in Asia: Trends and Policies*, Paris: OECD

Wickramasekera, Piri (2002) 'Asian labour migration: issues and challenges in an era of globalization', *International Migration Papers*, 57, Geneva: International Labour Office

Williams, George (2005) 'Balancing national security and human rights: lessons from Australia', *Borderlands*, 4:1

Williams, Michael C. (1999) 'The practices of security: critical contributions: reply to Eriksson', *Cooperation and Conflict*, 34:3, 341–4

Williamson, John (1994) 'In search of a manual for technopols', in J. Williamson (ed.), *The Political Economy of Policy Reform*, Washington, DC: Institute for International Economics

Winnefeld James A. and Mary E. Morris (1994) *Where Environmental Concerns and Security Strategies Meet: Green Conflict in Asia and the Middle East*, Santa Monica, CA: RAND

Wolfsthal, Jon B. (2006) 'Behind enemy reactors', *New York Times*, 14 October

Wong, Diana (1995) 'Regionalism in the Asia-Pacific – a response to Kanishka Jayasuriya', *The Pacific Review*, 8: 683–8

Woods, Lawrence T. (1993) *Asia-Pacific Diplomacy: Nongovernmental Organizations and International Relations*, Vancouver, BC: University of British Columbia Press

Woods, Lawrence T. (1997) 'Rediscovering security', *Asian Perspective*, 21, 79–102

Woods, Ngaire (2003) 'The United States and the international financial institutions: power and influence within the World Bank and the IMF', in R. Foot, S.N. MacFarlane and M. Mastanduno (eds), *U.S. Hegemony and International Organizations: the United States and Multilateral Institutions*, Oxford: Oxford University Press

Worthington, Ross R. (2003) *Governance in Singapore*, London: Routledge

Wright, Tony (2003) 'Our long path to war', *The Bulletin*, 29 April, 37–8

Wright-Neville, David (2004) 'East Asia and the "war on terror": why human rights matter', in A. Heijmans, N. Simmons and H. Van Den Veen (eds), *Searching for Peace in the Asia-Pacific*, Boulder, CO: Lynne Rienner

Wroe, David (2005) 'Iraq was motive for bombing: suspect' , *The Age*, 2 August

Wyn Jones, Richard (1995) 'Message in a bottle? Theory and praxis in critical security studies', *Contemporary Security Policy*, 16:3, 299–319

Wyn Jones, Richard (1999) *Security, Strategy and Critical Theory*, Boulder, CO: Lynne Rienner

Wyn Jones, Richard (2005) 'Emancipation: on necessity, capacity and concrete utopias', in Ken Booth (ed.) *Critical Security Studies and World Politics*, Boulder, CO: Lynne Rienner

Xinjiang, Xian (2002) 'China's "war on terror", *Foreign Affairs*, 81:4, 8–12

Xiong, Guangkai (2005) 'Coordinating our efforts to meet the challenges of non-traditional security threats' (in Chinese), available at: <http://jczs.sina.com.cn/2005-10-11/1124324596.html>

Yan Xuetong (1996) *An Analysis of China's National Interests*, Tianjin: Tianjin People's Press

Yan Xuetong (2000) *The American Hegemony and China's Security*, Tianjin: Tianjin People's Press

Ye Zicheng (2004) 'Reflections on the history and theory of China's strategy for multipolarity', *Studies of International Politics*, 1, 9–23

Yeoh, Brenda, Peggy Teo and Shirlena Huang (2002) 'Introduction', in Brenda Yeoh, Peggy Teo and Shirlena Huang (eds), *Gender Politics in the Asia-Pacific Region*, London: Routledge

Young, Oran (1989) *International Cooperation: Building Regimes for Natural Resources and the Environment*, Ithaca, NY: Cornell University Press

Young, Whan Kihl (1998) 'Seoul's engagement policy and US-DPRK relations', *The Korean Journal of Defense Analysis*, X:1: 21–48

Yu Xiaoqiu (2004) 'Non-traditional decurity: the new focus of national security', *World Knowledge*, 12, 42–3

Yuan, Jong-Dong (2005) 'Chinese perspectives and responses to the Bush doctrine', in M. Gurtov and P. Van Ness (eds), *Confronting the Bush Doctrine: Critical views from the Asia-Pacific*, New York: Routledge

Yuan Peng (2003) 'The war against Iraq and the prospect of the US hegemony', available at: <http://news.sina.com.cn/w/2003-04-14/1131994683.shtml>

Yuval-Davis, Nira (1997) *Gender and Nation*, London: Sage

Zacher, Mark (2001) 'The international territorial order: boundaries, the use of force, and normative change', *International Organization*, 55, 215–50

Zalewski, Marysia (1996) 'All these theories yet the bodies keep piling up', in Ken Booth, Steve Smith and Marysia Zalewski (eds), *International Theory: Positivism and Beyond*, Cambridge: Cambridge University Press

Zhang, Yongjin (1998) *China in International Society: Alienation and Beyond*, St Antony's-Macmillan Series, Basingstoke: Macmillan

Zhang, Yongjin (2001) 'Problematizing China's security: sociological insights', *Pacifica Review*, 13:3, 241–53

Zheng, Yongnian (2004) *Globalisation and State Transformation in China*, Cambridge: Cambridge University Press

Zolberg, Aristide, Astri Suhrke and Sergio Aguayo (1989) *Escape From Violence: Conflict and the Refugee Crisis in the Developing World*, Oxford: Oxford University Press

INDEX

Note: 'n.' after a page reference indicates the number of a note on that page

  proliferation 3, 5, 11–12, 29, 131–2, 135, 138, 183–4, 187, 191–4, 197, 211, 215, 233
  strategy 183, 186, 188